International Management

Manfred Fuchs

International Management

The Process of Internationalization and Market Entry Strategies

Springer Gabler

Manfred Fuchs
University of Graz
Graz, Steiermark, Austria

ISBN 978-3-662-65869-7 ISBN 978-3-662-65870-3 (eBook)
https://doi.org/10.1007/978-3-662-65870-3

This Springer Gabler imprint is published by the registered company Springer-Verlag GmbH, DE, part of Springer Nature.
The registered company address is: Heidelberger Platz 3, 14197 Berlin, Germany

Acknowledgments

This book is the result of decades of studying and teaching the fascinating subject of international business. I am indebted especially to Tilman Schiel, Otto Kreye, Folker Fröbel, and Jürgen Heinrichs of the Starnberg Institute for the Study of Global Structures, Developments, and Crises, in Starnberg, Germany, where I made my first and very formative experience researching the challenges and pitfalls of the global economy. I must also thank my long-time friend and colleague, Prof. Yang Dawei from Beijing, for his hospitality and many interesting discussions. I would also like to thank my colleagues and friends in the German Academic Association of Business Research, especially the section International Management. I must also thank Springer Verlag and in particular Ms. Christine Sheppard and Katharina Harsdorf for their patience and support. Admittedly all the shortcomings and mistakes in the implementation remain my responsibility.

Last but not least, I would like to thank my family for their love, especially Marlene, Anne, and Emilia.

Contents

List of Figures

List of Tables

Introduction

1

International business management studies how firms operate multiple cross-border business activities in uncertain and contingent foreign environments. It combines two significantly overlapping disciplines: international economics and international management (Dunning, 1988; Dunning & Lundan, 2008; Kutschker & Schmid, 2011; Macharzina & Engelhard, 1991; Oesterle, 2005). International business is closely related to international economics as a well-established field that studies international trade flows of goods and services at the country level (Buckley & Casson, 1996; Rugman & Verbeke, 2003). It examines factors that affect these trade flows and explains the specific regional and global patterns of trade (Feenstra, 1992; Gereffi, 2018; Rugman, 2005). It also focuses on foreign direct investment (FDI) and the rise and impact of large multinational firms on the world economy (Buckley et al., 2016; Doh, 2019; Pitelis, 2011; Shaver, 1998). On the other hand, international management is about how to organize the international firm and its multiple cross-border business activities. International management focuses on the evolution of firm strategies and structure and a key focus is the coordination and control of diverging activities within and across foreign subsidiaries. International management usually concentrates on the firm and the management making the decisions to internationalize (Andersen & Strandskov, 1997; Dow et al., 2018; Efrat & Shoham, 2013). It analyzes the behavior of the international firm through different cultural, economic, and political environments (Archer & Elder-Vass, 2012; Kirkman et al., 2017; Ng et al., 2007; Shenkar, 2001; Slangen & van Tulder, 2009). Unsurprisingly, international management is concerned with cross-border business activities, including the coordination and integration of various, and often diverging tasks performed by affiliated subsidiaries in distant and unfamiliar environments (Buckley, 2006, 2011; Medema, 1996; Schmid, 2018; Spulber, 2009). It also involves managing highly fragmented and spatially dispersed value-adding activities (Casson, 2013; Kano et al., 2020; McWilliam et al., 2019; Rugman et al., 2009).

M. Fuchs, *International Management*,
https://doi.org/10.1007/978-3-662-65870-3_1

International management is characterized by its effort to lead, motivate, plan, and control cross-border activities across multiple locations in contingent environments. Depending on the scale and scope of cross-border activities, firm experience, prevalent skills, and capabilities are exploited to manage different cross-border activities that include exports, imports, licensing, international joint ventures, or wholly-owned subsidiaries. Internationalization is a highly complex process that is not only affected by the liability of foreignness, uncertainty, and risks, but also by the constantly emerging opportunities in dynamic, unfamiliar and contingent environments (Aulakh & Kotabe, 1997; Brouthers & Hennart, 2007; Filatotchev et al., 2007; Morschett et al., 2010; Sanchez-Peinado & Pla-Barber, 2006; Xie, 2017; Zhao et al., 2017). International management is embedded in environments characterized by heterogeneous institutions and cultures, and puzzling habitual routines in home and host markets. Firm size and resources, existing managerial experience, and habitual practices affect the outcome of managing this evolving process. This process enables the firm to improve in adapting its products and services to co-evolving environments (Barkema & Vermeulen, 1997; Dow, 1998; Kirkman et al., 2006; Minkov & Hofstede, 2012; de Mooij, 2013).

This textbook describes the main issues in international business studies and elaborates on critical subjects of international management. However, it is not comprehensive and only thoroughly explores select issues. Each branch is hopefully viewed from different vantage points. One purpose is to offer a description of critical functions, but a significant focus is on asking and explaining key questions in international business research. The target audience is advanced students at universities and technical colleges who are interested in this subject. With this target group in mind, the aim is not to work through individual sub-areas and clearly outline core definitions and approaches, but rather to try to address also the common ambiguities.

The book is divided into seven chapters, with this introduction as the first chapter.

Chapter 2 deals with the world economy, globalization, and the relationships between different countries and regions. In this chapter, the world economy is presented as the overall macro-environment in which the business firm is organizing its ongoing processes of international activities. This section describes the structure and dynamic development of the world economy; it explains the key parts of the world economy's structure and analyzes the apparent pattern of trade relations and direct foreign investment, which are essential indicators that show the structural design of the world economy. This section also looks at the role of a multinational firm in the evolution of the world economy. Focusing on the multinational firm shows how its strategies, structure, and cross-border activities relate to the overall inter- and intra-firm trade and foreign direct investment pattern (Doz et al., 2001; Ernst, 2009; Gereffi, 2018; Jones, 2002; Mourtzis & Doukas, 2020; Rugman, 2005).

The world economy is not a uniform environment for the international business firm, as it is divided by nations, regions, provinces, cities, and neighborhoods. Economic activity is highly differentiated and unevenly distributed among these locations (Baldwin et al., 2003). Socio-economic and political geographies dynamically change their properties to compete with each other. The world economy is a geographical and political landscape populated by different people living in specialized cultural and socio-economic environments, which are hierarchically structured, but less global than the globality concept portrays (Ashenbaum, 2018; Bair & Gereffi, 2003; Gereffi & Fernandez-Stark, 2010; Hymer, 1970; Pearce & Papanastassiou, 2006).

Within and between core and periphery countries and regions, economic actors may upgrade their value-adding activities by migrating from one place to another. Firms expand into different countries by locating several value adding activities across multiple places. Regions can be trapped in a particular pattern of interaction in these often unequal core periphery relations, and some, will have limited control, may be weaker and less powerful than others (Beaverstock, 2009; Faulconbridge, 2007; Zhang, 2012). Core cities or regions never stay uncontested as their fragile position due to its hegemonial position disappears (Huygens, 2017; Saull, 2012). Regions are struggling to maintain attractiveness because each is administering all sorts of activities to attract investments (Atkins et al., 2009; Funck, 1995; Momaya, 2016).

Chapter 3 examines the main theories that help explain internationalization as a process and assesses theories that explain the strategies and structure of international firms. The focus on essential theories is determined by the general canonical knowledge framing current IB research and the so-called "big questions" in international business (Autio et al., 2005; Coviello et al., 2017; Forsgren, 2016; Fuchs & Horn, 2019; Pla-Barber et al., 2014; Reuber, 2016; Vahlne & Johanson, 2017). The theories elaborated are a reference to a body of a widely accepted, although disputed, theoretical knowledge generated in the last six decades in international business that examines and explains significant questions in IB research and international management. This section starts with a discussion of classical trade theories, which help establish a basic understanding of why trade between national economies is beneficial. This section notes that trade is not carried out by countries (national economies) but essentially by business firms. Thus, this section elaborates theories that explain the cross-border business activities of multinational firms, the reason for the multinational firm's growth, and the international firm's approaches in organizing heterogenous and multiple cross-border transactions. In addition, emphasis is placed on theories that reinstate a greater focus on the internationalization process and the managers' decision-making process (Aharoni, 2006; Aharoni & Brock, 2010; Devinney, 2011; Devinney et al., 2001; Lewin, 2011).

The focus on mainstream theories is twofold. First is the reference to a comprehensible body of widely accepted knowledge on how a particular phenomenon in international business is explained. Second is the understanding that any established theory that originated in a particular historical period with somewhat idiosyncratic problems might be outdated to some degree. In addition, each historical period shaped the way a core problem is approached and the methodological tools used to analyze it. However, each analysis and problem has evolved in a particular socio-economic and historical context. The theory's original contextual framework usually remains valid, but sometimes changes dramatically.

In the 1960s and early 1970s, a dominant theoretical body in international business studies centered on the rise, strategy, and structure of multinational firms emerged (Audretsch, 1983; Buckley, 2006; Inkpen, 2004; Rowthorn, 2006; Tallman, 2004). In the early 1990s, the perspective shifted to the overall impact that is largely associated with the dynamics of globalization (Dunning, 1989). In the 2000s, the focus shifted to the effects of global production networks and global value chains to the management of the international business firm (Asmussen et al., 2007; Buckley, 2009a; Buckley & Casson, 2014; Feenstra, 1998; Fernandez-Stark & Gereffi, 2019; Gereffi, 2018).

Mainstream theory is not meant to have a negative connotation. Rather, it stresses that theories are still widely used to analyze core issues in IB research at present. Mainstream theories enforce a widely accepted research paradigm and often imply a distinct research design in approaching a research question. These theories shape the way core subjects are taught in business schools (Buckley & Casson, 1998; Buckley et al., 2007; Doh, 2019; Egelhoff & Wolf, 2017; Kutschker & Schmid, 2011; Macharzina & Engelhard, 1991; Prahalad, 1995; Verbeke et al., 2016; Yamin, 2011).

Chapter 4 discusses foreign market entry choice, one of the most critical decisions in international management and a core subject in IB research and teaching. This section emphasizes the managerial decision-making process in international firms. The focus is laid on a critical reflection on apparent assumptions of rationality. The entry mode decision is considered vital in the process of internationalization and presents a complex challenge for both large and small firms. Most market entry decisions are made in a highly uncertain, unfamiliar and contingent foreign environment. Despite the importance of the decision-making process in entry mode research, it surprisingly remains poorly understood and neglected (Buckley & Casson, 2019; Buckley, 2014; Dow, 1998; Elia et al., 2019; Forester, 1984; Gigerenzer & Selten, 2002; Langlois, 1995; Surdu et al., 2020).

Chapter 5 elaborates the pros and cons of the international firm's several entry mode choices, including exporting, licensing, franchising, international joint ventures, or wholly-owned subsidiaries. This chapter describes major market entry strategies and provides an overview of entry mode strategies. Market entry strategies, also termed entry mode decisions, are core topics in international management research. Making an entry mode choice requires deliberate decisions regarding why, how, when, and where to internationalize. These four dimensions are considered major questions in international business (Schmid, 2018). "Why" encompasses the motives and strategic objectives guiding the intended internationalization. "How" is related to the most feasible entry mode in an unfamiliar business environment. "When" refers to choosing the ideal entry time. Several firms value finding the right moment to make an entry decision. Lastly, "where" allows a firm to select proper locations for its international efforts (Brouthers, 2013; Brouthers et al., 2003; Coviello et al., 2017; Erramilli & D'Souza, 1993; Hennart & Slangen, 2015; Jones & Coviello, 2005).

Most small firms and early adopters of internationalization may initially be attracted to exporting, which is an important part of foreign market entry strategies for almost all international firms. For many small and medium-sized enterprises (SMEs), exporting is the most common entry mode chosen for firm growth; although, "not necessarily [. . .] an orderly, systematic and sequential pattern" (Welch et al., 2018). Firms may start exporting in an ad-hoc, erratic pattern, passively reacting to meet customer demand. On the other hand, firms may actively and systematically explore export markets. Exporting is primarily attractive because it usually requires fewer resources compared to other entry modes and lowers the firm's risk exposure in foreign markets (Chen et al., 2016; Hultman et al., 2009, 2011). Many firms use the exporting strategy to grow while maintaining a low liability of foreignness (Cuervo-Cazurra et al., 2015; Hennart et al., 2019; Root, 1964, 1988, 1994). However, firms often use several entry modes simultaneously when expanding into multiple foreign markets. The challenge is to know the most appropriate entry mode and to gradually modify entry modes in a contingent foreign environment.

Chapter 6 tackles the challenges posed by the coordination and integration of cross-border activities on multinational firms, that are trying to balance the need to coordinate cross-border value-adding activities organized within and between firm boundaries (Buckley, 2009a; Casson, 1984; Caves et al., 2013; Dacin et al., 1999; Hassler, 2003; Mudambi & Venzin, 2010; Qiu & Donaldson, 2012; Stopford & Wells, 1972). However, this chapter goes beyond focusing on multinational firms as the lead actors in global value chains. This chapter analyzes the impact of global value-adding activities, the scale and scope of global value chains, and its effects in the management of the multinational firm. Multinational firms struggle to find a balance between value-added activities organized within firm boundaries and outsourced activities (transcending the boundaries of the firm). Multinational firms have been a major focus in analyzing the international division of labor between HQ and subsidiaries, and between country locations and regions. The global value chains (GVCs) approach radically extends the prevailing focus on the multinational firm as the most important nexus to explain the value-adding activities that are deployed within and beyond firm boundaries in a global network of intricate relationships (Casson, 2013; Fernandez-Stark et al., 2014; Gereffi, 2018; Gereffi & Fernandez-Stark, 2018).

The standard definition of the multinational firm as "an enterprise that engages in foreign direct investment (FDI) [which] owns or, in some way, controls value-added activities in more than one country" is generally still the "threshold definition" for any IB oriented analyses of international business activities associated with the theory of the firm (Dunning & Lundan, 2008: 3). However, identifying the determinant factors of the actual erosion of firm boundaries has become more complex and has made it impossible to stick to the widely used traditional perspectives about the inherent scale and scope of the multinational firm (Aggarwal et al., 2011; Goerzen & Beamish, 2003; Kirca et al., 2012; Thomas & Eden, 2004). Still, multinational firm theories are predominantly conceptualized applying transaction costs theory (Tallman, 2004; Verbeke & Kano, 2016) or through the use of the internalization paradigm (Buckley, 2009b, 2011; Buckley & Casson, 2009, 2010). Major causes for the existence of multinationals arise from the benefits of asset specificity and related agency problems that can be mitigated if cross border business activities remain within firm boundaries (Williamson, 1979, 1998, 2005). Furthermore, existing literature consider the role of incomplete contracts in both upstream and downstream activities as a key driver for the emergence and growth of multinational firms. These perspectives basically argue that asset specificity is empirically relevant to grasp the make or buy decisions in international business firms (Hubbard, 2018).

The last section, **Chap. 7**, deals with different models of managing multinational firms. The chapter initially discusses the strategy and structure, which are primary subjects in international business research and international management. It examines how the structure of the multinational firm has evolved, revealing the need to adapt to an ever-increasing complexity caused by multiple products and many foreign locations, to reach a balance between firm structure and strategy in a co-evolving environment. These challenges initiated several core questions in international business about how the multinational firm with multiple products and markets would be able to identify the proper organizational strategy to adapt to a more complex international business environment.

Both international business and international management are concerned with managing the cross-border operations, coordinating and integrating activities carried out in multiple foreign locations within and between multinational business firms. Although the central focus is on the business firm, specifically on how the international firm is managed within the traditional boundaries of the firm, a dominating feature for several decades has been the impact of spatially dispersed and highly fragmented global value chains which significantly affect the strategy and structure of international business firms (Bartlett & Ghoshal, 1998; Bartlett & Yoshino, 1998; Djodat & Knyphausen-Aufseß, 2017; Doz et al., 2001; Hennart, 1993; Inkpen, 2004; Mees-Buss et al., 2019; Prahalad & Doz, 1987; Rugman & Verbeke, 1992).

The world economy is not a uniform environment, as it affects the management of large and small-sized businesses differently. Though the world economy is the fundamental ecological environment for the business firm, there is a need to recognize how complex and dynamic effects evolve at different levels of society. Traditionally, the core focus in international business studies is understanding these complex environments. Focusing on the big issues in international business studies, it is important to understand how international activities can become more sustainable (Donaldson, 2001; Egelhoff & Wolf, 2017; Pearce & Papanastassiou, 2006; Qiu et al., 2012; Qiu & Donaldson, 2012; Wolf, 2020; Wolf & Egelhoff, 2002, 2013) .

International business focuses on the study of cross-border business transactions, while international management manages these international business transactions. Both approaches aim to analyze and explain how, why, when, and where cross-border business transactions arise. International business studies attempt to explain the inherent complexities associated with these four questions. A major perspective in international business is how firms decide on the allocation of scarce resources between different tasks within a complex network of activities. These questions are all crucial in understanding the complexities of international business transactions, not only because it is a challenge to decide how and when to enter foreign markets.

International management is a discipline that emphasizes the challenge of managing the international firm and coordinating its various overseas activities. Coordination in international firms is a challenge, not only because the different units of the firm in different geographical regions need to operate together, but also because each foreign activity is carried out in a complex, different and uncertain environment. International business analyzes the complexity of global markets and the effects of differences between individual national markets. Driven by the need to adapt to contingent and changing environments, international business focuses on how to manage heterogenous value adding activities operated at various stages within prevalent global production networks.

All these issues require unique theoretical approaches to explain the individual components and their mutually dependent relationships to each other, which are sometimes difficult to grasp.

Study Questions

1. Consider the differences and similarities in international business and in international management, and try to define the intersection of the two subjects.
2. Discuss the structure of the global economy with a colleague and think about how it affects your daily life.
3. Think about key management issues in international firms. What theories do you know that focus on these issues?
4. How do economists explain the decision-making process in a firm? Who is making decisions in a business firm?
5. What is the most challenging issue facing an international firm today?

References

Aggarwal, R., Berrill, J., Hutson, E., & Kearney, C. (2011). What is a multinational corporation? Classifying the degree of firm-level multinationality. *International Business Review, 20*(5), 557–577.

Aharoni, Y. (2006). Reassessing (home)regionalisation. *International Business Review, 15*(4), 439–446.

Aharoni, Y., & Brock, D. M. (2010). 50 years of IB research: What have we achieved, and what have we not yet achieved? *Journal of International Management, 16*(1), 3–4.

Andersen, P. H., & Strandskov, J. (1997). International market selection. *Journal of Global Marketing, 11*(3), 65–84.

Archer, M. S., & Elder-Vass, D. (2012). Cultural system or norm circles? An exchange. *European Journal of Social Theory, 15*(1), 93–115.

Ashenbaum, B. (2018). From market to hierarchy: An empirical assessment of a supply chain governance typology. *Journal of Purchasing and Supply Management, 24*(1), 59–67.

Asmussen, C., Pedersen, T., & Petersen, B. (2007). How do we capture "global specialization" when measuring firms' degree of globalization? *Management International Review, 47*(6), 791–813.

Atkins, K., Chen, J., Kumar, V. S. A., Macauley, M., & Marathe, A. (2009). Locational market power in network constrained markets. *Journal of Economic Behavior & Organization, 70*(1–2), 416–430.

Audretsch, D. B. (1983). A theory of multinational enterprise. By Jean-Francois Hennart. (Ann Arbor: The University of Michigan Press, 1982. xiv + 201 pp. $16.50.). *Business History Review, 57*(4), 575–576.

Aulakh, P. S., & Kotabe, M. (1997). Antecedents and performance implications of channel integration in foreign markets. *Journal of International Business Studies, 28*(1), 145–175.

Autio, E., Sapienza, H. J., & Arenius, P. (2005). International entrepreneurship. *Advances in Entrepreneurship, Firm Emergence and Growth, 8*, 9–42.

Bair, J., & Gereffi, G. (2003). Upgrading, uneven development, and jobs in the North American apparel industry. *Global Networks, 3*(2), 143–169.

Baldwin, R., Forslid, R., Martin, P., Ottaviano, G., & Robert-Nicoud, F. (2003). *Economic geography and public policy*. Princeton University Press.

Barkema, H. G., & Vermeulen, F. (1997). What differences in the cultural backgrounds of partners are detrimental for international joint ventures? *Journal of International Business Studies, 28*(4), 845–864.

Bartlett, C., & Ghoshal, S. (1998). *Managing across borders: The transnational solution*. Harvard Business School Press.

Bartlett, C., & Yoshino, M. (1998). *Corning glass works International (A)* (p. 18). Harvard Business School.

Beaverstock, J. V. (2009). International Encyclopedia of human geography. *Transactions of the Institute of British Geographers, 29*(2004), 162–163.

Brouthers, K. D. (2013). A retrospective on: Institutional, cultural and transaction cost influences on entry mode choice and performance. *Journal of International Business Studies, 44*(1), 14–22.

Brouthers, K. D., & Hennart, J.-F. (2007). Boundaries of the firm: Insights from international entry mode research. *Journal of Management, 33*(3), 395–425.

Brouthers, K. D., Brouthers, L., & Werner, S. (2003). Transaction cost-enhanced entry mode choices and firm performance. *Strategic Management Journal, 24*(12), 1239–1248.

Buckley, P. J. (2006). Stephen Hymer: Three phases, one approach? *International Business Review, 15*(2), 140–147.

Buckley, P. J. (2009a). The impact of the global factory on economic development. *Journal of World Business, 44*(2), 131–143.

Buckley, P. J. (2009b). Internalisation thinking: From the multinational enterprise to the global factory. *International Business Review, 18*(3), 224–235.

Buckley, P. J. (2011). International integration and coordination in the global factory. *Management International Review, 51*(2), 269.

Buckley, P. J. (2014). Adam Smith's theory of knowledge and international business theory and practice. *Journal of International Business Studies, 45*(1), 102–109.

Buckley, P. J., & Casson, M. (1996). An economic model of international joint venture strategy. *Journal of International Business Studies, 27*(5), 849–876.

Buckley, P. J., & Casson, M. C. (1998). Analyzing foreign market entry strategies: Extending the internalization approach. *Journal of International Business Studies, 29*(3). https://doi.org/10.1057/palgrave.jibs.8490006

Buckley, P. J., & Casson, M. C. (2009). The internalisation theory of the multinational enterprise: A review of the progress of a research agenda after 30 years. *Journal of International Business Studies, 40*(9), 1563–1580.

Buckley, P. J., & Casson, M. (2010). The multinational enterprise revisited. *The Essential Buckley and Casson, 2010*, 177–204.

Buckley, P. J., & Casson, M. (2014). *The multinational enterprise and the emergence of the global factory* (pp. 20–51). Springer.

Buckley, P., & Casson, M. (2019). Decision-making in international business. *Journal of International Business Studies, 50*(8), 1424–1439.

Buckley, P. J., Devinney, T. M., & Louviere, J. J. (2007). Do managers behave the way theory suggests? A choice-theoretic examination of foreign direct investment location decision-making. *Journal of International Business Studies, 38*(7), 1069–1094.

Buckley, P. J., Chen, L., Clegg, L. J., & Voss, H. (2016). Experience and FDI risk-taking: A microfoundational reconceptualization. *Journal of International Management, 22*(2), 131–146.

Casson, M. (1984). The theory of vertical integration: A survey and synthesis. *Journal of Economic Studies, 11*(2), 3–43.

Casson, M. (2013). Economic analysis of international supply chains: An internalization perspective. *Journal of Supply Chain Management, 49*(2), 8–13.

Caves, K. W., Holt, C. C., & Singer, H. J. (2013). Vertical integration in multichannel television markets: A study of regional sports networks. *Review of Network Economics, 12*(1), 61–92.

Chen, J., Sousa, C. M. P., & He, X. (2016). The determinants of export performance: A review of the literature 2006-2014. *International Marketing Review, 33*(5), 626–670.

Coviello, N., Kano, L., & Liesch, P. W. (2017). Adapting the Uppsala model to a modern world: Macro-context and microfoundations. *Journal of International Business Studies, 48*(9), 1151–1164.

Cuervo-Cazurra, A., Narula, R., & Un, C. A. (2015). Internationalization motives: Sell more, buy better, upgrade and escape. *Multinational Business Review, 23*(1), 25–35.

Dacin, M. T., Ventresca, M. J., & Beal, B. D. (1999). The embeddedness of organizations: Dialogue & directions. *Journal of Management, 25*(3), 317–356.

de Mooij, M. (2013). On the misuse and misinterpretation of dimensions of national culture. *International Marketing Review, 30*(3), 253–261.

Devinney, T. M. (2011). *Bringing managers' decision models into FDI research* (p. 15). Emerald Publishing.

Devinney, T. M., Rugman, A. M., & D'Cruz, J. R. (2001). Multinationals as flagship firms. *The Academy of Management Review, 26*(3), 462.

Djodat, N., & Knyphausen-Aufseß, D. (2017). Revisiting Ghoshal and Bartlett's theory of the multinational corporation as an interorganizational network. *Management International Review, 57*(3), 349–378.

Doh, J. P. (2019). MNEs, FDI, inequality and growth. *Multinational Business Review, 27*(3), 217–220.

Donaldson, L. (2001). *The contingency theory of organizations*. Sage.

Dow, D. (1998). A note on psychological distance and export market selection. *Journal of International Marketing, 8*(1), 51–64.

Dow, D., Liesch, P., & Welch, L. (2018). Inertia and managerial intentionality: Extending the Uppsala model. *Management International Review, 58*(3), 465–493.

Doz, Y., Santos, J., & Williamson, P. (2001). *From global to metanational. How companies win in the knowledge economy*. Harvard Business School Press.

Dunning, J. H. (1988). *Explaining international production*. Routledge. https://doi.org/10.4324/9781315739250

Dunning, J. H. (1989). The study of international business: A plea for a more interdisciplinary approach. *Journal of International Business Studies, 20*(3), 411–436.

Dunning, J., & Lundan, S. M. (2008). *Multinational enterprises and the global economy* (p. 10.18356/43ce1fe7-en). Edward Elgar.

Efrat, K., & Shoham, A. (2013). The interaction between environment and strategic orientation in born globals' choice of entry mode. *International Marketing Review, 30*(6), 536–558.

Egelhoff, W. G., & Wolf, J. (2017). *Understanding matrix structures and their alternatives. The key to designing and managing large, complex organizations* (pp. 43–74). Springer.

Elia, S., Larsen, M. M., & Piscitello, L. (2019). Entry mode deviation: A behavioral approach to internalization theory. *Journal of International Business Studies, 50*(8), 1359–1371.

Ernst, D. (2009). A new geography of knowledge in the electronics industry? Asia's role in global innovation networks. *SSRN Electronic Journal*. https://doi.org/10.2139/ssrn.2742923

Erramilli, M. K., & D'Souza, D. E. (1993). Venturing into foreign markets: The case of the small service firm. *Entrepreneurship Theory and Practice, 17*(4), 29–41.

Faulconbridge, J. (2007). Global shift, Fifth edition: Mapping the changing contours of the world economy. *Journal of Economic Geography, 7*(6), 777–779.

Feenstra, R. C. (1992). How costly is protectionism? *Journal of Economic Perspectives, 6*(3), 159–178.

Feenstra, R. C. (1998). Integration of trade and disintegration of production in the global economy. *Journal of Economic Perspectives, 12*(4), 31–50.

Fernandez-Stark, K., & Gereffi, G. (2019). *Global value chain analysis: A primer* (2nd ed.). Edward Elgar. https://doi.org/10.4337/9781788113779.00008

Fernandez-Stark, K., Hernández, R. A., Mulder, N., & Sauvé, P. (2014). *Introduction*. United Nation. https://doi.org/10.18356/b9138ae4-en

Filatotchev, I., Strange, R., Piesse, J., & Lien, Y.-C. (2007). FDI by firms from newly industrialised economies in emerging markets: Corporate governance, entry mode and location. *Journal of International Business Studies, 38*(4), 556–572.

Forester, J. (1984). Bounded rationality and the politics of muddling through. *Public Administration Review, 44*(1), 23.

Forsgren, M. (2016). A note on the revisited Uppsala internationalization process model – The implications of business networks and entrepreneurship. *Journal of International Business Studies, 47*(9), 1135–1144.

Fuchs, M., & Horn, S. (2019). Managerial decision making and the evolutionary process of internationalization. *Academy of Management Proceedings, 2019*(1), 14801.

Funck, R. H. (1995). *Urban agglomeration and economic growth* (pp. 227–255). Springer.

Gereffi, G. (2018). *Global value chains and development: Redefining the contours of 21st century capitalism* (Development trajectories in global value chains). Cambridge University Press. https://doi.org/10.1017/9781108559423

Gereffi, G., & Fernandez-Stark, K. (2010). The offshore services value chain: Developing countries and the crisis. *Policy Research Working Papers*. https://doi.org/10.1596/1813-9450-5262

Gereffi, G., & Fernandez-Stark, K. (2018). Global value chain analysis: A primer. In G. Gereffi (Ed.), *Global value chains and development: Redefining the contours of 21st century capitalism* (Development trajectories in global value chains) (2nd ed., pp. 305–342). Cambridge University Press. https://doi.org/10.1017/9781108559423.012

Gigerenzer, G., & Selten, R. (2002). *Bounded rationality: The adaptive toolbox*. MIT Press.

Goerzen, A., & Beamish, P. W. (2003). Geographic scope and multinational enterprise performance. *Strategic Management Journal, 24*(13), 1289–1306.

Hassler, M. (2003). The global clothing production system: Commodity chains and business networks. *Global Networks, 3*(4), 513–531.

Hennart, J.-F. (1993). *Organization theory and the multinational corporation* (pp. 157–181). https://doi.org/10.1007/978-1-349-22557-6_7

Hennart, J.-F., & Slangen, A. H. (2015). Yes, we really do need more entry mode studies! A commentary on Shaver. *Journal of International Business Studies, 46*(1), 114–122.

Hennart, J.-F., Majocchi, A., & Forlani, E. (2019). The myth of the stay-at-home family firm: How family-managed SMEs can overcome their internationalization limitations. *Journal of International Business Studies, 50*(5), 758–782.

Hubbard. (2018). *Firm boundaries (empirical studies): 4716*. Palgrave Macmillan UK. https://link.springer.com/content/pdf/10.1057/978-1-349-95121-5_1953-1.pdf

Hultman, M., Robson, M. J., & Katsikeas, C. S. (2009). Export product strategy fit and performance: An empirical investigation. *Journal of International Marketing, 17*(4). https://doi.org/10.1509/jimk.17.4.1

Hultman, M., Katsikeas, C. S., & Robson, M. J. (2011). Export promotion strategy and performance: The role of international experience. *Journal of International Marketing, 19*(4), 1739.

Huygens, A. D. (2017). *American decline and changing global hegemony*. IOWA State University. https://doi.org/10.31274/etd-180810-5777

Hymer, S. (1970). *The efficiency (contradictions) of multinational corporations*. https://doi.org/10.2307/1815843

Inkpen, A. C. (2004). Theories of the multinational enterprise: Diversity, complexity and relevance. *Advances in International Management, 2004*, 43–52.

Jones, G. (2002). Business enterprises and global worlds. *Enterprise and Society, 3*(4), 581–605.

Jones, M. V., & Coviello, N. E. (2005). Internationalisation: Conceptualising an entrepreneurial process of behaviour in time. *Journal of International Business Studies, 36*(3), 284–303.

Kano, L., Tsang, E. W. K., & Yeung, H. W. (2020). Global value chains: A review of the multi-disciplinary literature. *Journal of International Business Studies, 51*(4), 577–622.

Kirca, A. H., Hult, G. T. M., Deligonul, S., Perryy, M. Z., & Cavusgil, S. T. (2012). A multilevel examination of the drivers of firm multinationality. *Journal of Management, 38*(2), 502–530.

Kirkman, B. L., Lowe, K. B., & Gibson, C. B. (2006). A quarter century of culture's consequences: A review of empirical research incorporating Hofstede's cultural values framework. *Journal of International Business Studies, 37*(3), 285–320.

Kirkman, B. L., Lowe, K. B., & Gibson, C. B. (2017). A retrospective on culture's consequences: The 35-year journey. *Journal of International Business Studies, 48*(1), 12–29.

Kutschker, M., & Schmid, S. (2011). *Internationales management* (7th ed.). Oldenburg Wissenschaftsverlag.

Langlois, R. N. (1995). Do firms plan? *Constitutional Political Economy, 6*(3), 247–261.

Lewin, A. Y. (2011). The future of foreign direct investment and the multinational enterprise. *Research in Global Strategic Management, 15*, 301–313.

Macharzina, K., & Engelhard, J. (1991). Paradigm shift in international business research: From Partist and eclectic approaches to the GAINS paradigm. *Management International Review, 31*, 23–43.

McWilliam, S. E., Kim, J. K., Mudambi, R., & Nielsen, B. B. (2019). Global value chain governance: Intersections with international business. *Journal of World Business, 55*, 101067.

Medema, S. G. (1996). Coae, costs, and coordination. *Journal of Economic Issues, 30*(2), 571–578.

Mees-Buss, J., Welch, C., & Westney, D. E. (2019). What happened to the transnational? The emergence of the neo-global corporation. *Journal of International Business Studies, 50*(9), 1513–1543.

Minkov, M., & Hofstede, G. (2012). Hofstede's fifth dimension. *Journal of Cross-Cultural Psychology, 43*(1), 3–14.

Momaya, K. S. (2016). City clusters and break-out in corporate competitiveness: Patterns and perspectives focusing on innovation capabilities and India. *Competitiveness Review, 26*(4), 415–434.

Morschett, D., Schramm-Klein, H., & Swoboda, B. (2010). Decades of research on market entry modes: What do we really know about external antecedents of entry mode choice? *Journal of International Management, 16*(1), 60–77.

Mourtzis, D., & Doukas, M. (2020). The evolution of manufacturing systems: From craftsmanship to the era of customisation. In I. Management Association (Ed.), *Additive manufacturing:*

Breakthroughs in research and practice (pp. 446–477). IGI Global. https://doi.org/10.4018/978-1-5225-9624-0.ch019

Mudambi, R., & Venzin, M. (2010). The strategic nexus of offshoring and outsourcing decisions. *Journal of Management Studies, 47*(8), 1510–1533.

Ng, S., Lee, J., & Soutar, G. N. (2007). Are Hofstede's and Schwartz's value frameworks congruent? *International Marketing Review, 24*(2), 164–180.

Oesterle, M. J. (2005). Informations- und Kommunikationstechnik als Einflussfaktor der Internationalisierung. In M. J. Oesterle & J. Wolf (Eds.), *Internationalisierung und Institution*. Gabler Verlag. https://doi.org/10.1007/978-3-322-89667-4_8

Pearce, R., & Papanastassiou, M. (2006). To 'almost see the world': Hierarchy and strategy in Hymer's view of the multinational. *International Business Review, 15*(2), 151–165.

Pitelis, C. N. (2011). Globalization, development, and history in the work of Edith Penrose. *Business History Review, 85*(1), 65–84.

Pla-Barber, J., Villar, C., & León-Darder, F. (2014). Augmenting versus exploiting entry modes in soft services. *International Marketing Review, 31*(Issue 6), 621–636.

Prahalad, C. K. (1995). New view of strategy: An interview with C.K. Prahalad. *European Management Journal, 13*(2), 131–138.

Prahalad, C. K., & Doz, Y. (1987). *The multinational Mission*. The Free Press, MacMillan.

Qiu, J. X., & Donaldson, L. (2012). Stopford and Wells were right! MNC matrix structures do fit a "high-high" strategy. *Management International Review, 52*(5), 671–689.

Qiu, J., Donaldson, L., & Luo, B. (2012). The benefits of persisting with paradigms in organizational research. *Academy of Management Perspectives, 26*(1), 93–104.

Reuber, A. R. (2016). An assemblage-theoretic perspective on the internationalization processes of family firms. *Entrepreneurship Theory and Practice, 40*(6), 1269–1286.

Root, F. R. (1964). Strategic planning for export marketing. *The International Executive, 6*(4), 17–17.

Root, F. R. (1988). Managing export entry and expansion. *Journal of International Business Studies, 19*(1), 149–151.

Root, F. R. (1994). *Entry strategies for international markets*. Lexington Books.

Rowthorn, R. (2006). Stephen Hymer: An intellectual memoir. *International Business Review, 15*(2), 111–114.

Rugman, A. M. (2005). *International business and government relations in the 21stCentury*. Cambridge University Press. https://doi.org/10.1017/cbo9780511488597.016

Rugman, A. M., & Verbeke, A. (1992). A note on the transnational solution and the transaction cost theory of multinational strategic management. *Journal of International Business Studies, 23*(4), 761–771.

Rugman, A. M., & Verbeke, A. (2003). Extending the theory of the multinational enterprise: Internalization and strategic management perspectives. *Journal of International Business Studies, 34*(2), 125–137.

Rugman, A. M., Li, J., & Oh, C. H. (2009). Are supply chains global or regional? *International Marketing Review, 26*(4/5), 384–395.

Sanchez-Peinado, E., & Pla-Barber, J. (2006). A multidimensional concept of uncertainty and its influence on the entry mode choice: An empirical analysis in the service sector. *International Business Review, 15*(3), 215–232.

Saull, R. (2012). Rethinking hegemony: Uneven development, historical blocs, and the world economic Crisis. *International Studies Quarterly, 56*(2), 323–338.

Schmid, S. (2018). Internationalization of business, cases on strategy formulation and implementation. *MIR Series in International Business, 2018*, 1–25.

Shaver, J. M. (1998). Accounting for endogeneity when assessing strategy performance: Does entry mode choice affect FDI survival? *Management Science, 44*(4), 571–585.

Shenkar, O. (2001). Cultural distance revisited: Towards a more rigorous conceptualization and measurement of cultural differences. *Journal of International Business Studies, 32*(3), 519–535.

Slangen, A. H. L., & van Tulder, R. J. M. (2009). Cultural distance, political risk, or governance quality? Towards a more accurate conceptualization and measurement of external uncertainty in foreign entry mode research. *International Business Review, 18*(3), 276–291.

Spulber, D. F. (2009). *The theory of the firm* (pp. 367–416). Cambridge University Press.

Stopford, J. M., & Wells, L. T. (1972). *Managing the multinational enterprise: Organization of the firm and ownership of the subsidiaries*. Longman, Basic Books.

Surdu, I., Greve, H. R., & Benito, G. R. G. (2020). Back to basics: Behavioral theory and internationalization. *Journal of International Business Studies, 2020*, 1–22.

Tallman, S. (2004). *Theories of the multinational enterprise: Diversity, complexity and relevance* (pp. 53–64). JAI Press.

Thomas, D. E., & Eden, L. (2004). What is the shape of the multinationality-performance relationship? *Multinational Business Review, 12*(1), 89–110.

Vahlne, J.-E., & Johanson, J. (2017). From internationalization to evolution: The Uppsala model at 40 years. *Journal of International Business Studies, 48*(9), 1087–1102.

Verbeke, A., & Kano, L. (2016). An internalization theory perspective on the global and regional strategies of multinational enterprises. *Journal of World Business, 51*(1), 83–92.

Verbeke, A., Kano, L., & Yuan, W. (2016). Inside the regional multinationals: A new value chain perspective on subsidiary capabilities. *International Business Review, 25*(3), 785–793.

Welch, L. S., Benito, G. R. G., & Petersen, B. (2018). *Foreign operation methods: Theory, analysis, strategy*. Edward Elgar.

Williamson, O. E. (1979). Transaction-cost economics: The governance of contractual relations. *The Journal of Law and Economics, 22*(2), 233–261.

Williamson, O. E. (1998). Transaction cost economics: How it works; where it is headed. *De Economist, 146*(1), 23–58.

Williamson, O. E. (2005). *The economics of governance*. AEA Papers and Proceedings.

Wolf, J. (2020). *Organisation, Management, Unternehmensführung, Theorien, Praxisbeispiele und Kritik* (pp. 1–44). Springer.

Wolf, J., & Egelhoff, W. G. (2002). A reexamination and extension of international strategy–structure theory. *Strategic Management Journal, 23*(2), 181–189.

Wolf, J., & Egelhoff, W. G. (2013). An empirical evaluation of conflict in MNC matrix structure firms. *International Business Review, 22*(3), 591–601.

Xie, Q. (2017). Firm age, marketization, and entry mode choices of emerging economy firms: Evidence from listed firms in China. *Journal of World Business, 52*(3), 372–385.

Yamin, M. (2011). A commentary on Peter Buckley's writings on the global factory. *Management International Review, 51*(2), 285–293.

Zhang, J. (2012). Global shift: Mapping the changing contours of the world economy. *Economic Geography, 88*(3), 337–338.

Zhao, H., Ma, J., & Yang, J. (2017). 30 years of research on entry mode and performance relationship: A meta-analytical review. *Management International Review, 57*(5), 653–682.

The Global Economy as the Macro-Environment 2

International business (IB) examines the cross-national business activities and describes the internationalization of business firms. The behavior of international firms is embedded in a dynamically changing macro environment, which is defined as the global economy. This macro-environment affects the actions of individual actors, and these actors affect change in the environment through their actions (Archer, 2000).

The analysis of the global economy can be examined at different levels. It is important to acknowledge that an in-depth understanding of international business includes more than just the study of single components that constitute the general macro-environment; instead, it requires analyzing the global business activities of the international firm as parts of a more complex larger whole.

One of the critical elements that can be identified in this complex whole is the extent and structure of international trade relations between and within firms. Although international trade is aggregated at the country level, in fact the international business firms carry out all the imports and exports, creating the intricate pattern and structure of global trade. Studying the pattern of international trade helps to understand the actual cross-border activities of international firms. The pattern and structure of international trade demonstrate how dynamically and radically trade patterns have changed over the last decades.

Another critical feature of international business studies is to look at the structure and pattern of foreign direct investment (FDI). FDI is a capital transfer from a business firm headquartered in one country to a business firm located in another country.

Since the 1950s, the structure of FDI, measured by the inflow and outflow of capital, has changed radically (Buckley, 1989; Buckley & Casson, 2010). Analyzing the cyclical growth and pattern of FDI allows assessing how firm motives and strategies affect the structural pattern of FDIs. Studying FDI provides an insight into the dynamically evolving nature of global production networks (GPNs), another core feature of the global economy.

M. Fuchs, *International Management*,
https://doi.org/10.1007/978-3-662-65870-3_2

In addition, foreign direct investment patterns demonstrate how multinational firm strategies change over time.

The pattern of international trade and the structure of FDI in- and outflows are two dimensions to grasp the scope and scale of international business activities. It is important to note that international trade and the pattern of FDI are the outcomes of internationalizing firms, even though the data are usually aggregated at the national level.

International business activities are embedded in the global macro-structure but carried out by multinational firms. Multinational firms enact the structure and process of an overall global economy, both being mutually dependent (Castells, 2005). The macrostructure of the global economy simultaneously and significantly frames the behavior of international firms (Phelps, 2004; Rugman, 2005). Thus, it is essential to acknowledge the mutual dependency between the structure (the global economy) and micro-behavior of the single firm (agent). It is this interdependent joint development process between the macro-structure and micro-behavior of the agents that, as a whole, generates a dynamic pattern and evolutionary processes, defining the realm of IB (Archer, 2000, 2003).

2.1 Globalization or Internationalization?

Since the 1990s, globalization has emerged as a powerful narrative to describe significant features of the global economy. Its different effects on society portray the inherent nature of globalization. One major trigger is the assumed convergence of cultures and economies, related to an increasing disintegration of national politics. Kenichi Ohmae, managing director of McKinsey in Japan, declared in his bestseller *The Borderless World,* that for the success of the business firm, "country of origin does not matter. Location of headquarters does not matter [and] products [. . .] have become denationalized"(Ohmae, 1990: 94). Alternatively, globalization is defined as the great flattener that levels out barriers and removes all distances (Friedman, 2000).

Globalization

The term globalization describes the dynamic and cyclical development of the global economy. Globalization is defined as multifaceted processes transcending national borders. It is labeled a transnational process of multidirectional effects caused by several triggers. Globalization is characterized by its structure and is explained as an outcome of new communication technologies that unlock unforeseen opportunities. Focusing on the nation-state, globalization is defined by its effects on the national policies but refers to a hierarchical structure among strong and weak states. Globalization addresses the prevalent dominance of a particular trend in industries such as music, film, or cuisine, leading to an assumed convergence or divergence of cultures

(continued)

(Jameson, 2000). Globalization is not restricted to the multidirectional flow of goods and services (Ritzer, 2003). Globalization is a narrative about processes that transcend national and regional borders. In this context, transcendence is interpreted as rising above or reaching beyond national borders.

The term globalization was first used in the early 1970s and became a powerful narrative but eventually mutated into a buzzword that describes almost everything (Jameson, 2000; Ritzer, 2003). Although several camps refer to globalization as a culturally homogenizing force, others interpreted it primarily as an economic phenomenon. More pluralistic approaches claim, "despite its wide range of attributes and meanings, research on globalization has been characterized by more shared agendas than critics pointing to its alleged lack of coherence might assume" (Sachsenmaier, 2011: 66).

Stages of Globalization

Thomas Friedman, *a strong supporter* of globalization, describes it as a dynamic ongoing process that links distant nation-states, markets, people, and technologies "faster, deeper, and cheaper than ever before" (Friedman, 2000: 34). Friedman identified several stages of globalization. The first stage, baptized as Globalization 1.0, covers a historical period stretching 300 years from 1492 to 1800. The story Friedman is eloquently announcing is about how distances had been shrinking. He invokes Christoph Columbus as a crown witness, who bridged the distance between the West and the East. Maritime technologies, advanced techniques for navigation, and larger and faster ships revolutionized naval trade. However, Friedman's story offers only a selective account of what is conventionally accepted as historical fact, as it was not only the advance of maritime technologies, but also Portugal's and Spain's exploration based on the exploitation of distant colonies. It was not simply maritime technologies, but gunpowder ships reaching out into distant previously unknown territories across the Atlantic and the Pacific Ocean.

The next stage, Globalization 2.0, covers 200 years from 1800 to 2000, spanning from the advent of the industrial revolution and culminating in a radical revolution of communication and transportation technologies. However, it would be too simplistic to reduce the radical changes that have swept through these two centuries to have been caused by communications technologies and the personal computer alone. From 1820, corporate business developed into large industrial conglomerates and expanded faster and deeper into distant global markets. Several industries started to operate globally, crossing national borders and moving into unknown territories, spanning further existing distances. According to Friedman, the current phase, he entitled Globalization 3.0, emerged around the turn of the twenty-first century. This

(continued)

time the Internet is singled out as the central and all-revolutionizing technology. Distances shrinking further, and finally, metaphorically, borders vanished, enhancing the exploration and exploitation of the last idle territories on the globe. Friedman, the author, and creator of this bold categorization, presents us with one of his many witnesses, Netscape co-founder Marc Andreessen, who asserts enthusiastically: "[...] the most profound thing to me is the fact that a 14-year-old in Romania or Bangalore or the Soviet Union or Vietnam has all the information, all the tools, all the software easily available to apply knowledge however they want" (Friedman, 2005: 22).

These and many other stories created powerful narratives, which do not balance details, sources, and facts about Globalization. They reiterate a message widely accepted as the general truth. We may take offense at the overly optimistic portrayal, but that is not the point; rather, these perspectives apply only to one pervasive extent displaying a more complex phenomenon.

Globalization is a complex construct. But it seems like chasing an elephant from different perspectives, offering further insight and truth, each from its narrow scope, describing a particular aspect of reality, but never reaching the complex whole (Phelps & Fuller, 2000).

While globalization is a phenomenon profoundly affecting several areas of life in our societies, it is a much-distorted view accounting only for the gains. It negates the losses or inaccurately points out the failures. That can be easily illustrated by a few brief descriptions that mirror the paradox in the debate over globalization. Hyper-globalists (the proponents), like New York Times columnist Thomas Friedman, are fascinated by the sheer possibilities that globalization appear to create. Skeptics (the opponents) dispute that globalization is a new concept and focus almost exclusively on the negatives (Hirst & Thompson, 1999).

Global Cut Flower Industry

Let us assume a flower shop in a small town in Italy. The shop owner regularly purchases fresh flowers, such as roses and tulips, from a Dutch wholesaler delivered twice a week. The roses have been transported to the Netherlands by plane a few days before, from Latin America. On Valentine's Day, Airlines like Cargolux add extra capacities, approximately 20 flights per week to transport tons of flowers from Bogota to Miami, Florida, or Amsterdam (Muir, 2014). The flowers bought from the small neighborhood store in Italy were grown on large plantations in Bogota, Columbia. A large fraction of the total supply of cut flowers bought from the supermarket or small flower store around the corner comes from large plantations operated in Latin America or Africa. In Colombia, the first plantations were set up in

(continued)

the early 1970s, and they cover an area of approximately 5000 hectares, and employ 200,000 people working in that industry. Colombia, after the Netherlands, is the second-largest exporter of flowers. All this is made possible by a sophisticated trade system, which is the outcome of global production networks organized by a complex set of business relations (Beaverstock, 2009; Faulconbridge, 2007).

Countless other examples may illustrate the extent of the fragmented global division of labor, apparent in almost every industry, product or service, from shoes, apparel, food, personal computers, and many other consumer products. However, the single product or service visualize merely a snapshot or the tip of an iceberg hiding the actual scope and scale of the related global production networks (GPNs).

The common thread that runs through this account includes major issues in international business studies. Production and trade of goods and services is highly fragmented across different social, cultural, and economic worlds. The global economy is instituted in vibrant and powerful urban centers, surrounded by a weak and much less prosperous periphery, a spatial area performing a distinct role in these fragmented and highly dispersed global production networks. The core and periphery are intertwined across vast distances. Not only are economic activities highly differentiated, but their gains are also distributed unequally (Baldwin et al., 2003). The core and periphery regions are all subject to a permanent transformation. One central trigger is the ongoing, dynamically changing integration manifested by the extent of global value chains (GVCs), linking distant geographies and population, each dis-rooted and rooted in its habitat, bound in their native cultures and lifestyles, while at the same time alienated from them (Davis, 2019; Pearce & Papanastassiou, 2006; Zhang, 2012).

2.2 The Duality Between Structure and Agency

International business activities are analyzed by primarily focusing on business firms. However, each firm is embedded in a distinct social, political, cultural, and economic environment (Stopford, 2005; Strange & Humphrey, 2019; Strange & Newton, 2006; Streusand, 2018). One description of the environment focuses on the structural pattern and scope of the global economy, defined as a crucial macro-structure for the micro-behavior of the firm. The macro-structure of the global economy affects the scope of action for multinational firms and is the vital frame for national governments and several stakeholders, all contributing to the enactment of the macro-structure.

But it is important to acknowledge, that both structure and agency are conceptualized as significantly and mutually reciprocated. Because the individual actor (acting within its micro-structure) remains capable of making utterly deliberate choices.

However, many of the alternative options are predetermined by the macro-structure in which each action is likewise embedded. Note, the macro-structure did not develop independently from the agencies of individual actors. However, the outcome of past actions arising from the mutual interdependence between structure and agency, which gains some institutionalized stability over time, affects the current behavior of individual agents. However, the described effect is never understood as a rigid determination. Instead, it is in a constant and evolutionary process of enactment, affirmation, and modification, through gradual but slow transformations of existing institutional rules enacted by previous affirmative or non-affirmative actions. The interactions between the macrostructure (forces shaping the structural pattern and scope of the world economy) and the microstructure (forces shaping the scope and scale of individual action) enact a highly dynamic interdependent relationship between a constantly evolving world economy (macro-structure) in which individuals set their actions (micro-structure). Thus, in analyzing firm behavior and the dynamics of the global economy, it is essential to recognize the role of both structure and agency. They matter essentially because of their interdependent reciprocating mutuality (Archer, 1995, 2000; Archer & Elder-Vass, 2012; Cassell, 1993; North, 1991, 1993).

Examining the behavior of the multinational firm, it is assumed that the focus on the individual firm is sufficient, to explain the complex interaction between firm and macro-environment. Often the nature of the macro-environment, which is perceived as the appropriate approach in explaining the behavior of the individual firm is used to analyze key questions. In contrast, the agency of the individual firm is marginalized or neglected.

We need to reconcile the role of agency, how it interacts with the prevalent macro-environment, and how this mutually dependent interaction affects the evolution and pattern of the structure and agency. It is equally important that we do not conflate the explanation of individual agency with the explanation of the overall structure of the macro-environment. Realizing the importance of both –structure and agency– in explaining the behavior of the internationalizing firm and the evolution of the macro-environment, is necessary to understand the co-evolving dynamic of the mutual reciprocation.

2.2.1 Upward and Downward Conflation of Structure and Agency

What is meant by conflating structure and agency? When analyzing macro-structures and individual acts, we can identify various components. In the structure, we observe different levels, political, economic, social, or cultural spheres, each exerting a specific mutual influence. Each substructure interacts with the other and generates a particular effect on the other. All these structures are framing actions, which do not predetermine the activities of the individual actor but provide a general, broadly unquestioned framework.

The Co-evolution of Agency and Structure

Let us assume a car driver uses the car for commuting, every day, early in the morning from a small suburban house to the workplace downtown, in a nearby big city. They are using the car deliberately to drive the distance every working day. They consciously decided not to take the train because the rigid timetable of commuter trains does not match their flexible working hours. Here, the primary trigger of behavior can be easily explained by the motives of the individual actor's preferences for using the car. Arriving in the city, the driver steers their car into an inexpensive parking garage. Compared to other options, it is reasonably priced and approximately a twenty-minute walk away from her office. Depending on the arrival time, they often have to proceed down several floors in the parking garage to locate a free parking slot. Their elaborate search for a free parking slot is not really a deliberate decision, rather an outcome of their habit of using the car for commuting and an effect of arriving slightly late in the parking garage. However, although the individual behavior and search for a parking space can be explained by personal motives as well, they are equally affected by structural effects independently interacting with their actions. Here, some of the individual actions can be likewise explained by the superordinate structure, traffic congestions, overcrowded parking garage, limited supply of decent parking spaces, flexible working hours, and so forth. The overall availability of job alternatives shapes the need to commute to work. Therefore, it is no longer the individual motives that exclusively determine one's actions. The high price of parking space probably compels the driver to choose a parking lot twenty minutes away from the workplace. In this case, the individual's actions are influenced by a superordinate structure of available and affordable parking space as well, and they need to search for a free parking space for a longer period. These factors are also affected by the superordinate structure of the parking garage's occupancy, depending on the time of arrival. In the latter case, perhaps departing earlier could have removed the need to search for a free parking lot. However, whether leaving earlier is possible is unknown because of possible factors not elaborated here.

Structure and agency are always mutually interacting. However, analyzing these two interdependent effects is prone to two flaws. One is upward conflation. An example of the *upward conflation* of structure and agency is exemplified in an eloquent statement by John Stuart Mill: "Men in a state of society are still men. Their actions and passions are obedient to the laws of individual human nature. Men are not, when brought together, converted into another kind of substance with different properties, as hydrogen and oxygen differ from that of water". Mill was strongly swayed in that "the effects produced in social phenomena by any complex set of circumstances amount precisely to the sum of the effects of the circumstances taken singly" (Mill, 2006: 573).

Note, Mill explains the nature of human agency as a mere outcome of individual or idiosyncratic passions. Neither society nor social interaction matters much or alters the human nature. Mill endorses a concept of society that is defined as not more than the aggregate sum of isolated individual behavior.

Upward conflation is the flaw to put individual agencies into the center stage of any explanation (Archer, 1995: 4), a theory that conceptualizes the individual as the primary source of structure. Individual agency is assumed as the sole basis of causation that operates exclusively in a "one-way, upward direction" (Archer, 1995: 4). In its most extreme embodiment, the entire society is viewed as a macro-structure, perceived not more as the aggregate sum of all the individuals (Archer, 1995, 1996; Archer & Elder-Vass, 2012; Mill, 2006). The disappointing conclusion of this theoretical argument is that the macro-phenomenon must be explained by focusing on the individual agent. The fallacy of such an approach is that the social structure (or the entire macro-environment) is taken as not more than a passive outcome "incapable of acting back to influence individual activities" (Archer, 1995: 4).

In contrast, downward conflation is the other flaw. In this case, the macro-structure is deemed as the true generic source of all social reality and the primary foundation, trigger, or initial factor of the individual behavior. This other reductionism is called *downward conflation*. This compelling perspective was first put forward by the French sociologist Emilé Durkheim, who claimed "whenever certain elements combine, and produce, by the fact of their combination, new phenomena, it is plain that these new phenomena reside not in the original elements but in the totality formed by their union" (Archer, 1995: 3; Durkheim, 1962: xlvii). This penetrating and enduring thesis led to the belief that social structures do not explain but determine individual behavior, completely ignoring the motives and preferences that deliberately affect individual behavior (Archer, 1995: 3).

However, neither downward nor upward conflation is exclusively capable of explicating the mutual and steady interplay between both sources of causality. Their primary weakness is the neglect of the co-evolving *interplay* between structure and agency.

It is essential to acknowledge that structure is affecting the agency, and the agency is affecting the structure. Structure, even if capable of constricting individual behavior, does not abolish individual reflexivity or deliberate action. Likewise, individual behavior, despite its intentionality, cannot overturn or neglect structure.

2.2.2 Structure and Agency: A Morphogenetic Approach

Structure and agency are best understood by focusing on how each aspect is related to the other. It is misleading to ignore the problem of conflating structure and agency because we are constantly confronted with the fundamental question of how both agency and structure affect a particular phenomenon.

In IB research, the structure is often referred to as environment or institutional milieu. Entry mode choice is affected by the institutional environment. For example, the unfamiliarity and uncertainty in foreign markets is considered a major factor influencing market entry decisions, but the decision itself to enter the unfamiliar environment, and subsequent activity in these markets, affects the institutional environment through the actual interactions between the firm and its environment. In fact, firm behavior (by making a particular entry mode choice) is reciprocating with the external and co-evolving environment. Even if a pertinent rule cannot be changed, firms learn how to align their strategies to the rules and enact strategies to elude it or start lobbying to change the impact of the rules. All this deliberate behavior will affect the environment over time, albeit slowly.

Nobel laureate Douglass North described institutions as "humanly devised constraints that structure political, economic and social interaction." The meaning of this definition resides in the notion of "device," which is, to create, fabricate or produce the rules of action. Existing rules, values, and habits arise "from both informal constraints (sanctions, taboos, customs, traditions, and codes of conduct) and formal rules (constitutions, laws, property rights)." One of the primary functions is that institutions have been devised (intentionally) by human beings to create order and reduce uncertainty" (North, 1991: 97).

Rules and values, like habitual routines, became institutionalized over time by a complex and intricate (and still ongoing) process. However, individual agents do not blindly adhere to, follow, or disagree with these rules and values and are not addicted blindly to their habits. A cornerstone in institutionalism is that respective agents will be affected by a system of values. However, nobody blindly follows formal and informal rules that make up a common value system. Agents can deliberately question the value of a common rule and reflect upon presumably factual objective values and norms. Individuals are capable of reflecting on what is right or wrong. Each human agent can deliberately examine the legitimacy of motives, thoughts, preferences, and feelings. Consequently, human agents may accept rules and norms as legitimate or not.

The Emergence of a Rule Is the Outcome of Previous Social Interactions

It is important to note that the "emergence [of a rule or a value] takes time" (Archer, 1995: 14). It is the outcome of social interaction. Rules, values, and habits arise "from both informal constraints (sanctions, taboos, customs, traditions, and codes of conduct) and formal rules (constitutions, laws, and property rights)." (Archer, 1995: 14). For example, a cultural pattern that has emerged in the past results from a related but distinct set of functional conditions (which may have become obsolete or impractical). However, it remains that the cultural pattern "w[as] humanly devised to create order and reduce uncertainty" (North, 1991: 97). The functional property that creates order and reduces uncertainty may become increasingly autonomous from the "original conditional causative sources." Over time, the original rules and values will enact autonomously new rules and values (Archer, 1995: 14). Thus,

(continued)

existing structure pre-dates individual behavior and acting in accordance to these pre-existing rules and values, the performed action affects and moderates either the "reproduction or transformation" (Archer, 1995: 14). Human behavior framed by existing rules and values "necessarily post-dates the action sequences which gave rise to it" (Archer, 1995: 14).

It is this sequential and iterative duality that is characterized as a morphogenetic cycle constituted by the following processes: (1) "conditioning of structure"; (2) the "interaction" between structure and agents; and (3) the "structural elaboration" (Archer, 1995: 16). From this ontological position, it becomes evident that we cannot refer to a context (structural strata) without identifying the disposition of its agents. Following Ernest Gellner (1971), Archer claims, "we cannot identify the dispositions of 'voters' without referring to 'elections,' of 'soldiers' without 'armies,' or of 'bank tellers' without 'banks'" (1995: 15).

Applying this approach to IB studies, we need to recognize that we cannot analyze managerial behavior without considering the firm and its environment. Exploring the international scope and scale of multinational firms, we need to consider the effects of the institutional environment, which are much more subtle than the often-used and overly vague term "global economy." These propositions imply that we need to explain both the agent and structure as well as "the ties that bind all" (Archer, 1995: 17).

Then, the important questions are as follows: How does macro-structure affect firm behavior? What is the exact link between these two strata? To find an answer, it is common to start by attributing objective values to the structure and subjectivity to the agencies. Depending on the analytical approach and the theoretical grounding, either structure or agency is assigned the dominant role. For example, in IB research, firm behavior is assumed to be rational. Making a foreign investment is an outcome of a rational choice prepared by reasonable managers.

However, the notion of rationality is dependent on the institutional context. While rational action (firm behavior) and the institutional environment both exercise "quite different properties and powers," we need to accept that "structural and cultural factors ultimately emerge from people [contextually, in a business firm] and are efficacious only through people" (Archer, 2003: 2f).These properties and powers are embedded in different role models, of which, management is one.

Structure is the outcome of people's behavior, and in the effect, these emerged structures are carried out through people's actions (Weick, 2010).

The dual and reciprocating causation between agency and structure is mutually enacted by the "power of these social forms," while the structured body of law and other institutionalized rules, norms, and values "are mediated through agency" (Archer, 2003: 2).

We do not blindly adhere to rules and norms, and people do not blindly execute orders or follow rigid, existing institutional rules. All agents, weak and powerful, are capable of acting on their reflexive power. Individual agents can endorse rules, silently adhere to them, or intentionally refuse to accept them (Archer, 1995: 14).

The mutuality of agency and structure is a well-known phenomenon in organizational science, but neglected in its immediate implications for evolutionary change in institutional structure (Barnard, 1938). Two agents may have completely different interpretations of a widely accepted rule, behavior, or value.

Agents act through an existing structure that frames their deliberate behavior. However, as structure does not determine the outcome, the consequences of actions carried out by individual agents are contingent. We need to acknowledge that the objective structure shapes the agent's subjectivity. However, it does not determine their independent and contingent choice. Structural properties interact continuously through the deliberate powers of agents, who thereby elaborate properties of a pertaining structure. It is precisely this *generative mechanism* between structures and agency that matters (Archer, 1996, 2000, 2003). These reproductive, dynamic, and generative mechanisms between structure and agency need to be acknowledged.

2.3 Core–Periphery Relations and the New Economic Geography

Not surprisingly, studying firm behavior in IB is confronted with a complex, often opaque relationship, between macro-structure and the agency of business firms (Baldwin et al., 2003: 19). In international economics, the pervasive hierarchical relations between core and periphery in an established canonical knowledge and empirically demonstrated by several studies explaining agglomeration (Gordon & McCann, 2000; Mokyr, 1995; Rodríguez-Pose et al., 2013; Williamson, 1995).

Agglomeration

Agglomeration is defined as a spatial concentration of firms and their corresponding business activities within a close and relatively dense clustered regional area. Agglomeration effects were described in 1826 by German economist Johann Heinrich v. Thünen in his study "Der isolierte Staat in Beziehung auf Landwirtschaft und Ökonomie" (The Isolated State in Relation to Agriculture and Economy). Similarly, interdependent effects were painstakingly examined in 1909 by Alfred Weber in his study "Über den Standort der Industrien" (On the Location of Industries). Agglomeration effects describe the accelerating and reciprocating dynamic growth of core locations, such as industrial districts or urban centers,

(continued)

constantly attracting the colocation of mutually complementing and supporting economic activities. Agglomeration is triggered by various forces that accelerate the migration of people from the surrounding periphery to the core, supporting the growth of the core and depleting the periphery. Although the core appears to gain from migration and the periphery appears to lose, both remain interdependent.

2.4 Agglomeration and Gravity Equation

It is commonly reasoned that urban agglomeration, within more significant populations, is somewhat of a tautological process, because the duality of structure and agency is neglected. Agglomeration generates more opportunities, such as an expanding job market, better quality housing, superior health services infrastructure, and enhanced educational opportunities, attract more people from the peripheral regions. Thus, a larger population fuels the attractiveness of a location, further leading to additional business opportunities. Those industries attracted provide more jobs and stimulate further demand, attracting in addition, other industries. Thus, a self-reinforcing cycle is set in motion that translates into higher incomes and economic growth, creating further growth.

However, multiple interactions between core and peripheral regions characterize the dynamics of the global economy caused by trade flows, economic growth, and migration. In international economics, a number of theories sophistically explain the trade flows between different nations. The gravity equation (GE) model is a robust model that explains the volume and direction of bilateral world trade. The model assumes that trade dynamics between the core and periphery are significantly affected by trading costs (which are assumed to be low or high). Trade flows are further influenced by common borders, sizes of economies, and the (cultural and political) distance between trading entities (Anderson & van Wincoop, 2003).

Gravity equation models predict the size and pattern of trade flows between two countries, calculating the effects of a country's gross domestic product (GDP), the distance between the countries, and influences caused by a common border, language, or currency (Fratianni et al., 2011). The GE models test several cause-effect relations. One is geographical affinity, assuming that greater proximity between two countries, measured by the size a common border, is enhancing trade (Balistreri & Hillberry, 2007; McCallum, 1987). The size of economies, a proxy for income, measured using GDP, further affect bilateral trade flows, showing a positive significant relation to income (Fratianni, 2009). GE models of international trade empirically demonstrate how several forces and drivers significantly enact backward and forward linkages between trading countries (Baldwin et al., 2003: 28; Feenstra, 1998).

Initially, British economist Marshall (1920) described agglomeration as the effect of co-location of similar and supporting business firms in so-called industrial districts. He identified key contributory factors that increase agglomeration. Marshall argued that industries that co-locate in adjacent locations, attract workers with industry-specific talents, generating a shared labor market pool which is attractive to labor migration as it offers better job opportunities and greater flexibility in employment. In addition, the increased co-location of industries is a trigger for a more advanced supply of non-tradeable inputs. Co-location of industries creates a more sophisticated pool of technologies that can enhance existing production practices and trigger innovation within industry clusters, caused by spillover effects (Krugman, 1991).

However, the critical argument about the causation of agglomeration is that a substantial amount of demand is generated by the co-located clustered industries themselves. This circularity triggers a positive acceleration effect on market demand, attracting further forward and backward linkages in these industries. However, the created circularity of demand is based on the degree of specificity of the demand. Combined with low transportation costs between different regional clusters and industries, characterized by a large potential of economies of scale, the agglomeration effect is more robust in regions that have started early to attract industries (Krugman, 1991: 497).

The impact of urban clustering on the development of regional economies is a key focus in economic geography. Analyzing the pattern and structure of the global economy urban clusters and the shift in agglomeration remains an important concern. The enormous size of the population in the largest urban agglomerations worldwide illustrates such effects. A few urban agglomerations appear to have reached their urban peaks or limits, such as Tokyo or Osaka. Nevertheless, all other examples will double their size by 2035, according to the projections calculated by the UN Population Division. The sheer size of these agglomerations is an indication of economic magnitude. It raises elementary issues of how the infrastructure and public services will be designed under such large-scale agglomerations.

Urban Agglomeration

By 2035, urban areas will be the home of the majority of a country's population. Individual urban agglomerations such as New Delhi, populated by more than 30 million people in 2020, is projected to grow to 43 million inhabitants by the year 2035; In Japan, the Tokyo metropolitan area will be home to about 36 million people by 2035, approximately the same size as it was in 2020. Fast growing cities such as Kolkata, Manila, and Lahore, will inhabit approximately 20 million people in 2035, twice as much as today.

A few urban agglomerations appear to have reached their limits, such as Tokyo or Osaka. However, many are doubling their size within the next ten years or by 2035, according to the projections calculated by the UN Population Division. The sheer size of these agglomerations is an indication of the growing economic magnitude in such megacities (United Nations, World Population Prospects, 2018).

2.5 Interpreting the Data on the World Economy

> Per capita income of growth is not the only indicator of welfare. Over the long run, there has been a dramatic increase in life expectation. In the year 1000, the average infant could expect to live about 24 years. A third would die in the first year of life; hunger and epidemic disease would ravage the survivors. (Maddison, 2001: 17)

The expansion of the global economy is a story about the constant battle among competing regions and the rise and fall of powerful national economies. As indicated in the quote above, it is widely acknowledged that the growth of per capita income is not the only indicator of wealth. Moreover, growth, while steady, is also cyclical and interrupted periodically by severe shocks (Hart, 1999; Minsky, 2016). Thus, it is crucial to acknowledge that any interpretation of the past is dependent on the data available for a particular historical period. We further need to acknowledge that all measures used to operationalize aspects of the growth of an economy rely on a particular conception of prosperity and wealth, which is highly subjective and disputed.

The term development, while more accepted at first glance, reveals different meanings that affect how data are collected. Regardless of which indicator is chosen to measure development, the interpretation is not only dependent on the conception of how development is achieved, but equally on what development means. Presenting a balanced account on that issue, we need to differentiate how available data portray the success and failure of economies (Atkinson, 2015).

2.5.1 Gross Domestic Product: Its Pattern and Structure

2.5.1.1 Development of Gross Domestic Product

Total global GDP increased by a factor of 61 between 1960 and 2020, from USD 1.385 trillion in 1960 to USD 87.436 trillion in 2020 (World Bank). A difficult number to grasp, but it reveals the huge upsurge in disposable income and wealth. These numbers present an era in which IB activity increased significantly. We know that GDP is not a perfect estimate for the wealth and progress of national economies, but it has been widely used since 1937, when Simon Kuznets presented a feasible method for the measurement of GDP (Abramovitz, 1986).

How to Measure the Gross Domestic Product

GDP is measured annually as the sum of the value added by all resident producers in an economy plus product taxes minus subsidies. The annual GDP for a single economy is calculated by adding up the value of all final goods and services produced within the country. Alternatively, GDP can be measured by accounting for all expenditures on domestically produced goods and services. Another common

(continued)

approach to measuring GDP is calculating all income generated in the national economy by all its firms, that is, earnings from production, plus wages and salaries for employees, and all income generated through interests earned on capital, rents, and profits received from shares. All three methods will generally produce the same figure because the value of domestic goods and services equals aggregated spending (Krugman & Wells, 2017).

GDP is used to measure the size of an economy in a given period, and we can identify the growth of an economy by comparing its value across different periods. We use this information to compare the *measured* size of one economy with the size of other economies. This comparison is interpreted to mean that one economy either performs better or worse than the other. GDP is reliable provided that the same standard procedure is applied for all countries. While GDP is not without shortcomings, it is widely used to measure the size of an economy, especially compared to past periods, and contrasted with similar other economies.

2.5.1.2 Structure of GDP

There still are significant irregularities between the international standards practiced in calculating GDP, as the infrastructure and resources of many statistical agencies, particularly in developing countries, impose substantial constraints (OECD, 2006; Song, 2019). But looking at the impressive growth of the world's GDP in Fig. 2.1, it is easy to observe a steady growth and regular setbacks with more or less rapid recoveries. Information on how GDP is generated and distributed within economies is not presented in Fig. 2.1. However, if we take the distribution of a group of selected countries for the year 2019, we see that the United States of America (USA) with 26%, the European Union (EU) with 18%, and China with 15%, on a rounded basis, contribute to almost 59% of the world's GDP, and all the other countries contribute the remaining 41%. The data in Fig. 2.1 partially reveal that there is a significant gap between the group of high and low income countries, including the still substantial differences between and within regions across the globe. If one looks at the pattern of distribution of GDP within and between countries, a very uneven picture becomes apparent (World Bank, 2021). Annual data published by the World bank provides an accessible but selective account of how GDP is distributed among different regional aggregates. And it is important to acknowledge that the gap between high- and low-income economies remains remarkable.

However, GDP is a measure of national income; it does not reflect the amount of disposable income in individual households (Atkinson, 2015: 101f). The inequality within and across nations can be measured by the percentage of a country's population categorized as "absolutely poor." The measure termed "absolute poverty" illustrates how much of the total population is forced to live with less than 1.9 USD a day in a country (Allen, 2017). Focusing on this indicator, the share of people living in absolute poverty decreased from

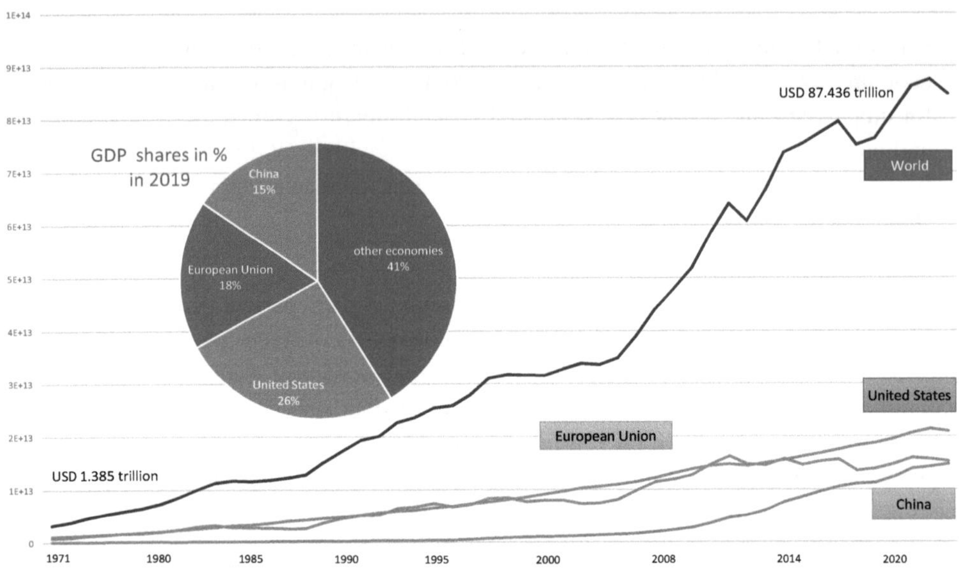

Fig. 2.1 World GDP (current prices, in trillion USD) from the year 1970 to 2020; selected regions. World Bank data, 2021, Creative Commons License (cc-BY 4.0)

approximately 42.7% to less than 10% in the last decades (World Bank, 2022). But the absolute number of people living in abject poverty is still around 1.4 billion. In high-income countries, less than 0.6% of the population is classified as absolutely poor. Some regions have been able to make amazing progress in recent decades, while others have been less fortunate. The most significant progress has been achieved in South Asia, where the share of people living in absolute poverty dropped from 58% to 26%, within the last four decades. In low-income countries and sub-Saharan Africa, the number of people living in abject poverty remains high: 40.4% in low-income countries and 46.8% in sub-Saharan Africa, where people still sustain on less than $1.9 per day. Even though this account is fairly selective, it provides a contrast to the overly optimistic impression of the overall GDP expansion that occurred within the last 60 years, illustrated in Fig. 2.1.

Arguing purely on the empirical basis of per capita income, we can readily observe a growing polarization and differentiation over the years, both between and within developed and developing countries (Easterly, 2002). Overall, the polarization that was first observed in the early 1970s solidifies the following account: The Third World as such remains highly fragmented. In the 1980s, a deeper segregation emerged within the group of Third World countries and revealed its most dramatic contours in sub-Saharan Africa, which remain prevalent to this day.

Capture the Inequality

Trying to capture the inequality within and between national economies, Antony Atkinson demonstrates that over the last hundred years, we can identify a period where the inequality within high-income countries was falling, but inequality between countries was growing. While today inequality within prosperous economies is rising, inequality between them is falling. However, Atkinson stresses that a comparison across such a long time cannot provide a broad picture. He reminds us that we need to acknowledge several dimensions of inequality: inequality among whom (e.g., between families and among generations) and inequalities of what (e.g., disposable household income and inequality of consumption) (Atkinson, 2015: 15–33). Indeed, since the 1950s, GDP has increased across all countries. However, a closer inspection of the relevant social and economic indicators for selected economies illustrates considerable disparities. In 2017, an average of 9.2 percent of the world's population was estimated to be living below the poverty line, earning only $1.90 per day—a threshold based on the average of the national poverty lines of the 15 poorest countries. This represents 689 million extremely poor individuals, 52 million fewer than in 2015 (World Bank, 2022).

Within the world economy as a whole, the disparities are significant, affecting not only distribution of income but multiplying social, economic, and political problems. Fröbel et al. (1991) observed that, since World War II, the gap between the industrialized and developing countries has been growing, especially in poor economies. Moreover, social and economic inequalities are reinforced not only between but also within countries (Atkinson, 2015).

2.5.2 World Trade: Its Pattern and Structure

A further pivotal dimension of the global economy is international trade. International trade is the cross-border export and import of goods and services. Trade data compiles the cross-border trade of goods (e.g., machines, automobiles, or energy), and services (Reinert, 2021; Reinert et al., 2009). Trade has always been an integral part of civilization and can be traced back to the earliest stages of mankind (Tracy & Chaudhuri, 1991).

2.5.2.1 Development of Trade

The uneven patterns of global economic development translate into a highly fragmented geographic distribution in which selected countries and regions participate in the global trade. The current pattern of world trade is the outcome of a highly idiosyncratic international division of labor. However, the international division of labor is equally the outcome and source of unequal trade relations between countries. Similar to GDP, international trade in goods and services has been growing at an astonishing rate for centuries. However, the rate of growth of global trade has been much greater than that of the GDP.

2.5.2.2 The Structure of Trade Between and Within Regional Economies

Aggregated data about international trade tells a success story. On average, since the year 1948, total merchandise trade has grown annually by approximately 8.7%. However, trade was interrupted cyclically. It stagnated at certain points, because of several recessions over the decades. Total merchandise trade accounted for 19 trillion USD in 2019 and approximately 17.6 trillion USD in 2020 (WTO database, 2021). Table 2.1 portrays the growth of total merchandise trade from 1948 to 2020. While the data illustrates a steady growth of trade between the year 1948 and 2019, it is instructive to focus on how the trade is distributed and how the contributions of selected economies and regions have changed over time. As illustrated in Table 2.1 European economies take the lion's share with approximately 37.7%. Asia, as a region, almost tripled the value of its exports from 1948 to 2019, while that of the North American region dropped by half. Whereas for the United States, the value of exports shrank from 21.6% to 9.0%. However, figures shown reveal the radical shift in the pattern and structure of world trade since 1948.

Taking a closer look, we can recognize a well-established pattern of import and export trade that has changed remarkably over the past decades. It is noteworthy that three regional geographical blocks, often referred to as the Triade-region, account for the bulk of all world trade. It deserves a special note that only 50 nations, out of 216, account for 93% of all global merchandise trade, and merely 33 economies still account for 80% in 2019.

While these statistics reveal that global trade tripled in size within each ten-year period, shares among regions changed substantially. Europe, North America, and Asia are dominating global trade. Strikingly, the respective shares of trade flows between the countries within the Triad, have shifted, illustrating the shrinkage of the once-potent economies.

China, the rising star, increased its share from 0.9% (1948) to 13.6% (2019) in a few decades; Asia's share more than doubled from 14% to 34%, exemplifying its rising economic power. The share of the US, the undisputed champion after World War II, declined substantially from 22% in 1948 to 9% in 2019. Europe appears to be doing better, its share increased slightly, from 35% to 38% in 2019, but peaked in 1973 when it contributed almost 50.9% to world trade. The trade figures presented in Table 2.1 show the percentage of world trade for several selected countries and regions. The figures reveal a remarkable change and dynamic in trading patterns, which portrays a fundamental transformation of the world economy. Behind that changing trade pattern is the extensive growth of sophisticated global production networks that developed over the last decades. Asia, as a region, and China, as a single national economy, stand out as the winning front-runners. However, the USA and the regional block of North America lagging behind.

The scale and scope of fragmentation in international trade is remarkable. Table 2.2. allows us to identify the real extent of the concentration and fragmentation of international

Table 2.1 World merchandise exports by region and selected economy in 1948, 1953, 1963, 1973, 1983, 1993, 2003, and 2019; value in billion USD and share in the percentage of total world value)

Year	1948	1953	1963	1973	1983	1993	2003	2019
	Value in billion USD at current prices							
World	**59**	**84**	**157**	**579**	**1838**	**3688**	**7382**	**19.004**
	Share in % of total merchanidse trade							
World	100.0	100.0	100.0	100.0	100.0	100.0	100.0	100.0
North America (USA and Canada)	28.1	24.8	19.9	17.3	16.8	17.9	15.8	13.9
USA	21.6	14.6	14.3	12.2	11.2	12.6	9.8	9.0
Brazil	2.0	1.8	0.9	1.1	1.2	1.0	1.0	1.2
Chile	0.6	0.5	0.3	0.2	0.2	0.2	0.3	0.4
Europe	35.1	39.4	47.8	50.9	43.5	45.3	45.9	37.7
Africa	7.3	6.5	5.7	4.8	4.5	2.5	2.4	2.5
Asia	14.0	13.4	12.5	14.9	19.1	26.0	26.1	34.0
China	0.9	1.2	1.3	1.0	1.2	2.5	5.9	13.6
Japan	0.4	1.5	3.5	6.4	8.0	9.8	6.4	3.8
India	2.2	1.3	1.0	0.5	0.5	0.6	0.8	1.8
Australia and New Zealand	3.7	3.2	2.4	2.1	1.4	1.4	1.2	1.7
Six East Asian traders	3.4	3.0	2.5	3.6	5.8	9.6	9.6	9.6
EU[a]	–	–	24.5	37.0	31.3	37.3	38.6	31.6
USSR, Former	2.2	3.5	4.6	3.7	5.0	–	–	–
GATT/WTO Members[b]	63.4	69.6	75.0	84.1	77.0	89.0	98.3	98.2

Note: Between 1973 and 1983 and 1993 and 2003, export shares were significantly influenced by oil price developments. Figures are significantly affected by including the mutual trade flows of the Baltic States and the CIS between 1993 and 2003

[a]Figures refer to the EEC (6) in 1963, EC (9) in 1973, EC (10) in 1983, EU(12) in 1993, EU(25) in 2003, and the European Union, excluding the United Kingdom, in 2019

[b]Membership as of the year stated. Source: WTO, World merchandise exports, WTO data, 2021, Creative Commons License 4.0

trade patterns. Nonetheless, the growth of international trade remains impressive. However, we need to acknowledge the apparent and substantial structural changes in the pattern of global trade. A major aspect of the change is the severe transformation of intrafirm and interfirm cross-border exchange of goods and services in the last four decades. Starting in the early 1980s, firms altered their production strategies, leading the more complex and fragile global value chains. This radical transformation of production strategies is part of an ever-greater expansion of cross-border intra- and interfirm trade organized by a few large key lead multinational firms (Castellani & Fassio, 2019; Ernst, 2009; Gereffi, 2018; Hassler, 2012; Perrow, 2009).

Table 2.2 World's leading merchandise exporters and importers in 2019 (value in billion USD and share in %, for the year 2020)

Rank	Exporters	Value	Share	Importers	Value	Share
1	China	2499	13.2	U.S.A.	2568	13.4
2	U.S.A	1646	8.7	China	2077	10.8
3	Germany	1489	7.9	Germany	1234	6.4
4	Netherlands	709	3.8	Japan	721	3.7
5	Japan	706	3.7	UK	692	3.6
6	France	570	3.0	France	651	3.4
7	Republic of Korea	542	2.9	Netherlands	636	3.3
8	Hong Kong, China	535	2.8	Hong Kong, China	578	3.0
	Domestic exports	15	0.1	Retained imports[a]	138	0.7
	Re-exports	517	2.7			
9	Italy	533	2.8	Republic of Korea	503	2.6
10	UK	469	2.5	India	484	2.5
11	Mexico	461	2.4	Italy	474	2.5
12	Canada	447	2.4	Mexico	467	2.4
13	Belgium	445	2.4	Canada	464	2.4
14	Russian Federation	419	2.2	Belgium	426	2.2
15	Singapore	391	2.1	Spain	372	1.9
	Domestic exports	184	1.0			
	Re-exports	206	1.1			
16	Spain	334	1.8	Singapore	359	1.9
				Retained imports[a]	153	0.8
17	Chinese Taipei	331	1.8	Chinese Taipei	287	1.5
18	India	324	1.7	Switzerland	277	1.4
19	Switzerland	314	1.7	Poland	262	1.4
20	United Arab Emirates[a]	280	1.5	United Arab Emirates[a]	262	1.4
21	Australia	272	1.4	Russian Federation[b]	254	1.3
22	Saudi Arabia[a]	269	1.4	Viet Nam	254	1.3
23	Viet Nam	264	1.4	Thailand	237	1.2
24	Poland	264	1.4	Australia	222	1.2
25	Thailand	246	1.3	Turkey	210	1.1
26	Malaysia	238	1.3	Malaysia	205	1.1
27	Brazil	223	1.2	Austria	185	1.0
28	Czech Republic	199	1.1	Brazil	184	1.0
29	Turkey	181	1.0	Czech Republic	178	0.9
30	Austria	179	0.9	Indonesia	171	0.9
31	Ireland	170	0.9	Sweden	159	0.8
32	Indonesia	167	0.9	Saudi Arabi[a]	142	0.7
33	Sweden	161	0.8	Hungary	120	0.6
34	Hungary	124	0.7	Philippines	113	0.6

(continued)

Table 2.2 (continued)

Rank	Exporters	Value	Share	Importers	Value	Share
35	Denmark	111	0.6	South Africa[a]	108	0.6
36	Norway	103	0.5	Ireland	98	0.5
37	South Africa	90	0.5	Denmark	98	0.5
38	Slovak Republic	90	0.5	Romania	97	0.5
39	Iraq[a]	89	0.5	Slovak Republic	90	0.5
40	Romania	77	0.4	Portugal	90	0.5
41	Finland	73	0.4	Norway	85	0.4
42	Qatar[a]	73	0.4	Israel	76	0.4
43	Philippines	70	0.4	Finland	74	0.4
44	Chile	70	0.4	Egypt	71	0.4
45	Portugal	67	0.4	Chile	70	0.4
46	Argentina	65	0.3	Greece	62	0.3
47	The State of Kuwait[a]	65	0.3	Ukraine	61	0.3
48	Nigeria[a]	62	0.3	Bangladesh[a]	60	0.3
49	Israel	58	0.3	Iraq (1)	57	0.3
50	Kazakhstan	57	0.3	Colombia	53	0.3
	Total of above[c]	17,617	93.3	Total of above[c]	17,675	91.9
	World[c]	18,889	100.0	World[c]	19,238	100.0

Source: WTO, Statistical Database, Metadata, 2021 (for Israel, Singapore, HK, and China, the data significant re-export and re-imports); Data from WTO data files, WTO, 2021; https://stats.wto.org/dashboard/merchandise_en.html; a) WTO Secretariat estimates; b) imports are valued f.o.b.; 3) includes significant re-exports or imports for re-export

The OECD estimate that the share of manufacturing intra-firm trade in the total manufacturing trade, increased from 60% in 1988 to almost 78% in 2000 (OECD, 2002a: 71). This pattern of trade is closely related to what Froebel, Heinrichs, and Kreye called the "new international division of labour" (Frobel et al., 1978; Snidal, 1982; Heron, 2012: 2f; Buckley & Casson, 2014; Gereffi, 2018; McWilliam et al., 2020; UNCTAD, 2011, 2012, 2021).

All these data about global trade indicate an evolving pattern, which is characterized as the outcome of a highly segregated, unequal, fragmented, and spatially branched out global division of labor, organized by large multinational business firms. This pattern of world trade portrays this unequal structure and demonstrates how few countries hosting a number of large multinational firms, account for the lion's share in the absolute value of exports and imports. Table 2.2 demonstrates a particular facet of this extreme fragmentation and how different economies participate in global trade. The figures illustrate the value (in billion USD) and share (in %) of merchandise exports and imports by the 50 leading economies, in the year 2019. From all the countries covered, slightly more than 25% or just 50 economies accounted for 93.3% of total exports and 91.9% of total imports, in 2019. China is at the top of this list, ranking number one in global merchandise exports accounting for 2.499 billion

USD, followed by the United States with 1.646 billion USD, and Germany ranks third with 1.489 billion USD worth of exports. However, the order reverses when it comes to the value of imports. The shift in the ranking of the two leading trading nations reveal the source of tension caused by the trade surplus for China, amounting at 422 billion USD, contrasted by the trade deficit of 922 billion USD for the United States in the year 2019 alone. The data in Table 2.2 demonstrate that the ten largest importers alone contributed to 51.3% of global imports. Similarly, the top ten exporters accounted for 53.4% of total merchandise trade. Additionally, the top 20 trading nations account for 73.5% of exports and 75.4% of imports in the year 2019.

These trade data are based on merchandise trade, but trade in services and trade segregated into product categories do not substantially alter this prevalent trade pattern. By and large, trade in services account for about 20% of world trade. It is important to note that the small and middle-sized business firms (SMEs) and the large multinationals located or headquartered in these economies are the actual entities responsible for carrying out the trade in exports and imports of goods and services.

2.5.3 Foreign Direct Investment: Its Pattern and Structure

2.5.3.1 The Development of FDI

While exports and imports are an important part of the international activities of the business firms, these firms actively invest assets in foreign countries to operate and control core business activities abroad. These international investment activities of firms are called foreign direct investments (FDIs). By and large, the pattern of trade is repeated in the structural pattern, dynamics, and development of FDI.

Foreign Direct Investment (FDI)

FDI is defined as "as an investment involving a long-term relationship and reflecting a lasting interest and control by a resident entity in one economy (foreign direct investor or parent enterprise) in an enterprise resident in an economy other than that of the foreign direct investor. FDI implies that the investor exerts a significant degree of influence on the management of the enterprise resident in the other economy. Such investment involves both the initial transaction between the two entities and all subsequent transactions between them and among foreign affiliates, both incorporated and unincorporated. FDI may be undertaken by individuals as well as business entities. Flows of FDI comprise capital provided (either directly or through other related enterprises) by a foreign direct investor to an FDI enterprise or capital received from an FDI enterprise through a foreign direct investor. FDI has three components: equity capital, reinvested earnings, and intracompany "loans." (UNCTAD, 1996: 219).

According to the above definition, FDI is a transfer of capital made to exercise a direct and long-lasting control over the operation of the capital receiving entity. FDI is defined by its intention to enact or maintain control. It is called *foreign* direct investment because of the cross-border transfer of capital facilitated by a business firm located in the home country to a business unit located in the host economy. The investors are assumed to act rationally, implying the expectation of maximizing returns on the investment made. However, the intention to exert a decisive influence on the management of the capital receiving enterprise is also equally significant.

Stephen H. Hymer noted in his pathbreaking study titled "International Operations of the National Firms" that "[c]ontrol is not an easy thing to define, and the dividing line between some control and no control is arbitrary" (Hymer, 1976: 1).

Depending on the country, a minority shareholding from 10% to 25% to a majority shareholding above 50%, allows the investor to exercise control. Most national regulations block FDI to a minority of 25% in corporations and joint-stock companies in the share capital.

FDI is studied as a bi-directional flow between distinct entities located in at least two different national economies. Traditionally it is assumed that international capital flows mitigate the risk an investing firm faces, because it diversifies investments across different institutional environments (Razin & Sadka, 2016).

In addition, FDI is analyzed by studying the investment behavior of multinational firms. The multinational firms are expected to exploit firm-specific advantages generated by superior efficiency gains or cost advantages due to prevalent economies of scale, such as technological advantages exploited by multi-plant operations or superior marketing and distribution capabilities (Helpman, 1984, 2006).

FDI includes the transfer of fixed assets, management services, or any transfer of firm-specific assets, based on organizational knowledge and entrepreneurial know-how, process technologies and machinery, and many other firm-specific assets and services.

Direct investment can be the transfer of trademarks and patent rights licensed to a wholly owned foreign subsidiary or to an international joint venture (IJV). The transfer refers to a parent company who is charging for the service delivered to a foreign-based subsidiary or joint venture, while the parent company continues to have a claim to its intangible intellectual property (IP) rights, such as trademarks or patents.

The parent companies may also supply intra-firm credits to its foreign subsidiaries by providing inter-subsidiary supply of intermediate inputs (supplies of goods, technologies, firm-specific know-how, or other management services).

Thus, the actual capital reported in the FDI statistics does not represent just the cross-border capital transfer but also loans or credits for services rendered by the parent firm or subsidiaries to other foreign affiliates or IJV firms.

In addition, earnings made in affiliate business enterprises can be re-invested in the profit generating entity or can be repatriated to the parent firm. The essential focus of the investor company is that the sustainable control over the transferred assets is not lost.

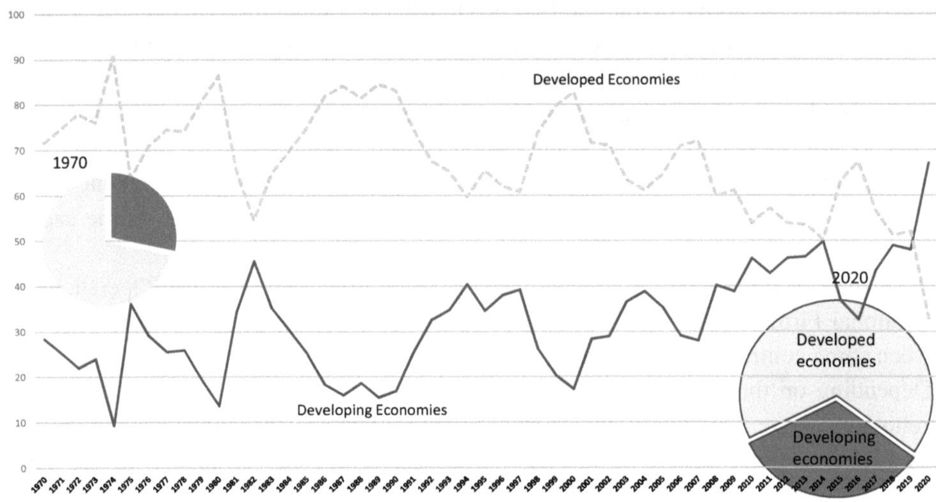

Fig. 2.2 Share of FDI inflow between developing and developed economies, years 1970 to 2019, data from UNCTAD (2021), author's compilation

2.5.3.2 Pattern and Structure of FDI

Analyzing the overall growth of FDI in detail, provides a pertinent picture. In the 1960s and 1970s, most FDI was invested within a relatively homogenous group of industries and among a relatively small number of similar industrial countries (Buckley, 1989; Buckley & Casson, 2002). In 1970, about 75% of all FDI (inflow) went to a fairly small number of allegedly developed economies, the industrial economies, and not more than 25% of FDI went to the developing economies (See Fig. 2.2).

Two decades later, in 1990, the group of industrial countries accounted for almost 83% of total FDI inflows (nearly billion USD 180) and approximately 15% of inflow went to the developed countries (United Nations, 1992: 313). However, at that time, the group of industrialized economies comprised only 25 countries and the developing world consisted of 120 countries. In 1998, the industrialized economies still accounted for 71.5% of total FDI inflows (USD 644 billion), and 25.8% went to the developing economies (UNCTAD, 1999: 20).

In 2019, approximately 52% of FDI inflow was received by developed economies, and the share of developing countries has increased to 44% of the total value of FDI. In 2020, owing to the dominance of China, this share increased further (UNCTAD, 2021). However, the actual percentage of FDI is highly concentrated in a few hotspots. Asia is still a highly attractive region for FDI inflow (China being the most important recipient). China has grown into a significant global competitor, and private and semi-state Chinese multinational firms have become a major source of FDI in technologically advanced industries located in developed countries. China has also become a major investor in several developing economies (Buckley et al., 2002; Wang et al., 2012).

The Distributive Pattern of FDI

The least developed countries accounted for not more than 0.7% of FDI inflows to developing countries between 1985 and 1989. On one hand, The UNCTAD (United Nations Conference on Trade and Development) contended that the "marginalization of least-developed countries, most of which are located in Africa, is likely to continue, since flows to developing countries are highly concentrated in newly industrializing and resource-rich economies" (United Nations, 1991: 13). The same report notes that the outflow of FDI from France (8%), Germany (7.8%), Japan (19.4%), the United Kingdom (20.2%), and the United States (14.3%) accounted for almost 70% of all FDI outflows. Between 1980 and 1989, these patterns remained fairly stable (United Nations, 1991: 10).

Prior to the 1980s, the UNCTAD reported that the FDI investment pattern was largely bipolar, with the US and the European Community (EU) dominating foreign-direct investment flows and stocks. However, in the 1990s a new pattern emerged, when Japan entered the scene as a major foreign-direct investor, changing the bipolar pattern into a fairly rigid tripolar pattern (United Nations, 1991: 36).

In 2000, UNCTAD described the transnational corporations and their international production strategies as the driving force of a shifting pattern in FDI flows. "Transnational" was a term used by the World Investment Report for multinationals to indicate that they were increasingly decaying their national character. The report estimated that there were 63,000 multinational companies operating some 690,000 foreign subsidiaries (UNCTAD, 2000: VX). In addition, the report concluded that cross-border mergers & acquisitions (M&As) are responsible for more than 80% of FDI flows. The M&As were described as the "fastest means of building up a strong position in a new market, gaining market power—and indeed market dominance—increasing the size of the firm or spreading the risk" (UNCTAD, 2000: XX). It is important to note that approximately 90% of all cross-border M&As took place in developed economies (UNCTAD, 2000: XXI).

For 2020, UNCTAD reports the lowest level of FDI since 2005, with a 35% decline over the previous year (UNCTAD, 2021: 2). The report is concerned about the uneven nature of recovery in FDI flows. Surprisingly, Asia has recovered from the COVID-19 crisis much better than Europe or the U.S. have, with declines of up to 40% in contrast to growth of 4% in Asia (UNCTAD, 2021: 18). The most important factor contributing to the significantly higher FDI inflows in Asia appear to be the greater stability of intraregional FDI flows within the region, especially compared to Europe and North America (UNCTAD, 2021: 33).

Considering the data portrayed in Fig. 2.2, FDI inflows and outflows (see Tables 2.3 and 2.4) are still not equally distributed.

In 2020, the top five host economies accounted for 31.3% of total global FDI, led by the US, Luxembourg, Germany, Ireland, and Sweden (UNCTAD, 2021: 71). Conversely, the least developed countries, described by the UNCTAD as "structurally weak, vulnerable and small economies," received only 2.4% of total global FDI, with China and France being the leading investors in these economies (UNCTAD, 2021: 80). Latin America and the Caribbean received 8.8% of the total global FDI, with Chile, Mexico, Colombia, Argentina, and Peru receiving the lion's share of this stake (UNCTAD, 2021: 54).

However, the developing economies of Asia appear to be the unleashed champions. Table 2.3 shows that Asia accounted for 57.9% of total global FDI inflows, led by China and Hong Kong, followed by India, Singapore, and the United Arab Emirates, as the primary recipients of FDI (UNCTAD, 2021: 46). Africa lags far behind, accounting for just 4% of the total global FDI inflow, with the largest five recipients being Egypt, Congo, South Africa, Nigeria, and Ethiopia (UNCTAD, 2021: 38).

A severe drop in FDI inflow can be identified in Europe, whose share is dropping from almost 40% in 1970 to less than 9% in 2020 (see Table 2.3 for detailed figures). Although, Tables 2.3 and 2.4 do not show the full impact of the COVID-19 crisis, it resulted in a substantial drop of almost 33% in FDI in- and outflow. In doing so, it revealed the obvious fragmentation of FDI prevalent from 1970 to 2020 and covering half a century. All this illustrates the rise of Asian economies.

The data in Table 2.3 concisely reveals a significant shift in the regional balance of power resulting from an apparent new international division of labor. It paints a picture of where the future core regions of the world economy are located. Although the UNCTAD concludes that the intra-regional investment will "grow over the coming years" (UNCTAD, 2021: 29), it is doubtful that such a dramatic regional shift will ever be reversed.

This overall transformation is the outcome of a turn, which will not lower the tension between regional blocks but steadily feed the growing inter-regional trade conflicts and widening inter-regional inequality, leaving Latin America and especially Africa, far behind.

The overall pattern is replicated in the figures depicted in Table 2.4, which demonstrate the size of regional distribution of FDI outflow.

Africa, as a single continent, is responsible for just 0.22% of total FDI outflows in the year 2020. The American continent have dropped its share from almost 60% in the year 1970 to just below 20% in 2020.

In contrast to this overall trend, Asia recorded an increase from just 2.5% to 68.8%, over the same period.

The decline in Europe is similar to that of North America, with its share falling from 36% to merely 11%. The evident shift toward Asia, away from the primary, dominant, and old industrial cores of Europe and America, is apparent and significantly manifested in figures shown and data presented in Tables 2.3 and 2.4.

The interpretation of the extent of this shift is not fundamentally corrected by the general decline in FDI triggered by the COVID-19 crisis.

Table 2.3 The regional distribution of FDI inflow in % for selected years, 1970, 1980, 1990, 2000, 2010, 2013, 2015, 2016, 2019, and 2020

Region	1970	1980	1990	2000	2010	2013	2015	2016	2019	2020
World	100	100	100	100	100	100	100	100	100	100
Africa	**9.56**	**0.74**	**1.39**	**0.77**	**3.39**	**3.48**	**2.85**	**2.24**	**3.08**	**3.98**
Northern Africa	3.29	0.28	0.56	0.24	1.13	0.88	0.61	0.67	0.90	1.01
Sub-Saharan Africa	6.27	0.46	0.82	0.53	2.26	2.61	2.24	1.57	2.18	2.97
Eastern Africa	0.61	0.36	0.19	0.16	0.78	1.12	0.70	0.62	0.77	0.95
Middle Africa	0.23	0.65	−0.17	0.11	0.31	−0.13	0.88	0.24	0.29	0.72
Southern Africa	2.52	0.24	0.04	0.09	0.31	0.64	0.16	0.14	0.35	0.33
Western Africa	2.91	−0.80	0.76	0.16	0.86	0.98	0.50	0.57	0.78	0.98
America	**34.64**	**53.36**	**31.49**	**33.96**	**27.78**	**31.47**	**32.87**	**30.57**	**30.70**	**26.81**
Northern America	23.26	41.78	27.33	28.07	16.26	18.63	25.16	24.00	20.21	18.05
Latin America and Caribbean	11.38	11.59	4.16	5.88	11.52	12.84	7.71	6.58	10.49	8.77
Caribbean	2.41	0.51	0.21	0.16	0.21	0.11	0.17	0.16	0.26	0.25
Central America	4.30	4.61	1.49	1.52	2.41	4.01	2.29	2.02	2.87	3.32
South America	4.67	6.47	2.46	4.21	8.90	8.72	5.25	4.39	7.36	5.19
Asia	**7.52**	**1.58**	**12.16**	**11.73**	**31.42**	**30.87**	**26.79**	**25.28**	**36.61**	**57.88**
Central Asia	..	..	..	0.11	1.25	1.02	0.48	0.65	0.52	0.66
Eastern Asia	2.05	2.31	5.34	8.85	14.39	15.39	15.78	14.05	16.76	30.24
South-eastern Asia	3.47	4.85	6.26	1.60	8.11	8.15	5.62	5.51	11.83	13.61
Southern Asia	0.73	0.52	0.10	0.36	2.50	2.45	2.52	2.63	3.86	7.11
Western Asia	1.27	−6.10	0.46	0.81	5.17	3.87	2.39	2.44	3.63	6.26
Europe	**39.42**	**40.05**	**50.13**	**52.39**	**34.63**	**29.96**	**35.98**	**39.38**	**26.76**	**8.90**
Eastern Europe	..	0.02	0.40	1.88	4.84	5.17	1.02	3.35	4.87	3.37
Northern Europe	13.72	19.98	17.77	15.84	8.37	7.68	13.35	15.66	11.44	8.44

(continued)

Table 2.3 (continued)

Region	1970	1980	1990	2000	2010	2013	2015	2016	2019	2020
Southern Europe	7.22	5.39	10.13	4.70	6.96	7.13	3.58	4.32	5.45	2.67
Western Europe	18.48	14.66	21.83	29.98	14.46	9.97	18.03	16.05	5.00	−5.57
Oceania	8.86	4.26	4.82	1.15	2.78	4.22	1.52	2.53	2.86	2.43

Source: UNCTAD Data Files, 2021, Author's compilation. Creative Commons License (cc-BY 4.0)

Table 2.4 The regional distribution of foreign direct investment outflow in % for selected years; 1970, 1980, 1990, 2000, 2010, 2013, 2015, 2016, 2019, and 2020

Year	1970	1990	1995	2000	2005	2010	2013	2015	2016	2019	2020
World	100.00	100.00	100.00	100.00	100.00	100.00	100.00	100.00	100.00	100.00	100.00
Africa	**0.13**	**0.27**	**0.82**	**0.13**	**0.25**	**0.74**	**0.76**	**0.54**	**0.50**	**0.40**	**0.22**
Northern Africa	0.01	0.06	0.04	0.02	0.03	0.34	0.03	0.08	0.09	0.14	0.15
Sub-Saharan Africa	0.12	0.21	0.79	0.11	0.22	0.40	0.73	0.46	0.41	0.26	0.07
Eastern Africa	..	0.01	0.01	0.00	0.02	0.12	0.08	0.02	0.03	0.07	0.06
Middle Africa	..	0.02	0.01	0.00	0.04	0.12	0.07	−0.03	0.03	−0.17	0.05
Southern Africa	0.12	0.02	0.71	0.02	0.12	−0.01	0.46	0.33	0.27	0.26	−0.26
Western Africa	..	0.17	0.05	0.08	0.05	0.17	0.12	0.13	0.08	0.10	0.22
America	**60.41**	**15.41**	**29.70**	**16.82**	**7.37**	**26.39**	**27.91**	**20.82**	**22.64**	**17.98**	**18.69**
Northern America	60.26	14.85	28.66	16.11	5.13	22.44	25.35	19.53	21.91	14.13	19.17
Latin America and Caribbean	0.15	0.56	1.04	0.71	2.24	3.94	2.56	1.29	0.73	3.85	−0.48
Caribbean	0.01	0.01	0.02	0.01	0.05	0.00	0.01	0.01	0.02	0.05	0.02
Central America	..	0.09	0.00	0.01	0.76	1.08	1.15	0.70	0.04	0.88	0.94
South America	0.14	0.45	1.02	0.69	1.43	2.86	1.40	0.58	0.68	2.93	−1.44
Asia	**2.58**	**25.47**	**19.00**	**9.80**	**16.63**	**26.16**	**35.57**	**30.85**	**35.02**	**49.12**	**68.83**
Central Asia	..	..	0.00	0.00	−0.02	0.57	0.16	0.05	−0.32	−0.21	−0.26
Eastern Asia	2.52	24.78	15.64	8.44	11.88	18.01	25.90	23.04	28.38	38.06	53.81
South-eastern Asia	..	0.95	3.34	0.77	2.40	4.55	5.75	4.06	3.00	5.94	8.26
Southern Asia	..	0.03	0.04	0.05	0.42	1.17	0.15	0.46	0.34	1.09	1.59
Western Asia	0.06	−0.29	−0.01	0.54	1.95	1.87	3.60	3.25	3.62	4.25	5.43
Europe	**36.03**	**57.80**	**49.29**	**72.95**	**80.17**	**45.22**	**35.62**	**48.34**	**41.68**	**31.72**	**10.88**
Eastern Europe	..	0.02	0.20	0.33	2.52	3.71	5.31	1.13	2.05	2.62	2.21
Northern Europe	14.17	15.73	18.67	29.04	20.80	8.61	8.08	8.22	2.12	1.41	−5.68

(continued)

Table 2.4 (continued)

Year	1970	1990	1995	2000	2005	2010	2013	2015	2016	2019	2020
Southern Europe	1.11	4.29	3.06	6.49	13.20	6.93	4.75	6.19	3.79	5.90	5.03
Western Europe	20.75	37.77	27.36	37.09	43.65	25.97	17.48	32.80	33.72	21.80	9.32
Oceania	**0.85**	**1.05**	**1.19**	**0.30**	**−4.43**	**1.48**	**0.15**	**−0.56**	**0.16**	**0.78**	**1.39**

UNCTAD Data Files, 2021, Author's compilation. Creative Commons License (cc-BY 4.0)

Against this background, the discussion of how FDI contributes to overall development, is more critical than ever. In general, FDI is widely acknowledged as a driver of economic growth (Doh, 2019; Farmer & Wendner, 1997; Streeten, 1972). It is also worth noting that approximately 80% of FDI is achieved through M&As, which means that firms are growing either by acquiring or merging with their competitors (Fubini et al., 2007: 1). FDI is usually treated as an indicator of the attractiveness of a business location and held as a source of dynamic growth of economies. Several authors have analyzed the intricate relationship between GDP and FDI. Hansen et al. found a significant relationship between FDI and growth using a sample of 31 developing countries, covering a period of 31 years (Hansen & Rand, 2006). Limited studies on this topic suggest that high GDP growth rates attract more FDI and this effect is much stronger than the causal link between increased FDI and GDP, suggesting that FDI is not initiating growth but might be a result of growth (Kosztowniak, 2016).

However, whether growth attracts FDI or FDI leads to growth, remains an open question. These two variables obviously influence each other, but how FDI leads to sustainable growth in the host economies remains a poorly understood and neglected issue in the relevant IB literature (Doh, 2019).

In addition, FDI indicates how particular industries shift their focus of operation from value-adding activities to more attractive locations. FDI is a significant indicator of the evolving integration of GVCs. However, the direct and indirect effects of FDI on long-term GDP growth remain ambiguous (Abbas et al., 2020; Sun et al., 2021; Swan, 1956).

Whether FDI has a positive and sustainable development effect on host economies depends on multiple factors and is widely disputed. Examining the details, it is evident that FDI activity shows a significantly positive relationship with growth but a more ambiguous causal relationship with the performance of smaller and medium sized firms (Lu & Beamish, 2006).

Evidence on the effect of FDI on exports is less controversial. Using panel data from 21 Asian economies, spanning from 1980 to 2013, Sothan demonstrates a significantly positive impact of FDI on export growth. They also identify a significant bidirectional correlation between FDI and growth (Sothan, 2015). However, this does not explain how the empirically observed bi directional causality between FDI and GDP operates.

Available data strongly suggest that FDI increasingly correlates with the prevalent inter- and intra-firm sales of foreign affiliates (UNCTAD, 2021: 22). Several studies found a positive effect of FDI on technology transfer from home to host countries (Basu et al., 2003; Hansen & Rand, 2006; Hwang & Kim, 2017; Kosztowniak, 2016; Sothan, 2015). However, there is no final and clear-cut conclusion explaining how FDI affects growth in host-economies. Nevertheless, it is a widely accepted truth that FDI is "an integral part of an open, efficient, and international economic system and an important driver of development" (OECD, 2002b: 3).

2.5.4 The Multinational Firm

The main source of FDI is the multinational firm. Large multinational firms are dominant and major players in the global economy. However, medium or small sized multinational firms also enter foreign markets, using FDI as an entry mode. For decades, large multinational enterprises (MNEs) have occupied a formative position in shaping the dynamics of the global economy and are treated as "either the heroes or villains" (Navaretti et al., 2020: IX) or the "beaut[ies] or beast[s]" (Forsgren, 2013: 1). The dominant scale and scope of the geographical organization of cross-border business activities by large multinationals remain disputed issues (Andersson, 1993; Casanova & Miroux, 2020; Davies & Markusen, 2021; Girma et al., 2005; Malgwi et al., 2006; Roddick, 1996; Solomon, 2000; Wheeler, 2012). Not surprisingly, a great deal of attention is almost exclusively focused on large multinational companies in international business research. The sheer size of some multinational firms is impressive and a significant indicator of their powerful impact on business and society.

In 1988, multinational firms located in ten industrialized high-income economies accounted for 97% of all FDI outflows (Dunning, 1993: 17; Dunning & Lundan, 2008). As aforementioned, multinational firms today account for "large portions of world production, employment, investment, international trade, research, and innovation" (Foley et al., 2021: 3).

For a long time, IB research has focused on the importance and impact of these large multinationals, paying relatively little attention to small and medium-sized international companies (Davies & Markusen, 2021; Oh, 2009).

The great trusts and conglomerates that emerged in the late nineteenth century, primarily in the US, exhibit several common features with today's large multinational firms. However, these big firms operated mostly in domestic markets. Firms like International Harvester, Singer, or Siemens managed their "international operation [...] by a loose federation of business leaders rather than by direct control from a corporate world headquarters" (Buckley & Casson, 2002: 1). Multinational firms have been criticized for their almost unlimited market power (Hymer, 1970; Pearce & Papanastassiou, 2006).

Studying the rise of multinational firms reveals the steady growth of the average number of subsidiaries established by multinational firms headquartered in the US, the UK, Europe, and Japan from 1914 to 1970. It suggests how firms, primarily headquartered in the US, dominated (with almost 80%) overseas investments (Buckley & Casson, 2002: 3ff; Vaupel & Curhan, 1973). Early research by IB scholars categorized multinational firms according to the following criteria: (a) the number of countries in which the MNC operates, and (b) the percentage of sales generated by foreign affiliates (Buckley & Casson, 2003).

It should also be noted that until the end of the 1960s, just before the rise of multinational firms, almost 80% of all multinational firms had affiliates in not more than nine countries and only 5 to 10% of MNCs operated in about 20 countries (Buckley & Casson, 2002: 14). In addition, a significant feature of these early years (covering the 1950s and 1960s) was that most foreign subsidiaries established by the US-headquartered multinational firms were established in Canada and Latin America, reaching a peak in the year 1960. After this, Europe became a favored location for foreign subsidiaries, along with the Asian-Pacific region.

Multinationality of Firms

From early categorizations, multinationality emerged as a term to approach the different scales and scope of multinational firms. In general, multinationality is captured through:

- The number and size of subsidiaries owned or controlled abroad
- The number of countries in which the multinational is controlling cross-border economic activities
- The ratio between a firm's assets, sales, and employees, between home and host locations
- The degree of management in international firms
- The extent of the international division of labor, controlled or owned
- The degree of superior efficiency gains caused by common governance and economies of scale (Dunning & Lundan, 2008)

These factors measure the degree of multinationality of the international firms, based on the premise that the chosen measures are related to the international exposure of the multinational firms. Measurements of the multinationality of the firm is based on the motivation to operate and control the cross-border activities of the multinational firm more effectively. However, over time, measures and concepts to operationalize the essence and nature of multinational firms changed considerably, reflecting a radical shift in the strategy and structure of multinational firms, based on a thorough transformation of the global division of labor (Pitelis, 2006, 2018; Pitelis & Teece, 2018).

Multinational firms are often defined by its superior firm-specific advantage (FSA). The core argument is that FSAs enable the firm to "own and control" activities in more than one country (Buckley & Casson, 2002: 1). While Hymer was worried about the monopolistic power of the large multinational firms, others addressed its efficiency gains (Buckley, 2006; Casson et al., 2009; Davies, 1980; Jiang et al., 2007; Kogut & Zander, 1993; Rowthorn, 2006).

The definition of the superior efficiency of multinational firms rests on three assumptions: First, a firm with an FSA is seeking to exploit these advantages abroad to maximize profits; second, the multinational firm seeks to exploit and explore opportunities arising from imperfect markets in foreign markets, and thus, it is the firm's internal capability (FSA) that bypasses (internalizing) imperfect markets; third, the internalization of imperfect cross-border markets is the original source of multinational firms, further augmenting its efficiency (Buckley & Casson, 2003: 33).

With this perspective, John H. Dunning portrays multinational firms by its capabilities to organize and operate multiple cross-border value-adding activities (Dunning, 1993; Dunning & Lundan, 2008). Stephen H. Hymer characterized FDI generated by the multinational firms as the major mechanism to exercise control (Hymer, 1970, 1976; Pilon-Lé, 1980). However, it is widely acknowledged that multinational firms do not only control foreign production but essentially extend control over its operations in unfamiliar foreign markets using equity and non-equity co-operative entry modes (Dunning, 1988).

Defining the Multinational Firm

Peter Buckley and Mark Casson defined a multinational firm "as an enterprise which owns and controls activities in different countries" (Buckley & Casson, 2002: 1). Stephen Herbert Hymer noted that a multinational firm is "a substitute for the market" and is "typically operating in imperfect markets" (Hymer, 1970: 441).

A multinational firm is conceptualized as a key mechanism to develop and augment firm-specific advantages (Birkinshaw et al., 1998).

John Dunning, an outstanding IB scholar, described a multinational firm as an "enterprise that engages in foreign direct investment (FDI) and owns or controls value adding activities in more than one country." However, he emphasizes the need to differentiate between multinational firms "undertaking foreign production" and the firms that "govern a group of largely independent multi-domestic foreign subsidiaries" (Dunning, 1988: 3).

2.5.4.1 The Impact of Large Multinational firms

In the 1980s, Raymond Vernon noted that "multinational enterprises have always been distinguished in the public mind by their sheer size. They are, for the most part, the giants of modern industry, commerce, and banking: the big oil companies such as Mobil, Shell, and Gulf; the leading chemical companies such as BASF and Du Pont; the major electrical-machinery producers such as AEG and General Electric; the largest drug companies such as Pfizer and Hoffmann-La Roche; and so on, through the upper ranks of Fortune's various lists of the world's leading firms" (Vernon, 1977: 19).

The ranking of the 100 largest non-financial multinational firms ordered according to the size of their foreign assets, is shown in Table 2.5. The table is a fixed feature of the World Investment Report, prepared annually by the UNCTAD since 1991, and provides an account of the largest multinational firms. However, each order offers one view of reality, from among a number of possible others. The ranking in Table 2.5 provides an order that takes into account the size and scope of international companies' foreign assets. Therefore, it is based on a biased view, because large mining and oil extraction multinationals that run capital-intensive facilities abroad are given greater weight in the ranking relative to other large firms such as Walmart, Apple, or Microsoft. Each ranking is the construct of a particular perspective that measures a phenomenon. Additionally, size is an important variable to describe multinational firms, but it is only one, among several others. In addition, it unclear whether size should be measured by the annual profits generated by the achieved sales or by the number of employees.

Nevertheless, the table is meaningful and it is built on the ratio between foreign and domestic assets to sales and employees. The average of these measures constitute the transnationality index (TNI) created by UNCTAD. In Table 2.5, multinational firms are ranked by foreign assets. The TNI is not a perfect measure, but it allows comparison between changes and fluctuations over a period of more than 30 years. Table 2.5 presents the 100 largest non-financial transnational firms compiled each year by the UNCTAD in Geneva.

Even though the TNI provides accessible and easy to compare information, it is not more than the ratio between foreign to domestic assets, sales, and employees. It does not discuss anything more about the hidden global spread and exposure of these multinational firms.

In 1994 the data for the largest 100 non-financial transnational firms showed that 29 of them are headquartered in the US, 16 in Japan, 12 in France, 9 in Germany, 9 in the UK, and more across Switzerland, Italy, Sweden, the Netherlands, Canada, and Belgium. These countries accounted for 96% of the 100 largest multinational firms (UNCTAD, 1994: 19ff.). For the year 2002, 90 of the top 100 non-financial transnational firms were headquartered in the EU economies, Japan, and the United States, with the US accounting for about 25% and Japan's share having declined to less than 10% (UNCTAD, 2004: 11f; 278).

Over the years, this picture has changed, slowly but considerably. Examining the rankings for the year 2020, 49 of the largest transnational firms are headquartered in the EU, excluding the UK, who has 12 firm headquarters, followed by 19 headquartered in the US and 11 in China. Asia, as a region, accounts for 22 firms. The number of multinational firms headquartered in emerging markets grew from 5 in 2015 to 15 in 2020, because of new giants emerging in China, such as e State Grid, China National, and Tencent (UNCTAD, WIR, 2021: 23ff.).

The data from Fortune Magazine's list of the GLOBAL 500 provides a closer perspective on the radical shift in large multinational firms. In 1995, the list contained 174 (34%) multinational firms from 21 EU countries; in 2021, they decreased to 127 (25%), demonstrating a dropout of 47 firms. In 1995, 148 firms were headquartered in the US (30%), but in 2021 this number decreased by 29 firms to 122 (24%), although these global firms tripled their revenues. In 1995, Japanese multinational firms accounted for 149 entries (approximately 30%); in 2021, only 53 (dropping to a share of 9%) made it to the list, demonstrating a decline of 25% in revenues. In 1995, only three multinational firms from China qualified for entry to the Global 500 (less than 1%), yet in 2021, the list contained 135 Chinese multinationals (approximately 27%) and their revenues had multiplied by a factor of 22 (Table 2.6).

Stephen H. Hymer conceived the multinational firm as a powerful vehicle to supersede the market mechanism (Hymer, 1970: 441). The sheer size of a multinational firm is considered an important attribute for its apparent influence. Since the 1960s, renowned

Table 2.5 The largest non-financial multinational firms, ranked by foreign assets; in 2020

The world's top non-financial multinational enterprises, ranked by foreign assets, 2019[a]

Ranked by Foreign Assets	TNI[b]	Corporation	Home economy	Industry[c]	Assets		Sales		Employment		TNI[b]
					Foreign	Total	Foreign	Total	Foreign[d]	Total	%
1	19	Royal Dutch Shell plc		Mining, quarrying & petroleum	376 417	402 681	276 518	331 684	59 000	83 000	82.6
2	46	Toyota Motor Corporation	Japan	Motor Vehicles	307 538	485 422	187 768	275 390	227 787	359 542	65.0
3	22	BP plc	UK	Pretrol. & Refining	259 860	295 194	215 203	278 397	58 900	72 500	82.2
4	41	Softbank Group Corp	Japan	Telecommunications	253 163	343 306	29 286	56 910	55 272	74 953	66.3
5	27	Total SA	France	Pretrol. & Refining	249 678	273 865	137 438	175 985	71 456	107 776	78.5
6	54	Volkswagen Group	Germany	Motor Vehicles	243 469	548 271	227 940	282 776	374 000	671 000	60.3
7	17	Anheuser-Busch InBev NV	Belgium	Food & beverages	192 138	237 142	44 352	52 251	148 111	171 915	84.0
8	29	British American Tobacco PLC	UK	Tobacco	184 959	186 194	25 232	32 998	31 196	53 185	78.2
9	56	Daimler AG	Germany	Motor Vehicles	179 506	339 742	163 875	193 357	124 842	298 655	59.8
10	60	Chevron Corporation	USA	Pretrol. & Refining	172 830	237 428	75 591	140 156	22 800	48 200	58.0
11	78	Exxon Mobil Corporation	United US	Pretrol. & Refining	169 719	362 597	123 801	255 583	35 058	74 900	47.4
12	13	Vodafone Group Plc	UK	Telecommunications	168 394	184 253	42 530	49 971	58 429	68 724	87.2
13	88	EDF SA	France	Electricity, gas & water	155 021	340 692	30 625	79 827	34 381	165 790	34.9
14	11	CK Hutchison Holdings Limited	HK, China	Retail Trade	143 367	155 523	32 556	38 163	279 000	300 000	90.2
15	33	Honda Motor Co Ltd	Japan	Motor Vehicles	143 180	188 541	16 150	137 382	153 215	219 722	76.7
16	71	Enel SpA	Italy	Electricity, gas & water	135 691	192 570	28 311	86 597	38 503	68 253	53.2
17	32	Siemens AG	Germany	Industrial & Commercial Machinery	134 634	163 598	77 280	97 957	269 000	385 000	77.0

18	96	China National Petroleum Corp (CNPC)	China	Mining, quarrying & petroleum	133 636	595 935	171 756	410 023	122 704	1 266 400	24.7
19	49	Deutsche Telekom AG	Germany	Telecommunications	132 443	191 723	62 605	90 140	116 422	210 533	64.6
20	63	BMW AG	Germany	Motor Vehicles	126 609	256 160	101 514	116 644	43 360	133 778	56.3
21	80	Microsoft Corporation	USA	Computer & Data Processing	117 460	286 556	61 644	125 843	59 000	144 000	43.6
22	45	Johnson & Johnson	USA	Pharmaceuticals	116 200	157 728	9 152	82 059	97 393	132 200	65.0
23	81	Apple Computer Inc	USA	Computer Equipment	114 719	338 516	157 908	260 174	47 928	137 000	43.2
24	9	Takeda Pharmaceutical Company Limited	Japan	Pharmaceuticals	113 414	118 140	24 828	30 283	45 595	47 495	91.3
25	64	General Electric Co	USA	Industrial & Commercial Machinery	112 676	266 048	55 850	95 215	135 000	205 000	55.6
26	36	Nissan Motor Co Ltd	Japan	Motor Vehicles	111 795	156 431	75 938	90 897	79 481	138 912	70.7
27	58	Eni SpA	Italy	Pretrol. & Refining	109 441	138 665	52 126	78 219	10 243	31 321	59.4
28	8	Nestlé SA	Switzerl&	Food & beverages	105 661	132 416	91 983	93 155	282 322	291 000	91.9
29	21	Glencore PLC	Switzerl&	Mining, quarrying & petroleum	105 588	123 568	134 032	206 882	154 828	159 345	82.5
30	31	Telefonica SA	Spain	Telecommunications	105 378	133 540	39 909	54 200	90 950	113 819	77.5
31	39	Iberdrola SA	Spain	Electricity, gas & water	102 889	137 462	22 597	40 786	25 787	35 374	67.7
32	43	Bayer AG	Germany	Pharmaceuticals	100 947	141 831	33 984	48 741	56 891	103 824	65.2
33	10	Hon Hai Precision Industries	Taiwan	Electronic components	96 897	110 865	169 254	172 842	863 183	987 613	90.9
34	79	Tencent Holdings Limited	China	Computer & Data Processing	95 453	137 037	2 420	54 589	40 723	62 885	46.3
35	23	GlaxoSmithKline PLC	UK	Pharmaceuticals	93 156	105 232	41 841	43 043	57 494	99 437	81.2
36	97	Sinopec - China Petrochemical Corporation	China	Pretrol. & Refining	90 492	328 607	132 500	443 308	39 658	423 543	22.3
37	82	Engie	France	Electricity, gas & water	89 247	179 502	40 111	67 224	26 201	160 301	41.9

(continued)

Table 2.5 (continued)

The world's top non-financial multinational enterprises, ranked by foreign assets, 2019[a]

Ranked by Foreign Assets	TNI[b]	Corporation	Home economy	Industry[c]	Assets		Sales		Employment		TNI[b]
					Foreign	Total	Foreign	Total	Foreign[d]	Total	%
38	30	Fiat Chrysler Automobiles	UK	Motor Vehicles	88 262	110 137	104 313	121 096	127 136	191 752	77.5
39	52	Samsung Electronics Co., Ltd.	Korea Rep.	Communications equipment	87 435	305 544	168 245	197 552	215 542	308 746	61.2
40	1	Rio Tinto PLC	UK	Mining, quarrying & petroleum	87 231	87 443	41 275	41 514	45 817	46 007	99.6
41	3	Medtronic plc	Irel&	Instruments & related products	86 701	89 694	30 466	30 557	87 065	90 071	97.7
42	92	Nippon Telegraph & Telephone Corporation	Japan	Telecommunications	85 984	212 063	20 460	109 488	123 000	319 039	32.6
43	16	ArcelorMittal	Luxembourg	Metals & metal products	85 125	88 092	70 509	70 509	119 735	208 503	84.7
44	70	IBM Corp	USA	Computer & Data Processing	82 388	152 186	40 873	77 147	190 885	352 600	53.8
45	7	Linde PLC	UK	Chemicals & Allied Products	82 205	86 612	26 575	28 228	69 624	79 886	92.1
46	99	China COSCO Shipping Corp Ltd	China	Transport & storage	81 190	315 020	22 786	114 465	8 091	173 300	16.8
47	20	Roche Group	Switzerl&	Pharmaceuticals	78 846	85 998	61 262	61 856	55 623	97 735	82.5
48	69	Orange SA	France	Telecommunications	76 795	119 415	26 958	47 278	59 682	147 000	54.0
49	77	Pfizer Inc	USA	Pharmaceuticals	76 273	167 489	27 898	51 750	40 211	88 300	48.3
50	87	Mitsubishi Corporation	Japan	Wholesale Petroleum & Fuels	76 196	166 318	53 867	135 990	15 985	77 478	35.4
51	86	Ford Motor Company	USA	Motor Vehicles	75 811	258 537	57 171	155 900	90 000	190 000	37.8
52	94	Walmart inc	USA	Retail Trade	74 653	236 495	121 432	523 964	700 000	2 200 000	28.9
53	83	Mitsui & Co Ltd	Japan	Wholesale Metals & Minerals	73 653	108 789	31 077	63 350	2 657	45 624	40.9

54	59	Airbus SE	France	Aircraft	69 722	128 521	53 601	78 887	73 200	134 931	58.8
55	89	China National Offshore Oil Corp	China	Mining, quarrying & petroleum	69 517	176 882	65 071	108 065	4 671	94 000	34.8
56	28	Christian Dior SA	France	Textiles, clothing & leather	68 261	105 403	54 785	60 074	129 608	163 309	78.4
57	38	Novartis AG	Switzerl&	Pharmaceuticals	68 049	118 370	47 755	48 624	51 127	103 914	68.3
58	84	Huawei Technologies Co, Ltd	China	Communications equipment	67 839	123 344	50 945	124 263	45 000	194 000	39.7
59	93	Amazon.com, Inc	USA	E-Commerce	67 166	225 248	85 384	280 522	237 953	798 000	30.0
60	42	Sanofi	France	Pharmaceuticals	65 149	126 641	38 828	42 121	54 699	100 409	66.0
61	18	Unilever PLC	UK	Food & beverages	64 569	72 350	43 783	56 040	124 000	153 000	82.8
62	68	Enbridge Inc	Canada	Electricity, gas & water	63 989	25 650	22 696	37 734	5 755	11 300	54.0
63	35	SAP SE	Germany	Computer & Data Processing	63 969	67 642	26 422	30 841	33 952	100 331	71.4
64	91	Alphabet Inc	USA	Computer & Data Processing	63 589	275 909	87 014	161 857	27 403	118 899	33.3
65	67	Procter & Gamble Co	USA	Chemicals & Allied Products	61 060	115 095	39 091	67 684	51 460	97 000	54.6
66	37	Robert Bosch GmbH	Germany	Motor Vehicles	60 199	100 011	69 429	86 995	265 489	398 150	68.9
67	55	Fresenius SE & Co KGaA	Germany	Health care services	60 188	75 271	22 645	39 634	128 272	294 134	60.2
68	90	Equinor ASA	Norway	Pretrol. & Refining	60 131	118 037	22 159	62 740	3 284	21 412	33.9
69	61	Atlantia SpA	Italy	Construction	59 548	91 685	7 452	14 120	16 965	30 633	57.7
70	47	BASF SE	Germany	Chemicals & Allied Products	59 018	97 675	53 346	66 394	63 600	117 628	64.9
71	12	Lafargeholcim Ltd	Switzerl&	Building materials	58 616	60 376	26 611	27 570	51 572	72 452	88.3
72	51	Renault SA	France	Motor Vehicles	57 983	137 240	46 660	62 164	131 587	179 565	63.5
73	53	Sinochem Group	China	Mining, quarrying & petroleum	57 275	71 200	75 201	89 308	11 023	65 271	60.5
74	50	China National Chemical (ChemChina)	China	Chemicals & Allied Products	54 090	117 011	2 768	34 433	86 025	167 000	64.3

(continued)

Table 2.5 (continued)

The world's top non-financial multinational enterprises, ranked by foreign assets, 2019[a]

Ranked by Foreign Assets	TNI[b]	Corporation	Home economy	Industry[c]	Assets		Sales		Employment		TNI[b]
					Foreign	Total	Foreign	Total	Foreign[d]	Total	%
75	34	The Coca-Cola Company	USA	Food & beverages	54 006	86 381	25 551	37 266	76 100	86 200	73.1
76	5	Anglo American plc	UK	Mining, quarrying & petroleum	53 703	55 922	26 580	28 727	61 000	63 000	95.1
77	85	Raytheon Technologies Corp	USA	Aircraft	53 551	139 716	29 737	77 046	93 215	243 200	38.4
78	25	Mondelez International, Inc.	USA	Food & beverages	53 093	64 549	19 243	25 868	68 000	80 000	80.5
79	73	RWE AG	Germany	Electricity, gas & water	51 725	72 110	9 274	14 691	3 474	18 244	51.3
80	72	Sony Corporation	Japan	Consumer electronics	50 915	212 295	53 270	76 000	77 000	128 400	51.3
81	100	Saudi Aramco	Saudi Arabia	Mining, quarrying & petroleum	50 558	398 434	69 871	329 809	8 866	69 867	15.5
82	65	Intel Corporation	USA	Electronic components	49 605	136 524	56 348	71 965	56 508	110 800	55.2
83	40	Unibail-Rodamco SE	France	Real Estate	49 099	73 021	2 445	3 784	2 542	3 625	67.3
84	48	National Grid PLC	UK	Electricity, gas & water	49 087	82 918	11 755	18 461	16 414	23 024	64.7
85	4	John Swire & Sons Limited	UK	Transport & storage	48 751	51 317	13 121	14 109	131 670	133 000	95.7
86	6	Altice Europe NV	Netherl&s	Telecommunications	48 255	53 000	16 288	16 561	41 343	45 409	93.5
87	66	Peugeot SA (PSA Peugeot Citroen)	France	Motor Vehicles	47 869	78 371	64 578	83 648	56 118	208 780	55.1
88	98	Comcast Corp	USA	Telecommunications	47 137	263 414	22 476	108 942	34 000	190 000	18.8
89	14	Danone Groupe SA	France	Food & beverages	47 099	50 957	25 853	28 304	76 799	102 398	86.3

90	26	Schneider Electric SA	France	Electricity, gas & water	47 058	50 554	28 534	30 398	81 883	151 297	80.4
91	76	Vinci SA	France	Construction	46 754	102 339	24 695	54 570	121 348	222 397	48.5
92	44	TC Energy Corp	Canada	Electricity, gas & water	46 428	76 404	6 930	9 989	4 750	7 300	65.1
93	74	Legend Holdings Corporation	China	Computer Equipment	46 331	89 647	41 968	56 702	24 360	87 000	51.2
94	57	Compagnie de Saint-Gobain SA	France	Building materials	46 204	56 148	9 889	47 653	137 888	180 941	59.7
95	15	AstraZeneca PLC	UK	Pharmaceuticals	45 886	61 126	21 699	23 451	59 900	67 300	85.5
96	24	Air Liquide SA	France	Chemicals & Allied Products	45 416	49 052	21 474	24 536	41 664	67 200	80.7
97	62	Petronas - Petroliam Nasional Bhd	Malaysia	Mining, quarrying & petroleum	45 031	153 978	43 580	62 177	34 000	48 001	56.7
98	95	General Motors Co	USA	Motor Vehicles	45 008	228 037	26 623	137 237	68 000	164 000	26.9
99	75	Repsol YPF SA	Spain	Pretrol. & Refining	44 936	65 036	25 916	55 214	7 522	24 634	48.9
100	2	Barrick Gold Corporation	Canada	Mining, quarrying & petroleum	43 803	44 392	9 412	9 717	42 585	43 511	97.8

Source: UNCTAD, World Investment Report, 2021; Unctad data base. Creative Commons, CY4

[a]Preliminary results based on data from the companies' financial reporting; corresponds to the financial year from 1 April 2019 to 31 March 2020

[b]TNI, the **Transnationality Index**, is calculated as the average of the following three ratios: foreign assets to total assets, foreign sales to total sales & foreign employment to total employment

[c]Industry classification for companies follows the United States St&ard Industrial Classification as used by the United States Securities & Exchange Commission (SEC)

[d]In a number of cases foreign employment data were calculated by applying the share of foreign employment in total employment of the previous year to total employment of 2019

[e]Data refers to 2018

Table 2.6 Number of top 500 multinational firms in selected country and regions, Fortune Magazine, 2021, Global 500, Listing for the year 1995 and 2021 (number of firms and revenues in billion and trillion USD); authors compilation, Source: Fortune Magazin, 2021

Number of top 500 multinational firms in selected country and regions, Fortune Magazine, 2021, Global 500, Listing for the year 1995 and 2021 (number of firms and revenues in billion and trillion USD); authors compilation, Source: Fortune Magazine, 2021.

Country/region	Year 1995	Revenue (USD)	Year 2021	Revenue (USD)
China	3	41.26 bill	135	8.92 trill
Asia	16	207.28 bill	43	2.33 trill
Japan	149	3.81 trill	53	2.94 trill
Europe	174	3.27 trill	127	7.01 trill
USA	151	2.94 trill	121	9.65 trill
Americas	12	139.62 bill	20	834.19 bill

Source: Global 500 List, Fortune Magazine; (https://qlik.fortune.com/global500/)

researchers have forecasted the dominance of multinational enterprises (Forsgren, 2007, 2018; Winiecki, 1980; Yamin & Forsgren, 2006).

A multinational firm is characterized by its operations abroad. However, the terms "operations" or "business operations" are highly generic. They can include exports and imports or several other activities, such as licensing and franchising. The international operations of a multinational firm include strategic alliances and non-equity forms of cooperation in highly fragmented and spatially dispersed value-adding activities. Multinational firms operate closely with prevalent competitors, employing cross-licensing agreements with rival firms.

Therefore, controlling and operating business activities in two or more national economies can be manifold, complex, and a great challenge. Its success depends on internal resources and capabilities or external factors affecting the organization and outcomes of IB operations. To some extent, multinationality itself is treated as a source of superior efficiency, allowing the multinational firm to increase its leverage arising out of operational flexibility (Benito et al., 2019; Kogut & Zander, 2003; Taliman, 2003).

The basic definition of a multinational business revolves around the fact that the firm "operates or controls value-adding activities in more than one country"(Dunning, 1993: 3). However, there are various ways to operate, and multiple concepts are involved in controlling a business activity abroad. Although FDI is made with the intention to control—a key definitional dimension—large multinationals control business activities across a wide variety of stages in GVCs, without having direct stake or ownership in key suppliers and subcontractors. As it is their dominant role, the sheer size of the multinational firm remains important as a leverage to control key nodes in the highly fragmented and complex GPNs.

To define a multinational firm is an ambiguous endeavor. The assumed superior efficiency of the large multinational firm generated within its own firm boundaries arises from its capability to efficiently explore and exploit gains generated outside its firm boundary.

In addition, controlling and operating a value-adding activity in more than one national location can provide access to generous tax exemptions and subsidized infrastructure. As a result, multinational firms can have a significant advantage over uni-national operating firms because of their leveraged operational flexibility by the exploitation of scale economies in cross-border vertical and horizontal integration of value-adding activities. Operational flexibility may not only minimize costs but also reduce risks with the associated liability of foreignness (Kogut, 1984).

2.5.4.2 The Prolonged Power of the Multinational Firm

The immense power of multinational firms has been at the center of a debate since Hymer (1976), who critiqued multinational firms for being economically too powerful, and was concerned that the world economy could be dominated by a few giant firms (Graham, 2006: 149). Even though Hymer is acknowledged as a "pioneer of modern analysis of a multinational enterprise" his approach "has not received the attention it merits" (Yamin & Forsgren, 2006: 166). The current pattern and structure of global trade and FDI closely resembles what Hymer described multinational firms as "... islands of conscious power in an ocean of unconscious cooperation," a phrase borrowed from D. H. Robertson and quoted by Ronald Coase in 1937 (Coase, 1937; Hymer, 1970: 441).

In the 1950s, large firms grew larger by increasing direct control of value-adding activities by vertically integrating forward and backward stages in the production, especially in the expanding extractive industries. Today the production process, from the supply of raw material to the final distribution, is organized along a highly fragmented and spatially dispersed global production, controlled by large multinational firms in both producer and buyer driven GVCs (Gereffi, 2018).

These multinational firms efficiently lead and control key technologies, essential intermediary products, and major services embedded in the global business network, operated by a mix of wholly owned affiliates, independent firms, highly dependent contractors, and non-affiliate subcontracting entities scattered across countries and regions (Dicken, 2017).

The scope and scale of global trade and cross-border FDI flows are significant for business activities, contributing to an extensive, highly fragmented and unequal international division of labor, embodied in global value-adding activities (Sturgeon, 2008).

In the past, the role of the multinational firm was analyzed primarily by studying its strategy for international production and the pattern and growth of FDIs (UNCTAD, 2012: 124). A more thorough perspective needs to include not only the extent of managerial control but also multinational firms' exercise in GPNs (UNCTAD, 2012). Multinationals generate sophisticated strategies to indirectly control the complex and spatially dispersed value-adding activities using non-equity forms of co-operations, contractors, and affiliates. Non-equity modes of managing key value-added activities are signifying a new form of governance that slowly emerged in the last two decades. It includes contract manufacturing, service outsourcing, contract farming, franchising, and licensing, to control and coordinate highly complex value-adding activities across the globe (UNCTAD, 2011).

The conception of large and leading business firms governing the operations within a large network of competing firms, including suppliers and key customers, rests on the assumption that the lead firm is more efficient in the execution of the strategy adopted in GPNs (Buckley & Casson, 2014; Devinney et al., 2001; Girod & Rugman, 2005; Rugman & D'Cruz, 1997).

For a long time, a multinational firm has been conceptualized as an alternative governance design resulting from the failure of imperfect markets. The argument is based on the notion that within firm boundaries, the necessary control and coordination is more efficient. Unsurprisingly, markets and business firms appear as two antithetical concepts in orthodox neoclassical theory of firms, but the dividing line between the two governing modes appears somewhat blurred.

In this chapter we examined the world economy with some of its main structural features, such as GDP, world trade, and FDI. These structural features of the world economy represent the macro-environment and the micro-behavior of agents operating in the world economy. Under these conditions, firms operate internationally and establish their activities facing different, mostly unfamiliar and uncertain environments. The macro-environment affects the micro-behavior of agents (firms, governments etc.) but micro-behaviors are impacting the macro-environment as well. A look at the core structural features of the world economy uncovered a highly typified, uneven pattern of distribution of income, global trade, and FDI. Indeed, it is a highly concentrated pattern magnifying the structural effects between core and periphery regions. However, these centuries old structural patterns have changed significantly with new core regions emerging and old ones not disappearing but becoming increasingly weaker or less dominant. One of the most striking features of the global economy is that large multinational firms can be identified as the major drivers of international trade and investment. The intrafirm and interfirm trade organized by these giant multinational firms are unequally supported by many small and medium sized enterprises, embedded in a vast network of business relations. It is the outcome of a highly fragmented and spatially dispersed global division of labor between firms operating in the core and periphery regions. It is important to examine this pattern of trade and investment: The outcome of an intricate mutually dependent relationship between the macro-environment (the global economy) and the micro-behavior of the individual agents. The macro-environment as the pre-given structural constraint has not been generated independently from the individual agent (the firm, manager, and individual). Neither the macro- nor the micro-level, being the context of our behaviors, is rigidly determining

(continued)

each other. Both are mutually dependent, with rules, values, and habits enacted if they fit the existing situational environment. Each agent in this global economy is capable of making a deliberate decision despite being constrained by the existing rules and values prevalent in the seemingly rigid institutional environment.

Study Questions

1. Try to identify the most important features of the world economy. What is a pattern that typifies today's world economy? Why and how did you choose the "important feature" of the world economy?
2. How does globalization work? Think about a thing you recently bought and analyze how it was produced. Where did the raw materials come from? Where and how was the product manufactured? Who is selling the product?
3. Try to summarize the major structural patterns of global trade.
4. Think about a recent trade conflict. What is the major source of the conflict? How could it be resolved?
5. Identify major recipients (countries/regions) of FDI. Think about the major source of FDIs made recently. Try to identify a pattern of distribution between FDI in- and outflows. Use the recent World Investment Report published by the UNCTAD (United Nations Conference on Trade and Development) in Geneva. https://unctad.org/webflyer/world-investment-report-2021
6. Think about a large multinational firm and discuss with a friend how it affects you. What product is this multinational firm producing, and how is it manufactured? How is the production process of this multinational firm affecting the global environment?

References

Abbas, H. S. M., Gillani, S., Ullah, S., Raza, M. A. A., & Ullah, A. (2020). Nexus between governance and socioeconomic factors on public service fragility in Asian Economies. *Social Science Quarterly, 101*(5), 1850–1868.

Abramovitz, M. (1986). Simon Kuznets 1901–1985. *The Journal of Economic History, 46*(1), 241–246.

Allen, R. C. (2017). Absolute poverty: When necessity displaces desire. *American Economic Review, 107*(12), 3690–3721.

Anderson, J. E., & van Wincoop, E. (2003). Gravity with gravitas: A solution to the border puzzle. *American Economic Review, 93*(1), 170–192.

Andersson, T. (1993). The global race for Foreign Direct Investment. *Prospects for the Future, 1993*, 205–231.

Archer, M. S. (1995). *Realist social theory*. Cambridge University Press. https://doi.org/10.1017/cbo9780511557675

Archer, M. S. (1996). *Culture and agency: The place of culture in social theory* (2nd ed.). Cambridge University Press. https://doi.org/10.1017/CBO9780511557668

Archer, M. S. (2000). For structure: Its reality, properties and powers: A reply to Anthony King. *The Sociological Review, 48*(3), 464–472.

Archer, M. S. (2003). *Structure, agency and the internal conversation*. Cambridge University Press.

Archer, M. S., & Elder-Vass, D. (2012). Cultural system or norm circles? An exchange. *European Journal of Social Theory, 15*(1), 93–115.

Atkinson, A. B. (2015). *Inequality. What can be done?* Harvard University Press.

Baldwin, R., Forslid, R., Martin, P., Ottaviano, G., & Robert-Nicoud, F. (2003). *Economic geography and public policy*. Princeton University Press.

Balistreri, E. J., & Hillberry, R. H. (2007). Structural estimation and the border puzzle. *Journal of International Economics, 72*(2), 451–463.

Barnard, C. (1938). *The function of the executive*. Harvard University Press.

Basu, P., Chakraborty, C., & Reagle, D. (2003). Liberalization, FDI, and growth in developing countries: A panel cointegration approach. *Economic Inquiry, 41*(3), 510–516.

Beaverstock, J. V. (2009). International Encyclopedia of human geography. *Transactions of the Institute of British Geographers, 29*(2004), 162–163.

Benito, G. R. G., Petersen, B., & Welch, L. S. (2019). The global value chain and internalization theory. *Journal of International Business Studies, 50*(8), 1414–1423.

Birkinshaw, J., Hood, N., & Jonsson, S. (1998). Building firm-specific advantages in multinational corporations: The role of subsidiary initiative. *Strategic Management Journal, 19*(3), 221–242.

Buckley, P. J. (1989). The multinational enterprise. *Theory and Applications, 1989*, 3–23.

Buckley, P. J. (2006). Stephen Hymer: Three phases, one approach? *International Business Review, 15*(2), 140–147.

Buckley, P. J., & Casson, M. (2002). *The future of the multinational enterprise. 25th Anniversary Edition*. Palgrave Macmillan.

Buckley, P. J., & Casson, M. (2003). The future of the multinational enterprise in retrospect and in prospect. *Journal of International Business Studies, 34*(2), 219–222.

Buckley, P. J., & Casson, M. (2010). *The multinational enterprise revisited. The essential Buckley and Casson* (pp. 177–204). Palgrave.

Buckley, P. J., & Casson, M. (2014). *The multinational enterprise and the emergence of the global factory* (pp. 20–51). Springer.

Buckley, P. J., Clegg, J., & Wang, C. (2002). The impact of inward FDI on the performance of Chinese manufacturing firms. *Journal of International Business Studies, 33*(4), 637–655.

Casanova, L., & Miroux, A. (2020). *The era of Chinese multinationals* (pp. 3–25). Elsevier.

Cassell, P. (1993). *The Giddens reader* (pp. 88–175). Springer.

Casson, M., Dark, K., & Gulamhussen, M. A. (2009). Extending internalisation theory: From the multinational enterprise to the knowledge-based empire. *International Business Review, 18*(3), 236–256.

Castellani, D., & Fassio, C. (2019). From new imported inputs to new exported products. Firm-level evidence from Sweden. *Research Policy, 48*(1), 322–338.

Castells, M. (2005). Global governance and global politics. *Political Science & Politics, 38*(1), 9–16.

Coase, R. (1937). The nature of the firm. *Economica, 4*(16), 386–405.

Davies, S. (1980). Minimum efficient size and seller concentration: An empirical problem. *The Journal of Industrial Economics, 28*(3), 287.

Davies, R. B., & Markusen, J. R. (2021). What do multinationals do? The structure of multinational firms' international activities. *The World Economy, 44*(12), 3444–3481.

Davis, J. B. (2019). Economics and economic methodology in a core-periphery economic world. *SSRN Electronic Journal*. https://doi.org/10.2139/ssrn.3324569

Devinney, T. M., Rugman, A. M., & D'Cruz, J. R. (2001). Multinationals as flagship firms. *The Academy of Management Review, 26*(3), 462.

Dicken, P. (2017). *Global shift. Mapping the changing contours of the world economy*. Sage.

Doh, J. P. (2019). MNEs, FDI, inequality and growth. *Multinational Business Review, 27*(3), 217–220.

Dunning, J. H. (1988). The theory of international production. *The International Trade Journal, 3*(1), 21–66. https://doi.org/10.1080/08853908808523656

Dunning, J. H. (1993). *Multinational enterprise and the global economy*. Addison-Wesley.

Dunning, J., & Lundan, S. M. (2008). *Multinational enterprises and the global economy*. Edward Elgar Publisher. https://doi.org/10.18356/43ce1fe7-en

Durkheim, E. (1962). *The rules of sociological method*. Free Press.

Easterly, W. (2002). *The elusive quest for growth*. MIT Press.

Ernst, D. (2009). A new geography of knowledge in the electronics industry? Asia's role in global innovation networks. *SSRN Electronic Journal*. https://doi.org/10.2139/ssrn.2742923

Farmer, K., & Wendner, R. (1997). *Wachstum und Außenhandel, Eine Einführung in die Gleichgewichtstheorie der Wachstums- und Außenhandelsdynamik* (pp. 47–71). Springer.

Faulconbridge, J. (2007). Global shift, fifth edition. Mapping the changing contours of the world economy. *Journal of Economic Geography, 7*(6), 777–779.

Feenstra, R. C. (1998). Integration of trade and disintegration of production in the global economy. *Journal of Economic Perspectives, 12*(4), 31–50.

Foley, C. F., Hines, J. R., & Wessel, D. (2021). *Multinational corporations in the 21st century economy*. Brookings Institutions Press.

Forsgren, M. (2007). Foreign direct investment, location and competitiveness. *Progress in International Business Research, 2007*, 29–50.

Forsgren, M. (2013). *Theories of the multinational firm. A multidimensional creature of the global economy*. Edward Elgar.

Forsgren, M. (2018). The development of international business: A narrative of theory and practice. *Journal of International Business Studies, 49*(6), 774–777.

Fratianni, M. (2009). The gravity equation in international trade. In A. Rugman (Ed.), *The Oxford handbook of international business* (pp. 72–89). Oxford University Press.

Fratianni, M. U., Marchionne, F., & Oh, C. H. (2011). A commentary on the gravity equation in international business research. *Multinational Business Review, 19*(1), 36–46.

Friedman, T. L. (2000). *The Lexus and the Olive Tree*. Macmillan.

Friedman, T. L. (2005). It's a flat world, after all. *The New York Times Magazine*. Retrieved from https://www.nytimes.com/2005/04/03/magazine/its-a-flat-world-after-all.html

Frobel, F., Heinrichs, J., & Kreye, O. (1978). Export-oriented industrialization of underdeveloped countries. *Monthly Review, 30*(6), 22–27.

Fröbel, F., Kreye, O., Heinrichs, J., & Fuchs, M. (1991). *Diversity and unity in the third world*. Research Report. Volkswagen Stiftung.

Fubini, D., Price, C., & Zollo, M. (2007). *Mergers, leadership, performance and corporate health* (pp. 102–117). Springer.

Gellner, E. (1971). Holism versus individualism. In M. Brodbeck (Ed.), *Readings in the philosophy of the social sciences* (p. 267). Macmillan.

Gereffi, G. (2018). *Global value chains and development*. Cambridge University Press. https://doi.org/10.1017/9781108559423

Girma, S., Thompson, S., & Wright, P. (2005). Globalisation and productivity growth. In *Theory and evidence* (pp. 79–91). Springer.

Girod, S. J. G., & Rugman, A. M. (2005). Regional business networks and the multinational retail sector. *Long Range Planning, 38*(4), 335–357.

Gordon, I. R., & McCann, P. (2000). Industrial clusters: Complexes, agglomeration and/or social networks? *Urban Studies, 37*(3), 513–532.

Graham, E. M. (2006). Comment on Peter J. Buckley: "Stephen Hymer: Three phases, one approach?". *International Business Review, 15*(2), 148–150.

Hansen, H., & Rand, J. (2006). On the causal links between FDI and growth in developing countries. *The World Economy, 29*(1), 21–41.

Hart, J. S. (1999). Origins of economic instability: Real, financial or both? - Part II: An appraisal of Minsky's financial instability hypothesis. *South African Journal of Economic and Management Sciences, 2*(2), 188–206.

Hassler, M. (2012). Macroregional economic integration in Southeast Asia: AFTA and the automobile industry from a Thai perspective. *Singapore Journal of Tropical Geography, 33*(1), 124–136.

Helpman, E. (1984). Chapter 7. Increasing returns, imperfect markets, and trade theory. In: *Handbook of international economics* (Vol. 1, pp. 325–365). Academic Press.

Helpman, E. (2006). Trade, FDI, and the organization of firms. *Journal of Economic Literature, 44*(3), 589630.

Heron, T. (2012). *The global political economy of trade protectionism and liberalization: Trade reform and economic adjustment in textiles and clothing* (1st ed.). Routledge. https://doi.org/10.4324/9780203114940

Hirst, P., & Thompson, G. (1999). *Globalization in question* (2nd ed.). Polity Press.

Hwang, S. I., & Kim, N.-D. (2017). The relationship between GDP and FDI. *The Journal of Foreign Studies, 42*, 505–530.

Hymer, S. (1970). The efficiency (contradictions) of multinational corporations. *American Economic Review, 60*(2), 441–448. https://doi.org/10.2307/1815843

Hymer, S. H. (1976). *The international operations of national firms: A study of direct foreign investment*. The MIT Press.

Jameson, F. (2000). *Globalization and political strategy*, 4. Retrieved from https://newleftreview.org/issues/ii4/articles/fredric-jameson-globalization-and-political-strategy

Jiang, M. S., Aulakh, P. S., & Pan, Y. (2007). The nature and determinants of exclusivity rights in international technology licensing. *Management International Review, 47*(6), 869–893.

Kogut, B. (1984). Normative observations on the international value-added chain and strategic groups. *Journal of International Business Studies, 15*(2), 151–167. https://doi.org/10.1057/palgrave.jibs.8490488

Kogut, B., & Zander, U. (1993). Knowledge of the firm and the evolutionary theory of the multinational corporation. *Journal of International Business Studies, 24*(4), 625–645.

Kogut, B., & Zander, U. (2003). Knowledge of the firm and the evolutionary theory of the multinational corporation. *Journal of International Business Studies, 34*(6), 516–529.

Kosztowniak, A. (2016). Verification of the relationship between FDI and GDP in Poland. *Acta Oeconomica, 66*(2), 307–332.

Krugman, P. (1991). Increasing returns and economic geography. *Journal of Political Economy, 99*(3), 483–499.

Krugman, P., & Wells, R. (2017). *Essentials of economics* (pp. 535–575). Macmillan.

Lu, J. W., & Beamish, P. W. (2006). SME internationalization and performance: Growth vs. profitability. *Journal of International Entrepreneurship, 4*(1), 27–48.

Maddison, A. (2001). *The world economy. A millenium perspective*. OECD Development Centre. OECD. https://doi.org/10.1787/9789264189980-en

Malgwi, C. A., Owhoso, V., Gleason, K. C., & Mathur, I. (2006). Who invests in the least developed countries? *Journal of African Business, 7*(1–2), 201–227.

Marshall, A. (1920). *The principles of economics* (8th ed.). Macmillan.
McCallum, J. (1987). Unemployment in Canada and the United States. *The Canadian Journal of Economics, 20*(4), 802.
McWilliam, S. E., Kim, J. K., Mudambi, R., & Nielsen, B. B. (2020). Global value chain governance: Intersections with international business. *Journal of World Business, 55*(4), 101067.
Mill, J. S. (2006). *A system of logic, rationcinative and inductive*. Liberty Fund.
Minsky, H. P. (2016). Longer waves in financial relations: Financial factors in the more severe depressions II. *Journal of Economic Issues, 29*(1), 83–96.
Mokyr, J. (1995). Urbanization, technological progress, and economic history. In H. Giersch (Ed.), *Urban agglomeration and economic growth*. Publications of the Egon-Sohmen-Foundation. Springer. https://doi.org/10.1007/978-3-642-79397-4_1
Muir, J. (2014). Roses are red, violets are blue, air cargo flies flowers for you. *Air Cargo Week*. Retrieved from https://www.aircargoweek.com/roses-red-violets-blue-air-cargo-flies-flowers/
Navaretti, G. B., Venables, A. J., Barry, F. G., Ekholm, K., Falzoni, A. M., et al. (2020). *Multinational firms in the world economy*. De Gruyter. https://doi.org/10.2307/j.ctv10crfcz
North, D. (1991). Institutions. *Journal of Economic Perspectives, 5*(Winter), 97–112.
North, D. (1993). *Rationality, institutions and economic methodology* (Vol. 19933353). Springer. https://doi.org/10.4324/9780203392805.ch10
OECD. (2002a). *Intra-industry and intra-firm trade and the internationalisation of production*. OECD. https://doi.org/10.1787/data-00095-en
OECD. (2002b). *Foreign direct investment for development. Maximising benefits, minimising costs*. OECD.
OECD. (2006). *Alternative measures of well-being*. OECD. https://doi.org/10.1787/growth-2006-7-en
OECD. (2008). *Evolution of GDP* (pp. 40–41). OECD.
Oh, C. H. (2009). The international scale and scope of European multinationals. *European Management Journal, 27*(5), 336–343.
Ohmae, K. (1990). *The borderless world: Power and strategy in the interlinked economy*. Harper Business.
Pearce, R., & Papanastassiou, M. (2006). To 'almost see the world': Hierarchy and strategy in Hymer's view of the multinational. *International Business Review, 15*(2), 151–165.
Perrow, C. (2009). Modeling firms in the global economy. *Theory and Society, 38*(3), 217–243.
Phelps, N. A. (2004). Triangular diplomacy writ small: The political economy of the Indonesia–Malaysia–Singapore growth triangle. *The Pacific Review, 17*(3), 341–368.
Phelps, N. A., & Fuller, C. (2000). Multinationals, intracorporate competition, and regional development. *Economic Geography, 76*(3), 224–243.
Pilon-Lé, L. (1980). Cohen, Robert B., et al, (eds.) «The multinational corporation : A radical approach », Papers by Stephen Herbert Hymer, 1979, Cambridge University Press, 323 p. *Études Internationales, 11*(3), 560–561.
Pitelis, C. (2006). Stephen Herbert Hymer and/on the (theory of the) MNE and international business. *International Business Review, 15*(2), 103–110.
Pitelis, C. N. (2018). *The Palgrave Encyclopedia of strategic management* (pp. 686–691). Springer.
Pitelis, C. N., & Teece, D. J. (2018). The new MNE: 'Orchestration' theory as envelope of 'internalisation' theory. *Management International Review, 58*(4), 523–539.
Razin, A., & Sadka, E. (2016). *Foreign direct investment: Analysis and aggregate flows*. Princeton University Press.
Reinert, K. A. (2021). *International economics. New perspectives on the world economy*. Cambridge University Press.

Reinert, K. A., Rajan, R. S., Glass, A. J., & Davis, L. S. (2009). *The Princeton Encyclopedia of the world economy* (Two Volume Set). Princeton University Press. Retrieved from http://search.ebscohost.com/login.aspx?direct=true&db=nlebk&AN=329822&site=ehost-live

Ritzer, G. (2003). Rethinking globalization: Glocalization/grobalization and something/nothing. *Sociological Theory, 21*(3), 193–209.

Roddick, A. (1996). Resolving international conflict: What role for business? *Business Strategy Review, 7*(3), 43–50.

Rodríguez-Pose, A., Tselios, V., Winkler, D., & Farole, T. (2013). Geography and the determinants of firm exports in Indonesia. *World Development, 44*, 225–240.

Rowthorn, R. (2006). Stephen Hymer: An intellectual memoir. *International Business Review, 15*(2), 111–114.

Rugman, A. M. (2005). *International business and government relations in the 21st century*. Cambridge University Press. https://doi.org/10.1017/cbo9780511488597.016

Rugman, A., & D'Cruz, J. (1997). The theory of the flagship firm. *European Management Journal, 15*(4), 403–412.

Sachsenmaier, D. (2011). A term and a trend: Contours in the United States. In *Global perspectives on global history: Theories and approaches in a connected world* (pp. 59–109). Cambridge University Press. https://doi.org/10.1017/CBO9780511736544.003

Snidal, D. (1982). The new international division of labour: Structural unemployment in industrialized countries and industrialization in developing countries. *American Journal of Sociology, 87*(5), 1218–1220.

Solomon, R. C. (2000). Business with virtue: Maybe next year? *Business Ethics Quarterly, 10*(1), 339–341.

Song, X. (2019). *Understanding Chinese GDP* (pp. 233–247). McKinsey.

Sothan, S. (2015). Foreign direct investment, exports, and long-run economic growth in Asia: Panel Cointegration and causality analysis. *International Journal of Economics and Finance, 8*(1), 26.

Stopford, J. (2005). *International business and government relations in the 21st century* (pp. 103–116). Cambridge University Press.

Strange, R., & Humphrey, J. (2019). What lies between market and hierarchy? Insights from internalization theory and global value chain theory. *Journal of International Business Studies, 50*(8), 1401–1413.

Strange, R., & Newton, J. (2006). Stephen Hymer and the externalization of production. *International Business Review, 15*(2), 180–193.

Streeten, P. (1972). *The frontiers of development studies*. Macmillan.

Streusand, D. E. (2018). *Islamic gunpowder empires* (pp. 291–298). Springer.

Sturgeon, T. J. (2008). Mapping integrative trade: Conceptualising and measuring global value chains. *International Journal of Technological Learning, Innovation and Development, 1*(3), 237.

Sun, C., Abbas, H. S. M., Xu, X., Gillani, S., Ullah, S., et al. (2021). Role of capital investment, investment risks, and globalization in economic growth. *International Journal of Finance & Economics*. https://doi.org/10.1002/ijfe.2514

Swan, T. W. (1956). Economic growth and capital accumulation. *Economic Record, 32*(2), 334–361.

Taliman, S. (2003). *The significance of Bruce Kogut's and Udo Zander's article, "Knowledge of the firm and the evolutionary theory of the multinational corporation"* (Vol. 34). University of Manchester. https://doi.org/10.1057/palgrave.jibs.8400061

Tracy, J. D., & Chaudhuri, K. N. (1991). *Reflections on the organizing principle of premodern trade* (pp. 421–442). Cambridge University Press.

UNCTAD. (1994). *World investment report 1994. Transnational corporations, employment and the workplace*. https://unctad.org/system/files/official-document/wir1994_en.pdf

UNCTAD. (1996). *World investment report 1996. Investment, trade and international policy agreement.* https://unctad.org/system/files/official-document/wir1996_en.pdf
UNCTAD. (1999). *World investment report 1999.* UNCTAD. https://doi.org/10.18356/8e79f24c-en
UNCTAD. (2000). *World investment report 2000. Cross-border mergers and acquisitions and development.* https://unctad.org/system/files/official-document/wir2000_en.pdf
UNCTAD. (2004). *World investment report 2004. The shift towards services.* https://unctad.org/webflyer/world-investment-report-2004
UNCTAD. (2011). World Investment Report 2011: Non-equity modes of international production and development: Key messages – FDI trends and prospects (overview). *Transnational Corporations, 20*(2), 113–146.
UNCTAD. (2012). *World investment report 2012. Towards a new generation of investment policies.* https://doi.org/10.18356/5f5c0728-en
UNCTAD. (2021). *World investment report 2021. Investing in sustainable recovery.* https://doi.org/10.18356/9789210054638c005
United Nations. (1991). *World investment report 1991. The Triad in foreign direct investment.* https://unctad.org/system/files/official-document/wir1991overview_en.pdf
United Nations. (1992). *World investment report 1992. Transnational corporations as engines of growth.* https://unctad.org/system/files/official-document/wir1992_en.pdf
Vaupel, J. W., & Curhan, J. P. (1973). *The world's multinational enterprise.* Harvard University.
Vernon, R. (1977). *Storm over the multinationals* (pp. 219–252). Harvard University Press.
Wang, C., Hong, J., Kafouros, M., & Boateng, A. (2012). What drives outward FDI of Chinese firms? Testing the explanatory power of three theoretical frameworks. *International Business Review, 21*(3), 425–438.
Weick, K. E. (2010). Reflections on enacted sensemaking in the Bhopal disaster. *Journal of Management Studies, 47*(3), 537–550.
Wheeler, K. (2012). *Fair trade and the citizen-consumer, shopping for justice?* (pp. 1–13). Palgrave Macmillan.
Williamson, J. G. (1995). Migration and city growth during industrial revolutions. In H. Giersch (Ed.), *Urban agglomeration and economic growth.* Publications of the Egon-Sohmen-Foundation. Springer. https://doi.org/10.1007/978-3-642-79397-4_3
Winiecki, J. (1980). The role of multinationals in the world economy. *Intereconomics, 15*(5), 231–234.
World Bank. (2022). World Bank data. Poverty headcount ratio in percent of population. Between 1985 and 2021. https://data.worldbank.org/topic/poverty
WTO. (2021). *World trade statistical review.* https://www.wto.org/english/res_e/statis_e/wts2020_e/wts20_toc_e.htm
Yamin, M., & Forsgren, M. (2006). Hymer's analysis of the multinational organization: Power retention and the demise of the federative MNE. *International Business Review, 15*(2), 166–179.
Zhang, J. (2012). Global shift: Mapping the changing contours of the world economy. *Economic Geography, 88*(3), 337–338.

Theories of Internationalization

3

In the early 1960s, Kurt Lewin, psychologist, pioneer and founder of social psychology noted, "there is nothing more practical than a good theory" (Lewin, 1952: 169). His message focused on the contention that a theory should offer new insights to understand a given problematical situation and he maintained that a good theory will help to understand so-called practical problems (Vansteenkiste & Sheldon, 2006). He was convinced that solving complex issues relies on a thorough understanding, which is *only* provided by a good theory. Good theories allow us to make sense of phenomena prevalent in the real world (Bello & Kostova, 2012).

In addition, it seems necessary to acknowledge that if a simple theory explains the same phenomenon as well as a complex theory, it is better to stick to the simple theory. However, in most cases, theories often illuminate only a tiny fraction of a more complex whole, and reality is rarely as simple as postulated by an established and widely accepted theory (Archer, 1995; Bhaskar, 1975).

Many research questions are developed on the basis of uncritically adopted assumptions, of widely accepted theories, or seem to be guided by the availability of data. Strong theories offer a convincing logic that is used to define core concepts which make up the problem analyzed (Bello & Kostova, 2012). A good theory, one which is per definition important and widely used is tested many times, but often referring to stylized facts that are not directly observable. Models derived from theories are often overloaded with variables which are highly abstracted proxies of a phenomenon, fitting a sound measurement model (Reeb et al., 2012).

It is a key issue what data is used in research, if the key variable cannot be observed. It is often critiqued that the pertinent focus on mere facts "may encourage searching vast quantities of data for statistical significance rather than producing good research"

The original version of this chapter was revised with updated figure caption for Figure 3.1. A correction to this chapter can be found at https://doi.org/10.1007/978-3-662-65870-3_8

M. Fuchs, *International Management*,
https://doi.org/10.1007/978-3-662-65870-3_3

(Lounsbury & Beckman, 2015: 290). Thus, it is essential to specify the measurement of core variables, because the proposed cause–effect relationships are often compromised by a mis-specification of measures, and hypotheses tested often lack an in-depth nomological grounding. It is also crucial to note that, in the social and behavioral sciences, we cannot create theories based on eternal natural laws (Jarvis et al., 2010; Podsakoff et al., 2003). So-called "hard-core" theories are relatively immune to falsification because the theory itself is applied in highly abstract and general terms (Qiu et al., 2012).

Whether hypothesized cause–effect relationships are supported by empirical research, in each case, the rationale underlying the design of the hypothesized relationship needs to explicate how a given theory is presumably a better fit to explain the analyzed problem. Mostly scientists apply theories that are powerfully generated in a prevailing research paradigm and invest a lot of effort to elaborate, extend, and refine the dominant theory. A theory can be applied primarily because it is attractive, and much less or no effort is made to clarify the essence of the explanatory power of a theory, which is chosen for a particular empirical research design.

However, a good theory cannot explain a poorly understood cause–effect relationship. We know that a good theory focuses on only a small fraction of an often much bigger problem. Nevertheless, it is important to elaborate on why a theory is used in a given context, it must be explicitly spelled out, and the empirical observations that are to be used to substantiate single hypotheses that are coherently related to the core meaning of the theory in question cannot be merely shrugged off with a reference to the significance of the theory. Theories in use significantly define the conception and design of a study, and can not only guide a discussion but also prescribe its direction and how to interpret an outcome. A theory may become a formative paradigm, implying that it is being treated as "the only valid" way to approach a research problem (Nickles et al., 2002; Qiu et al., 2012).

We will discuss in this section theories that allow us to gain a deeper understanding of the international business activities organized by international firms. It is worthwhile to start with a summary of the early theories of international trade. These theories were primarily orientated to explain trade between national economies. Discussing these early theories allows us to look at the still valued impact of some of their fundamental assumptions. Core ideas from these early theories about international trade can be found in modern trade theories.

Economists differentiate between classical and neoclassical theories that explain international trade. They continue to be a bedrock of international economics. Many insights in international business research are built on these well-established and proven theories.

The focus on mainstream theories is twofold. First, we can refer to a comprehensive body of widely accepted knowledge on how a particular phenomenon is explained. Second, we need to recognize that any established theory that has originated in a particular historical period dealing with an idiosyncratic problem will be, to some extent, outdated. Each historical period shaped how a professed question was being approached and what methodological design were used to study the particular research problem. Moreover, each analysis and problem studied has evolved in a particular socio-economic or situational context which may have changed substantially in the last decades. But, sometimes the original context has changed dramatically.

Mainstream Theories Matter

We can see that a dominant theoretical body of knowledge concerned with the rise, strategy, and structure of the multinational firm that is still applied in international business studies emerged in the 1960s and early 1970s (Audretsch, 1983; Buckley, 2006; Inkpen, 2004; Rowthorn, 2006; Tallman, 2004). However, a shift in perspective occurred in the early 1990s due largely to the dynamics of globalization (Dunning, 1989). Finally, since the turn of the twenty-first century, the focus has increasingly been on the effect of global production networks and global value chains on the management of international business firms (Asmussen et al., 2007; Buckley, 2009a; Buckley & Casson, 2014; Feenstra, 1998; Fernandez-Stark & Gereffi, 2019; Gereffi, 2018a).

The phrase "mainstream theory" employed in this work is not meant to have a negative connotation; rather, it stresses on what historical, often path-dependent grounds a theory is widely used to analyze the core issues in IB research. It seems necessary to acknowledge that a particular focus of these theories is both their strength and weakness. However, we need to accept that these mainstream theories also force upon us a widely accepted research paradigm and often imply a distinct well-accepted research design when addressing a particular research question. Of course, these theories inevitably shape the way we understand our world and how we teach the core subjects in business schools.

3.1 Foreign Trade Theories and International Business

One of the core subjects in international economics is international trade. From its very beginning, trade theory aimed to provide a coherent answer "Why do nations trade?"

At the same time, these early theories focused on one big question: "How is foreign trade between national economies mutually beneficial?" A thorough understanding of these theories is helpful not only to better understand international trade but allow us to appreciate more deeply the major activity of internationalizing firms as major actors.

Traditionally, international economics discuss classical and neoclassical trade theories, as both elaborate on how trade between at least two countries (involving exchange of at least two commodities) can be explained. Most trade theories use parsimonious models, highly restricted to a few constructs (production factors, such as labor, land, and capital). These models are adopted to explain one particular output, such as how two different goods are to be exchanged. In order to keep things simple, the number of countries is limited.

Model

A model, used in economics, is a theoretical construct that illustrates a set of stylized processes through a list of variables and an assumed logical sequence of relationships among those variables. The economic model is a simplified, often panglossian framework designed to illustrate more complex processes. The model addresses only a small slice of a much more complex reality, but claims to explain a central portion of this complexity.

The theories presented in this section will allow us to promote a basic understanding of the general perspectives in the IB domains. We will start with the classical and neoclassical theories. We need to limit this discussion because our major aim is to establish a basic understanding of how these theories explain international trade. We use these insights to discuss international firms and the process of internationalization. Theories about the internationalizing firms and those about international trade have much in common. Trade theories focus on countries, but it is actually not the country, but firms that are producing the goods and services that are traded. It is largely within and between firms that most of the international trade is organized. Global trade is characterized by cross border inter- and intrafirm trade. This is not trivial, because it will substantially affect the proposed understanding of the dynamics and patterns of the global economy.

We are not primarily concerned with why foreign trade occurs and how foreign trade benefits or harms a country, but rather focus on how international firms are affected by and are affecting the international trade structures and patterns.

Still, to avoid any misconceptions, the underlying question in this chapter is: How does the internationalization of multinational firms, the global value chains and the international production networks contribute not only to the success of the firm but how does firm behavior and the highly fragmented process of global value chains affect the development of the global economy?

3.1.1 Classical and Neoclassical Trade Theory

Classical trade theories consider how goods produced by one country are exchanged for goods produced in another country. These theories focus on nations as the major unit of analyzing the factors that explain the extent of trade and look at locational factors prevalent in a particular nation to explain why and how a nation is being affected by trade. The big question all along has been how trade determines a nation's wealth (Calvo, 2020; Feenstra, 1992; Gaynulina, 2020; Shen & Shang, 2019).

One major fact about early trade theories that emerged around the seventeenth century was that the payment for imported goods, which was made with precious metals, was perceived as a major drawback for the state's wealth. The fact that imported goods had to be paid for in precious metals was a thorn in the flesh of the sixteenth century absolutist monarchies since they professed it as a detriment to have their wealth drained abroad to pay for the goods. All trading businesses during these times would have received some exclusive rights from monarchies that put them into a somewhat superior position compared to other trading parties. This negative contention was again and again nurtured by absolutist rulers who suffered from constant financial shortages caused by expensive wars they continuously waged and their excessive and lavish lifestyle. In those times, international trade was treated as an instrument for filling the state budget. Thus, a trade surplus was deemed good, and a deficit was considered bad. Mercantilism consequently emerged as the political doctrine used to carry out multiple measures legitimizing all forms of protectionism and it is by no means outdated.

3.1.2 Mercantilism

Mercantilism flourished and became the pre-dominant economic worldview nurtured by nationalist governments in the seventeenth century. The term "mercantilism" was coined by Adam Smith in 1776 by referring to the compelling ideas of the English Merchant Thomas Mun (1571–1641). Mercantilism is a policy popularized by the French Jean-Baptiste Colbert (1619–1683). Colbert, the Prime Minister of King Louis XIV, projected several dogmatic principles to promote domestically industrial development and perceived foreign trade as a mechanism to strengthen the French state. He believed in developing France by setting high tariffs and favoring public works. His measures included the promotion and establishment of industrial manufacturing, protecting inventors, and the promotion of the influx of foreign labor, but also to constrain the migration of French workers. A more radical version of mercantilism used to reorganize the French absolutist state was supposed to boost exports to bring silver and gold into the king's coffers. Colbert succeeded in reforming the French economy and saved the state from bankruptcy. The mercantilist states did not seek to shut off their national economies from foreign trade totally, but rather strove to protect domestic industries, but mercantilists were somewhat blind to the fact that excessive protection did not promote the growth of those sheltered industries.

Example

That intricate motivation to protect domestic industries is portrayed and criticized by Adam Smith in his *Wealth of Nations* where he noted: "in Great Britain Silesian lawns may be imported for home consumption, upon paying certain duties. But

(continued)

French cambricks and lawns are prohibited from being imported, except into the port of London, there to be warehoused for exportation" [...].

Adam Smith's critique, recounting a host of different tariffs noted, "the French in their turn have, I believe, treated our goods and manufactures just as hardly [...] though I am not so well acquainted with the particular hardships which they have imposed upon them. Those *mutual restraints* have put an end to almost all *fair commerce between the two nations*, and *smugglers are now the principal importers*, either of British goods into France, or of French goods into Great Britain" (Smith, 1976: 473 Book I).

Adam Smith clearly realized that protecting the domestic industry amounted merely to the import of inferior goods at higher prices. He emphatically reasoned that if Britain were to tame its *animosity and national prejudices*, it might buy better wine from France instead of the inferior produce from Portugal, and better linen instead of the poorer-quality materials from Germany (Smith, 1976: 474; Book I).

Smith conveys in these quotes his deep-seated aversion and rejection of mercantilism, simply because it is an unfair trade practice. It does not help it harms. He knew that the French mercantilism grew from a general and deep-rooted mistrust against traders. It was an old and long-lived stereotype expressed by Francoise Quesnay (1694–1774), a French Physiocrat who assumed that trading was not a productive activity. Quesnay reasoned trade adds no value to the economy. Mercantilism is a reference to Mercury, the god of traders, but he is also the god of cheaters and swindlers. Mercantilism was applied in the belief that it would strengthen (or protect) the absolutist states. Mercantilist policies were widely implemented in Europe between the sixteenth and eighteenth centuries.

Mercantilists aimed only to secure state finances by maximizing exports and limiting imports. The rationale behind was the simple belief that as much gold and silver as possible should flow into the state coffers. The export industry was encouraged by granting privileges, but the export of raw materials was restricted, as was the import of finished products. Consequently, colonies were exploited mercilessly. How fruitless this endeavor was to build a healthy national budget is described by an anonymous commentator as follows: "all the gold and silver that is brought falls, as it were, into a sack full of holes, because France is like a canal through which water flows inexorably" (Braudel, 1986: 213).

Adam Smith presumed that free, but not unregulated trade, would promote prosperity much more effectively than the shortsighted protectionism hailed by mercantilists. Smith was deeply convinced that a country should focus on those economic activities where it has the greatest absolute advantage.

3.1.3 From Mercantilism to Deregulation

Smith became the classical counterproposition to the uncompromising stance of mercantilism. Smith explained in detail that not the precious metals, but the productive resources, namely land, labor and capital is the source of wealth. A question that focused on how value is created. The idea of unrestricted trade that concerned Adam Smith and later David Ricardo, is considered an original source of laissez-faire liberalism. Adam Smith's condemnation of the blunt regulation of commerce was based on his belief that the true source of wealth lies in the productive use of resources, especially land and labor. Keeping in mind this original message puts a different light on the notion of laissez-faire.

Laissez-Faire, Laissez-Passer
The original vernacular "laissez-faire, laissez-passer," literally means "let them do and pass." Its intended meaning was to let the children go and enable them to become inventive and self-aware individuals. The phrase was later adopted by Physiocrats as motto to demand more commercial freedom and deregulate existing trade restriction. Decades later, in the mid-twentieth century, the original meaning became a dogma bluntly celebrating the message that the governments should keep their hands off regulating or interfering with economic matters at all.

But all too often, when arguments are used single-sided, the notion of the original message is inevitably lost. If Adam Smith (1976) is quoted as a proponent of laissez-fair policies, he is quoted without recognizing the deeper meaning of his carefully elaborated words. Smith does not blame to the state. Rather, he conceives an increased competition among firms needed to discipline businesses in order to force them to better serve customers.

3.1.4 From Country-Specific Factors to Factor-Specificity in Trade

Many arguments in international trade theories are often better understood by considering their classical roots. Adam Smith and David Ricardo, and the subsequent neoclassical foreign trade theory, measured the success of foreign trade by its effect on national wealth. According to Smith, the inherent source of the wealth of nations was built on expanding the division of labor within and between nations. In addition, the division of labor and the extension of markets was seen as a major cause for the expansion of trade.

The notion of absolute advantage became a cornerstone of explaining the pattern of trade. Smith defined the concept as follows: "If a foreign country can supply us with a commodity cheaper than we ourselves can make it, better buy it of them with some part of the produce of our own industry, employed in a way in which we have some advantage" (Smith, 1976: 424 quoted by (Reinert, 2021: 28).

Absolute Advantage

A country is assumed to have an **absolute advantage** over another country in the production of goods or services if it is capable of producing this product or service with fewer inputs. Major input is capital and labor, but also land.

Consequently, free trade would promote the exchange of those goods and services where the absolute advantage is greatest. The concept of absolute advantage, which is important to acknowledge, was originally an argument to support a policy introducing rules that favor free trade. But it is also used to argue that a country should focus on exploiting its productive opportunities using resources, in which it is more efficient. Efficiency in that argument rests not exclusively on the abundance of a country's resources, but also on its capability to use a better technology in producing a good or service (Reinert, 2021: 28; Teece, 1980). The concept of absolute advantage as it was used by Adam Smith is still a useful tool to understand how trade between *different* countries contribute to the wealth of nations. But it is misleading to take the principle of absolute advantage that everyone within the respective countries will gain from trade. And not all trade can be taken to contribute to the welfare, such as the arms trade or the international trade in narcotic drugs (Reinert, 2021: 37).

3.1.5 Comparative (Cost) Advantages

David Ricardo (1772–1823) seemed uncomfortable with that explanation and offered a more elaborated argument on how an advantage in one area of production can contribute to a theory of international trade. In 1817, in his famous book *The Principles of Political Economy and Taxation* Ricardo claimed: "No extension of foreign trade will immediately increase the amount of value in a country, although it will very powerfully contribute to increase the mass of commodities [available in that country], and therefore [increase] the sum of enjoyments" (Ricardo, 1817: 128; chap. VII On Foreign Trade).

Yet, the above quote does not tell us why and how international trade between two countries would be mutually beneficial. But in a *single quote* in his classical account about the Principles of Political Economy Ricardo asserts: "If Portugal had no commercial connection with other countries, instead of employing a great part of her capital and industry in the production of wines, with which she purchases for her use the cloth and hardware of other countries, she would be obliged to devote a part of that capital to the manufacture of those commodities, which she would thus obtain probably inferior in quality as well as quantity" (Ricardo, 1817: 134). Ricardo seems fully convinced that (in this special case) trade is beneficial for Portugal, and this unique insight remains a cornerstone of international trade theory (Eaton & Kortum, 2012).

Both Smith and Ricardo placed great emphasis on the specific endowment of countries with factors of production that are believed to be somewhat prototypical. They both assumed that the price differences of the individual production factors (capital, labor, and land) lead to different production costs of a particular good or service. It is important to see that the argument about cost advantages assumes that a country producing goods or services is always using the same fixed factor proportions of inputs. This factor proportion do not change over time, a perspective that implies there is no technological progress, and it assumes the absence of learning. Two aspects that will become essential cornerstones in the many theories explaining trade between a set of countries. It is important to know that Ricardo, for example did not neglect the technology and skills, but it was treated as a somewhat static factor of production. Ricardo knew that it was less important for a country what absolute advantage it can exploit in producing a good or service for export. Instead, he placed greater weight on how a country was capable to gain from specializing in those activities in which it has a relative advantage and how it would gain to export those products to pay for imports. This shift to the effects of specialization related significantly to the idea of opportunity costs.

In His *Principles of Political Economy and Taxation* Ricardo Offers the Following Account on that Matter:

> the quantity of wine which she [Portugal] shall give in exchange for the cloth of England, is not determined by the respective quantities of labour devoted to the production of each, as it would be, if both commodities were manufactured in England, or both in Portugal. England may be so circumstanced, that to produce the cloth may require the labour of 100 men for one year; and if she attempted to make the wine, it might require the labour of 120 men for the same time. England would therefore find it her interest to import wine, and to purchase it by the exportation of cloth. To produce the wine in Portugal, might require only the labour of 80 men for one year, and to produce the cloth in the same country, might require the labour of 90 men for the same time. It would therefore be advantageous for her to export wine in exchange for cloth. This exchange might even take place, notwithstanding that the commodity imported by Portugal could be produced there with less labour than in England. Though she could make the cloth with the labour of 90 men, she would import it from a country where it required the labour of 100 men to produce it, because it would be advantageous the other rather to employ her capital in the production of wine, for which she would obtain more cloth from England, than she could produce by diverting a portion of capital her capital from the cultivation of vines to the manufacture of cloth. Thus, England would give the produce of the labour of 100 men, for the produce of the labour of 80 men (Ricardo, 1817: 135).

Portugal holds an absolute advantage over England in producing both wine and wool. Portugal needed the labour of 80 men to produce wine and 90 to produce cloth, whereas England required the labour of 120 men for wine and 100 for cloth. Portugal was obviously more efficient in producing wine and wool than England. Nonetheless, both would mutually benefit if Portugal focused on producing wine and England on the manufacture of cloth. How is this possible? To understand the logic behind this argument, we need to focus on what became known as the "four magic numbers" (Gehrke, 2015).

How did Ricardo demonstrate that both countries would gain from trade? Ricardo argued that the focus needed to be on the comparison between how much labor is needed to produce the total amount of exports and the quantity of labor needed to produce the total amount of imports. The core of the argument is constructed around the idea of how much labour is needed to produce a unit of wine and cloth, which is different in Portugal and England.

In fact, we don't know how much wine or cloth is produced, only the amount of labor needed for producing wine and cloth in 1 year is given. Note there had been several different interpretations or readings developed over time (Gehrke & Kurz, 2002; Sraffa & Einaudi, 1930). The major argument, how Ricardo's curious insight is illustrated is usually focusing on two goods and two countries, such as in his classical account of Portugal and England exchanging wine and cloth. All we know are these *four magic numbers*.

Applying these four numbers, the opportunity costs of switching to wine or cloth production for Portugal would be $90/80 = 9/8$ while $120/100 = 5/6$ for England. Note Ricardo did not mention how much is produced or how much is exported. In this account the price of labor is not given and no currency is used to pay for imports.

Assuming X is the fabric exported by England and Y is the wine imported, we need to know how much labor is used in each country compared to the other. Comparing these two ratios we see something new, which has become defined much later as the opportunity costs. The question then, how much cloth in terms of wine England exchanges is stated in the following equation.

$$(100/\mathrm{X})/(120/\mathrm{Y}) = (5/6)\ \mathrm{Y}/\mathrm{X}.$$

For Portugal, the opportunity costs for wine in terms of cloth are $(80/Y)/(90/X) = (9/8)/(Y/X)$. Although we don't know the price of the exported goods and we don't know how the specialization on the manufacture of one product (wine or cloth) increases the productivity, the calculated opportunity costs remain the same across all produced outputs (Maneschi, 2008: 206).

$$(9/8)\ \mathrm{Y}/\mathrm{X} > \mathrm{Y}/\mathrm{X} > (5/6)\ \mathrm{Y}/\mathrm{X}.$$

The above equation demonstrates that the price of the imported good decreases in each country if they concentrate on the production of those products, they own a comparative advantage (Andrea Maneschi, in Reinert et al., 2009: 201; Maneschi, 2008).

The ***ultimate question posed in this section*** is to explain how the capability (or the firm-specific organizational capability) contributes to the performance of the internationalizing firm. For example, the question of how a firm generates an advantage by specializing in a particular production is likely to have a profound impact on its ability to internationalize. Yet, we also need to know the specific context in which specialization takes place. How is a firm utilizing its machinery and skills? In addition, we cannot only look at the firm as the primary unit explaining trade, we need to look equally at how country-specific institutional and location factors interact in the formation of firm-specific advantages? We will deal with this question in more detail later in this chapter.

It is no coincidence that the questions of competitiveness of individual firms rest on this classical account of comparative advantage, because firms focus on the activities which they believe will generate the greatest gains or the least losses (applying the concept of opportunity costs). The concept of comparative advantage is additionally important to inform the decision on whether to develop a value-generating activity within firm boundaries or acquire it from another firm or on the market. However, in Ricardo's classical account, nothing is said about the special effects that accrue through specialization. Likewise, little is said about how we can learn from concentrating on a specialized activity, and generating routines and habits that allow us to get better in that particular activity. These and other pertinent questions will be answered much later in management studies and IB research by exploring the notions of resources, capabilities, and dynamic capabilities (Helfat & Peteraf, 2015; Hodgson & Knudsen, 2004; Teece, 1996; Wernerfelt, 1984, 1995; Whittington, 2008).

3.2 Foreign Direct Investment and the Theory of the Multinational Firm

In the following sections, a particular focus will be given to the multinational firms and their international scope and exposure, where the link to these old and classic insights related to comparative advantage should be kept in mind when discussing firm-specific advantages (Birkinshaw et al., 1998; Pitelis & Verbeke, 2007; Reddy & Naik, 2011).

It is far beyond the scope of this text to elaborate more how much the neoclassical trade theories, such as the Stolper-Samuelson Theorem or the Leontief Paradox, have been implicitly affected by the theory of the multinational firm that emerged in the late 1950s and 1960s. However, neoclassical trade theory assumes that countries have access to similar or equal technology and that production factors are usually mobile within but not between countries. Likewise, many researchers and practitioners used to believe that consumer preferences are homogeneous, or that there is no uncertainty on the part of producers in the two countries and on the part of the consumers (see Iletto-Gilles, 2005).

Starting from these assumptions, a new theory of multinational enterprise must at least critically reflect on the reasoning behind them. As we will see below, these arguments re-emerge in modern theories of the multinational firm and play an important role in our ability to gain a deeper understanding of multinational firms.

Stephen Herbert Hymer is acknowledged as the seminal contributor to the theory of the multinational firm (Buckley, 2006; Pitelis, 2002, 2006). Hymer is recognized as a pioneer since he established the solid grounds for the modern theory of the multinational firm (Dunning & Pitelis, 2008; Hymer, 1970; Kindleberger, 2002).

In Stephen Herbert Hymer's doctoral thesis finished in 1960, and published posthumously in 1976, he uttered a famous question: Why is a national firm going to operate internationally despite additional costs, multiple risks and hazards expecting abroad?

One of Hymer's key contributions to the modern theory of the multinational firm is related to his skepticism about the prevalent theory of how cross-border portfolio investment is explained. He argued that differential interest rates, the common and widely accepted answer, offered no coherent explanation for the scale and scope of international capital flows in the 1950s. He rather opined that it is more important to understand the real disparity between FDI and foreign portfolio investment (FPI). The insight he had was that the differences in pattern and scope between the structure of FDI and FPI cannot be explained by mere differences in real interests between countries.

When choosing FDI instead of portfolio investment, the decision is grounded in the intention to retain control over the investment. The motivation of control at the time was to "ensure the safety of [the] investment"—a safety needed in an unfamiliar foreign location (Hymer, 1976: 23), described as liability of foreignness.

But it is by no means only control that matters. Firms making FDIs intend to assert their influence by means of investing abroad and can leverage this influence across multiple locations. This intention to control, according to Hymer, is a pertinent feature of a second type of FDI. Hymer thus noted control "is desired in order to remove competition between that foreign enterprise and enterprises in other countries" and he added control is used to "appropriate fully the returns on certain skills and abilities" (Hymer, 1976: 25). Consequently, foreign direct investment allows the investor the highest degree of control over the repatriation of the expected profits generated by the use of firm-specific assets abroad.

Hymer recognized that within firm boundaries, so-called firm-specific advantages are exploited more efficiently. Part of his argument was built on the inefficiency of intermediary markets and he knew that the "possession of advantages [are] a cause of international operations" (Hymer, 1976: 41). Thus he additionally asked: "Why does a firm use the advantage itself instead of licensing it?". His answer, "[t]he firm is a practical institutional device which substitutes for the market. The firm internalized or supersedes the [imperfect] markets" (Hymer, 1976: 48).

Hymer echoes the ideas put forth by Ronald Coase about the benefits of joint production organized within the firm hierarchy contrasting it to the costs of market transactions (Coase, 1937). But Hymer's tone and intent are more radical, and to this day these premises remain strongly embedded in industrial economics (Scherer, 1986; Shepherd, 2017).

Hymer considered why ***FDI is more attractive*** compared to other forms of market entry, such as licensing, and argued that FDIs are also beneficial for controlling firm-specific assets more efficiently. For example, selling firm-specific advantages is difficult, because of the need to specify a license and to retain control over the licensee, which can be more costly than "to undertake the operations itself" (Hymer, 1976: 49).

Hymer noted that managerial control is a highly effective tool to exercise the firms' superior efficiency abroad to exploit existing firm-specific advantages in more than one country. He criticized the multinational firm that exploit its monopolistic power for collusive bargaining, (Fiocco & Gilli, 2016). Contrasting FDI with portfolio investments Hymer explained how "the capital movement is needed to acquire a share of the foreign enterprise and thus obtain the desired control. The motivation for the investment is not the higher interest rate abroad but the profits that are derived from controlling the foreign enterprise" (Hymer, 1976: 26). All in all Hymer prepared for the first time the ground for a deeper understanding of why FDI is more likely in imperfect markets, where "the owner may not be able to appropriate fully the returns [. . .] unless he controls its use" (Hymer, 1976: 26). He added "that it is sometimes profitable to control enterprises in more than one country in order to remove competition" and cautioned that "[s]ome firms have advantages in a particular activity, and they may find it profitable to exploit these advantages by establishing foreign operations" (Hymer, 1970: 33).

Hymer's claim that the "international operations of the national firms is part of the theory of the firm" marks the beginning of a key question in international management. His insight that the international operation of the national firm, which "is concerned with various relations between enterprises of one country and enterprises of another [country]" is dealing with the need of integration cross-border activities, its costs and its advantages. In fact, he sees that the international operations is both, causing additional costs resulting from the complexity of increasing the scope of international operations and at the same time a source of advantages (Hymer, 1970: 27).

Hymer recognized that the international firm is confronted with higher costs caused by "different governments, different laws, different languages, and different economies" (Hymer, 1976: 33). However, different governments, different laws and different economies are used by the multinational firm as a leverage to increase the bargaining power with host-country governments (Hymer, 1976: 41).

Still, Hymer knew that it is not only the additional costs of communications but also the "lack of integration" (Hymer, 1976: 28f) that was a major problem for exercising control within the multinational firm.

Many aspects of **Hymer's findings** were reproduced in subsequently developed theories about the multinational firm, and several notable authors appreciate his contributions without bias. However, his critical perspective, which focused on the negative effects of multinational firms in developing countries, has been either neglected or marginalized in IB research (Buckley, 2006; Dunning, 2006; Graham, 2006; Pilon-Lé, 1980; Pitelis, 2006; Rowthorn, 2006; Strange & Newton, 2006).

Hymer's claim that for the multinational firm it is profitable "to control enterprises in more than one country to remove competition between them" (Hymer, 1976: 33) is largely undisputed. His ideas experienced a renaissance in many studies exploring the exploitation and exploration of firm-specific advantages abroad (Jin et al., 2016; Lengnick-Hall & Inocencio-Gray, 2013; Sousa et al., 2020; Uli, 2018; Volberda & Lewin, 2003). Hymer recognized early the tradeoff between different entry modes and argued that some firms can license firm-specific advantages to other firms.

Yet, any examination of Hymer's work must take into account his contribution to the theory of multinational enterprise and his input to the "political economy of MNEs" (Pitelis, 2002: 10). His core arguments on the first subject can be found almost entirely in his dissertation. The second much more critical perspective on how multinational firms operate abroad is elaborated in his later work. But Hymer's concern how the growth of the multinational firm is related to the unequal development in many regions, is somewhat neglected and marginalized in IB research (Buckley, 2006; Graham, 2006; Hymer, 1970; Pilon-Lé, 1980; Pitelis, 2002, 2006).

3.3 Technology, Product Lifecycles, and the Internationalization of Business Firms

Stephen Hymer was concerned with the growing power of multinational firms. Other economists initially studied the behavior of multinational firms, drawing upon insights gained from industry studies in international economics in the 1950s and 1960s. International economists, such as Kuznets, Posner, and Hufbauer (Cheng, 1984; Forrester, 1976; Hufbauer, 1966, 2002; Kuznets, 1926; Posner, 1961, 1993) had cardinal doubts about the validity of the neoclassical trade models, despite their technical elegance (Cheng, 1984; Forrester, 1976; Hufbauer, 1966, 2002; Kuznets, 1926; Posner, 1961, 1993). These group of economists were particularly dissatisfied with the rigorous assumptions build into the world of the Heckscher–Ohlin factor cost theorem and its subsequent version (Cheng, 1984; Forrester, 1976; Hufbauer, 1966, 1976, 2002; Posner, 1961).

Indeed, Nobel laureates Bertil Ohlin and Eli Heckscher excluded technological change and learning from their trade model. Yet their critics wondered how technological differences among trading countries and the cycle of product development affect international trade (Cheng, 1984). This critique led to the question of how international trade is initiated. The focus led to the analyzes how development of a product and the subsequent market demand relate to the emerging structures and patterns of trade and foreign direct investments.

The major outcome of this new perspective was the study of the product lifecycle (PLC). The product life cycle became a common research topic in the 1950s and 1960s and extended the focus of these early theories by asking how the rapid growth of multinational firms and their international expansion is related to the product life cycle and how the diffusion of technology affected international trade pattern (Klepper, 2017; Levitt, 1965).

3.3.1 Technological Gaps and the Learning Curve Inconsistencies Across Countries

These new approaches focusing on prevalent technological gaps and different learning capabilities were motivated by the need to include technical skills and their dynamic development to explain the actual structure of international trade in the late 1960s (Hufbauer, 1966; Posner, 1961).

One aim of these studies was to offer a more realistic explanation of the emerging pattern of trade between apparently similar economies. Harvard economists Gary Hufbauer and Michael Posner noted that technology and technological capabilities are not equally distributed among firms (Hufbauer, 2002). The core of the argument proffered by Hufbauer and Posner was that each firm owns different capabilities to exploit seemingly similar technologies and this difference substantially affects firm growth and international trade.

How does technology affect international trade? Posner questioned a number of core assumptions needed to design the logical consistency of neoclassical trade models. He first reasoned that not all trade can be explained by differential factor endowments as predicted by Heckscher Ohlin (Helpman, 2006).

The **Heckscher-Ohlin theorem** is based on the central assumption that countries export goods whose production requires predominantly those factors (land, labor, capital) that are more abundant in a country relative to other factors. By contrast, countries import those goods whose production requires factors that are relatively scarce in the (importing) country. The theorem predicts that the prices of these different factors of production will tend to be equalized between countries that trade with each other, even if the factors of production are not mobile across borders.

(continued)

"The notion of factors of production is a central part of microeconomics and reflects the field's recognition of resource scarcity. Factors of production are types of resources that are used in production processes. They appear as independent variables in production functions, with firm's outputs as the dependent variables." (Reinert, 2021: 60).

Empirical data about the size of trade in manufactured goods between developed countries did not really fit into the world of neoclassical trade models. Hufbauer (1966) tested empirically the pattern of trade carried out in industries that manufactured synthetic fibers. He observed that assumptions of the Heckscher-Ohlin theorem were inconsistent with his empirical findings. His industry data demonstrated how trade originated first in firms that applied advanced technologies. These firms then started exporting goods to other similar countries and exports were growing as long as the demand in the importing country was increasing. But sooner or later, the exports declined, because domestic firms in the importing country started manufacturing similar products substituting imports.

Equally Michael V. Posner felt uncomfortable with the existing trade theory, because "the common analytical framework [. . .] is leading to elegant analysis and interesting conclusions, [but] may not provide the whole answer to the question at issue" (Posner, 1961: 323). His first concern was that existing trade models do not account for the acknowledged fact that new products will substitute old products. Note, a new product will sooner or later replace a whole range of older products, because the technology used to manufacture new products will slowly be diffused within industries and across countries.

Posner further argued that the manufacturing processes and products will be improved as a result of changing technologies, either because new technologies will be invented or existing processes and new products will be developed. The outcome of these evolving process is that new technologies will destroy existing ones. And he additionally pointed at the fact that these new technologies will substantially change the pattern of investment in industries (Posner, 1961).

Posner knew that his new focus questioned the established way how orthodox trade theory explained the pattern of international trade. Retrospectively, his questions are immediately understood. But in the 1960s they were new and radical. Increasingly it became accepted that the dynamic growth of technologies and its use, its diffusion across different industries, learning between and within firms how to apply these new technologies significantly affected the pattern of international trade.

Although Posner was primarily concerned with explaining trade between countries, industrial firms were his real focal point, specifically he wanted to understand how a particular firm learns to apply a new technology. However, he knew from his empirical observations that any "technical progress takes time to evolve" (Posner, 1961: 329). That is a firm needs time to develop the capabilities to handle efficiently new technologies. A firm does not easily establish a new routine in an established process of manufacturing. It takes time not only to manufacture a product, but it takes time to explore and exploit new technologies.

While Posner did not use the term *exploitation and exploration of technological capabilities*, he argued that a firm "draw[s] on its [past] experience" and develops "new methods independently of its previous experience" (Posner, 1961: 329). His insight is not trivial. Based on his far-sighted analyses he concluded, firms rely on their past experience to generate new knowledge, but additionally noted that generating new knowledge and inventing new technologies is a random process. He discovered that it is not simply "pure knowledge" (a term later coined as "explicit knowledge") that is more or less easily distributed "freely" but rather "'know-how' [which] is overwhelmingly [more] important" (Posner, 1961: 329). He demonstrated that in *cohesive industries*, these gaps between new knowledge, existing knowledge, and applied knowledge are closed faster than in others, anticipating network effects, which were only addressed much later (Andersson et al., 2007; Low & Johnston, 2012; Rugman & Verbeke, 2003). But more important, especially in the context of international business theory, he defined the context, in his word the *cohesiveness* within and between firms that explain the diffusion and degree of adaptability of unique firm assets (Cheng, 1984; Posner, 1961: 331).

Figure 3.1 illustrates Posner's key message on the internationalization of technologically new products using a two-country example. There are two countries, X with the more advanced technologies and products and Y that imports these products. Country X will sooner or later try to export products made with this technology, depending on the domestic market and other factors. Once production has started (t_0), it will take some time until demand in the foreign market takes off (t_1). The gap between these two periods is called the demand gap. At period t_1, the firm located in country X is able to start with exporting the new product to country Y. The dashed line in the graph shows the curve of the production quantity for the product in country X. The solid line displays the curve of the quantity of the product sold in country Y. With the start of exporting (t_1), not only consumers learn about the new product in Y, but also domestic firms located in Y start imitating the product. It can be assumed that these domestic firms in country Y will try to substitute this new product. Posner refers to the period between t_1 and t_2 as the learning gap, which, once closed, allows the firm in country Y to become increasingly self-sufficient in supplying demand for the previously imported product. From time t_3 on, the assumption is that the firms in country Y have managed to fully substitute the imports and production in country X decreases. Accordingly, the export pattern, represented by the dotted curve, shows a decline for country Y from time t_2 and ends at time t_3.

Posner characterized the demand gap plus the learning gap as the total imitation gap. Each industry is affected by a typical learning gap and the prevalent demand gap, whereas the absolute size differs from industry to industry.

According to Posner, there are different sources of time lags. One is caused by the time needed for a new product to become known in the foreign country Y before the relevant industry in country X will start exporting the product to country Y (t_1) and it will do so until the the total imitation lag is closed by products from industries country Y (t_3).

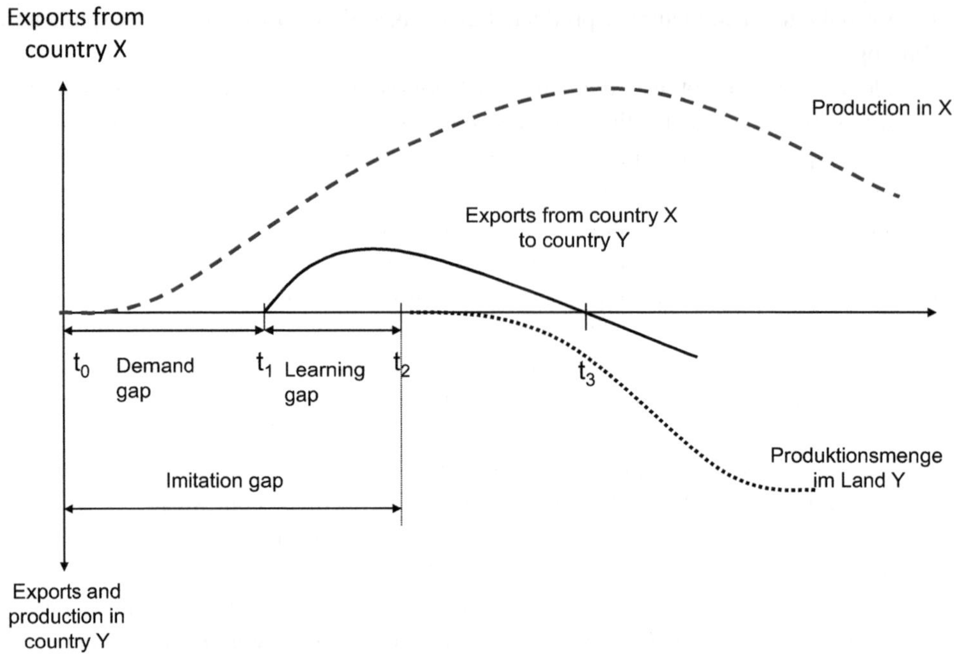

Fig. 3.1 International Trade and technology gaps (reprinted with permission from Oldenbourg Verlag. Copyrights by Kutschker & Schmid, 2012:397)

In this scenario, several consequences arise. If the entrepreneurial industries in the imitating country are quick, the reaction lag will be shorter. If the imitating industry is learning fast, the learning gap (the time between t_1 and t_2) will allow country Y sooner to start producing locally a similar product.

Time lags may differ due to differences in capabilities across industries and product demand, and if potential entrepreneurs in country Y are slow or less motivated, or simply incapable of imitating new technologies.

Posner's approach to this issue is remarkable because traditional trade models assume a linear production possibility curve, implying constant scale effects in producing goods, and do not consider the effect of imitators in the importing country that sooner or later develop substitutes (Scherer et al., 1975). Posner's approach eventually allows us to explain the speed of imitation within and between industries, which was later elaborated and linked to the size of the market and the optimal plant size in industrial economics (Scherer, 1973).

Michael Posner argued that the value of the new product reduces sooner or later the value of the old product to zero. The relative size of this effect depends on the size of the learning gap and the imitation gap. However, the substitution effect seems equally important for explaining the pattern and the dynamics of exchange between the country X and Y. Moreover, plant size, market size, cultural differences, and the readiness to switch from old to a new technologies and products will additionally affect the size of technological gaps and the slope of the learning curve, which would in turn affect the speed of imitation.

All this factors substantially effect the rhythm, speed and pattern of internationalization of firms. All in all Posner observations (1961) contribute to a more general body of research that focused on the growth stages or cycles in product development that have been empirically observed.

Nevertheless, product life cycles (PLCs) have never been fully elaborated in detail and tend to be regarded within IB research as a mere (albeit important) footnote or simply as a "forerunner" of Vernon's product life cycle (PLC) approach (Dunning & Lundan, 2008: 85).

3.3.2 Product Lifecycle

The product lifecycle (PLC) approach considers the evolution of a product passing through different stages in its life cycle (Almor et al., 2006; Hirsch, 1976, 2009). PLC approaches conceptualize the development of a product comprising of three stages. (1) The first stage is predominantly generated by factors affecting the invention and innovation of a product and how a new product is introduced in a market. The next critical stage (2) describes the process how the product starts to grow, more and more, and then eventually matures. This process is often split into two periods, called the major growth and maturing phase. The final stage (3) of a product life is dealing with the declining market demand for the product before it will be substituted and become obsolete.

The concept of PLC illustrates how the cyclical growth of a product market, and how product development affects its growth. Seev Hirsch noted that approaches focusing on the influence of "technology gaps, neo-technology, and product cycle models" do not necessarily offer "mutually exclusive explanations" (Hirsch & Bijaoui, 1985: 239).

Still, PLC approaches have been extensively applied and gave rise to two closely related research streams, respectively related to (1) the analyzes of antecedents that determine the development of new products and the factors affecting the extent of the different lifespans of product cycles (learning and imitation gaps), and (2) attempts to explicate how different product stages affected the entry pattern of internationalizing firms, in other words the propensity to export (Hirsch & Bijaoui, 1985: 241). PLC concepts were initially used in economics by Edwin Mansfield (Stead, 1976) who empirically observed the rise and decline of market shares in leading industries, such as automobile and aircraft industries (Cohen, 2005; Scherer, 2004; Stead, 1976). But PLC approaches help to explain the relative propensity to export in certain industries and also the difference in export performance between innovative and non-innovative firms (Hirsch, 2009; Hirsch & Bijaoui, 1985: 244).

Yet, PLC approaches are conceived as a byproduct of the debate about the structure-conduct-performance paradigm in industrial organization (Scherer, 1986)—the idea based on the assumption that a potentially high market growth triggers product innovation. However, firms are not equally capable to innovate. And in addition, not every external institutional environment supports innovating firms equally. It is also worth noting that all innovation cycles will eventually reach a peak, whereby rising market entry barriers and declining demand for the product affect the size and number of competing firms capable to operate profitable in a given market with its limited demand (Klepper, 1996: 562).

3.3.3 PLC Affecting the Internationalization of the Multinational Firm

Against this background, Vernon (1966) extended the theory of FDI by applying the concept of product lifecycles. PLCs, according to him, explain the origin and pattern of FDI made by US companies in the 1970s. He built his argument on the conviction that US firms enjoy easily accessible capital and a great reservoir of research-led innovations as well as friendly infrastructure for entrepreneurial industries. Vernon claimed that similar technology does not translate mechanically into "generate[ing] of new products" (Vernon, 1966: 191). Vernon's initial idea was how the timing of innovation, economies of scale, and uncertainty is affecting the pattern of international trade (Vernon, 1966: 190). He believed that a major trigger is how "entrepreneurs, wherever located" take randomly emerging "entrepreneurial opportunities, wherever they arose" and justified this faith in the positive effect of clustered research labs, agglomerated in close proximity, accordingly "profoundly affecting the outcome" of generally available scientific knowledge (Vernon, 1966: 192). But it seems the abundance of skill, much more than capital, which is the major determinant of exports in Vernon's study (Hirsch, 2009: 305). But Vernon assumed that each entrepreneur is "equally conscious of and equally responsive" (Vernon, 1966: 192) to surfacing opportunities. Note, Vernon assumed somewhat similar internal firm resources existing in enterprises operating in the same industry. From that contention he hypothesized that the size of the US market was a driver for many [contingent] opportunities seized by these entrepreneurial firms. In his view, market size and the existing stock of knowledge (skills and talent) determined "a consistently higher rate of expenditure on product development" (Vernon, 1966: 193). The invention of new products, and the growth rate of such innovations was claimed to be an essential antecedent for the propensity to innovate, supported by the large size of US consumer markets and the high per capita income. High per capita income and the strong segmentation of consumer markets was deemed important because the absolute size of each market allows firms to identify specialized and smaller customer segments that can achieve a critical market size soon after introducing a new product. However, Vernon argued that the real driving force that keeps innovation rates high is the entrepreneurial firm (Vernon, 1966: 199, 203).

Figure 3.2 shows, a PLC divided into four stages. Stage 1 is defined by its role in product development, in which the skills and technical know-how are the source of the exploratory nature in this more experimental phase of product development. Vernon's understanding of this first phase was informed by presuming that at this early stage a much greater degree of freedom enabled innovative firms to modify and experiment with existing factor inputs. New products need to be adapted. They are changed repeatedly in this early stage to fit emerging customer needs. This early stage attracts only a few customers,

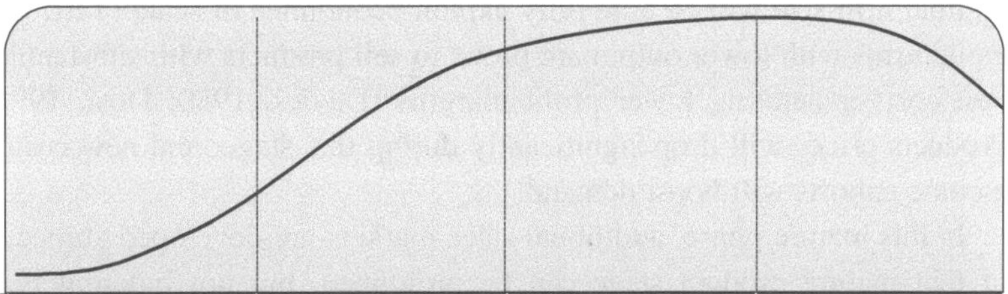

Stage	Initial	Growth	Maturity	Decline
Demand	Low demand, few buyers	Growing number of buyers	Peak demand	Degression, steep fall
Technology	Short production cycles, rapid changes	Introduction of mass production techniques, some variation but less change	Long production cycles and stable technologies	
Capital intensity	Low	high	Stable at the beginning, because of exiting firms	
Industry structure	Entry is driven by the know how, small number of firms, highly specialized	Number of competitors is increasing	Number of firms starts to decline	Firms get obsolescent
Critical produciton factors	Knowledge, technology and innovation skills	Managerial efficiency & high capital needs	Semi- and low skilled labor	

Fig. 3.2 Product life cycle and market characteristics

therefore the capability to respond quickly to feedback from these new markets increases the speed and success of product adaptation in that juvenile market. Vernon described this first stage as critical and claimed that the high degree of uncertainty about future success in the product development process requires a high degree of entrepreneurial knowledge about future market potential (Klepper, 1996).

In stage 2, product demand starts to grow slowly and then more rapidly. In that period of accelerating market growth firms are required to invest vast amounts of capital to standardize production. This highly capital-intensive stage, during which the full product growth progresses, some firms may leave the market and new entrants may succeed in building up full production capacity, resulting in an ever-increasing competition among incumbent industries. Industry studies demonstrated that, as soon as a highly efficient production process is established, a small number of firms will sooner or later dominate the market.

While early entrants face fewer and lower hazards, in extreme scenarios, the number of firms can decline by 90% within 15–20 years, despite vigorous growth rates in markets (Klepper & Simons, 2000, 2005). Yet, at that stage the dominant product design and economies of scale forces incumbent industries to invest more in standardized mass manufacturing, while incentives for further product innovation will decline rapidly (Mourtzis & Doukas, 2020; Scott & Ziebarth, 2015; Smirnov et al., 2002).

However, extant studies analyzing innovation rates and firm survival offer mixed results (Ortiz-Villajos & Sotoca, 2018). Vernon calls this product phase “the mature stage” (Vernon, 1966: 196) in which a few firms start dominating the market demand. Incumbent firms try to increase efficiency by vertical integration. Enterprises operating with minimal optimal firm size will be able fully exploit economies of scale (Tarr, 1984; White, 1971), while firms with lower output are prone to sell products with substantially higher production costs generating lower profit margins (Davies, 1980; Dosi, 1992; Scherer, 1973). Products prices will drop significantly during this stage, and new customers from lower-income cohorts will boost demand.

In this mature phase, additional sales markets are developed abroad, and the extension of that mature product stage can be prolonged, but not indefinitely by exploring and exploiting new export markets. If market demand in foreign countries is large enough, firms begin to relocate production capacities abroad, a major argument put forward by Vernon.

But soon a number of firms will try to imitate or develop new product features or may substitute fully existing products. At the same time, stage 3 is the beginning, when product demand touches its final peak, from now on, product demand inevitably levels off. Growth rates become zero and quickly negative. New products increasingly replace obsolete products. Often these new products are manufactured from innovative imitators, offering cheaper and better products. Depending on the cost of market exit, older firms with massive manufacturing capacity will have big troubles to change or overcome their systemic inertia to initiate an exit (Klepper, 2017; Levitt, 1965).

Raymond Vernon (1976) applied the PLC approach to explain how industries start to establish new production plants in major importing countries. Assuming rational management, Vernon argues that as long as the marginal cost of production including the transport cost for exports are lower than the "prospective production costs in the market for import" the firm will refrain from such an investment. Yet, Vernon knew that such a decision depends on the capability to make a fully rational, that is a realistic calculation about potential markets "in which factor costs and the appropriate technology differ from those at home" (Vernon, 1966: 197). However, referring to Otis Elevator and Singer, Vernon hypothesized, if overseas demand is "highly standardized" and "sufficiently large" for exploiting scale economies abroad firms will choose to establish a manufacturing plant abroad to serve the market in the foreign country (Vernon, 1966: 198).

3.4 Neo-Institutional Approaches Explaining Diversification and Internalization

The inherent dynamics of a market environment, the structure of markets, and firm-specific advantages became increasingly important in the subsequent decades to study the international business activities of the firm. Classical trade theories have been based on the conviction that either absolute or comparative advantage are the primary triggers for existing trade patterns. In the 1970s, these questions dominated the search for a general theory capable of explaining how firm-specific advantages (FSAs) and the resulting organizational efficiency evolve within the international firm. The existence of the multinational firm was basically explained by its superior efficiency (Casson et al., 2009;

Fransson et al., 2011; Kogut & Zander, 1993). At the same time, the pattern of international trade based on the traditional division of labor between industrialized economies and developing economies began to change (Casson, 2013; Dicken, 2017; Fröbel et al., 1980; Gereffi, 2018b).

Beginning in the late 1960s, business firms started to outsource and relocate labor-intensive portions of their value chains. These firms relocated particular activities to newly created export production zones (EPZ) established by governments from developing countries seeking to attract foreign direct investments as part of a strategy to push forward the export oriented development (Elia et al., 2019; Lewin & Volberda, 2011).

Export production zones (EPZs) and special economic zones (SEZs) started to be established as enclaves in host economies supplying cheap, disciplined, and abundant labor. Foreign firms were also attracted by attractive tax regimes. However, at the beginning, most business firms expanding into these new EPZs and SEZs relocated only fractions of their manufacturing processes, as outputs generated in these special zones were supposed to be exported and not used for local consumption or supply. Most of such intra-firm trade rested on a fundamental reorganization of the manufacturing processes, driven by computer aided design (CAD) and/or computer aided manufacturing (CAM) that enabled highly vertically integrated industrial enterprises to redefine the concept of manufacturing within traditional firm boundaries (Ariyawardana & Collins, 2013; Contractor et al., 2009; Fröbel et al., 1978, 1980; Momaya, 2016; Roza et al., 2011) This more general shift in the way firms have started to radically reorganize their business activities and expand into new and unfamiliar foreign geographies has been closely mirrored by a gradual but significant transformation of the institutional environment that has impacted the governance of global firms. The outcome of this radical transformation of the multinational business firm was a fundamental change how these firms organized their vertically integration production networks.

3.5 Vertical Integration and Horizontal Expansion

Large multinational firms that succeeded in maintaining efficient growth during the 1960s and 1970s were increasingly faced with the problem of managing a growing and more complex, diversified enterprise. Especially in cases where growth was achieved by vertical integration, these firms needed to alter their management, because of the complexity of an ever more sizeable and more complex administrative structure.

Vertical integration is defined as the forward or backward integration of value-adding activities across different production stages. For example, a steel producer vertically integrates by buying an iron ore mine to increase the efficiency of its

(continued)

coking plant. A firm is vertically forward-integrated when it purchases a formerly independent service provider to carry out post-production services, such as after-sales services and maintenance for its products. A firm is vertically forward-integrating when it acquires a wholesaler, with an established distribution system.

If there is a high degree of uncertainty about the quality and quantity of the necessary inputs (the iron ore), it is more likely that a firm would seek to vertically integrate the supply of these inputs. Integrating a supplier can lead to cheaper inputs, or to a more secure flow of supplies. For example, a shoe or handbag manufacturer may buy different qualities of leather skins by different suppliers promising to deliver high quality of hides. However, the more differentiated the input is in production (i.e. the degree of how significant the input is for the output), the greater the potential motive and advantage for integrating the supply. Integration can be a friendly or hostile takeover, or can be achieved by a merger. A manufacturer can grow if it merges with an established firm that processes its output. For example, if a manufacturer of consumer electronics invests in a distribution network or buys controlling shares in a large retail chain, it can probably increase its efficiency and margins (Scherer et al., 1975). By and large it is a major assumption that vertical integration increase the efficiency of the firm, an argument that is built upon the idea of better control of activities within firm boundaries.

But controlling large complex and highly diversified firms became a major challenge. Harvey Leibenstein studying efficiency, a core concepts in economics, demonstrated that size was not mechanically associated with superior efficiency, but in fact, increasingly the source of X-Efficiency, a term coined by Leibenstein, who analyzed a number of cases, where firms lost significantly their capability to organize many and complex multi-divisional plants (Frantz, 1988; Leibenstein, 1966; Perelman, 2011). Leibenstein was concerned about the assumption that integration more or less automatically increases the allocative efficiency of large firms. He argued that in fact the efficiency in the day-to-day operation of large firms was demonstrating a large gap between the ideal assumed efficiency in theory and the realized practice (Frantz, 2015; Harris, 1995). But his critique equally focused on the need that increasing integration requires the capability to change diseconomies of the acquired entity (Leibenstein, 1966: 397).

Yet, all these decisions to integrate along different stages of production, are intended to add business activities in order to maintain or increase efficiency. Efficiency is, however, only one trigger, because integration also serves to increase market power and the control over suppliers and buyers, a problem that occupied Stephen Hymer (1970, 1976). Consequently, each firm that intends to grow substantially needs to find an appropriate organizational structure. Each structure needs to be implemented and operated efficiently. While in theory a structure may promise a fit, in practice several factors may actually affect the often suboptimal outcome (Gugler et al., 2003).

Vertical Integration in the Steel Industry
The textbook example of vertical integration is steel production, in which individual production stages are combined due to technological interdependence. In the production of crude steel, the further processing of the hot crude steel is integrated in a proprietary rolling mill, as it will save considerable energy costs. The example of the forward-looking vertical integration of a crude steel producer leads to a reduction of energy and transport costs because the crude steel does not have to be reheated for rolling in the mill. In this case, not only energy costs are saved, but also the acquisition costs of additional heating furnaces (Bain, 1956).

The example illustrates how integration increases the efficiency across several stages of a production line based on technological interdependencies. These technological interdependencies can be the source of firm-specific advantages.

Obviously, a large industrial enterprise would integrate forward or backward across national borders in order to increase their productivity or reduce uncertainties. The cross-border vertical integration—i.e., the backward integration of raw material processors in extractive capital-intensive industries (like mining or oil)—is often justified primarily quoting the efficiencies in technological interdependencies. Not surprisingly, vertical integration can be typically observed in industries that exhibit features of a natural monopoly (Aulakh et al., 2010; Jiang et al., 2007; Rowthorn, 2006).

Note that the degree of integration in the industry significantly affects the structure of markets and constrains its ability to function.

Market structure is defined by

- The number and size of established firms that operate in a market
- The degree of product differentiation exercised by these firms
- The nature of the barriers to market entry for the new entrants
- The nature of barriers to exit existing markets

Firms integrate horizontally by merging or acquiring with other firms producing different products. Joe Bain (1912–1991), who is considered the father of industrial economics is treated as the originator of the structure-conduct-performance paradigm in industrial economics, but his special interests was the analysis of how a small dominating group of firms, a group of oligopolies in an industry, affected new entry and competition in the markets they dominated. He studied how economies of scale and the number of firms active in a prevalent market influenced the performance and behavior of firms in an industry, assuming that the structure of the market is affecting the conduct (strategies of the firm) and strategies that fit the market structure are resulting in better performance.

The major factors used to explain the prevalent market structure and the existing behavior of incumbent firms was the idea of absolute cost advantages, product differentiation, and the size of the firm in a given industry (Shepherd, 2017), especially the number and size of firms, which shape the entry of new firms and determine the behavior of established firms in a given structure of markets.

In **capital-intensive industries in fast-growing markets**, firms enlarge their predominant position by horizontally merging with other firms for several reasons. One common cause can be exploitation the existing product differentiation in other product groups. For example, a renowned vacuum cleaner manufacturer may be able to convince its customers relatively quickly that it knows how to produce good refrigerators, while a new firm producing a refrigerator will have to put much more effort to gain a new customer. It is plausible at first sight that a firm would expand its market coverage by horizontal integration, for example acquiring a renowned producer of refrigerators. Thus, product differentiation can be a significant entry barrier (Kaufer, 1980).

The current pattern of horizontal integration in large multinational firms show that horizontal FDI can be observed in industries with pronounced product differentiation. That pattern is confirmed by the boom in mergers especially in the beverages, pet foods, and pharmaceutical industries. Industrial economics had a formative influence on the dictum that market structure affects firm behavior and performance, giving rise to the structure-conduct-performance paradigm (Hoskisson et al., 1999; Scherer, 1986; Tallman, 2004). But it was later criticized for neglecting the internal firm capabilities as a source for change and innovation. Nevertheless, analyzing FDI data, the growth of multinational firms seems still driven by vertical and horizontal mergers and acquisitions.

3.6 Property Rights, Externalities, and Ronald Coase

A vantage point that radically changed the existing theoretical focus to look at the firm had been initiated much earlier by Ronald Coase. Coase published three essays making an outstanding contribution. One article started with an in-depth discussion about "The Nature of the Firm" (1937), which was followed by an essay dealing with "The Marginal Cost Controversy" (1946), and finally his masterpiece "The Problem of Social Cost" (1960). Coase is widely known for his clear and detailed account of the foundations of the modern theory of the firm. The core arguments were built from a radical rejection of a perspective that implicitly dominated neoclassical economics, assuming zero costs in market transactions. Although he radically challenges existing neoclassical assumption, he never doubted perhaps the most central assumption, namely rationality.

The Coase theorem purports that, whenever externalities arise, fully rational agents may find an efficient solution to the problem. Note rationality assumes that agents have access to all relevant information. While bounded rationality acknowledge that agents are required to make a choice with fairly limited information, Coase proposed that any possible solution negotiated by agents depends on (a) the existence of clear property rights and presence of negotiating parties who will enjoy the full disposition over these property rights, irrespective of how these property rights are distributed. Although the Coase theorem does not inform us of the means by which a solution may be reached, it posits that a solution is possible (Galiani et al., 2014; Jaffe, 1975). The Coase theorem remains highly influential despite notable controversies (Medema, 2020: 1046). One controversy relates to the fact that agents are assumed to be fully rational and transaction costs are non-existent. Nonetheless, Coase clearly recognized that property rights are necessary to solve the problem of externalities. In practice, however, each agent is also required to share all important information.

Property Rights

Property is a central institutional concept in economics. Existing property rights are a core element that enables the efficient exchange of goods and services. The term "property" is defined by the physical ownership of a good. It is important that the physical ownership of a good can be fully transferred from one person to another. Effective and efficient exchange requires the transferability of property rights.

3.7 Transaction Costs and Ronald Coase

Ronald Coase's impact on the development of the modern theory of the firm is undisputed. His radical departure from orthodox knowledge is widely acknowledged. And yet, as he pointed out in the late 1980s, it is startling that it took more than four decades for the original idea to be recognized as a significant contribution. Any re-reading of "The Nature of the Firm" does help to separate that original insights from the prevailing use today in neo-institutional theories. In the first lines of his essay, Coase complains, how neoclassical economists had failed to delineate some of their core assumptions (Coase, 1937). One major discomfort is how the traditional perspective in economics is designing markets.

How a Market Works

> The normal economic system works itself. For its current operation it is under no central control, it needs no central survey. Over the whole range of human activity and human need, supply is adjusted to demand, and production to consumption, by a process that is automatic, elastic, and responsive (Coase, 1937: 387).

The assumption that the economic system is working by itself puzzled Coase. Why did Coase mistrust the widely accepted definition how an economic system works. First and foremost, he was not convinced by the alleged automatism and magical self-organization of markets. He was not convinced that the automatism is produced by an invisible hand. Invisible forces operating in markets, were claimed to be able to fix all the coordination glitches that arise in matching supply and demand. He knew that the assumed spontaneous alignment between supply and demand is not generated by the market alone. His odd insight centered on the fact how trade is accomplished. And, he emphasized that each genuine exchange, each transaction will depend on the actions of real people, of entrepreneurs seeking to trade a product or service in a given, but unfamiliar and uncertain market.

What Coase particularly objected to was the prevailing belief of economists that "the economic system is being co-ordinated by the price mechanism and society becomes not an organization but an organism" (Coase, 1937: 387).

Coase did not accept the assumption that a market system works without the "planning [made] by individuals" (Coase, 1937: 387). Of course, Coase knew that the automatic alignment between supply and demand operates on the basis of price information. But he pointed at the fact that this price information is not free of charge. Market participants, suppliers and buyers invest considerable time and effort to obtain accurate information about the price and the quality of a product. In addition, Coase knew that much of the coordination is accomplished only by making further an extra effort to plan, seek, evaluate and instruct all activities that cause further costs related the transactions. Moreover, any information gathered is processed to check the quality and price of product needed to conclude a transaction is not free.

Coase used a quote by D.H. Robertson (Plant, 1932: 85) to illustrate the problem: "[we find] islands of conscious power in this ocean of unconscious co-operation"(Coase, 1937: 388). According to this view, mindful agents influence and carry out deliberately a number of transactions, in order to achieve their goals through an anonymous market, implying a costly and conscious coordination between often unequal albeit independent agents.

But Coase elaborated in detail an important second argument that contrasted markets and firms and how both achieved coordination:

The Entrepreneur-Co-ordinator

Outside the firm, price movements direct production, which is co-ordinated through a series of exchange transactions on the market. Within the firm, these market transactions [...] is substituted [by] the entrepreneur-co-ordinator, who directs production (Coase, 1937: 388).

It is important to comprehend that the price information remains a significant part of coordination. But price can be an incomplete and insufficient information. Thus coordination within the firm supplants the price mechanism. If the price tag alone is not a sufficient criterion to coordinate supply and demand, than the firm can potentially replace the missing mechanism. From this assessment, Coase designs his unique contribution to the theory of the firm. Coase conceptualizes the firm as a major mechanism that coordinate several independent activities not supplied by markets. But the efficient operation of the firm is a mechanism depending on the deliberate decision-making of the "entrepreneur-co-ordinator" (Coase, 1937: 389).

Within the firm, the so-called entrepreneur co-ordinator is the specific nexus that organizes the coordination, often carried out by the manager or the owner-entrepreneur. The owner-entrepreneur thus becomes the significant figure in making deliberate decisions.

Accordingly he defines the firm as a "system of relationships which comes into existence when the direction of resources is dependent on an entrepreneur" (Coase, 1937: 393). The firm is replacing the market as a mechanism to coordinate transactions.

In other words the entrepreneurial co-ordination steps in where the market does not provide an efficient mechanism to coordinate exchange. Coase notes it is the extended power over other people willing to be directed by the owner-entrepreneur that allows to explain the existence of the emergence of the firm substituting apparent market failures (Coase, 1937: 390). But firms may also eliminate markets, because they are capable to exercise more control and direct several resources more flexible (Coase, 1937: 391).

There are several reasons why a firm is superseding the market as a mechanism for carrying out transaction. As a consequence, these reasons equally define the boundaries of a firm. Coase did in fact generate a definition of the boundaries of the firm, arguing that the firm would organize internally transactions within their boundaries as long as the marginal costs are smaller than or equal to cost of market transactions. But this definition only works if we assume that for each transaction the full information about the real costs are known.

In other words, firms face costs using the price mechanism. Comparing the growth of the firm with the prevalent efficiency of markets Coase argued, firms will grow as long as the costs of organizing an additional transaction is smaller within the firm than the costs of organizing the exchange by the markets (Coase, 1937: 397).

Note, entrepreneurs that rely on specialized traders can reduce costs of transactions, but these traders sell their service for a fee. There are also costs arising from putting up contracts and negotiating prices with potential buyers and sellers. In a single market transaction, these costs can be minimized, but they cannot be eliminated completely (Coase, 1937: 391). All these reasons contribute to the emergence of the firm, as long as the costs of organizing a transaction within the firm is lower than using the price mechanism. Although very radical in his thoughts, Coase does not depart from the narrow framework of neoclassical economics. He concludes that a firm is established if the joint organization within its boundaries is less costly than market transactions and the firm will grow as long as any additional transaction can be carried out more advantageously within the firm. A firm will stop growing if it is cheaper to carry out additional transactions through the price mechanisms available in the markets (Coase, 1937: 393).

3.7.1 Enforcing Control and the Costs of Transaction

Transaction cost economics remains indebted to these insights made by Ronald Coase (1937). The theory of the multinational corporation imported much of the Coasian concepts in the early 1980s. A great number of approaches applying the transaction costs approach are based on the assumptions that the firm can offer a superior efficiency compared to markets. A major contribution was developed by McManus (1975), he addressed the question posed by Coase asking:

> Why is the firm "chosen in preference to a price system to allocate resources" (McManus, 1975: 334). The easy answer to that question was built around the idea of efficiency, the more complex one, is looking at the problem, why, how and when the firm is more efficient than markets.

McManus observed that a number of difficulties in market transactions are due to products or services that cannot be easily defined, as well as quality issues that are difficult to identify or accurately measured (McManus, 1975). He knew that several mechanisms can be used to measure standard product quality. In cases where it is difficult to measure the quality of a product or service exchanged in a market, firms may be the preferred and organizational form to enforce the necessary control. Control is used by McManus basically as a metaphor for monitoring and measuring the constraints on the individual behavior. Note the idea to monitor and measure these behavioral constraints imply the assumption to find a rational solution to that problem within the organizational mechanism of the firm to fix or mitigate these problems. The answer offered by McManus focused on how to enforce a workable mechanism that directs how each actor performs in a joint effort. But he also knew that: „we are incurring costs to enforce behaviour constraints by monitoring or measuring the activity of another individual" (McManus, 1975: 336).

What Coase called the power to exercise control still matters. But McManus elaborated the argument that enforcing mechanisms that constrain harmful behavior will increase the quality of services or products jointly generated but these efforts are costly and not always applicable.

Assuming perfect markets McManus endorsed the argument that independent producers will jointly increase the output and maximize their profits. Perfect markets, however do not really exist and instead, so the argument, in international markets, the multinational firm is a feasible and efficient alternative to enforce effective control (Hennart, 1982: 25). Yet, enforcing is costly, hidden action and moral hazards prevail, and generate extra transaction costs. It is plausible pointing at the fact that "the life of a newly constructed road [...]

depend[s] upon the costs of inspecting the contractor's work" (McManus, 1975: 337). It is equally convincing that enforcing control may produce a positive effect on the quality of output, even if the control is suboptimal or inefficient.

However, the general argument about the efficiency of the firm seems to revolve around the fact that transaction costs matter. Whereas control exerts a direct effect on the quality of services supplied through joint efforts enforcing control or being capable to control is not just a matter of transaction costs.

McManus knew that measurement costs increase "with the precision of the measurement" and he noted, "there will be some error in measurement that will not be worthwhile [. . .] to eliminate" (McManus, 1975: 337). In other words, the costs of enforcing control can be nullify potential gains (Hennart, 1982: 32).

It seems trivial to appreciate that the cost of enforcing is a matter of control, but it is non-trivial to know exactly whether the actual enforcing costs will be greater than the benefits generated by implementing a control mechanism. Although enforcement costs are difficult to measure there is no way to identify the outcome of control (Alchian & Demsetz, 1972; Ghoshal & Moran, 1996). The argument elaborated by McManus is that if the enforcement of control about the actual performance of contracting parties is difficult, potential partners may refrain from establishing a joint production. Likewise, if the measurement of the quality of a transaction is too costly or impossible in relation to the price of the good or service, no exchange will occur in markets. A core premise behind these arguments is that if the enforcement of quality measurement is not possible, market transactions may never be successfully implemented or may not occur between rational agents. But then, still the question remains to be answered, why and how the firm is the superior mechanism to deal with those problems.

3.7.2 The Firm as a Nexus of Contracts and Transaction Costs

Nobel laureate Oliver Williamson (1932–2020) was concerned throughout his lifetime contributions with the question which governance structure provides an efficient organizational design. And most, if not all his work concentrated on merging insights gained from his studies of law, economics, and organizational practice to find an answer to that question. Nevertheless, he bemoaned the latent hostility and prevailing ignorance in each discipline toward the other which prevent prevailing insights from being brought together. His research interests have thus been guided by the belief that transaction costs are the most significant problem and that an optimal governance mechanism is designed to reduce transaction costs across a wide range of exchange relationships.

In his approach to transaction costs, the firm is conceived as a nexus of contracts, as he recognized that the existing frictions in exchange relationships—viewed from the perspective of transaction cost economics—are caused by prevailing conflicts among humans, which could be attributed to suboptimal agreements between two or more parties attempting to organize the exchange of specific assets in uncertain situational contexts (Langlois, 2019; Williamson, 1979, 1985, 2005). Frictions are assumed to be the main source of costs in asymmetric relations. The frictions were assumed to arise from an ineffective, suboptimal organizational designs. Thus the questions is how to find and implement an effective organizational design, described by Williamson as governance mechanism.

What is special about the contribution of Oliver Williamson is his emphasis "that the social context in which transactions are embedded" matter. He was convinced and throughout his many contribution this remains an important notion that the "customs, mores, [and] habits" have an substantial effect and these differences in institutional contexts "need to be taken into account" (Williamson, 1985: 22).

Frictions as a Source of Inefficiency

Frictions are assumed to be the main source of costs in asymmetric relations and these frictions are the source of any ineffective, suboptimal organizational designs.

Williamson's effort to develop an elaborated theory to explain how transaction costs affect the efficiency of exchange relationships should not be read as a prescription or recipe for the ideal design of contracts in asymmetric relationships. It is important to highlight that it is not feasible to solve all the problems related to contracting in a contingent world. But his focus is different, because he reminds us that incomplete contracts in a complex, contingent world are not the exception but rather the rule. Thus, he loved to describe his approach as the "study of good order and workable arrangements" making an emphasis on workable (Williamson, 2005: 1).

The ***economics of governance*** is an effort to implement the study of good order and workable arrangements, where good order includes both spontaneous order in the market, which is a venerated tradition in economics and intentional order, of a conscious, deliberate, purposeful kind. Also, I interpret workable arrangements to mean feasible modes of organization, all of which are flawed in comparison with a hypothetical ideal (Williamson, 2005: 1).

Note the difference between the hypothetical ideal world and the feasibility of workable arrangements. Williamson conceptualized transaction as a transfer "across a technologically separable interface", which he did not elaborate, but noted, this means essentially that "one stage of activity terminates, and another begins" (Williamson, 1985: 1). The key notion here is that the transfer of a good, service, or a resource occurs from one separate unit to another, whereas the units are located either within the boundaries of a hierarchical organization, between a market and a firm, or between firms. The physical transfer will induce costs. The core argument is that the efficiency of transactions is affected significantly by three basic dimensions that define the nature of a transaction. This inherent nature of a transaction depends on (1) the degree of ***uncertainty***, (2) ***frequency of exchange***, and (3) the level of ***asset specificity***.

The important point here is that, across several value-adding activities, the physical transfer of one activity—which can be a material good or an immaterial service—is handed over to someone else.

3.7.3 Asset Specificity, the Frequency of a Transaction, and Uncertainty

As Ronald Coase claimed, there are no zero transactions costs, so even in a trivial transaction, like buying a cup of coffee, even though the complete transfer of the assumed good should occur without much friction, a few transactions costs will accrue.

If a ***transaction*** involves a material good, let's assume it is a cup of coffee, then the transfer from the person who sells the cup of coffee to the one who will consume it does not cause many problems. The cup of coffee is a ***standardized*** product and placing an order and specifying how the coffee should be prepared does not incur significant transaction costs (time and effort). Nonetheless, you need to look for a coffee shop and you need to tell the barista how you like your coffee, and you will have to place your order. And last but not least you need to go to your preferred coffee shop.

In this special case, the low degree of asset specificity is one reason why the transaction is fairly simple and transactions costs are low or negligible. But still, transaction costs arise when you search for a coffee shop that sells the coffee you like. If you are new in a town, you need to search for a shop and you may collect information about your most favorite brand. Then, you need to communicate to the barista how your coffee should be prepared, and you need to reach an agreement, so some time will be invested for that purpose, usually not much, but an informal negotiation is needed. Once you receive your coffee, you can taste it and assess its quality. Being able to assess the quality of the product is an essential part of enforcing and monitoring the efficiency of a transaction, but this informal assessment is part of the unceremonious agreement.

The Costs of Transactions

Each transaction, both difficult or simple, will generate (a) search and information costs, (b) costs that arise from the efforts and time invested in bargaining and

(continued)

decision-making, and (c) costs of enforcing and monitoring the actual transaction (Richter & Furubotn, 2010: 51).

Transactions involving standardized products (i.e., everyday consumer goods, as well as standard services, such as a haircut) do not require great effort to search, bargain, and enforce the exchange. Williamson described transactions as nonspecific if standard equipment or material is purchased. The important aspect of a standardized transaction is that a fairly great number of similar products with a comparable or equal quality is offered. The effort required to specify the preferred quality of a standardized product or service is usually low. Yet, there are never zero transaction costs in any exchange, neither in markets nor within organizations. When purchasing nonspecific goods or services, the frequency of exchange, our second major criteria, will affect the scope of transaction costs. A standardized products purchased only occasionally likely incurs gradually higher information costs, as there is a need for searching for a trusted supplier to deliver the good or service. If purchases occur in recurring pattern, the buyer acquires knowledge about the quality and service of a preferred shop useful in future transactions.

Even nonspecific transactions established through repeated purchasing would result in a mutual and reciprocal relationship of trust that will make any future transactions simpler. Therefore, the rate of repeating a particular transaction significantly reduce information costs, negotiation costs, and monitoring costs. Still, the real problem is the degree of asset specificity in a transaction, which can be low or high (Williamson, 1985: 52). Without the issue of asset specificity, contracting could be easy.

Thus, a generic proposition for standardized, nonspecific transactions is that it is likely that all three types of transaction costs will be small. For transactions characterized by mixed asset specificity, they tend to be higher compared to nonspecific transactions, but compared to idiosyncratic transactions characterized by high asset specificity they will be substantially lower. Although asset specificity can be low (standardized, nonspecific), mixed (purchasing customized goods and services), or high (idiosyncratic, highly specialized products and unique services provided according to the needs of a single or unique client) the boundaries between these categories can be arbitrary.

Uncertainty is the third major dimension that significantly affects the level of transaction costs affecting an exchange. Frank H. Knight (1921: 231) defined uncertainty by its inherent ambiguity. He was convinced that uncertainty cannot be reliably discounted unless it is reduced to risk. Thus, considering the meaning of uncertainty in transaction costs, we need to separate uncertainty from risk. Knight (1921) defined risk as a situation in which the probability of an outcome is known. For instance, in a dice game, each player knows the probability of rolling a certain number. In other words, although the chance is small, it can be transformed into a probability. However, throwing a die and knowing the probability of getting a six in each throw does not mean that your next throw will bring the number you need. Thus, uncertainty cannot be converted into a probability, as Knight has alluded.

Converting uncertainty to risk is an inaccurate estimate and the numerical result will not help much in a decision-making process under uncertainty (Mousavi & Gigerenzer, 2014). Important, uncertainty is about contingencies.

Example

Dealing with the impact of uncertainty and how it will be related to transaction costs is illustrated by the following fictional example of a customer who is looking for a custom-made suit. Asset specificity is mixed, and the making of a customized suit will require a closer exchange between the client and the tailor than simply buying a ready-made suit in a retail store around the corner. The apparent transaction will require more time and effort on both sides. The client needs to search for an appropriate tailor and collect some information about the reputation and quality of several dressmakers before selecting those that are worth considering. Even if the customer manages to acquire limited information at this stage, from the moment he enters a tailor's shop, a great deal of uncertainty will be resolved during the upcoming bargaining process. The dressmaker will probably advise the client on the choice of a proper fabric, and his uncertainty about the texture and visual quality will disappear. The point here is that, if the client is uncertain about the quality of the product, he could probably refrain from buying a suit. But simply by interacting with the tailor most if not all details about her uncertainty about how the new suit will look like can be resolved in a process of negotiating. But negotiating in that case is not only about setting the details of a contract, is also about coming to terms what both, the buyer and the tailor is expecting.

So, the question here is how uncertainty affects the realization of a transaction. Our fictional customer will spend some time visiting several dressmakers, which will allow him to learn more about her preferences and wishes. The dressmaker she finally choses will likewise have the chance to adapt and change the fit of the tailor-made suit several times. Thus, asset specificity is only one dimension affecting transaction costs, and not a static one. The frequency of exchange is an important factor, but the moderating effect may vary depending on how the specific relationship between buyer and seller evolves during subsequent stages of dealing with each other. Thus, the particular quality of an exchange relationship will allow both parties to deal with multiple options to cope with the prevalent uncertainty in exchange relations, which is the third dimension that affects transactions. In sum, several types of transaction costs will be affected by several interacting effects.

All three aforementioned dimensions, asset specificity, the frequency of exchange, and uncertainty, relate to an outcome that is contingent, as it evolves into different trajectories affected by the evolutionary dynamic of interacting agents engaged in dynamic social relationships (Williamson, 1985: 85). The costs in our example of a custom-made product are higher than in the case of acquiring standardized product (off-the-peg suit). Nonetheless, because of the closer interaction between the client and the supplier, the specification of the service is not a big problem, but essential for carrying out a successful transaction. In a transaction such as the one just described, as it occurs only once, the effort for both sides appears higher compared to a repeatedly returning client.

A special case seem to be idiosyncratic transactions, being defined "where the human and physical assets required for the production are extensively specialized" (Williamson, 1985: 76).

Although our hypothetical dressmaker needs extensive specialized skills developed for the special purpose of tailoring, the difference with respect to a highly idiosyncratic asset specificity stems from the fact that these unique skills remain basically the same irrespective of the number of clients served. If the investment is made again for each specialized order, transaction costs are significantly higher. The tailor is not forced to acquire for each new order his skill anew. Skills and tools, so-called transaction cost-specific materials, or capabilities can be utilized again for each additional transaction. Highly idiosyncratic transactions characterized by its extreme asset specificity are different, because a producer is forced to make *transaction-specific investments*, exclusively for the order, specialized machinery to deliver a unique component or service will be needed. And transaction-specific investment can include the hire and training of special human capital, skills and capabilities that have to be learned first, for becoming capable of delivering the product or service.

The nature of these transaction cost-specific investments forces both clients and suppliers to enter into an expensive exchange relationship, where the outcome is open or highly uncertain. Contracting parties are forced to invest an extra effort into the sustainability of the relation (Williamson, 1979; Burt, 2007).

> If goods and services in highly **idiosyncratic transactions** are produced by deploying highly specialized human skills and capabilities developed only for a narrow and particular activity, the transaction is likely to yield an expected outcome. For example, gasoline is a fungible commodity, and will usually have the expected standardized quality predetermined in the given market. Conversely, idiosyncratic highly specific assets are either very hard to substitute or cannot be replaced by other products or services.
>
> Idiosyncrasy is used by Williamson to signify that a transaction-specific activity (personalized human skills, specialized equipment) cannot be easily replaced by suitable alternatives. Consequently, entering a contract characterized by high asset specificity to fulfill these transactions almost inevitably induces sunk costs. If the uncertainty of achieving a asset-specific transaction is too high, such transactions will rarely take place (Williamson, 1985, 1998).

In each of our three scenarios—related respectively to standardized (nonspecific), mixed, or highly idiosyncratic asset specificity—the transaction cost differs considerably (see Table 3.1). Most nonspecific transactions cause low transaction costs and can usually be carried out as arm-length market transactions. The difference between occasional and recurrent transactions is that the latter enable both the customer and the seller to learn over time about each other and both will expect any future transaction to replicate the previous experiences.

In cases of mixed asset specificity, a client may use the information provided by other customers, or feedback available on the internet about the reputation of the provider of a good or service. If a good or service is only occasionally obtained, he/she may rely on other customers' feedback to reduce uncertainty about the expected quality of a service. In recurrent relations, both parties can count on their previous reciprocating experience.

Transaction cost approaches, however, employ an overly narrow focus on costs. Generally, it is assumed that each transaction is embodied in the existing bulk of formal and informal norms and rules. It is generally acknowledged that transactions are embedded in social fabric of communities (firms, organizations, clubs, markets). These institutional landscapes exert considerable effects on the scope of transaction costs because they provide the reciprocating framework for developing a habitual routine in carrying out exchange relations. Some institutional rules may cause friction if they seem outdated. Likewise, if they become superfluous as an effective frame of reference for the behavior they presumably once successfully guided. Institutional rules are ignored or replaced when they have become obsolete. But change and replacement is a slow and often costly process, and is prone to conflicts.

However, institutional norms and rules do not only cause tensions, as they essentially provide a frame of reference developed over centuries, which is often deeply embedded in informal cultural habits that prescribe rules and duties each agent abide by simply participating in society as a member. These prescribed rules and habits are important for effective carrying out most exchange relations in society.

Therefore, it is important to acknowledge that, although the efficiency of transactions are affected by the degree of uncertainty, the frequency, and the asset specificity, they are

Table 3.1 Types of transactions

Types of transaction affected by asset specificity and the frequency of exchange				
		Investment characteristics		
		Nonspecific	Mixed	Idiosyncratic
Frequency	Occasional	Purchasing standard equipment	Purchasing customized equipment	Constructing a plant
	Recurrent	Purchasing standard materials	Purchasing customized materials	Site-specific transfer of an intermediate product across successive stages

Source: Williamson (1985: 73), own compilation

moreover affected by the more general institutional rules, norms and values prevalent in society.

Transaction cost economists demonstrate that any transaction implies cost of searching for and acquiring information. Economic agents invest a great deal of time and effort in gathering information about potential products and services. They need to compare available alternatives and have to make a choice about the quality of the product. All of these decisions are boundedly rational and often based on biased information. In bargaining and decision-making, costs arise from the fact that agents have no incentive to disclose all information, and withholding important information can significantly affect the exchange. Thus, each transaction requires monitoring and enforcing efforts, the extent of which will differ significantly depending on whether issues arise ex-ante or ex-post of contracting a transaction.

Why Transaction Costs Matter

Transaction costs approaches strongly rely on the work of J.R. Commons (1862–1945), considered the founding father of institutional economics, who pointed at the need to arbitrate between often conflicting interests (Williamson, 1985: 29). Arbitration is initiated to settle a dispute, or to reconcile between presumably different stakes. Its aim is finding a balance that everyone can accept, or to borrow a phrase from Barnard (1938), with which everyone could be *satisficed* with.

Furthermore, human behavior is only limited rational. Agents intend to be rational, but lack key information about the alternatives they are required to consider when making a decision. Transaction costs economists assume that agents are opportunists, and that the true nature of their behavior is shaped by the pursuit of "self-interest with guile" (Williamson, 1985: 30). Yet, if all human behavior is motivated primarily by self-interest with guile, almost all exchange relations would result in conflict. Yet, asymmetric relationships, even among anonymous agents, can be based on trust and reciprocity. Admittedly, the conception of human nature "is stark and rather jaundiced" (Williamson, 1985: xiii). Although seemingly narrow, this approach is widely applied to define the core aspects of rational human behavior as it is generally assumed that humans are not acting altruistically in exchange relations.

Williamson perceives the modern firm as an efficient alternative to imperfect markets, where high uncertainty or high transaction costs render market transactions excessively expensive or impossible. And it is right, that a firm can internalize these transactions and can bypass the uncertainty, provided that the internal behaviors can be organized efficiently.

Finally, transaction costs are not a static concept. During each bargaining process, the relationship between buyer and seller, employer and employee, and between

(continued)

principal and agents inevitably changes. But change is based on forces affecting the relationship that are endogenous, emerging within somewhat tacit qualities generated by the mutual interdependence in exchange relations.

3.8 Internalization Theory

Early theories of the multinational firm have concentrated on the use and abuse of firm power (Hymer, 1970, 1976). Other approaches focused on how product lifecycles and technologies affected the internationalization of multinational corporations (MNCs) (Hufbauer, 1966; Posner, 1961; Vernon, 1966). More recent approaches explain the existence of the multinational firm primarily in terms of its superior efficiency, arguing that it can exploit firm-specific advantages abroad by leveraging the effects of multinationality (Kirca et al., 2012).

Mostly the aim of explaining how firm-specific advantages evolve is paradoxically based on the argument that firms are more efficient if they carry out transactions within their own boundaries rather than using alternatively so-called imperfect markets.

Theories that address the problem of uncertainty in markets assume that the internalization of a transaction that is subject to uncertainty is the central rationale for the existence of the multinational firm (Buckley & Casson, 2009, 2010, 2014).

Internalization is a term used to describe the integration of a transaction within the hierarchical boundaries of the firm. The idea of internalization is based on the conviction that the hierarchical organization of joint activities of some transactions can be more efficient than the market because the internal hierarchy allows the firm to coordinate and operate activities more efficiently. However, internalization is motivated by more than efficiency. It is also driven by the need to internalize a particular transaction that is not offered by a market, or in which markets fail to produce a supply simply because uncertainty is too high, and thus the market mechanism is insufficient since no one has an interest in bearing the prevailing uncertainty.

Internalization theory has had a major impact on IB research and has become the dominant paradigm. The theory was developed by Buckley & Casson (1976) by extending the transaction costs approach advanced by Ronald Coase (1937).

Firms that need or intend to produce highly specialized value-adding activities, based on idiosyncratic asset specificity (Williamson, 1985, 2005) are therefore forced to produce these services in-house (Buckley & Casson, 2009). Internalization of this type is a major trigger for cross-border vertical or horizontal mergers. Any internalization based on efficiency gains from producing a particular value-added product or service internally as compared to cost of using the market mechanism is based on the premise that a firm's efficiency in cross-border activities leads to the creation of multinational firm. This is also the dominant thought in IB noting that the multinational firms is the champion capable of more efficiently operating international business activities, i.e. including foreign direct investment (Clougherty et al., 2016; Clougherty & Skousen, 2019).

The other argument behind the internalization approach is that multinational firms are more efficient in the cross-border exploitation of existing firm-specific advantages (Verbeke et al., 2018). The organizational hierarchy is presumed to enable these firms to exploit much better an uncertain and difficult to specify product development process. The core of the argument rests on the fact that some, if not most, of the efficiency gains are based on a more effective control of existing firm-specific advantages. In addition, internalization theory has propelled the perspective that hierarchy as a governance mechanism used by the large multinationals in their business networks enables them to exploit existing advantages more efficiently (Grindley & Teece, 1997; Teece, 1980, 1996).

Internalization and Market Power

Internalization is not simply initiated to mitigate the impact of uncertainty prevalent in many business activities, but is often pursued to allow a greater control of apparent contingencies in and across different stages of value-adding activities that evolve during the process of internationalization.

If a firm is capable of controlling a particular stage of value-adding activity in-house and this results in greater output productivity, exploiting economies of scale and scope, the efficiency argument is correct. But the theoretical rationale that in-house value-adding activities are carried out as long as the marginal costs are lower than relying on market transactions can be tricky or impossible to test in reality, because the multinational firm and its management, although intentionally acting rational are embedded in a contingent environment.

However it is important to note the internalization theory is assuming that "the boundaries of a firm are set at the margin where the benefits of further internalization of markets are offset by the costs" (Buckley & Casson, 2009: 1564). In addition, internationalization is based on the argument that the firm is seeking to operate particular business operations in locations that offer the least-costs.

In theory, several factors affect the logic of internalization (Buckley, 2009b)

- If there is a sizable time lag between the process of inventing a product and its final completion. If a firms need to coordinate several "multistage process" in product development, markets may be imperfect and firms consequently will seek to maintain internal control over these subsequent stages (Buckley, 2009b: 224).
- If there is a high degree of uncertainty about the final success of product development, it is unlikely that product development will be initiated by markets. Consequently, highly uncertain product development will only take place if firms can internalize this uncertainty (e.g., have a secure future sales forecast or can cover investment costs through long-term protected property rights).
- Market failures often emanate from information asymmetries and subsequent agency problems which the firm can mitigate by internalizing.
- If foreign governments do not provide or have not established proper institutional rules to protect intellectual property (IP) rights it is unlikely that related cross-border business activities will be externalized or outsourced to contractors (Buckley & Casson, 2002).

In general, multinational firms are considered to be more capable of controlling, developing, and promoting knowledge embedded in intangible, multistage, and spatially dispersed value-creation activities. Large multinational firms are capable of bearing the extra costs of timely product development processes and can arbitrate costs and benefits across several locations (Buckley, 2009b). Then, foreign direct investments basically serve not only to minimize transaction costs of international business activities, but help internalize or buffer the contingencies that arise from imperfect or uncertain markets. All these propositions are built on the assumption that the management of business firms is capable of making fully rational choices, while considering productivity gains of internal value-adding activities against the costs (i.e. loss of control) or benefits of licensing or outsourcing these transactions (Buckley & Casson, 2009).

3.9 Edith Penrose's Theory of the Firm

Edith T. Penrose's major contribution in her "Theory of the Growth of the Firm" (1959) is explicitly acknowledged in IB research.

> The business firm as a "collection of productive resources" (Penrose, 1959: 31).

She conceptualized the firm as an administrative unit capable of organizing the prevalent and unique bundle of productive resources. An important aspect of Penrose's argument is that the firm "owns resources together with other resources acquired from outside" and both internal and external resources are used by the firm to produce and sell goods and services (Penrose, 1959: 31). Thus, she is not focusing exclusively on the firm, but on how the firm is using its internal resources by complementing these with external resources. It is not only the resources the firm owns but the mix of internal and external resources, that enable the growth of the firm.

She acknowledged, that the structure of the firm is created by those "who run it" and she defined this structure as the product that "arose from the past" challenges. Penrose pointed at these challenges, because she knew these problems and opportunities "shaped largely [the] conscious attempts to achieve a 'rational' organization"(Penrose, 1959: 31).

It is important to acknowledge that firm capabilities are the outcome of past challenges, resulting in a structure, that has been designed by the management, i.e. the owner-entrepreneurs, who run the firm.

Penrose contends that the management of the firm is "attempting to act rational," a major purpose, but not always achieved. It is particularly noteworthy that, according to Penrose, the "productive opportunity" of the firm rests on "entrepreneurs" (ibid). But the entrepreneur as the core agent and the organizational structure are both, mutually dependent. She identifies both the agent and the structure, which is the administrative body of a firm that has evolved from past efforts to master emerging challenges, and the individual agency (the entrepreneur), which is characterized by its role seeking and taking productive opportunities fitting existing firm resources. How much an entrepreneurial agent is motivated, willing, or capable to respond to an opportunity is determined by the existence of "competent management" (Penrose, 1959: 32), which is based less on "sober calculations" than on a "general entrepreneurial bias in favour of growth" (Penrose, 1959: 33). Thus, a major characteristic of a firm's success is the level of entrepreneurial spirit, ambition, and motivation of the management.

Yet, Penrose argues that motivation and ambition may not necessarily correlate with the competence of the management. She is skeptical about an almost too narrow focus on the "mere specialization of managerial knowledge and ability" which will not necessarily increase the needed capability of many executives lacking the "imaginat[ion], knowledge and ability" to lead or manage the productive use of firm's resources (Penrose, 1959: 35).

The Bundling of Resources Matters

Penrose claimed eloquently that "it is never *resources* themselves that are the 'inputs in the production process, but only the *services* that the resources can render" (Penrose, 1959: 25). She continues: "the important distinction between resources and services is [. . .] the fact that resources consist of a bundle of potential services and can [. . .] be defined independently of their use" (Penrose, 1959: 25). What Penrose elaborates here is that a firm's resources may matter, but without using these resources for productive purposes (which implies physically doing something) firms will not attain success. Penrose further claims that the firm is "something more

(continued)

than a collection of individuals – it is a collection of individuals who have had experience in working together" (Penrose, 1959: 46). It is this collective experience of individuals and the gradual development of their somewhat intricate and tacit "working relationship" that makes the firm profitable, because these bundled experiences embedded in a working relationship in fact enable "each other to provide [. . .] the services that are uniquely valuable" in a firm (Penrose, 1959: 46). According to Penrose, it is these bundled experiences that enable the firm to carry out any "effective operation" and enable the firm to use its productive resources (Penrose, 1959: 47).

Although, this is just a short summary of the approach Edith Penrose (1959) adopted to develop a particular version of the theory of the firm, it should be read as an addition, rather than as a contrasting perspective to the transaction cost or internalization approaches. However, there is one major difference, while transaction cost oriented approaches are mainly interested in explaining the costs of transactions that occur in different settings, Penrose is primarily concerned with how firms utilize existing resources. Penrose allows us to acknowledge the inert nature of the way bundled firm resources are effectively used. More importantly, a firm needs to be capable of organizing its collective experience and enact the embedded knowledge using this experience by sustaining productive working relationships (Foss, 1999; Hodgson, 1998; Nason & Wiklund, 2018; Pitelis, 2007; Rugman & Verbeke, 2004).

3.10 Firm Specificity, Location, and Internalization: The "OLI" Paradigm

John H. Dunning characterizes "international production as production owned or controlled by multinational enterprises (MNE)" and it is the multinational firm which is coordinating value adding activities by "internaliz[ing] intermediate product markets across national boundaries" (Dunning, 1995: 79). John Dunning decisively contributed to and shaped the development of IB research. One major contribution is his OLI paradigm to incorporate existing theories about FDI and the multinational firm, which he conceived as too particularistic, into a more general cohesive framework. His OLI framework postulates that the scope and scale of cross-border activities is affected by three basic categories described as (O) ownership, (L) locational, and (I) internalization advantages.

He argues that these three advantages allow a more holistic explanation of FDIs made by multinational firms. These variables are defined by (Dunning, 1995: 81):

- Ownership advantages (O) arising from the stock of assets, owned or controlled by the multinational firm

- The locational advantages (L) generated by the existing factor costs which can be exploited in a potentially selected foreign location
- The extent to which in the selected foreign market advantages of internalization (I) can be exploited by the internationalizing business firm

The OLI framework (Fig. 3.3) describes how a somewhat ideal entry mode choice can be made, accounting for the differential effects of exploiting ownership, locational, and internalization advantages (Dunning, 1988). Dunning's intention was to synthesize the partial strands of existing international business theories. He originally argued that the OLI paradigm "explain all types of foreign direct investment and [...] most other forms of international economic" activity (Dunning, 1988: 13). Dunning basically differentiates largely between three groups of entry modes: FDI, export, and contractual entry modes, such as licensing.

FDI is the first choice by a multinational firm capable of exploiting all three OLI advantages, because FDI allows the exploitation of ownership, locational, and internalization advantages (see Fig. 3.3). If a firm can exploit ownership advantages and internalization advantages, but cannot utilize prevalent locational benefits abroad, it will stick to exporting as the ideal entry mode strategy. Finally, if a firm capitalizes only on ownership advantages and cannot exploit the foreign locational advantage nor is it capable to realize internalization benefits, it will have to choose a contractual entry mode, such as licensing.

Ownership advantages are generated by the MNEs because these entities can exclusively exploit unique firm-specific assets, but this raises the question of the extent to which the firm is capable of coordinating these assets across national boundaries without losing these assumed efficiency gains. However, firm specific advantages are not independently generated from locational factors. Although ownership advantages can be explained by combining several exclusively owned assets generated in joint production stages (Dunning,

Fig. 3.3 OLI framework as a decision tree (Dunning, 1988)

1988), it is important to acknowledge, that the core assumption here is that the multinational firm is capable of controlling and operating these ownership advantages (0) abroad more efficiently than other, domestic firms. Ownership advantages can be the outcome of superior common governance embedded in an extended network of affiliates operated and controlled by the multinational firm. Yet, the question is also how these ownership advantages should be allocated within and across firm boundaries or be shared across the extended network within the firm.

However, if advantages are generated exclusively by value-adding activities situated within the firm's own boundaries, they are also not independent from internalization advantages (I). In that case, it does not make sense to lease out these assets, because the efficiency gains will be lost.

Further, if O and I can be generated independently by the multinational firm and if both allow the firm to exploit the existing advantages in foreign locations (L), the firm will not, but must choose FDI as an entry mode. Dunning assumed that the greater the product diversity and international scope of a multinational firm, the greater the gains arising from exploiting ownership advantages.

Dunning further argues that the superior efficiency of multinational firms is not only generated by their ability to exploit O, but also by their capability to internalize (I), arguing that in fact the efficiency gains evolve from the common governance, mostly by fostering vertical and horizontal integration (Dunning, 1988). From that perspective, O and I can be the outcome of overlapping activities.

The gains from locational benefits (L) are generated by multinational firms because these organizations are more capable of exploiting or leveraging existing advantages embedded in foreign locations, such as low labor costs, or tariff and tax credits. Moreover, multinational firms can exploit relatively better the presumably immobile locational merits abroad and own a greater leverage in exploiting the arbitrage between multiple locations seeking to attract FDIs.

Dunning further argues that the special configuration of O, L, and I advantages allows multinational firms to exploit the greatest range of efficiencies maintained by operating abroad (Dunning, 1988). From these three gains that can be attained by enacting OLI advantages, four major observations matter:

- Multinational firms coordinate various R&D activities across borders.
- They operate in different environments and manage these activities differently, suggesting that they differentiate between host and home locations.
- By applying these three advantages, multinational firms can arbitrage between different country locations using means of transfer-pricing, exploit gains from different exchange rates, and leverage benefits from multi-plant operations.
- Multinational firms enjoy different international environments to exercise a global strategy. (Dunning, 1988: 40)

Although the OLI paradigm offers an integrated approach for analyzing multiple sources of the superior efficiency generated by multinationality, it has its limitations. Most of the factors cannot easily be identified before making an entry mode decision.

3.11 Internationalization as an Evolving Process

Most of the theories discussed so far have branched out from neoclassical economics and rely on the several assumptions that are held as undisputed truths. Although economists acknowledge that agents, described as homo oeconomicus, never have access to perfect information and do not always maximize expected utility, rationality remains the cornerstone on which these theories rest.

Based on **a highly specific model of human behavior**, internationalization of the firm is often explained as a mere choice among alternative entry modes. Each choice made by rational entrepreneurs or managers and the selection made is rational, if the agent is capable of selecting the most appropriate entry mode for internationalizing firm.

But assumptions needed to construct a model of rational behavior could be criticized as overly static and very difficult to meet. It is increasingly accepted that human agents are severely limited in their capacity to be rational, or to foresee what might happen and in fact humans are fairly imperfect in selecting an appropriate behavior in a given situation (Kreps, 1988). In addition, managers and firms change, alter or even retract from choices previously made, their preferences are often ambiguous and change continuously. Consequently, it seems obvious that internationalizing is a dynamic and constantly evolving process.

In the early 1970s, the behavioral theory of the firm emerged as a starkly contrasting model to explain firm behavior from a different perspective. The difference consisted in a new and alternative conception of human behavior. The alternate approach rested primarily on the work of Cyert and March (1963) who considered the firm as a "coalition of managers, workers, stockholders, customers and others, each with their own goal" (1963, 61). What was novel was the observation that single selfish individuals are not isolated in satisfying their odd intentions, but in almost all life situations they are in a coalition with other individuals in fulfilling their objectives (Cyert & March, 1963).

Cyert and March argued that in organizations these coalescing individuals, with their different interests need to be integrated, and finding a feasible way how to cooperate, is framed by a fragile organizational design. Obviously, some fractions "exert greater influence and make greater demands [. . .] than others" but all in all members of an organization need to interact. The firm, therefore "tends to focus sequentially" on one goal and then on another, while others will be forgotten or neglected, or intentionally ignored (Cyert & March, 1963: 61).

The **behavioral theory of the firm** perceived organizations, not as overtly smooth running systems constructed to execute machine-like the designed choices made by rational decision makers, but rather as living organic bodies that articulate different expectations and prioritize different choices.

It is crucial to keep in mind in all endeavors to explain the international firm and its business operations abroad, to note that Cyert and March (1963: 68) focused on how organizations learn when faced with the ambiguity of making choices. Thus, the study of the "actual decision making processes requires a thorough description of the firm's decision in terms of a specific series of steps used to reach [a] decision" (Cyert & March, 1963: 11). In this approach, two prevalent assumptions define the problem of making a rational decision within the firm. One is that firms seek to maximize profits. The other is that they operate with perfect knowledge (Cyert & March, 1963: 18). Although the authors are concerned about these assumptions, they propose a more radical perspective, namely that maximizing profit is just one objective in a business firm (ibid). Any theory of the firm that focuses only on that goal falls short.

Not, surprisingly the sequential nature of decision making, the evolutionary nature of the decision making as a process should be on the center stage. Thus, organizational "motives grow out of interaction" between different members of the organization and this interaction does not necessarily generate one stable preference function (Cyert & March, 1963: 19).

From that perspective, learning emerged as a significant research question within the behavioral theory of the firm because the approach did not comprehend actions as singular and static, but addressed their processual and sequential nature. Organizational learning was thus considered important because firms need to adapt continuously to contingent environments. It is further noted that knowledge, which in organizations is not independently created from past experience, has to be constantly adapted to new contexts. From that contention, Cyert and March speak about organizational memory which is not uniform, but varies across individuals and subunits. They further contended that this organizational memory is embedded in a firm-specific context of incentives and motivations which do not materialize independently from "pre-existing understandings, beliefs, and attitudes" (Cyert & March, 1963: 68).

The behavioral theory of the firm allows us to appreciate the foolishness of organizational decision-making (March, 1978), and Cyert and March acknowledge that decisions are intendedly rational, but their outcome is often not (Puranam et al., 2015; Simon, 1991).

It is important to note that the firm's **management is intendedly rational** in the process of making a decision to entry of foreign market, but due to the lack of information, caused by different forms of distances, because of the uncertainty and contingency about the future that lies ahead, and the constraints imposed by past knowledge and experience made in other situational contexts, it will often rely on suboptimal or even wrong entry mode choices.

It is worthwhile taking into account that organizational objectives emerge from or are the outcome of an often conflicting interaction among multiple participants, with unstable and multiple preferences in ambiguous worlds. Not surprisingly, within a business firm, multiple objectives exist and agents are seeking to find a substitute for the lack of perfect knowledge traditionally assumed in orthodox theory. A number of these concerns elaborated by the behavioral theory of the firm have been imported by a small number of Scandinavian scholars who started to analyze the internationalization of the firm as a process, evolving gradually, affected by the firm's capability to learn from past and current experiences.

3.11.1 Reijo Luostarinen: The Internationalization of the Firm

Reijo Luostarinen (1939–2017) from the School of Economics in Helsinki introduced his doctoral dissertation published in 1979 with the verdict: "This study is the *product of a long learning* and *development process*" and claimed he did not "only select a topic" but "develop[ed] a theoretical framework which is the result of *interaction between myself and the environment*" (Luostarinen, 1989: vii).

In this introductory remark, Luostarinen reminds us that objectives grow often slowly, they are the outcome of a process, and this process is guided by the capability (or willingness) to learn. In addition, he accentuates that internationalization can only be explained conclusively taking seriously the interaction between the firm and its environment. He knew that from his own struggle and the distinctive approach to write his doctoral thesis. It is not incidental how he experienced to carry out a study about the process of internationalizing, which is itself an on-going process significantly affected by the mutually dependent interaction between author and environment. His study may be read as a response to the fact that until the 1980s all major studies in IB were carried out in the US and focused almost exclusively on large multinational firms. Yet the seemingly alternative approach of Luostarinen, who offered a holistic perspective to analyze the internationalization of business firms, remains relatively unknown to date.

The major objective of Luostarinen's doctoral thesis was to analyze the phenomenon of internationalization how the internal organization of the business firm is trying to cope with the problems arising from its external relations and how these interactions affected the problems of planning and decision-making, driven by different organizational and functional challenges.

The study identified key differences between the domestic and the foreign enterprise and attributed these differences to the outcome of being embedded in both environments. But it was noticed that these two situational contexts were not isolated from each other, but interdependent, affecting each other dynamically. One of his key insights was that a changing environment induces a modification in the internal activity of the firms.

Thus, Luostarinen acknowledged that the sources of change were a trigger of activities that are related to the accumulated and constantly, but slowly growing stock of knowledge in firms interacting with that environment. He further noticed that firms do not only adapt to change but rather try to anticipate it. However, he knew equally that firms are characterized by severe rigidities and time lags, and that any change is often initiated by the management in order to innovate (Luostarinen, 1989).

Luostarinen concluded from all these observations that the traditional neoclassical theory of the firm is not of great help to solve the puzzle of internationalization and focused on how systems theory, the theory of the growth of the firm (Penrose), and the behavioral theory of the firm (Cyert and March) can be used to analyze the rich data he had gathered as a part of his longitudinal study about internationalizing firms.

His in-depth study allowed him to analyze the idiosyncratic facets of his sampled firms. And he thought about how he could succeed to elucidate how these factors interact with the environment. So he started to study how major units that served the domestic market interacted with the need to serve new emerging international markets and diagnosed how limited the ability of the management is to look beyond their entrenched operational scope.

Luostarinen concluded that the narrow operational perspective is an outcome of the past challenges the firm management has been confronted with, which is one of the core behavioral constraints he diagnosed for managerial decision-making. So, he hypothesized that this limited scope or narrow focus did significantly affect the initial or early stages of internationalization (Luostarinen, 1989: 46).

Reijo Luostarinen's motivation to understand how firms can overcome the prevalent rigidities generated by its domestic activities that dominated their habitual routines led him directly to think about factors that influence the process of learning occurring in firms that are shaped by the close mutually dependent interaction with the environment.

Further, adapting insights made by Edith T. Penrose (1959), Luostarinen argued that if the firm focuses on adjusting its growth alternatives by balancing the internationalization process (Luostarinen, 1989: 65) it may augment its productive capacities and technologies to attain a more appropriate (i.e., successful) internationalization (Luostarinen, 1989: 90).

But unlike the seemingly similar Uppsala School, Luostarinen emphasized that firm performance will depend on how the firm succeeds in adapting its products to the unfamiliar, largely different international market environment, implicitly pointing to the inherent evolutionary nature of the process of internationalization.

He further noticed that firms need to focus on the adaptation of an existing "product-operation market mix" (POM) to gain a fit in international environments (illustrated in Fig. 3.4). Luostarinen moreover conceptualized *distance* as a term that cause several "impediments and restricting forces" (Luostarinen, 1989: 129), barriers that the firm needs to overcome. He opined that this distance "prohibit the flow of general knowledge from the target country to the home country" (Luostarinen, 1989: 132) and began to operationalize other distances, such as cultural and economic distance between the home and host countries (Luostarinen, 1989: 146).

He then tested a number of hypotheses positing the effects of these distances (from close to distant) on specific marketing operations of the internationalizing firm and concluded, that firms need to know how they may bridge the gaps caused by several distances, but also highlighted the necessity being capable to learn from unfamiliar environments.

Figure 3.4 illustrates how these three dimensions affect the pattern and process of internationalization. The idiosyncratic firm-related factors (1) in the upper right quadrant interact with home (2) and target country factors (3) resulting each from the two different environments. All three dimensions influence how a firm is coping with factors that impact the evolving managerial decision-making process (4). In the lower-left quadrant, the product operation mix (5) used to internationalize is moderated on two levels. One moderation is caused by factors influencing directly the decision-making process, related to the evolving context in home and target markets.

The initiated pattern of internationalization is in early periods the input, generated by the feedback provided, which in turn, leads to needed modifications based on the internal firm-related factors. But these internal capabilities and firm-related factors are the results of the anterior and current interaction between home and target country-related factors, which subsequently feedback (6) on the process of managerial decisions aiming to find a feasible fit of the product-oriented mix for the international target markets.

Luostarinen's model implies, although not explicitly articulated, that the decision to internationalize is embedded in an iterative, dynamically changing, and co-evolving environment, driven by feedback loops that force the firm continuously to adapt its internationalization pattern according to a co-evolving environmental landscape (Luostarinen, 1989; Welch & Luostarinen, 1988).

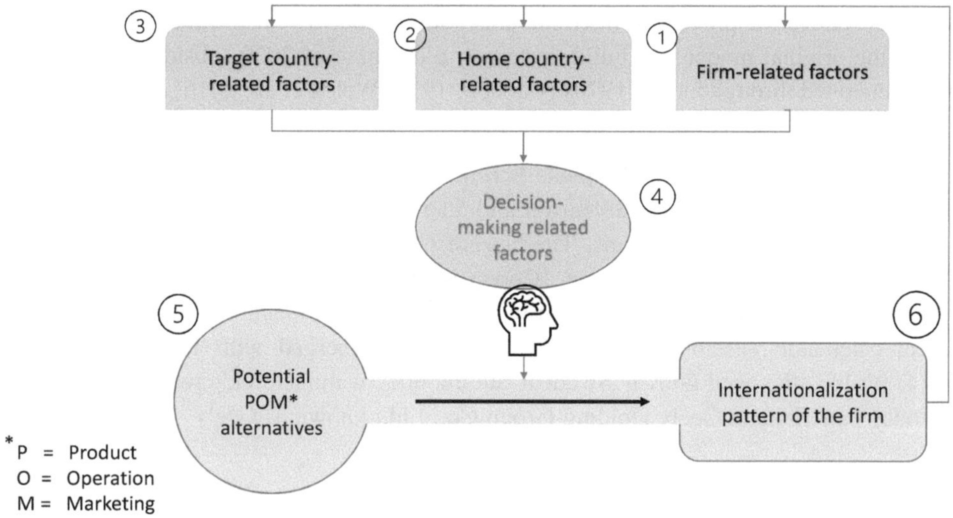

Fig. 3.4 Factors affecting the internationalization process of the firm (Luostarinen, 1989: 198)

3.11.2 Johanson and Vahlne: The Process of Internationalization

Jan Johanson from the University of Uppsala and Jan-Erik Vahlne from the Stockholm School of Economics developed a popular, similar and widely accepted model of internationalization as a process that shaped international business studies. Retrospectively, the Uppsala model contrasted the static managerial decision-making approach of entry mode choice with a more dynamic, gradual, or incremental process view.

Their original contribution in 1977, one of the most cited articles published in the Journal of International Business Studies (JIBS), is an approach that answers the questions of why and how firms internationalize gradually step by step, describing the fact that a firm's "internationalization is the product of a series of incremental decisions" (Johanson & Vahlne, 1977: 23).

The term **incremental** in this specific context means that the decision is not one single big choice, but actually occurs in a number of small increments, understood as a series of consecutive steps in a larger process, that takes time to evolve. Thus, incrementality is a key feature of a proliferating, successively augmenting reciprocating process, emphasizing that internationalization is not based on a single, but rather on a series of sequential interrelated decisions.

The original study focused on how four prototypical firms started to internationalize and how each firm developed a distinctive pattern of how it expanded abroad. Although the model described the process of internationalization of four Swedish firms, the insights on which the original model was build, rested on a database of 2000 subsidiaries that have been generated throughout the 1970s (Carlson, 1974; Welch et al., 2016).

The Original Study of the Uppsala School

In their widely cited study, Johanson and Vahlne analyzed the internationalization process of four Swedish firms. These were (1) Sandvik AB, originated in 1862, (2) Atlas Copco, a steel producer, Copco is the acronym made from Compagnie Pneumatique Commerciale, founded in 1873, (3) Facit, a manufacturer of mechanical calculators, established in 1922, which later merged with Electrolux, and (4) Volvo, the well-known Swedish automobile manufacturer, created in 1927, today part Hejiang Geely Holding Group Co., Ltd., known as Geely.

The core insight of this early approach is that internationalization "is a process in which the firms gradually increase their international involvement" and that the special characteristics of this "process influence the pattern and pace" of the internationalization of firms (Johanson & Vahlne, 1977: 23).

The pattern of internationalization is used in the extant literature as a major characteristic of the process of internationalizing and is termed establishment chain. The characterization as an establishment chain suggests that one step is relying on the previous step, whereby the step is understood as a preceding stage initiating the next stage of expansion. Using the idea of a step or a stage implies an incremental progress, from irregular to regular export activities, or from indirect to direct exporting. The concept of an establishment chain can induce a somewhat misleading interpretation that the process of internationalization proceeds in a rigid order from simpler entry modes (export) to more elaborated and more demanding entry modes. Because it can be misleading to assume some automatism between steps or stages, but the idea of gradual changes, the notion of accumulating progressively knowledge from the experience made by the firm in each previous stage is highly important. The gradualism supposed in the Uppsala model is meant to signify that a firm is learning from its past and current activities, which is a substantial input for the achievement in successive stages.

Although it is correct to categorize export as a mode of market entry which is less demanding than the establishment of a foreign production plant, the conclusion that a firm would automatically progress gradually, step by step, from the bottom to the top, to an increasingly more sophisticated form of market entry is not that straightforward. Basically because we need to refrain from treating entry mode choice as a fully rational activity. Entry modes are more a mixture of several entry modes, consisting of exports, probably shared with an International Joint Venture (IJV), and supplemented by a licensing agreement. Note, firms actually utilize several entry modes simultaneously, and often rely on a mix of entry modes in each foreign market (Welch et al., 2018).

It is important to note that the establishment chain suggests that firms may learn from less prolific entry modes such as exporting, and they may gain experiential knowledge from their current activities in foreign markets, whereby this incrementally growing experiential knowledge allows them to pursue more elaborated entry modes at a later stage or adapt the current ones.

The establishment chain identified by the Uppsala School should be not read as a strict guideline or program on how to internationalize, but is rather a pattern identified in the original study conducted in 1977 based on the original four Swedish firms.

The incremental pattern observed in many firms revealed that irregular exports marked the beginning of internationalization, whereby firms moved on to selling via sales agents in more attractive markets. In large markets, firms established sales subsidiaries or production plants. But all four Swedish firms soon exploited a mixture of market entry modes.

The entry modes, starting from irregular exports switching to sales agents, and later shifting to wholly owned sales subsidiaries and/or production plants led, as mentioned above, to a narrow interpretation of the observed pattern of internationalization (Johanson & Vahlne, 1977: 25). But still, the Johanson and Vahlne did not claim that a firm necessarily needs to start with exports before switching to more demanding and advanced entry modes. Thus, we need to acknowledge the historical context, the late 1950s and early 1960s, in which the study was conducted. But this early study demonstrated that early exports and sales generated by sales agents were instrumental in "gradually [. . .] gaining experience in starting and managing [foreign] subsidiaries" (Johanson & Vahlne, 1977). In other words, through the incremental process, firms acquire new experiences and insights, and equally generate new capabilities through its current activities.

The processes and the dynamics of gradual and incremental progress in internationalizing firms revealed that these firms have limited knowledge about target markets abroad at the time of entry. Johanson & Vahlne witnessed firms not only lacking information and routines to operate abroad but are prone to fix sporadic and irregular problems unforeseen in the unfamiliar environment (Johanson & Vahlne, 1977).

The original Uppsala model illustrating how all these dimensions interact is shown in Fig. 3.5. On the right side, the state aspect, market knowledge and market commitment are exhibited. These two variables, market knowledge and market commitment are described as state factors. Johanson and Vahlne argue that firm behavior is dependent on an existing stock of knowledge related intrinsically to the degree of market commitment. These state factors designate the condition from which the business firm launches the internationalization based on its present knowledge and commitment. It is important to acknowledge, that a firm does not own an unlimited stock of experience and knowledge prior to the entry, rather it is experiencing a lack of information, resources and skills. This initial state of knowledge

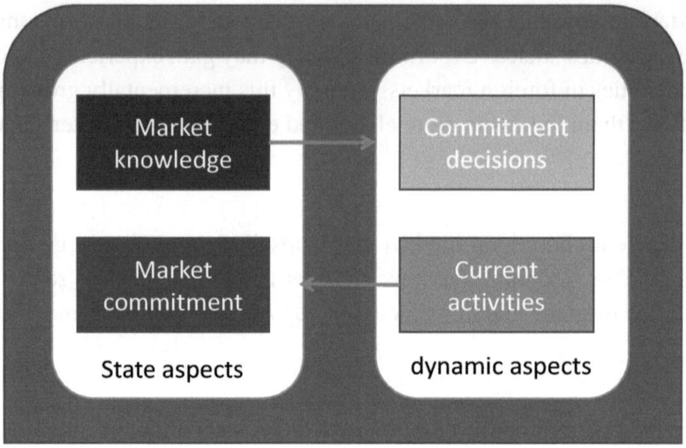

Fig. 3.5 Basic mechanism in the process of internationalizing (Johanson & Vahlne, 1977)

and commitment will frame any further activity carried out by the firm in a prospective foreign market.

In the model, the meaning of market commitment is rooted in the assumption that firms that internationalize will have to make a commitment decision about how to allocate resources, including capital, products, technological skills, and human resources to serve markets (existing and potentially new ones). Note, firm resources are committed not only to new activities deployed to internationalize, but also to current markets. So, the baseline of the depicted mechanism in internationalization is influenced by the existing state of market knowledge and the market commitment. These two factors have a considerable impact on how the commitment decision is made. Further, these state aspects can be defined as the dimensions that significantly affect the way a firm perceives its potential opportunities (Johanson & Vahlne, 2006).

The notion of commitment is important because a firm is required to make additional decisions how to allocate its resources in an ongoing process of internationalization. But how these decisions are made is equally influenced by the current activities, which are the "prime source of experience" (Johanson & Vahlne, 1977: 29). Although experience can be acquired by hiring experts, the core aspect lies in the fact, that the current business activity allows the firm to generate its own experiential knowledge in markets in which it is operating. The gained experiential knowledge will create the input for further change and adaptation. Current activities may force firms to adapt previously designed objectives and substantially alter the degree of market commitment (see lower left side in Fig. 3.5 where market commitment is impacting at the lower right side of the model).

Firms then, increase their market knowledge, based on the current activities and may change the commitment as foreign environments may need additional or alternative resources to exploit emerging market opportunities (Jones & Coviello, 2005). The second change aspect is characterized by "the decision to commit resources to foreign operations"

(Johanson & Vahlne, 1977: 29). This commitment decision is basically affected by two factors, the available resources and the factors that influence how a firm is making the commitment decisions (Welch et al., 2016). The capability to learn from the experience made in carrying out current activities may alter previous commitment decisions. This interactive process is the outcome of the dynamic and interdependent character of the two layers, described as static and dynamic factors.

Considering that Johanson and Vahlne (1977) generated most of these observations using the behavioral theory of the firm (Cyert & March, 1963) we need to acknowledge that the commitment of resources to a particular activity mostly generates tension between current and alternative uses. On the other hand, market knowledge is assumed to directly affect the "opportunities or problems [...] to initiate decisions" (Johanson & Vahlne, 1977: 27).

Thus, one key insight of the Uppsala model is that limitations can be compensated by dynamic changes triggered by challenges and new experiential knowledge gained in an unfamiliar environment. In addition, Johanson and Vahlne recognized the problem of dealing with a time gap, a gap caused by the need to learn operating with existing resources in that new and unfamiliar environment. They called it "a lag between [...] current activities and their consequences" which in turn take time to acknowledge (Johanson & Vahlne, 1977: 28). Still, this does not automatically imply progress in the process of internationalization, as firms may learn in later stages how to adapt to a foreign environment (Coviello et al., 2017; Jones & Coviello, 2005).

Another key variable in the Uppsala model is the distance between the home and host markets. Johanson and Vahlne define this distance as psychic distance, because they assume that it is not only the objectivity of facts, but the subjective perception how these facts matter. As a consequence, the degree of distance is not based on an objective measure alone, as it is also influenced by the experienced gap caused by the assumed distance. Psychic distance is defined as the "sum of those factors preventing the flow of information from and to the market" generated by "differences in language, education, business practices, culture, and industrial development" (Johanson & Vahlne, 1977: 24). A consequence related to psychic distance is that a firm tend to expand first in nearby markets, because of the assumed smaller gap between domestic and foreign market. In the IB literature distance became a debated issue, however, its role in the *process* of internationalization remains somewhat marginalized, especially how the prevalent lack of knowledge about foreign markets affect the evolving process of internationalization (Child et al., 2009; Dow, 1998; Evans et al., 2008; Welch et al., 2016).

3.11.3 Modifications and Extensions of the Original Uppsala Model

The Uppsala model has been modified several times, which is one aspect of its enduring success. The original model was built around the concept of learning and how it will affect the process of internationalization. However, the concept of learning was not fully explained in this first classical version. Thus, one critique on the original Uppsala model was that firms do not need to learn everything by themselves, but may acquire external expertise and knowledge. In response to this critique, Johanson and Vahlne imported key notions of the business network theory to augment and extend their original model.

The idea that networking matters (Atkins et al., 2009; Håkansson & Snehota, 2006; Lee et al., 2001; Meschi & Wassmer, 2013) was a response to the changing pattern in the global economy, where not a single firm controls and carries out highly fragmented value-adding activities across the globe, but rather an extended number of affiliated firms embedded in a tight business network (Forsgren, 2016).

Against that background, Johanson and Vahlne argued that "markets are networks of relationships in which firms are linked to each other" (Johanson & Vahlne, 2009: 1411) From that observation, they hypothesized that firms which operate in an extended business networks can mitigate the effect of what the authors called "liability of outsidership." (Johanson & Vahlne, 2009).

The notion of outsidership used by Johanson and Vahlne in extending their original framework bears a close conceptual similarity with their approach to measuring the effect of psychic distance on the process of internationalizing. Assuming that a firm is capable of maintaining trusted relationships in an extended network of business firms, these firms can exploit these relations to gain access to valuable and new knowledge generated by others in the network. Thus, the business network is conceptualized as a source of knowledge and learning (Forsgren, 2016; Håkansson & Snehota, 2006; Vahlne & Johanson, 2021). Depending on the network position more or less additional knowledge will be acquired. Firms then, develop further their capability to learn within and from that network. The capability to learn is somewhat de-coupled from the current activities exercised by the single firm, which can deliberately exploit and explore knowledge embedded in its business network. However, the business network as an extension of the original model of Johanson and Vahlne still emphasizes that learning remains a core construct.

The new business network version of the original model in fact did not substantially change the definitions of the core variables, as market knowledge became knowledge opportunities. Likewise, market commitment was changed to network position, addressing the fact that the knowledge gained in a network is significantly related to the position in an existing network (see Fig. 3.6). The commitment decision was converted into the relationship commitment decisions. Addressing the notion that a firm in an extended international network needs to continuously make new commitments to sustain a stable network position. The old dimension designated as current activities became learning and creating trust-building, referring to the fact that in social networks each network position is both an opportunity to learn and an opportunity to maintain trust to keep benefitting from the network.

The business network extension of the original Uppsala model could be interpreted as an acknowledgement of the growing importance of tapping into networks of business firms, which became more important to ensure firm's success in the process of internationalizing. However, networking has become somewhat a metaphor for learning and access to unique knowledge (Parmigiani & Rivera-Santos, 2011; Welch, 2016; Yli-Renko et al., 2001).

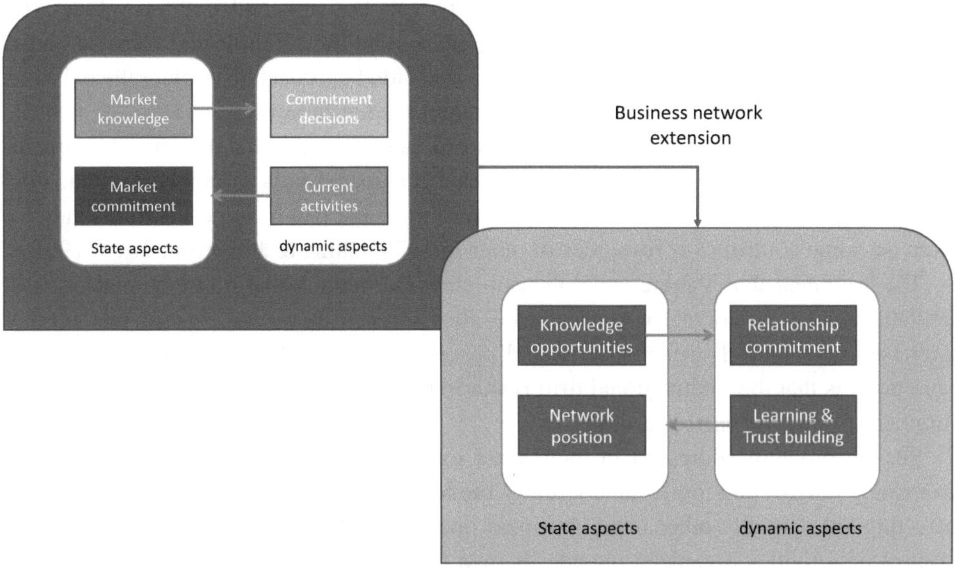

Fig. 3.6 The business network internationalization process model (2009 version, Johanson & Vahlne, 1977, 2009)

Nonetheless, the network theory demonstrates that usually only similar knowledge is exchanged among members of a network, and the closer the network the greater the similarity. And the question is how much *insidership* is affecting the *liability of outsidership* (Johanson & Vahlne, 2009).

One new aspect that the business network extension elaborates is the growing importance of the intrafirm and interfirm relationships that a business firm builds in order to operate effectively in global markets. Thus, the transformation of the original model seems immediately obvious. In Fig. 3.6 the left quadrant describes the two variables that define the state aspects, now called knowledge opportunities and network position. It is important to acknowledge that network theories assume that the capability and opportunity to learn, and also the acquisition of new knowledge are dependent on the density of network relations (Borgatti & Carboni, 2007; Borgatti & Cross, 2003; Cross & Borgatti, 2001). Johanson and Vahlne argue in their updated version that knowledge opportunities depend largely on the commitment decision to build and sustain viable relationships. The overarching argument is that any decision to devote additional resources (time and effort) to creating a more sustainable and more stable network of business relationships will affect future capabilities that are needed for the "ongoing inter-organizational processes of learning, creating, and trust-building" (Vahlne & Johanson, 2013: 200).

Johanson and Vahlne further extended their model in 2013 (Vahlne & Johanson, 2013, 2017). This last extension offers an alternative to the eclectic paradigm embedded in a more general discussion of the question as to what is the proper approach to analyze the internationalization of the firm. In their third extension a specific outlook how the evolution of the multinational business enterprise (MBE) can be explained without relying (too much) on the dominant internalization paradigm. Essentially, Vahlne and Johanson argue that a severe limitation in theory is based on a one-sided approach to explain the existence of the multinational firm as an answer to apparent market failures.

The argument that the firm "control and coordinate resources that it owns while the use of other resources is governed by the market mechanism" fails to emphasize that firms never can "fully control the use of their own resources and that in some situations they can exercise some control over resources of other firms" (Vahlne & Johanson, 2017: 190).

The argument that Vahlne and Johanson elaborate here is that multinational firms do neither exclusively control nor coordinate all resources they own, but in fact need to exercise some control over resources and processes organized by other firms. Thus, the core point is that the multinational firm is sharing the control of business processes with a number of other *uncontrolled* firms.

So, the problem addressed in their latest extension of the original model is that by exercising control and implementing entry mode choices, a multinational firm is not only affecting substantially other firms' business operations, but needs to implement a shared control of activities organized outside its own firm boundaries. It is this prevalence of a need to control business activities transcending firm boundaries, on which Vahlne and Johanson justify their contentions that a "more realistic and dynamic approach is needed" (Vahlne & Johanson, 2013: 190).

A careful reading of the 2013 extension allows us to conclude that multinational firms control and coordinate "heterogeneous resources" (Vahlne & Johanson, 2013: 191) that are not exclusively owned by these multinational firms, but which are embedded in extended global business networks. In addition, Vahlne and Johanson argue that firms cannot act fully rationally or reduce prevalent uncertainty in imperfect markets by internalizing all these activities. Multinational firms act in a non-ergodic world, they need to cope with this increased complexity which "is the driving force [in an ongoing] evolutionary process" (Cantwell et al., 2010: 567, quoted in Vahlne & Johanson, 2013: 192).

The latest extension of the model is illustrated in Fig. 3.7. If we focus on the four variables of the original design of the model, we can see that market knowledge has been renamed to dynamic capabilities generated within an evolving business network. The commitment decision is now defined as an effort how to reconfigure and change the firm's position in its business network. In this new version learning is the outcome of ongoing inter-organizational processes. The commitment is extended to the effects generated by the intra- and interorganizational network position of the firm in its process of internationalization. These commitment decisions of the firm "will have an impact of subsequent knowledge development" (Vahlne & Johanson, 2013: 200). Thus, commitment is concerned with leveraging ongoing inter-organizational processes of learning and trust building. Note, learning is now portrayed as a process involving two or more organizations (transgressing the narrow firm boundaries into a much larger inter- and intra-organizational context). It is conceived now as a process based on multiple ties within the inter-organizational network. Consequently, the process of learning is conceptualized by Vahlne

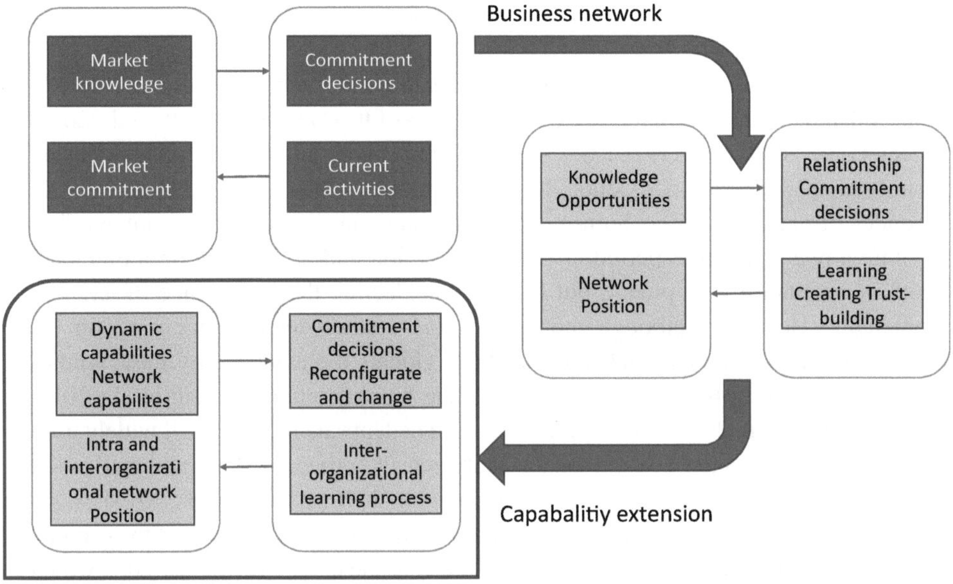

Fig. 3.7 Internationalization from internalization to coordinating networks and capability generation (Vahlne & Johanson, 2013)

and Johanson (2013: 200) as an inter-organizational dyadic relationship. New knowledge is then created, and new insights emerge from the scope of inter-organizational business activities.

The state variables on the left side of the diagram describe the current state of knowledge as an output of the prevalent network position. From this network position, the firm is sustaining and developing its capabilities. It is defined as a dynamic process because the new knowledge will affect the range of opportunities on which the firm can rely on. Firm capabilities are conceived as cause for learning and knowledge accumulation but in turn also its outcome. The commitment decisions (now on the lower quadrant on the left side of Fig. 3.7) signify how important it is to reconfigure the allocation of resources for new projects that will in turn impact the scale and scope of inter-organizational learning.

Vahlne and Johanson argue that the whole dynamic of the process is driven by the effort to exploit and explore the means available in these inter-organizational business processes, providing unforeseen entrepreneurial opportunities. The idea that internationalization is driven by firm capabilities is an implicit reference to the process of effectuation (Sarasvathy, 2001; Vahlne & Johanson, 2013: 200).

Conclusion

The Uppsala model has attracted criticism, because entry mode decisions seemed to be explained more conclusively by transaction cost theories (Morschett et al., 2010; Puck et al., 2009; Shaver, 2013). Likewise, criticism by authors of studies focusing on *born globals (BG)*(Coviello, 2015; Kuivalainen et al., 2007; Rennie, 1993; Zander et al., 2015). The born-global firms internationalize into distant markets within a relatively short period after their inception and do not rely on the gradual and incremental development, but basically neglecting the importance of learning gradually. However, although more and more studies emerged focusing on the assumably rapid internationalization of born globals the evidence by these studies fail to contradicts the core assumptions of the Uppsala approach (Jin et al., 2018; Kuivalainen et al., 2007; Zander et al., 2015). The Uppsala model is still widely used and supported as an effective tool for analyzing the process of internationalization (Dzikowski, 2018; Fletcher, 2001; Freeman et al., 2010; Zander et al., 2015).

Much of the criticism it has attracted to date ignores a central aspect of the original model. First and foremost, Johanson and Vahlne argue that market knowledge which the firm gradually acquires relates to market commitment remains a key part to reach a conclusive explanation for evolving pattern and scope of the *process* of internationalization. Based on their original data, Johanson and Vahlne explained that the existing market knowledge about a target country affects the entry mode decision, but subsequent current activities in these new foreign markets are essentially embedded in the firms' learning capabilities generated by the on-going internationalization (Carlson, 1974; Johanson & Vahlne, 1977).

In their model, they focused on an incremental and more elaborated intricate stimulus–response pattern between existing (often biased knowledge) and new knowledge evolving from learning by doing acquired in the current experiential practices carried out by the firm.

The elaborated dynamic in the Uppsala model is not simply a story of blunt resource committed to a chosen target, but reflects the notion that what matters is not the *stock of resources* but what is generated from the existing bundle of resources (Penrose, 1959). Firm success depends not only on the decision how to allocate resources, but how these resources are deployed in current activities. Johanson and Vahlne did not explain in detail how firms learn, but they did point at the dynamic and evolving nature of the process of incremental change.

Another important insight yielded by the Uppsala school is that internationalization is not the outcome of a single, isolated decision, but based on a series of elaborated successive interdependent and sequential commitment decisions.

These different versions adapted from the original Uppsala model signify how radically the international business context has changed over the last 40 years.

(continued)

Reading through these different adaptations, it should be noted that the Uppsala model was initially developed to explain the process of internationalization as an incremental and gradual one. Although the latest extension may need still some further elaboration, it is a focus that has been extended beyond the narrow boundaries of the international business firm.

Study Questions

1. Think about the essence of absolute and comparative cost advantages in early trade theories. Compare the two concepts and discuss how they explain the benefits of international trade.
2. How does Stephen Herbert Hymer define foreign direct investment?
3. Think about the concept of product life cycles and how it affects international trade.
4. Discuss the theory of the firm of Ronald Coase and describe how it fits into the theory of the multinational firm.
5. Discuss the difference and commonality of the theory of internationalization and transaction costs economics in international business.
6. Define the concept of process in Johanson and Vahlne's Theory of internationalization.

References

Alchian, A. A., & Demsetz, H. (1972). Production, information costs, and economic organization. *The American Economic Review, 62*(5), 777–795.

Almor, T., Hashai, N., & Hirsch, S. (2006). The product cycle revisited: Knowledge intensity and firm internationalization. *Management International Review, 46*(5), 507–528.

Andersson, U., Forsgren, M., & Holm, U. (2007). Balancing subsidiary influence in the federative MNC: A business network view. *Journal of International Business Studies, 38*(5), 802–818.

Archer, M. S. (1995). *Realist social theory*. Cambridge University Press. https://doi.org/10.1017/cbo9780511557675

Ariyawardana, A., & Collins, R. (2013). Balancing industry needs against global competitiveness: A challenge for the Australian vegetable industry. *Outlook on Agriculture, 42*(3), 155–161.

Asmussen, C., Pedersen, T., & Petersen, B. (2007). How do we capture "global specialization" when measuring firms' degree of globalization? *Management International Review, 47*(6), 791–813.

Atkins, K., Chen, J., Kumar, V. S. A., Macauley, M., & Marathe, A. (2009). Locational market power in network constrained markets. *Journal of Economic Behavior & Organization, 70*(1–2), 416–430.

Audretsch, D. B. (1983). A theory of multinational enterprise. By Jean-Francois Hennart. (Ann Arbor: The University of Michigan Press, 1982. xiv + 201 pp. $16.50.). *Business History Review, 57*(4), 575–576.

Aulakh, P. S., Jiang, M. S., & Pan, Y. (2010). International technology licensing: Monopoly rents, transaction costs and exclusive rights. *Journal of International Business Studies, 41*(4), 587–605.

Bain, J. S. (1956). *Barriers to new competition*. Harvard University Press. https://doi.org/10.4159/harvard.9780674188037

Barnard, C. I. (1938). *The function of the executive*. Harvard University Press.

Bello, D. C., & Kostova, T. (2012). From the editors: Conducting high impact international business research: The role of theory. *Journal of International Business Studies, 43*(6), 537–543.

Bhaskar, R. (1975). *A realist theory of science*. Leeds Books.

Birkinshaw, J., Hood, N., & Jonsson, S. (1998). Building firm-specific advantages in multinational corporations: The role of subsidiary initiative. *Strategic Management Journal, 19*(3), 221–242.

Borgatti, S. P., & Carboni, I. (2007). On measuring individual knowledge in organizations. *Organizational Research Methods, 10*(3), 449–462.

Borgatti, S. P., & Cross, R. (2003). A relational view of information seeking and learning in social networks. *Management Science, 49*(4), 432–445.

Braudel, F. (1986). *The perspective of the world: Civilization and capitalism*. 15th–18th Century (Vol. 3). Harper Collins.

Buckley, P. J. (2006). Stephen Hymer: Three phases, one approach? *International Business Review, 15*(2), 140–147.

Buckley, P. J. (2009a). The impact of the global factory on economic development. *Journal of World Business, 44*(2), 131–143.

Buckley, P. J. (2009b). Internalisation thinking: From the multinational enterprise to the global factory. *International Business Review, 18*(3), 224–235.

Buckley, P. J., & Casson, M. C. (1976). *The future of the multinational enterprise*. (25th Anniverary Edition). Palgrave Macmillan.

Buckley, P. J., & Casson, M. (2002). *The future of the multinational enterprise*. 25th Anniversary Edition. Palgrave Macmillan.

Buckley, P. J., & Casson, M. C. (2009). The internalisation theory of the multinational enterprise: A review of the progress of a research agenda after 30 years. *Journal of International Business Studies, 40*(9), 1563–1580.

Buckley, P. J., & Casson, M. (2010). *The multinational enterprise revisited. The essential Buckley and Casson* (pp. 177–204). Palgrave.

Buckley, P. J., & Casson, M. (2014). *The multinational enterprise and the emergence of the global factory* (pp. 20–51). Springer.

Burt, R. S. (2007). Secondhand brokerage: Evidence on the importance of local structure for managers, bankers, and analysts. *Academy of Management Journal, 50*(1), 119–148.

Calvo, C. W. (2020). *The emergence of capitalism in early America* (pp. 1–26). Springer.

Cantwell, J., Dunning, J., & Lundan, S. (2010). An evolutionary approach to understanding international business activity: The co-evolution of MNEs and the institutional environment. *Journal of International Business Studies, 41*, 567–586. https://doi.org/10.1057/jibs.2009.95

Carlson, S. (1974). International transmission of information and the business firm. *The Annals of the American Academy of Political and Social Science, 412*(1), 55–63.

Casson, M. (2013). Economic analysis of international supply chains: An internalization perspective. *Journal of Supply Chain Management, 49*(2), 8–13.

Casson, M., Dark, K., & Gulamhussen, M. A. (2009). Extending internalisation theory: From the multinational enterprise to the knowledge-based empire. *International Business Review, 18*(3), 236–256.

Cheng, L. (1984). International competition in R&D and technological leadership: An examination of the Posner-Hufbauer hypothesis. *Journal of International Economics, 17*(1–2), 15–40.
Child, J., Rodrigues, S. B., & Frynas, J. G. (2009). Psychic distance, its impact and coping modes. *Management International Review, 49*(2), 199–224.
Clougherty, J. A., & Skousen, B. R. (2019). The efficiency and market-power interpretations of the multinational enterprise: Two out of three ain't bad. *Global Strategy Journal, 11*(3), 356–379.
Clougherty, J. A., Kim, J. U., Skousen, B. R., & Szücs, F. (2016). The foundations of international business: Cross-border investment activity and the balance between market-power and efficiency effects: The foundations of international business. *Journal of Management Studies, 54*(3), 340–365.
Coase, R. (1937). The nature of the firm. *Economica, 4*(16), 386–405.
Coase, R. H. (1946). The marginal cost controversy. *Economica, 13*(51), 169–182. https://doi.org/10.2307/2549764
Coase, R. H. (1960). The problem of social cost. *The Journal of Law & Economics, 3*, 1–44. http://www.jstor.org/stable/724810
Cohen, W. M. (2005). *Essays in honor of Edwin Mansfield, the economics of R&D, innovation, and technological change* (pp. 217–231). Springer.
Contractor, F. J., Kumar, V., Kundu, S., & Pedersen, T. (2009). *Global outsourcing and offshoring* (pp. 3–47). Springer.
Coviello, N. (2015). Re-thinking research on born globals. *Journal of International Business Studies, 46*(1), 17–26.
Coviello, N., Kano, L., & Liesch, P. W. (2017). Adapting the Uppsala model to a modern world: Macro-context and microfoundations. *Journal of International Business Studies, 48*(9), 1151–1164.
Cross, R., & Borgatti, S. (2001). A social network view of organizational learning. *Academy of Management Proceedings, 2001*(1), 1–1.
Cyert, R. M., & March, J. G. (1963). *A behavioral theory of the firm*. Prentice Hall.
Davies, S. (1980). Minimum efficient size and seller concentration: An empirical problem. *The Journal of Industrial Economics, 28*(3), 287.
Dicken, P. (2017). *Global shift. Mapping the changing contours of the world economy*. Sage.
Dosi, G. (1992). *Recent developments in the theory of industrial organization* (pp. 34–57). Springer.
Dow, D. (1998). A note on psychological distance and export market selection. *Journal of International Marketing, 8*(1), 51–64.
Dunning, J. H. (1988). *Explaining international production (Routledge revivals)*. Routledge. https://doi.org/10.4324/9781315739250
Dunning, J. H. (1989). The study of international business: A plea for a more interdisciplinary approach. *Journal of International Business Studies, 20*(3), 411–436.
Dunning, J. (1995). *The globalization of business*. Routledge.
Dunning, J. H. (2006). When I met Hymer: Some personal recollections. *International Business Review, 15*(2), 115–123.
Dunning, J., & Lundan, M. S. (2008). *Multinational enterprises and the global economy*. Elgar Publishers.
Dunning, J. H., & Pitelis, C. N. (2008). Stephen Hymer's contribution to international business scholarship: An assessment and extension. *Journal of International Business Studies, 39*(1), 167–176. https://doi.org/10.1057/palgrave.jibs.8400328
Dzikowski, P. (2018). A bibliometric analysis of born global firms. *Journal of Business Research, 85*, 281–294.
Eaton, J., & Kortum, S. (2012). Putting Ricardo to work. *Journal of Economic Perspectives, 26*(2), 65–90.

Elia, S., Massini, S., & Narula, R. (2019). Disintegration, modularity and entry mode choice: Mirroring technical and organizational architectures in business functions offshoring. *Journal of Business Research, 103*, 417–431.

Evans, J., Mavondo, F. T., & Bridson, K. (2008). Psychic distance: Antecedents, retail strategy implications, and performance outcomes. *Journal of International Marketing, 16*(2), 32–63.

Feenstra, R. C. (1992). How costly is protectionism? *Journal of Economic Perspectives, 6*(3), 159–178.

Feenstra, R. C. (1998). Integration of trade and disintegration of production in the global economy. *Journal of Economic Perspectives, 12*(4), 31–50.

Fernandez-Stark, K., & Gereffi, G. (2019). *Global value chain analysis: A primer* (2nd ed.). Springer. https://doi.org/10.4337/9781788113779.00008

Fiocco, R., & Gilli, M. (2016). Bargaining and collusion in a regulatory relationship. *Journal of Economics, 117*(2), 93–116.

Fletcher, R. (2001). A holistic approach to internationalisation. *International Business Review, 10*(1), 25–49.

Forrester, J. W. (1976). Business structure, economic cycles, and national policy. *Futures, 8*(3), 195–214.

Forsgren, M. (2016). A note on the revisited Uppsala internationalization process model – The implications of business networks and entrepreneurship. *Journal of International Business Studies, 47*(9), 1135–1144.

Foss, N. (1999). Edith Penrose, economics and strategic management. *Contributions to Political Economy, 18*(1), 87–104.

Fransson, A., Håkanson, L., & Liesch, P. W. (2011). The underdetermined knowledge-based theory of the MNC. *Journal of International Business Studies, 42*(3), 427–435.

Frantz, R. S. (1988). *X-Efficiency: Theory, evidence and applications* (pp. 37–60). Springer.

Frantz, R. (2015). Antitrust and X-efficiency. *The Antitrust Bulletin, 60*(3), 221–230.

Freeman, S., Hutchings, K., Lazaris, M., & Zyngier, S. (2010). A model of rapid knowledge development: The smaller born-global firm. *International Business Review, 19*(1), 70–84.

Fröbel, F., Heinrichs, J., & Kreye, O. (1978). The world market for labor and the world market for industrial sites. *Journal of Economic Issues, 12*(4), 843–858.

Fröbel, F., Heinrichs, J., & Kreye, O. (1980). *The new international division of labour*. Cambridge University Press.

Galiani, S., Torrens, G., & Yanguas, M. L. (2014). *The Political Coase Theorem: Experimental evidence*. Working Paper 19943. National Buerau of Economic Research. https://doi.org/10.3386/w19943

Gaynulina, R. (2020). The revival of protectionism in the modern world: Case study of Uzbekistan. *Scientific Conference on Economics and Entrepreneurship Proceedings, 0*, 17–23.

Gehrke, C. (2015). Ricardo's discovery of comparative advantage revisited: A critique of Ruffin's account. *The European Journal of the History of Economic Thought, 22*(5), 791–817.

Gehrke, C., & Kurz, H. D. (2002). Keynes and Sraffa's "Difficulties with J. H. Hollander". *The European Journal of the History of Economic Thought, 9*(4), 644–671.

Gereffi, G. (2018a). *Global value chains and development*. Cambridge University Press. https://doi.org/10.1017/9781108559423

Gereffi, G. (2018b). *Global value chains and development* (pp. 343–380). Springer.

Ghoshal, S., & Moran, P. (1996). Bad for practice: A critique of the transaction cost theory. *Academy of Management Review, 21*(1), 13–47.

Graham, E. M. (2006). Comment on Peter J. Buckley: "Stephen Hymer: Three phases, one approach?". *International Business Review, 15*(2), 148–150.

Grindley, P. C., & Teece, D. J. (1997). Managing intellectual capital: Licensing and cross-licensing in semiconductors and electronics. *California Management Review, 39*(2), 8–41.

Gugler, K., Mueller, D. C., Yurtoglu, B. B., & Zulehner, C. (2003). The effects of mergers: An international comparison. *International Journal of Industrial Organization, 21*(5), 625–653.

Håkansson, H., & Snehota, I. (2006). No business is an island: The network concept of business strategy. *Scandinavian Journal of Management, 22*(3), 256–270.

Harris, G. (1995). Allocative inefficiency, X-inefficiency, bureaucracy and corruption in developing countries. *Journal of Interdisciplinary Economics, 6*(1), 55–79.

Helfat, C. E., & Peteraf, M. A. (2015). Managerial cognitive capabilities and the microfoundations of dynamic capabilities. *Strategic Management Journal, 36*(6), 831–850.

Helpman, E. (2006). Trade, FDI, and the organization of firms. *Journal of Economic Literature, 44*(3), 589630.

Hennart, J.-F. (1982). *A theory of multinational enterprise*. The University Of Michigan Press.

Hirsch, S. (1976). An international investment theory of the firm. *Oxford Economic Papers, 28*(2), 258–270.

Hirsch, S. (2009). The product cycle model of international trade. *Oxford Bulletin of Economics and Statistics, 37*(4), 305–317.

Hirsch, S., & Bijaoui, I. (1985). R&D intensity and export performance: A micro view. *Weltwirtschaftliches Archiv, 121*(2), 238–251.

Hodgson, G. M. (1998). Competence and contract in the theory of the firm 1 This article is dedicated to the memory of Edith Penrose. *Journal of Economic Behavior & Organization, 35*(2), 179–201.

Hodgson, G. M., & Knudsen, T. (2004). The firm as an interactor: Firms as vehicles for habits and routines. *Journal of Evolutionary Economics, 14*(3), 281–307.

Hoskisson, R. E., Hitt, M. A., Wan, W. P., & Yiu, D. (1999). Theory and research in strategic management: Swings of a pendulum. *Journal of Management, 25*(3), 417–456.

Hufbauer, G. C. (1966). *Synthetic materials and the theory of international trade*. Harvard University Press.

Hufbauer, G. C. (1976). *International trade and finance*. Springer. https://doi.org/10.1017/cbo9780511895685.007

Hufbauer, G. C. (2002). International economic law in times that are stressful. *Journal of International Economic Law, 5*(1), 3–16.

Hymer, S. (1970). *The efficiency (contradictions) of multinational corporations*. Springer. https://doi.org/10.2307/1815843

Hymer, S. H. (1976). *The international operations of national firms: A study of direct foreign investment*. The MIT Press.

Ietto-Gilles, G. (2005). *Transnational corporations and international production. Concepts, theories and effects*. Elgar Publishers.

Inkpen, A. C. (2004). Theories of the multinational enterprise: Diversity, complexity and relevance. *Advances in International Management, 2004*, 43–52.

Jaffe, J. F. (1975). The "Coase theorem": A reexamination—comment. *The Quarterly Journal of Economics, 89*(4), 660.

Jarvis, C., MacKenzie, S. B., & Podsakoff, P. M. (2010). A critical review of construct indicators and measurement model misspecification in marketing and consumer research. *Journal of Consumer Research*. https://doi.org/10.1086/376806

Jiang, M. S., Aulakh, P. S., & Pan, Y. (2007). The nature and determinants of exclusivity rights in international technology licensing. *Management International Review, 47*(6), 869–893.

Jin, J. L., Zhou, K. Z., & Wang, Y. (2016). Exploitation and exploration in international joint ventures: Moderating effects of partner control imbalance and product similarity. *Journal of International Marketing, 24*(4), 20–38.

Jin, B., Chung, J.-E., Yang, H., & Jeong, S. (2018). Entry market choices and post-entry growth patterns among born globals in consumer goods sectors. *International Marketing Review, 35*(6), 958–980.

Johanson, J., & Vahlne, J.-E. (1977). The internationalization process of the firm—A model of knowledge development and increasing foreign market commitments. *Journal of International Business Studies, 8*(1), 23–32.

Johanson, J., & Vahlne, J.-E. (2006). Commitment and opportunity development in the internationalization process: A note on the Uppsala internationalization process model. *Management International Review, 46*(2), 165–178.

Johanson, J., & Vahlne, J.-E. (2009). The Uppsala internationalization process model revisited: From liability of foreignness to liability of outsidership. *Journal of International Business Studies, 40*(9), 1411–1431.

Jones, M. V., & Coviello, N. E. (2005). Internationalisation: Conceptualising an entrepreneurial process of behaviour in time. *Journal of International Business Studies, 36*(3), 284–303.

Kaufer, E. (1980). *Industrieökonomik. Eine Einführung in die Wettbewerbstheorie*. Vahlen.

Kindleberger, C. P. (2002). Stephen Hymer and the multinational corporation. *Contributions to Political Economy, 21*(1), 5–7. https://doi.org/10.1093/cpe/21.1.5

Kirca, A. H., Hult, G. T. M., Deligonul, S., Perryy, M. Z., & Cavusgil, S. T. (2012). A multilevel examination of the drivers of firm multinationality. *Journal of Management, 38*(2), 502–530.

Klepper, S. (1996). Entry, exit, growth, and innovation over the product life cycle. *JSTOR, 86*(3), 562–583.

Klepper, S. (2017). *The new Palgrave dictionary of economics* (Vol. 1–8, pp. 5178–5179). Palgrave.

Klepper, S., & Simons, K. L. (2000). The making of an oligopoly: Firm survival and technological change in the evolution of the U.S. Tire industry. *Journal of Political Economy, 108*(4), 728–760.

Klepper, S., & Simons, K. L. (2005). Industry shakeouts and technological change. *International Journal of Industrial Organization, 23*(1–2), 23–43.

Knight, F. H. (1921). *Risk, uncertainty, and profit*. Hart, Schaffner & Marx, Houghton Mifflin Co.

Kogut, B., & Zander, U. (1993). Knowledge of the firm and the evolutionary theory of the multinational corporation. *Journal of International Business Studies, 24*(4), 625–645.

Kreps, D. (1988). *Notes on the theory of choice*. Routledge.

Kuivalainen, O., Sundqvist, S., & Servais, P. (2007). Firms' degree of born-globalness, international entrepreneurial orientation and export performance. *Journal of World Business, 42*(3), 253–267.

Kuznets, S. (1926). *Cyclical fluctuations: Retail and wholesale trade, United States, 1919–1925*. Adelphi. Retrieved from https://books.google.at/books?id=HPhaQwAACAAJ

Langlois, R. N. (2019). *The corporation is not a nexus of contracts: it's an iPhone*. Palgrave. https://doi.org/10.4337/9781785365003.00019

Lee, C., Lee, K., & Pennings, J. M. (2001). Internal capabilities, external networks, and performance: A study on technology-based ventures. *Strategic Management Journal, 22*(6–7), 615–640.

Leibenstein, H. (1966). Allocative efficiency vs. "X-Efficiency". *The American Economic Review, 53*(3), 392–415.

Lengnick-Hall, C. A., & Inocencio-Gray, J. L. (2013). Institutionalized organizational learning and strategic renewal. *Journal of Leadership & Organizational Studies, 20*(4), 420–435.

Levitt, T. (1965). Exploit the product life cycle. *Harvard Business Review, 43*(6), 81–94.

Lewin, K. (1952). *Field theory in social science: Selected theoretical papers by Kurt Lewin*. Tavistock.

Lewin, A. Y., & Volberda, H. W. (2011). Co-evolution of global sourcing: The need to understand the underlying mechanisms of firm-decisions to offshore. *International Business Review, 20*(3). https://doi.org/10.1016/j.ibusrev.2011.02.008

Lounsbury, M., & Beckman, C. M. (2015). Celebrating organization theory. *Journal of Management Studies, 52*(2), 288–308.

Low, B., & Johnston, W. (2012). Emergent technologies, network paradoxes, and incrementalism. *Journal of Business Research, 65*(6), 821–828.

Luostarinen, R. (1989). *Internationalization of the firm: An empirical study of the internationalization of firms with small and open domestic markets with special emphasis on lateral rigidity as a behavioral characteristic in strategic decision making*. Helsinki.

Maneschi, A. (2008). How would David Ricardo have taught the principle of comparative advantage? *Southern Economic Journal, 74*(4), 1167–1176. https://doi.org/10.1002/j.2325-8012.2008.tb00886.x

March, J. G. (1978). Bounded rationality, ambiguity, and the engineering of choice. *The Bell Journal of Economics, 9*(2), 587.

McManus, J. C. (1975). The cost of alternative economic organizations. *The Canadian Journal of Economics, 8*(3), 334–350.

Medema, S. G. (2020). The Coase theorem at sixty. *Journal of Economic Literature, 58*(4), 1045–1128.

Meschi, P.-X., & Wassmer, U. (2013). The effect of foreign partner network embeddedness on international joint venture failure: Evidence from European firms' investments in emerging economies. *International Business Review, 22*(4), 713–724.

Momaya, K. S. (2016). City clusters and break-out in corporate competitiveness: Patterns and perspectives focusing on innovation capabilities and India. *Competitiveness Review, 26*(4), 415–434.

Morschett, D., Schramm-Klein, H., & Swoboda, B. (2010). Decades of research on market entry modes: What do we really know about external antecedents of entry mode choice? *Journal of International Management, 16*(1), 60–77.

Mourtzis, D., & Doukas, M. (2020). *Additive manufacturing* (pp. 446–477). Springer.

Mousavi, S., & Gigerenzer, G. (2014). Risk, uncertainty, and heuristics. *Journal of Business Research, 67*(8). https://doi.org/10.1016/j.jbusres.2014.02.013

Nason, R. S., & Wiklund, J. (2018). An assessment of resource-based theorizing on firm growth and suggestions for the future. *Journal of Management, 44*(1), 32–60.

Nickles, T., Barker, P., Chen, X., & Andersen, H. (2002). *Kuhn on concepts and categorization* (pp. 212–245). Cambridge University Press.

Ortiz-Villajos, J. M., & Sotoca, S. (2018). Innovation and business survival: A long-term approach. *Research Policy, 47*(8), 1418–1436.

Parmigiani, A., & Rivera-Santos, M. (2011). Clearing a path through the Forest: A meta-review of interorganizational relationships. *Journal of Management, 37*(4), 1108–1136.

Penrose, E. T. (1959). *The theory of the growth of the firm*. Blackwell.

Perelman, M. (2011). Retrospectives: X-Efficiency. *Journal of Economic Perspectives, 25*(4), 211–222.

Pilon-Lé, L. (1980). Cohen, Robert B., et al. (eds.) «The Multinational Corporation : A Radical Approach », Papers by Stephen Herbert Hymer, 1979, Cambridge University Press, 323 p .Cohen, Robert B., et al. (eds.) «The Multinational Corporation : A Radical Approach », Papers by Stephen Herbert Hymer, 1979, Cambridge University Press, 323 p. *Études Internationales, 11*(3), 560–561.

Pitelis, C. N. (2002). Stephen Hymer: Life and the political economy of multinational corporate capital. *Contributions to Political Economy, 21*(1), 9–26.

Pitelis, C. (2006). Stephen Herbert Hymer and/on the (theory of the) MNE and international business. *International Business Review, 15*(2), 103–110.

Pitelis, C. (2007). Edith Penrose and a learning-based perspective on the MNE and OLI. *Management International Review, 47*(2), 207–219.
Pitelis, C., & Verbeke, A. (2007). Edith Penrose and the future of the multinational enterprise: New research directions. *Management International Review, 47*(2), 139–149.
Plant, A. (1932). Trends in business administration. *Economica, 35*, 45.
Podsakoff, P. M., MacKenzie, S. B., Lee, J.-Y., & Podsakoff, N. P. (2003). Common method biases in behavioral research: A critical review of the literature and recommended remedies. *Journal of Applied Psychology, 88*(5), 879–903.
Posner, M. V. (1961). International trade and technical change. *Oxford Economic Papers, 13*(3), 323–341.
Posner, R. A. (1993). Nobel Laureate: Ronald Coase and methodology. *Journal of Economic Perspectives, 7*(4), 195–210.
Puck, J. F., Holtbrügge, D., & Mohr, A. T. (2009). Beyond entry mode choice: Explaining the conversion of joint ventures into wholly owned subsidiaries in the People's Republic of China. *Journal of International Business Studies, 40*(3), 388–404.
Puranam, P., Stieglitz, N., Osman, M., & Pillutla, M. M. (2015). Modelling bounded rationality in organizations: Progress and prospects. *The Academy of Management Annals, 9*(1), 337–392.
Qiu, J., Donaldson, L., & Luo, B. (2012). The benefits of persisting with paradigms in organizational research. *Academy of Management Perspectives, 26*(1), 93–104.
Reddy, Y. V., & Naik, S. S. (2011). Determinants of Goan SME firms going global: Theoretical and empirical approach. *Vikalpa: The Journal for Decision Makers, 36*(2), 45–58.
Reeb, D., Sakakibara, M., & Mahmood, I. P. (2012). From the editors: Endogeneity in international business research. *Journal of International Business Studies, 43*(3), 211–218.
Reinert, K. A. (2021). *International economics. New perspectives on the world economy*. Cambridge University Press.
Reinert, K. A., Rajan, R. S., Glass, A. J., & Davis, L. S. (2009). The Princeton Encyclopedia of the world economy. (Two Volume Set). Princeton University Press. Accessed September 6, 2022.
Rennie, M. W. (1993). Born global. *The McKinsey Quarterly, 4*, 45–52.
Ricardo, D. (1817). *The works and correspondence of David Ricardo, Vol. 1 Principles of political economy and taxation*. Liberty Fund.
Richter, R., & Furubotn, E. G. (2010). *Neue Institutionenökonomik*. Mohr Siebeck.
Rowthorn, R. (2006). Stephen Hymer: An intellectual memoir. *International Business Review, 15*(2), 111–114.
Roza, M., den Bosch, F. A. J. V., & Volberda, H. W. (2011). Offshoring strategy: Motives, functions, locations, and governance modes of small, medium-sized and large firms. *International Business Review, 20*(3), 314–323.
Rugman, A. M., & Verbeke, A. (2003). Extending the theory of the multinational enterprise: Internalization and strategic management perspectives. *Journal of International Business Studies, 34*(2), 125–137.
Rugman, A. M., & Verbeke, A. (2004). A final word on Edith Penrose. *Journal of Management Studies, 41*(1), 205–217.
Sarasvathy, S. D. (2001). Causation and effectuation: Toward a theoretical shift from economic inevitability to entrepreneurial contingency. *The Academy of Management Review, 26*(2), 243. https://doi.org/10.2307/259121
Scherer, F. M. (1973). The determinants of industrial Plant sizes in six nations. *The Review of Economics and Statistics, 55*(2), 135.
Scherer, F. M. (1986). Mainstreams in industrial organization, Book I. Theory and international aspects. Book II. Policies: Antitrust, deregulation and industrial. In *Studies in industrial organization* (pp. 5–22). Springer.

Scherer, F. M. (2004). Edwin Mansfield: An appreciation. *The Journal of Technology Transfer, 30*(1–2), 3–9.

Scherer, F. M., Beckenstein, A., & Kaufer, A. (1975). *The economics of multiplant operations*. Harvard University Press.

Scott, P., & Ziebarth, N. (2015). The determinants of plant survival in the U.S. Radio Equipment Industry during the great depression. *The Journal of Economic History, 75*(4), 1097–1127.

Shaver, J. M. (2013). Do we really need more entry mode studies? *Journal of International Business Studies, 44*(1), 23–27.

Shen, W., & Shang, S. (2019). Tackling local protectionism in enforcing Foreign Arbitral Awards in China: An empirical study of the supreme people's court's review decisions, 1995–2015. *The China Quarterly, 241*, 144–168.

Shepherd, W. G. (2017). *The new Palgrave dictionary of economics* (Vol. 1–8, pp. 331–332). Palgrave.

Simon, H. (1991). Organizations and markets. *Journal of Economic Perspectives, 5*(2), 25–44.

Smirnov, A., Pashkin, M., Chilov, N., & Levashova, T. (2002). Moving into mass customization. *Information Systems and Management Principles, 2002*, 155–175.

Smith, A. (1976). *An inquiry into the nature and cause of the wealth of nations*. Oxford University Press. reprint Liberty Fund.

Sousa, C. M. P., Li, R. Y., & He, X. (2020). The impact of exploitation and exploration on export sales growth: The moderating role of domestic and international collaborations. *Journal of International Marketing, 28*(4), 1–20.

Sraffa, P., & Einaudi, L. (1930). An alleged correction of Ricardo. *The Quarterly Journal of Economics, 44*(3), 539.

Stead, H. (1976). The costs of technological innovation. *Research Policy, 5*(1), 2–9.

Strange, R., & Newton, J. (2006). Stephen Hymer and the externalization of production. *International Business Review, 15*(2), 180–193.

Tallman, S. (2004). Strategic management and the role of the MNC in a postindustrial world market. In M. A. Hitt & J. L. C. Cheng (Eds.), *Theories of the multinational enterprise: Diversity, complexity and relevance* (Advances in international management) (Vol. 16, pp. 53–64). Emerald Group Publishing Limited. https://doi.org/10.1016/S0747-7929(04)16004-6

Tarr, D. G. (1984). The minimum efficient size steel plant. *Atlantic Economic Journal, 12*(1), 122–122.

Teece, D. J. (1980). Economies of scope and the scope of the enterprise. *Journal of Economic Behavior & Organization, 1*(3), 223–247.

Teece, D. J. (1996). Firm organization, industrial structure, and technological innovation. *Journal of Economic Behavior & Organization, 31*(2), 193–224.

Uli, V. (2018). A co-evolutionary perspective on business processes. *Business Process Management Journal, 24*(3), 00–00.

Vahlne, J.-E., & Johanson, J. (2013). The Uppsala model on evolution of the multinational business enterprise – From internalization to coordination of networks. *International Marketing Review, 30*(3), 189–210.

Vahlne, J.-E., & Johanson, J. (2017). From internationalization to evolution: The Uppsala model at 40 years. *Journal of International Business Studies, 48*(9), 1087–1102.

Vahlne, J.-E., & Johanson, J. (2021). Coping with complexity by making trust an important dimension in governance and coordination. *International Business Review, 30*(2), 101798.

Vansteenkiste, M., & Sheldon, K. M. (2006). There's nothing more practical than a good theory: Integrating motivational interviewing and self-determination theory. *British Journal of Clinical Psychology, 45*(1), 63–82.

Verbeke, A., Coeurderoy, R., & Matt, T. (2018). The future of international business research on corporate globalization that never was.... *Journal of International Business Studies, 49*(9), 1101–1112.

Vernon, R. (1966). International investment and international trade in the product cycle. *The Quarterly Journal of Economics, 80*(2), 190–2917.

Vernon, R. (1976). Introduction. In *Japan's multinational enterprises* (pp. xv–xviii). Harvard University Press. https://doi.org/10.4159/harvard.9780674866393.intro

Volberda, H. W., & Lewin, A. Y. (2003). Co-evolutionary dynamics within and between firms: From evolution to co-evolution. *Journal of Management Studies, 40*(8), 2111 2136.

Welch, L. S. (2016). The emergence of a knowledge-based theory of internationalisation. *Prometheus, 33*(4), 1–14.

Welch, L. S., & Luostarinen, R. (1988). Internationalization: Evolution of a concept. *Journal of General Management, 14*(2), 34–55.

Welch, C., Nummela, N., & Liesch, P. (2016). The internationalization process model revisited: An agenda for future research. *Management International Review, 56*(6), 783–804.

Welch, L. S., Benito, G. R. G., & Petersen, B. (2018). *Foreign operation methods: Theory, analysis, strategy*. Edward Elgar.

Wernerfelt, B. (1984). A resource-based view of the firm. *Strategic Management Journal, 5*(2), 171–180.

Wernerfelt, B. (1995). The resource-based view of the firm: Ten years after. *Strategic Management Journal, 16*(3), 171–174.

White, L. J. (1971). *The automobile industry since 1945* (pp. 38–53). Springer.

Whittington, R. (2008). Alfred Chandler, founder of strategy: Lost tradition and renewed inspiration. *Business History Review, 82*(2), 267–277.

Williamson, O. E. (1979). Transaction-cost economics: The governance of contractual relations. *The Journal of Law and Economics, 22*(2), 233–261.

Williamson, O. E. (1985). *The economic institutions of capitalism*. Free Press.

Williamson, O. E. (1998). Transaction cost economics: How it works; where it is headed. *De Economist, 146*(1), 23–58.

Williamson, O. E. (2005). The economics of governance. *AEA Papers and Proceedings*.

Yli-Renko, H., Autio, E., & Sapienza, H. J. (2001). Social capital, knowledge acquisition, and knowledge exploitation in young technology-based firms. *Strategic Management Journal, 22*(6–7), 587–613.

Zander, I., McDougall-Covin, P., & Rose, E. L. (2015). Born globals and international business: Evolution of a field of research. *Journal of International Business Studies, 46*(1), 27–35.

Market Entry Decisions

4

4.1 Entry Mode Choice

The foreign market entry choice is one of the most important decisions for the internationalizing firm. It is a complex challenge, because entry mode decisions are characterized by high uncertainty arising from the unfamiliarity of foreign market environments. Firms can decide to internationalize for the first time or change the current scope of business, or add new markets when internationalizing.

Four Major Aspects of the Entry Mode Decision
Making an entry mode choice requires a deliberate decision regarding why, how, when, and where to internationalize. These four dimensions are major questions in international business. The "Why" encompasses the motives and strategic objectives guiding the intended internationalization. The "How" is related to the question of which entry mode is the most feasible in an unfamiliar business environment. What matters is to find the right moment in time to make an entry decision. The question of "when" refers to choosing the ideal entry time. In addition, a firm needs to select a proper location or locations for its international efforts ("where").

These four decisions cannot be made in a mechanistic way, but a quick and sustainable solution cannot be fabricated by applying an abstract models or recipe. Each of these four aspects affects the entry mode decision in the context of a firm's limited resources, which encompass limited managerial resources, the lack of information and knowledge, and frequently limited capabilities. The mere ownership of resources and capabilities will not suffice (Penrose, 1959; Pitelis, 2004). A firm need to exploit and explore its resources,

M. Fuchs, *International Management*,
https://doi.org/10.1007/978-3-662-65870-3_4

often by converting current routines learned in the past to fit a new, but unfamiliar environment (Chung et al., 2012; Coviello et al., 2017).

Often, all four dimensions are mixed with ill-defined goals, perhaps randomly generated from idiosyncratic experiences, multiplying the difficulty of an already complex decision-making process.

Entry mode strategies either emerge from ambiguous and poorly understood internal or external antecedents or are based on a set of well-designed and comprehensive goals. Further, firm behavior can be defined as a proactive or reactive response to these triggers. In addition, firms can be categorized how readily they respond, early or late, to an emerging opportunity to internationalize. These aspects and many more boil down to a decision-making process that is about seeking, selecting, and implementing an entry mode (Schmid, 2018; Zhou & Wu, 2014).

Overall, how management makes these decisions is poorly understood in international business (Fuchs & Horn, 2019; Maitland & Sammartino, 2015; Oliver & Roos, 2005). There are countless entry mode studies and many excellent reviews, each looking at important factors affecting the entry mode choice. These studies analyze how a selected set of factors affects the performance, pattern, time, and scope of internationalization. However, not much is known about the actual decision-making process, which has been a point of criticism in several studies (Aharoni & Brock, 2010; Aharoni et al., 2011; Devinney, 2011).

4.1.1 The Rational Decision Maker in Entry Mode Choices

A **decision maker is neither omniscient nor omnipotent** (Gigerenzer & Gaissmaier, 2011; Mousavi & Gigerenzer, 2017). Most of the time, managers lack information, are biased and face significant cognitive boundaries in making rational choices (Kahneman & Thaler, 2005; Kahneman & Tversky, 1996). Firms and managers making rational decisions face severe limitations. Preferences that guide these decisions are not stable, and the motifs and the values on which they are built change.

It is assumed that a rational manager generates a decision-making process to maximize profits. The behavior of rational agents is defined by their primary goal of maximizing expected utility. Maximizing is a proposition based on the theory of rational expectation. That theory assumes that agents (individuals, firms, organizations) make decisions based on the expectation that their choices will optimize the expected outcome (Benassy, 1992; Krugman & Wells, 2006). But expectations, optimization, choices, and values are not objective facts.

It is widely acknowledged that agents mostly have access to limited information about the range of alternative choices (Cristofaro, 2017; Puranam et al., 2015; Sent, 2005). Experiments have shown that individuals making choices are biased in how information is collected and used (Gigerenzer & Selten, 2002; Kahneman & Tversky, 1996; Mousavi & Gigerenzer, 2014). Part of being rational is to minimize the costs of collecting information, and agents stop sampling information if they become satisfied with the perceived output of this process.

Theories used in IB, such as internalization theory, transaction cost economics (Buckley et al., 2007; Hennart, 2007) or the OLI paradigm (Dunning, 1988) consider a choice rational if—despite the apparent lack of knowledge about the actual outcome—the best possible alternative is chosen among all the options available. Making a choice without knowing much about the outcome seems paradox, but remains a key proposition in rational choice.

The **conception of rationality** depends on rigorous assumptions that are never met in many real decision-making contexts. For instance, individual preferences are not stable, as they change over time. The perceived expectations about entry mode alternatives are often not based on objective facts but biased by past experience, easy access to information, and objectives are vaguely defined or ambiguous. At the time an entry mode decision is made, the final outcome is, in fact, unpredictable (Ellis, 2010; Ellis & Taylor, 2006; Knight, 1921; Mousavi & Gigerenzer, 2014).

IB research recognizes that only a "few [entry] strategies follow reasonable rules" (Buckley et al., 2007). In fact, it is acknowledged that management decisions are "apparently chaotic" and characterized as "trial-and-error processes" (Hutzschenreuter et al., 2007) or motivated less by its rationality than by a process of called "muddling-through" (Binmore & Samuelson, 1997; Forester, 1984; Lindblom, 1979; Makkonen et al., 2012; Schweizer, 2012).

4.1.2 A Descriptive or Prescriptive Approach

A decision-making process is analyzed using either descriptive or prescriptive theories. A descriptive theory about decision-making recounts what actually happens when making a decision. A prescriptive theory is based on a normative model that shows how an optimal decision should look. Normative theories rest on assumptions that abstract from 'noisy' day-to-day situational contexts in which any real decision is embedded (Damnjanović & Janković, 2014; Gold et al., 2011; Mellers, 2006).

Analyzing decision-making in an experimental setting in a laboratory attempts to mimic important elements of real decision-making processes, but does not replicate real day-to-day decision-making processes. These experiments test a small but essential piece of the whole process of decision-making. Manipulation of a single variable shows how it affects the behavior of agents making a decision, and thus it delivers valid proof of the effect analyzed in this setting but not beyond. The external validity of such experiments is low (March et al., 1991; Yan, 2014).

Normative theories argue that a rational choice is intentional, which is defined as a decision made to generate an expected outcome. From that, rational behavior is conceived as maximizing the expected value.

However, there is a problem: Many decisions do not lead to the expected outcome. There is a considerable time lag between action and consequence. Intentionality can cause several unexpected results (Brown, 1975).

Making a selection among available discrete alternatives is usually an easy choice, especially if the ready-made alternatives are lined up before you. The rational decision maker will choose the option with the greatest perceived utility. However, the problem is not making a choice from off-the-shelf ready-made options, but making a decision when the outcome cannot be predicted.

4.1.3 Uncertainty

Many, if not most, entry mode decisions are characterized by high uncertainty (Knight, 1921). In international business, uncertainty is a major problem in decision-making that needs to be addressed (Liesch et al., 2011). Uncertainty arises because of the lack of information about the actual outcome of a selected alternative. It refers to the fact that options branch out into unforeseen contingencies (North, 1990). A contingency is defined as something that might occur. It is an outcome that cannot be foreseen and is caused by a random or unexpected emerging events or exigencies which cannot be controlled.

In his reputed opus magnum, "Risk, Uncertainty and Profit," Frank H. Knight (1921: 231) defined uncertainty by its inherent ambiguity. He argued that uncertainty cannot reliably be discounted unless it is reduced to risk, which he claimed is not correct. In many situations, agents are confronted with uncertainties or risks. The major difference between uncertainty and risk is that the latter can be calculated. It is no great deal to compute the chance to win in a lottery. The outcome of a lottery can be precisely calculated, which is not the case with uncertainty.

Risk is defined as a situation in which the probabilities of the potential outcome are known. For instance, in a dice game, each player knows the probability of rolling a certain number. Each player also knows that with each roll, the probability of getting the number desired stays the same. However, with each throw, the probability can be specified exactly. Even if the chance is so small or almost meaningless, we can put it

(continued)

into a number. Risk is calculated by applying probability theory, but this method cannot convert uncertainty into tangible numbers, as Knight has alluded (Knight, 1921).

Converting uncertainty to risk is an impractical and inaccurate estimate. It can be done, but the result will not describe uncertainty (Mousavi & Gigerenzer, 2014).

Uncertainty is a different concept than risk. In a situation of uncertainty, the outcome is left open. In addition, we do not know, or have any accurate information, how many outcomes may evolve as a consequence of our actions. If we throw a die, the chance to get one out of six outcomes is the same for every single roll. If we repeat the rolls many times, we will inevitably see an even distribution of all possible options. However, we still do not know the outcome of a roll will be. We can throw a die six times and never roll the number we desire. However, we may roll the same number six times in a row. The results are randomly distributed and we cannot calculate the expected pattern from the past results. We can describe uncertainty as low or high, but we are still betting on a contingent, random event.

It is crucial to accept the fact that the entry mode decision is prone to uncertainty regarding the outcome of a selected entry mode because there are several contingencies that affect the outcome. But, the decision maker, which is uncertain about the contingency of upcoming (unforeseen) opportunities affecting the entry mode, can be prepared to react and adapt to the changing context. In many entry mode studies, a thorough differentiation between risk and uncertainty is left open. Remember, in cases of uncertainty, we can never be sure about the expected outcome.

However, accepting the significant impact of uncertainty in entry mode decisions, we do not deny deliberate decision-making. In contrast, deliberation is a pivotal property of human agency. In any decision processes that are constrained by uncertainty, we deliberately can decide what we do.

The major proposition is that entry mode decisions cannot be squeezed into a numerical calculation of risk in uncertain environments. Because the future is uncertain and the outcome of the selected prospects is contingent, a more dynamic and evolutionary approach to decision making is required in entry mode research. If we accept that proposition rather than the adhere to the orthodox meaning of rationality, then entry mode decisions become a very different challenge.

To avoid any misinterpretation, we are not proposing that management is not making a rational choice, but the framing of decision-making is totally different in the context of uncertainty.

Firms that are making entry mode decisions are confronted continuously with the need to adapt to an evolving environment. They may need to change intentions in pre-entry stages as they prepare to make the decision, they may alter their strategies after the decision has been implemented, or switch their objectives during later stages as they are forced to change, re-start or withdraw from pre-planned operations.

If an entry mode fails, the failure is partly related to a suboptimal entry mode choice, but it is equally a failure to miss the opportunity to change or adapt the selected entry mode. Firms need to be flexible in changing to other entry modes, switching between a mixture of modes, or withdrawing from selected target markets (Benito & Welch, 1993; Davis et al., 2000; Morschett et al., 2010; Welch et al., 2018).

A major proposition is that the actual outcome of a market entry mode decision is contingent and that the outcome will emerge in the future. The outcome of an entry mode is not decided at a single moment in a pre-entry stage but is evolving continuously along different post-entry stages and is affected by multiple contingencies.

It is crucial to acknowledge this to get a more realistic picture of entry mode choices and the process of internationalization (Coviello et al., 2017; Jones & Coviello, 2005).

The difference between uncertainty and risk is then that the decision maker can identify a loss. If the decision-making process allows management to identify losses, management can deliberately respond and change that situation by exploring alternatives that seem feasible to reduce the apparent loss. We need to keep in mind that risk refers to the capability to specify the probability of a loss (or gain), but the real challenge in decision-making emanates from an ambiguous world of contingencies to which we need to adapt. If we cannot calculate the probability of an outcome, it is better to refer to uncertainty. If a firm cannot expect whether a specific outcome is achieved by a specific action, the outcome is left open, or it is uncertain. The ambiguity and uncertainty in entry mode choices is important to understanding the sequential, gradual, or incremental nature of the process of internationalization.

4.1.3.1 Uncertainty and Sequential Nature of Entry Modes

Entry mode choices can be separated into several sequential stages. Making a choice before entry is more ambiguous than making a choice after entry. In each stage of this decision-making process, the decision maker has access to different levels of information (Fuchs & Horn, 2019). At each stage, the firm can experientially learn from the current activities, and the agent (firm or its management) can improve his or her knowledge and information about a decision already made and about the need for subsequent decisions (Hult et al., 2020).

However, not only is the agent changing but also the decision-making processes, which are characterized by an evolving relationship between the firm (referring to the qualities and properties of the decision maker) and external factors (the environment). Both the firm and the environment interact and are interdependent, and both are evolving and affecting each other (Gigerenzer & Selten, 2002; Luostarinen, 1989; Vuori & Vuori, 2014; Welch & Luostarinen, 1988).

Entry Mode Choice and Unfamiliarity

When firms make an entry mode choice in an unfamiliar international environment, they are confronted with a lack of knowledge and limited information about the expected outcome. Each stage in the decision-making process is highly contingent. Firms need to adapt to these contingent realities. A selection between a direct export and the establishment of a sales subsidiary can be made, for example, and a firm will try to make a decision that fits its current resources and meets its objectives in the target market (Chung et al., 2012; Uli, 2018). However, the firm does not have all the information on how each of these prevailing choices will develop, because the outcome is an evolving process. Internationalization is the *beginning of a journey*, a *journey* into an unfamiliar environment. Prior to making a choice, a firm is confronted with a biased picture of the environmental conditions. After entry, firms are forced to learn how to operate effectively in that environment (Welch et al., 2018).

The entry mode decision is not only a decision about why, how, when and where to enter a foreign market (Kutschker & Schmid, 2011); it is a decision to start an ongoing process, which will be a somewhat uncertain voyage into an unfamiliar territory (Sanchez-Peinado & Pla-Barber, 2006). It is the start of a complex and challenging tour in which firms will have the opportunity to learn, enact organizational routines, or change them (Lundan & Li, 2019; Pla-Barber et al., 2014). An entry mode choice is the beginning of a journey, and the success of the chosen entry mode depends on the capabilities and the scope of changes enacted. In managing these processes, firms require resources, often restrained by current activities, and the firm needs to make choices regarding how to divide limited resources between competing objectives (Fuchs, 2011; Fuchs & Köstner, 2015, 2016).

IB research has always been engrossed in the question of how to select the best entry mode, which is a frontier issue (Morschett et al., 2010; Shoham, 1999; Taylor et al., 2000). However, firms cannot resort to ready made tools in making their choices. Each entrant firm must focus on multiple challenges.

A firm is a diverse social body of different groups, variously engaged and contrarily concerned with making an entry mode decision, although all are affected but in many entry mode studies, only the management of the firm is the ultimate focal address of studying the process of decision-making.

In entry mode studies, every problem is narrowly defined as a managerial problem (Buckley et al., 2007; Devinney, 2011; Shoham, 1999). Managers are charged with selecting the right time, adapting to the external environment, dealing with uncertainty, designing and articulating goals and objectives and dealing with constraints.

Managerial Decision Making as a Co-evolving Process

Managerial decision making is defined as "a decision complicated by noisy, ambiguous information and high uncertainty", and "we know little about how managers make sense of foreign environments, and whether and how their perceptions and analyses affect internationalization decisions" (Maitland & Sammartino, 2015: 733). Management, we agree, is the focal point of many important decisions, but each decision made will be affected by how a firm frames, supports, understands, and implements decisions. A firm is as well a social entity (Cyert & March, 1963; Fligstein, 2001, 2018; Fligstein & White, 2003). A decision made at the top is supposed to trickle down to those who will put the decisions into practice. It is important to note that management is affected significantly by the "nature and character of the management process, including aspects such as control, coordination and staffing" (Welch et al., 2018). The paradox seems to be that, although management has been the focal point of decision- making studies for five decades, "Little is known about how managers actually choose "(Benito et al., 2009: 1467).

4.1.3.2 Contingency and Uncertainty

Entry into new foreign markets is complicated by a new, unfamiliar and difficult-to-control reality prevalent in a distant environment. Entrant firms need time to become acquainted with that unfamiliar environment (Kabongo & Okpara, 2019; Tuppura et al., 2008). During the process of adapting and operating in unfamiliar environments, firms seek to reduce or avoid uncertainty. As mentioned, uncertainty is one of the essential characteristics of entry mode choices. Uncertainty and risk are often mistakenly conflated. The momentous difference between the meaning and scope of uncertainty and risk is important. Uncertainty cannot be punched into a calculus of risk, no matter how hard we try.

Thus, making an entry mode decision is a sequential activity over time (Coviello et al., 2017; Forsgren, 2016; Vahlne & Johanson, 2013). Different periods are categorized in pre-, entry and post-entry stages. Each stage is characterized by unknown contingent opportunities. Once a selected entry mode is implemented, a consistent and well-prepared plan can become inappropriate. Firms then may stick to the original plan or stray from projected goals. Firms are not robotlike machines executing routine operations; they are social bodies capable of learning, adapting and changing their behaviors in a contingent and co-evolving environment (Brown & Duguid, 2001; Kogut & Zander, 1993; Taliman, 2003).

In strategy research, it is widely accepted that contingencies affect the performance and strategy-making process of organizations. However, the contingency approach is not undisputed (Drazin & de Ven, 1985). Common to all contingency concepts is the premise that the chosen strategy and structure need to have a good fit to achieve proper performance. Contingency is not only about a match between strategy and structure. It implicitly refers to emergent contingencies evolving over time. Firms need to change their strategies and subsequently implement changes in structure to continuously maintain this fit in evolving environments (Chung et al., 2012; Fry & Smith, 1987; Fuchs & Köstner, 2014; Hultman et al., 2009).

Contingency theory explains why a firm is changing its organizational structure as a response to a changing variable. A major assumption of contingency theory is that a misfit/fit significantly affects performance.

How organizations can productively react to changing contingencies determines their overall performance (Donaldson, 2001; Qiu et al., 2012). If the performance is low, the organization will ideally respond to this information to modify the structure. A trigger to change is that the organization needs to concede that the level of performance is low or unsatisfying (Donaldson, 2001). Alfred Chandler (1962) suggested that undiversified firms operating with a functional structure exhibit a greater fit than firms with diversified products; likewise, diversified firms with divisionalized structures operate with a greater fit than undiversified firms. Donaldson empirically showed that the cause-effect relationship on performance is significant (Donaldson, 1987).

Contingency approaches remind us that firms need to translate unsatisfying performance levels into a motivation for change. "Change is triggered by the feedback from the low performance caused by the misfit" (Donaldson, 2001: 13). The contingency approach is often interpreted ambiguously in organizational research. Contingency theory implies that there is not *one solution* to a misfit but several options for a resolution (Qiu et al., 2012). The interaction between structure, the efficiency of organizational processes and the environment is a core proposition (Langley et al., 2013; de Ven & Poole, 1995).

4.1.3.3 Misfit of Entry Modes

The argument that internationalization and entry mode decisions are part of a contingent and complex process leads to several important questions: How can a firm be capable of changing a clear misfit arising from a suboptimal entry mode choice? To answer this question, it is important to acknowledge the different stages that allow a firm to collect information about the performance of a previous action. An entry mode decision made and implemented produces information and feedback about how the entry mode operates in the foreign environment with a time lag (Fuchs & Horn, 2019).

Will the sequential nature of internationalization processes enable the firm to recognize the fit or misfit of a previously chosen entry mode? The answer depends on several factors affecting that problem.

Firms can react early or late to an ostensible misfit. How firms adjust, alter or retrace their steps to previous decisions is a key characteristic of entry mode choices. However, existing entry mode studies seem to deal with these questions indirectly by assuming that a higher control in a selected entry mode is simply better than less control.

4.2 Planning the Entry Mode Choice

The decision to enter a foreign market is typically assumed to be, but not always, a rational and well-prepared choice. Each choice is frequently constrained by a lack of time and a lack of resources. It is generally conceived that small- and medium-sized firms (SMEs) lack resources, especially international experience, and have limited personnel resources compared to large multinational firms (Hong, 2016; Javalgi et al., 2012; Khan et al., 2020; Schweizer, 2012; Williams, 2014).

It is a general assumption that a well-prepared choice is better than any ad hoc approach to internationalize. An entry mode choice is related to a well prepared organizational strategy of exploiting and exploring new and unfamiliar foreign markets. However, strategies (Chia & Holt, 2009) are not always the product of an intentional design (Mantere & Sillince, 2007), and entry mode choices can be rationally planned, the outcome of an emergent strategy, or simply follow a random or erratic decision (Benhabib & Day, 1981). Expanding into unfamiliar markets is without question a critical decision and consumes considerable firm resources (Brouthers & Hennart, 2007). Entry mode decision is a matter of designing a dynamic organizational structure capable to adapt routine operations to emerging contingencies unknown at the time of entry mode decision (Erramilli et al., 2002; Fuchs & Horn, 2019; Morschett et al., 2010; Puck et al., 2009; Shaver, 1998).

In addition, firms entering a foreign market need to exercise and maintain control (Anderson & Gatignon, 1986: 3). How much control a particular entry mode will allow after entry is difficult, if not impossible, to know prior to entry. But control is assumed a major antecedent to make a reasonable entry mode choice (Anderson & Gatignon, 1986; Blomstermo et al., 2006; Erramilli & Rao, 1993; Giachetti et al., 2019).

It is a major assumption that more unfamiliar markets require a greater degree of control (Beugelsdijk et al., 2014; Kogut & Singh, 1988; Maseland et al., 2018).

Entry Mode Choice

The **entry mode choice** literature largely assumes that **costs of control** in penetrating a foreign market can be managed by selecting the most appropriate entry mode (Brouthers, 2013; Elia et al., 2019a).

We fully agree with this assumption, but are less optimistic about determining the appropriate level of control. We need to acknowledge that at the time when an entry mode decision is made, firms do not have all the information they need to make quasi-optimal rational decisions, and they are forced to make decisions when vital information is not yet available (Fuchs & Horn, 2019; March, 1978, 1991). Many empirical studies show how complex and difficult entry mode decisions are. Even large multinational firms fail to select appropriate entry modes. But contrary to a small firm, they have access to much more resources and time to overcome inappropriate choices that cause considerable losses.

However, it is not only the cost of failure that matters but the fact that an unprepared and suboptimal entry into foreign markets consumes considerable resources.

Thus, textbooks and practical guides offer elaborate advice on how to enter a foreign market. Numerous guides claim to assist practitioners in addressing complex foreign market entries (Root, 1964, 1968, 1988). The genre of literature in IB intends to aid managers in making prudent and thoughtful entry decisions (Andersen & Strandskov, 1997; Brouthers et al., 2009a; Nowak, 1997; Papadopoulos & Martín, 2011; Sakarya et al., 2007). Most of these publications propose a structured approach to foreign market entry to escape the most obvious traps, which will be discussed in the following section.

4.2.1 Franklin Root and the Entry Strategy

Franklin Root's pioneering approach to "Entry Strategies for International Markets" advocates a strategy grounded in thoroughly planning several successive and interdependent stages (Root, 1994). Similar to other approaches, Root distinguishes between external and internal factors that affect entry mode decisions (Root, 1994; Welch & Luostarinen, 1988, 1990).

The relationship between internal and external effects and its impact on entry mode decisions, according to Root (1994: 9–15), is illustrated in Fig. 4.1. The figure shows that the market (size); environmental factors such as political, economic, and cultural characteristics of the target country; and location factors that affect production (i.e., labor costs and location specific assets) in the target market are related to each other. These three dimensions, combined with the home country characteristics (broadly defined at the same level as the target country factors) make up a set of influences that need to be considered when choosing a feasible entry mode. Factors existing in the home location that may affect the entry mode choice are the size and competitive structure of the home market (Luostarinen, 1989; Welch & Luostarinen, 1988). All four dimensions describe the environment of the firm that is intending to internationalize, and the size and several other factors will substantially affect the choices made by the firm that is motivated to expand internationally. However, each firm is characterized by firm-specific factors that differentiate it from other firms, and these idiosyncratic properties affect how it prepares and carries out an entry mode choice for a target market.

Firm-specific factors that can affect the entry mode decision are product-related qualities such as differentiated products (i.e., product loyalty and high quality), reputed brands and firm resources, or capabilities and commitment (management, capital, technologies, skills). Root implicitly describes the firm as a bundle of resources, including its products and services, similar to Penrose (1959). This is important because an entry strategy, considering the interdependence between external and internal factors demonstrates that an emerging strategy is a mixture of objective and subjective factors (Welch & Luostarinen, 1993; Wrona & Trąpczyński, 2012).

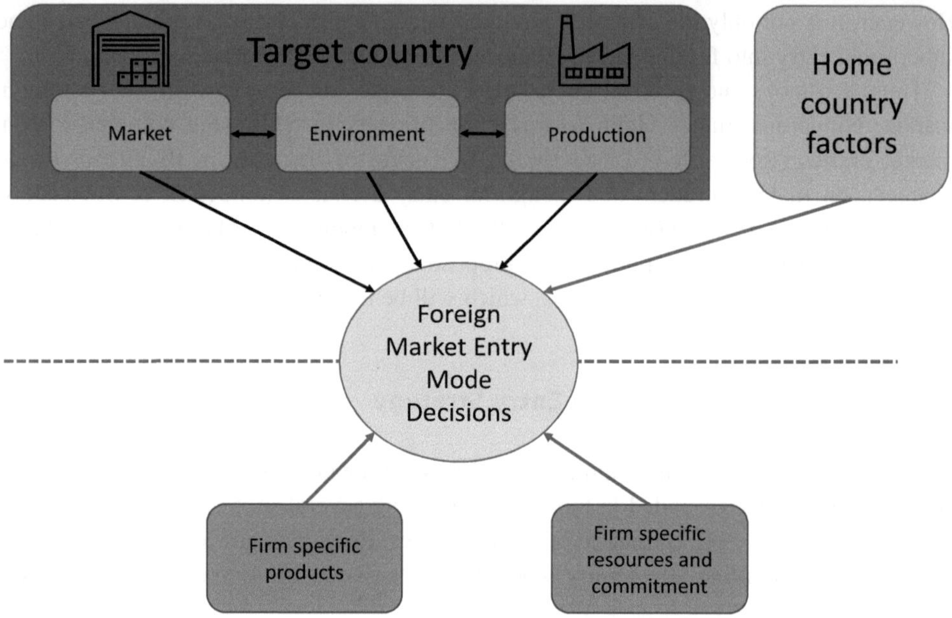

Fig. 4.1 Factors affecting entry mode choice (Root, 1994: 9)

Against the background of his conceptual approach, Root suggests five stages to prepare for an entry mode decision. At each stage (see Fig. 4.2),

1. the firm prepares to make a preliminary selection of the target market and what product to sell.
2. Next, it needs to specify the goals and objectives for the selected market.
3. With these two sets of information, a firm is ready to make a preliminary selection of which entry mode will fit best with the goals and objectives drafted in stages 1 and 2. Matching the entry mode with goals and objectives applies the proposed model of internal and external factors affecting that choice.
4. In the next stage, the firm needs to elaborate upon how it will approach the marketing for the selected product in the chosen market. The marketing approach will depend on existing operational routines and how a firm markets its product in the home market, but the key question will be how much these operational routines and habits need to be adapted to the new market selected. The firm will substantially depend on the availability of accurate information about the still unfamiliar and new market that it intends to enter but has no firsthand experience with.
5. In the final stage, the firm needs to operate a system of controls to monitor the performance.

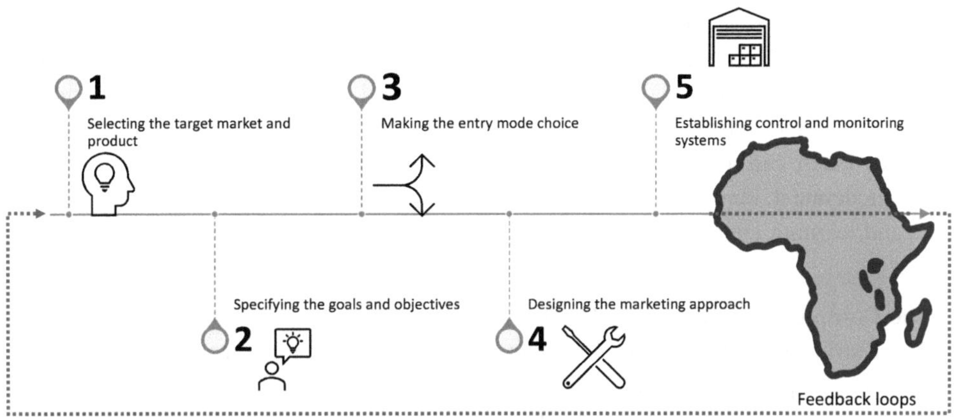

Fig. 4.2 A structured entry mode approach (Root, 1994: 219)

The quality of the outcome of that approach depends on the degree to which the information, resources and capabilities of the firm will fit into the newly selected market. Assuming that the fit will not be perfect during the early stages of internationalization, the question will be how capable the firm is in adapting its prevailing operational routines and resources to match the unfamiliar context in the target country or in dealing with contingencies in the new environment.

Overall, the model designed by Franklyn Root is a reference to early studies of internationalization (Johanson & Wiedersheim-Paul, 2007; Welch & Wiedersheim-Paul, 1979; Wiedersheim-Paul et al., 1978). Wiedersheim-Paul et al. (1978) demonstrated that internationalization and decision-making are sequential processes operating on two interdependent levels between internal aspects characterizing the firm and the external firm environment.

Root's contention is that preparing a sound plan requires a set of clear objectives wrapped in a consistent strategy to accomplish projected goals in the selected target markets. In addition, each preparation for an intended entry mode can lead to a new and more critical appraisal of existing products, services and firm routines and may start a process for a more objective assessment of current strengths and weaknesses in a firm (Dichtl et al., 1990).

An assessment may change an already rigid internal view of what is right and wrong, and it may initiate the perspective of how a decision-making process is affected by the past experience and value system that makes up the firm's context. This change, in turn, may raise the level of awareness and attention and provide input for entry mode choice (Wiedersheim-Paul et al., 1978). However, the implicit assumption of this approach is that a structured planning process can match existing strength and weaknesses in a firm with the most appropriate entry mode strategy. A choice that is made basically before actually accomplishing the entry.

However, the evocation of how these decision-making processes are triggered by internal (firm) and external (firm environmental) factors is moderated by the idiosyncratic character of the decision maker and the organizational culture of the firm, the industry environment, and other subjective interpretations of seemingly objective factors. An objective factor can affect a firm independent of how management perceives that factor or can moderate it, considering that the importance of gradual change, adaptation, commitment and learning are prone to subjective perception (Welch & Luostarinen, 1988).

The Complexity of Planning Market Entry Strategies

These structured approaches for an entry strategy do not automatically lead to sound analyzes of seemingly objective facts. Awareness of and attention to factors affecting the decision are highly subjective. Preparing a thorough analysis of how to achieve something and then "persevering, striving, paying with effort as we go, hanging on, and finally achieving our intention" are two very different things (Sarasvathy, 2001: 243).

Wiedersheim-Paul, Olson and Welch studied how an existing product portfolio shapes the goals and objectives of an entry mode strategy and how the propensity to internationalize depends on internationalization as a viable firm strategy (Wiedersheim-Paul et al., 1978). The study concludes that a product line requiring a small flow of information between the seller and buyer may lead to the choice to export. A more complex product line which depends on a more sophisticated information flow between the seller and buyer, caused by a high service content, requires a greater presence in the foreign market. Wiedersheim-Paul et al. have also been concerned with how the past experience of a firm and the perception of the distance between home and host markets (1978: 51) affects the export inclination. Thus, emphasizing a focus on the subjective attitudes and values of decision makers and how they perceive several influencing variables that affect their decision to internationalize. However, they categorize these perceptions as affecting the decision-making process on the one hand, and they consider these perceptions are one thing and that the implementation of specific measures is another, even though they are connected to each other.

Franklin Root's Approach

Root's structured approach to entry mode choice can be interpreted as follows: Additional information can be accumulated stage by stage in sequence. New information may trigger a re-evaluation of current measures, and the outcome of prior stages can be adjusted. However, there is no simple mechanism available that ensures

(continued)

incremental learning, change, commitment, and adaptive behaviors will occur automatically.

Since Root describes ideal decision-makers as the architects of a planned and structured strategy, he assumes an abstract model of the rational decision maker, which appears stripped of personal constraints and capabilities. To some extent, Root's approach treats the decision-maker as an agent capable of creating *ex ante* justifications to match the unfamiliar environment in the target market. His approach pretends rational and consistent decision making throughout all five stages but concedes that change and adaption may be required. He claims what matters is "the idea of planning [the] entry strategies" because "[o]nce management accepts that idea, it will find feasible means to design an international market entry, however limited company resources may be" (Root, 1994: 3). Root assumes a great flexibility in how firm resources can exploit prevailing competitive advantages in a new and unfamiliar environment. The above quote illuminates that the *intention to plan* is already assumed to matter for the expected outcome because Root argues that thorough planning triggers a more conscious response to how prevailing *resources may be allocated* among possibly conflicting goals. The overall message of that approach is that although any systematic planning can be imperfect and inconsistent, the mere effort to make a plan is preferable to no plan.

4.2.2 Way Station Model to Entry Mode Choices

Likewise, the so-called Way Station Model, an approach that has been developed from synthesizing and extending other approaches, explicitly assumes that a structured approach aids newly internationalizing firms in avoiding apparent difficulties in unfamiliar foreign markets (Yip et al., 2000). The name of the approach suggests that a well-prepared map for a route between pre-defined stations will enable firms to escape the greatest pitfalls of unsystematic and ad hoc approaches to entering foreign markets. The Way Station Model is not so different from Root's approach, but it is more concerned with how a firm exploits its initial advantages throughout the process of internationalizing and how it can gain new and additional competencies that will affect the overall performance of the entry approach.

The Way Station Model claims that many smaller firms tend to drop into new foreign markets relying on "unsystematic, ad hoc efforts", and the study argues that many ad hoc entries fail (Yip et al., 2000: 10).

Several approaches share this contention (Aharoni, 1966; Root, 1994). However, exactly how the structured approach is a trigger for success is still elusive.

The Way Station Model claims that the real problem of ad hoc market entries is that a firm does not know what it does not know (Yip et al., 2000: 10).

Not knowing what one does not know cannot be solved by searching for information (Bilkey & Tesar, 1977; Patterson et al., 1997). We agree with that argument, and the preparation of market entries logically makes sense only if the problems a firm will face in unfamiliar markets are known (Aharoni, 2010). But how a firm resolves not knowing remains mysterious. The Way Station model contends that small and inexperienced firms often have ambiguous motives or lack the motivation to internationalize (Yip et al., 2000: 10).

However, inexperienced firms also enter markets by exploiting ad hoc opportunities, tapping into unexpected market opportunities and encountering unforeseen contingencies (Cuervo-Cazurra et al., 2015). Thus, a lack of experience and ambiguous motivation are not sufficient to explain the failure to internationalize.

4.2.3 Choosing One Entry Mode or Combining Several Entry Modes

In a similar fashion, Root (1994: 159) devised three pragmatic rules regarding how firms develop entry strategies. Firms follow a *naïve rule* if they depend "only on one way to enter a market". They do not consider the heterogeneity of foreign markets and miss much of the growth potential in the market they enter by neglecting other entry options. Managers who stick to this naïve rule have a fairly narrow view of internationalization and are inflexible or unaware of the huge possibilities and differences in foreign markets. A firm depending on a naïve rule can be successful in its chosen entry mode as long as the selected market and firm resources are a decent fit, but their "long-term profitability" is limited (Root, 1994: 159).

Firms that follow a *pragmatic rule* choose low-risk entry modes, such as exports. Managers with no or little international experience will start internationalizing by choosing exporting as the most feasible entry; only if exporting is not a clear option for the firm it may search for other entry modes that might work. That pragmatic rule will minimize the risk of choosing an entry mode that does not fit the firm's resources and capabilities; however, after entry, these firms often cannot adapt the mode because of their belief that the chosen mode still works and delivers satisfactory performance. However, this contentment with the apparent performance is the problem of the pragmatic rule because firms do not search for better, more profitable entry modes. Firms applying the pragmatic rule stay away from riskier markets, miss more profitable opportunities and, may sacrifice the growth potential of the firm. Root claims that "the entry mode that works may not be the right entry mode" (Root, 1994: 160).

Root proposes as the *golden rule* what he calls the *strategy rule*. The strategy rule is more difficult than the pragmatic rule because it requires thorough analyzes of possible options and is based on a systematic evaluation of potential entry modes. The final outcome of applying the strategy rule is that the firm is able to generate an entry mode strategy that fits the external and internal factors affecting the entry mode choice. A firm applying the strategy rule systematically compares the "multiplicity of entry modes: the several variations in exports, contractual, and investment modes and the several combinations of these modes to form mixed modes" (Root, 1994: 161).

The strength of the strategy rule rests on exploiting the multiplicity of entry modes and the possibility of combining several entry modes in selected markets. The strategy rule accounts for multiplicity, heterogeneity, and dynamism of entry mode choice and emphasizes that *one entry mode* is probably not going to provide as good a fit in a target market as the *combination of several modes*. The entry mode decision is then not an either/or choice.

Root's structured approach to market entry is much more than how to develop an entry mode for a selected market but also how a firm can embrace a mix of entry modes for several selected markets. Reading Root's approach carefully, it becomes apparent that he does not talk about how a firm will find a single entry mode by comparing options but how the firm might find a mixture, a combination of workable entry modes. Although Root maintains that comparing the strengths and weaknesses of entry mode options is demanding and requires a sophisticated assessment by management, a selection of target markets and entry modes with high scores is seemingly the best choice for entry (Root, 1994: 159–163).

There is a wide range of entry mode options in international markets that "offer considerable scope [...] to fine tune the way [to] operate" and to allow firms to "flexibly [use] mode combination and stretching strategies" (Welch et al., 2018: 468).

This complex notion of endorsing a flexible combination of entry modes and thereby leveraging the means of exploring and exploiting international markets is often neglected in many entry mode studies.

4.3 Entry Mode Studies

Several excellent studies and reviews about entry mode choice provide fairly good insight into the scope and richness of this genre (Ahi et al., 2016, 2017; Aulakh & Kotabe, 1997; Canabal & White, 2008; Chen & Chang, 2011; Dow & Larimo, 2009; Elia et al., 2019b; Hennart & Slangen, 2015; Morschett et al., 2010; Nakos & Brouthers, 2002; Puck et al., 2009; Shaver, 2013; Zhao et al., 2017). A thorough and balanced review of all entry mode studies would be a valid contribution but seems difficult considering the number of existing studies.

Any selection based on core topics would still be extensive and tentative. Each choice will always remain a subjective and highly limited choice.

The overall **aim of entry mode studies**, being a part of strategy research, is how specific strategies (entry mode choices) "lead to superior performance", and the message is that a firm can increase its performance if selected entry modes demonstrate significant effect sizes. However, the choice of strategy is influenced by a number of endogenous factors (Shaver, 1998: 571).

Thus, we need to carefully interpret the results of entry mode studies because the measured effect can also be largely related to unobserved or unobservable variables not considered in the measurement model. It is important to clarify the underlying logic or argument on which the measurement model of assumed cause-effect relationships is based. Furthermore, it is also meaningful to know how the supposed cause-effect is measured and how the measurement is theoretically explained, that is, how it is grounded in sound theory. Note, it is one thing to observe a cause-effect relationship, and it is another to explain it.

Several meta-studies have focused on how external antecedents affect entry mode choice (Morschett et al., 2010). Other studies have tested what factors impact export performance or how the entry mode choice affects performance (Brouthers & Nakos, 2004; Brouthers et al., 2009b; Nakos & Brouthers, 2002).

Before we start to review a number of core entry mode studies, we need to look at the question of what is the focus of entry mode research. This question is not easily answered. For instance, Myles Shaver, an expert in entry mode research, provocatively asked, "Do we really need more entry mode studies?" (Shaver, 2013). The reply was "Yes, we really do need more entry mode studies" (Jean-Francois Hennart & Slangen, 2015).

Shaver criticized entry mode research narrowly focused on "playing the R^2", adding just another variable to the existing sets of factors, and he condemned the idea that most studies depend on large samples for "the sake of sampling" and that the measurement and the underlying conceptual arguments rely on restrictive assumptions or simply substitute one "set of assumptions for another [equally restrictive set] not progressing the field" (Shaver, 2013: 24–25).

However, he did not mean that we do not need any more entry mode studies, but future research should focus on how much "entry mode choices are interdependent". Further, he cautioned that we should not narrowly focus on what companies should or might be doing, but refine "our understanding of entry mode choice – especially if our underlying goal is to guide practice effectively" (Shaver, 2013: 25). His outlook for future research options is the real critique, indicating that we need more insights into what firm management can learn in making entry mode choices and that future research should focus more on the ongoing change in entry modes during the process of internationalization.

The articulated reply by Jean-Francois Hennart and Arjen Slangen does not support the harsh critique but does come to fairly similar conclusions. Hennart and Slangen suggest that entry mode studies still need to focus more on three aspects:

1. How do firms change suboptimal entry mode choices? What determines the evolution of foreign operations resulting from suboptimal choices?
2. What factors motivate multinational firms to replicate past entry mode choices?
3. What processes are structuring entry mode selection? (Hennart & Slangen, 2015: 114).

4.4 Institutional, Cultural and Transactional Costs Affecting Entry Mode Choice

Any particular effect of institutional, cultural or transaction costs on entry mode strategies is often not easy to separate from other effects. Rules, values and laws in a country are not independently developed from cultural patterns, and transaction costs are affected by the rules and institutional environment in a country.

In a seminal paper by Keith Brouthers entitled "Institutional, Cultural and Transaction Cost Influences on Entry Mode Choice and Performance" (Brouthers, 2002), several factors are tested to determine how they influence the entry mode choice. In this study, the author tested several hypotheses about the effects on entry mode choices and how the choice of entry mode affects performance. Brouthers (2002) postulated that firms perceiving high transaction costs in international markets choose wholly owned subsidiaries (WOS). Firms noticing low transaction costs tend to choose international joint ventures (IJVs). This assumed effect on the choice of an entry mode is extended by the assumption that firms with a high degree of firm-specific assets prefer WOS and those with low firm-specific assets choose IJVs. The study observed that firms chose WOS in markets with low restrictions and preferred IJVs in markets with high restrictions. Other factors were tested in that study, where the influence of high growth potential in selected markets and low risk affected the prevalence of WOS, while low growth and high risk favored IJVs (Brouthers, 2002: 207).

It seems obvious that the choice of an entry mode is affected by these five factors, as summarized in Table 4.1. However, a recap of the underlying argument of the cause-effect relationship is needed to answer the question of why firms perceiving high transaction costs choose a WOS. It is widely accepted that transaction costs impact the governance structure used to organize economic exchange relations. Each governance mode is related to varying costs of organizing activities. Remember, there are no zero transaction costs. The argument about transaction costs specifies that a firm's governance mode, the formal and informal system of relations, is dependent on the size and degree of possible alternative costs of market transactions for the same activity. Therefore, the argument is that if the perceived transaction costs are lower for a wholly owned subsidiary compared to other modes, a firm

Table 4.1 Factors affecting entry mode choice of WOS or IJV

Factors affecting the entry mode choice between WOS and IJV		
	High	Low
Transaction costs (perception)	WOS	IJV
Asset specificity (firm-specific assets)	WOS	IJV
Legal restrictions (in target country)	IJV	WOS
Market growth (potential)	WOS	IJV
Risk assessment (by the firm)	IJV	WOS

Source: Brouthers (2002: 203)

will choose the WOS. However, the original Coasean approach to transaction costs was based on marginal utility, and it was assumed that a firm would grow as long as additional activity organized within the firm generated a greater advantage than using the price mechanism in the market. Thus, transaction costs depend on the efficiency of firms organizing its several business activities applying different entry modes.

However, it is not only (a) the perception of transaction costs but also (b) the degree of asset specificity that affect transaction costs. It is a core assumption that the specificity of an activity affects the costs of transactions. High asset specificity increases the complexity of transactions (Williamson, 2002: 190). Transaction costs economics (TCE) assumes that agents have different risk aversion levels and that in-depth information sharing, which may reduce the effects of asset specificity, depends on the quality and strength of relational ties (ibid). In turn, asset specificity can lead to a negative effect in any relationship if one party is capable of acquiring more information than the other and exploits this asymmetry. Studies have found that high asset specificity is associated with a greater degree of integration (Erramilli & Rao, 1993). The argument is that high asset specificity increases the uncertainty in market transactions, and firms therefore tend to select entry modes with a high degree of ownership; this tendency is replicated in market environments with low property rights protection (Delios & Beamish, 1999).

Thus, transaction costs are affected by asset specificity, but the relationship is also affected by several other factors (i.e., the frequency of exchange and the degree of trust).

Thus, the argument about why transaction costs and asset specificity affect the performance and choice of an entry mode can be very different. For example, Brouthers (2002: 205) could not support the assumed effects of WOS preference in high asset specificity investments or for IJV preference in low asset specificity investments.

Another factor in entry mode studies influencing the entry mode choice is (c) the low restrictions in foreign markets (Brouthers, 2002; Delios & Beamish, 1999: 919). In markets with low legal restrictions related to entry modes, firms tend to prefer WOS; in markets with high legal restrictions, firms prefer IJV. However, firms with more international experience can compensate for the presumed disadvantages caused by host country unfamiliarity (Delios & Beamish, 1999: 920; Makino & Delios, 1996).

In addition, the entry mode is related to the perception of (d) risk. Brouthers (2002) argued that firms seeking to enter markets with low risks for investments choose WOS, while they prefer IJV in markets with high investment risks. Brouthers (2002: 213) did not find empirical support for WOS in low-risk environments but for IJV preference in high-risk environments.

Then, there is (e) the potential growth in the respective foreign markets to consider in choosing an entry mode. The underlying logic of the selection based on these factors is either WOS or IJV. In summarizing the implications, the study argues that the five factors (a to e) do "a good job" predicting the entry mode choice (Brouthers, 2002: 215). The findings of the study significantly support a, c, and d but not b and e.

The Problem of Measuring Transaction Costs

Keith D. Brouthers measured the *perception* of transaction costs using Likert scales asking how hard it was to find and negotiate with potential partners and how difficult it was to enforce contracts in the foreign market. Asset specificity was measured by R&D expenditures as a percentage of sales. Institutional context (legal restrictions) was measured by responses to the question, "Were there legal restrictions on the choice of entry mode at the time you entered?" (Brouthers, 2002: 211). The risk assessment was measured with four items, asking about how difficult it is to convert and repatriate profits, the risk of being 'nationalized', the degree of cultural similarity and the stability of the country.

The underlying logic of the effects on entry mode choice (Brouthers, 2013) is that the institutional environment, the perception of risk, and the firm-specific assets that determine transaction costs affect the entry mode choice. This popular and widely cited study was predated, followed, replicated, and extended by many other studies that tested these supposed relationships. In the *Journal of International Business Studies*, one of the leading forums, 482 articles are listed under the subject of entry modes and how they relate to transaction costs.

4.4.1 Lack of Knowledge About Feasible Markets and the Problem of Distance Measures

Firms preparing the entry mode decision-making can put much effort into collecting information about the target market in pre-entry stages, hoping to be better prepared, or they can plan to be prepared to learn in a new unfamiliar environment.

Many entry mode studies point to the lack the knowledge among firms as a severe impediment to successful internationalization (Wilkinson et al., 1980) and argue that superior firm-specific advantages can compensate for this shortcoming (Benito, 2015; Crick & Chaudhry, 1997; Cuervo-Cazurra & Narula, 2015).

However, the critical question here is, knowledge of what? Operational experience is generated by carrying out activities that are embedded to a large degree in organizational routines. Routine is the outcome of past learning and experiences. Firm-specific advantages have evolved and are the result of past and current organizational practices, and it can be difficult to transplant these embedded practices one-on-one into a different context. This problem is widely admitted.

Firms face multiple difficulties when entering a new and unfamiliar foreign market (Cuervo-Cazurra et al., 2007), especially how to transfer firm-specific advantages to foreign markets. Firms are confronted with major time lags when transferring tacit knowledge within the firm (Boisot, 2013; Child et al., 2014; Szulanski, 1996, 2000; Szulanski & Jensen, 2006).

Conventional approaches to a market entry decision separate the process of internationalization into stages. All these approaches assume that firm management can assess the internal potential for expanding abroad, and then management relies on a more or less adequate picture of the readiness to enter foreign markets. However, that assessment can be highly biased.

Many firms systematically analyze potential foreign markets and rely on several planning tools. A key assumption of planning can curb or at least reduce these perturbations and aberrations. Corporate readiness can be a highly abstract concept, although it is often not more than a crutch, but it remains a much used tool in finding the right entry mode choice (Slick, 2001). Collecting information about the assumed capability of a firm is different from analyzing how well firm capabilities will fit in an unknown environment.

The attractiveness of these approaches rests on the assumption that success is determined by the selection of an optimal entry mode (Brouthers, 2013; Erramilli, 1990; Erramilli et al., 2002). This assumption is firmly held as the rock-solid cornerstone of market entry decisions.

However, the degree to which the proposed entry strategy evolves after entry is less dependent on a pre-entry choice and more on how much the firm will be capable of flexibly adapting to emerging contingencies in the new foreign environment. Anderson and Gatignon (1986) recap the choice of an entry mode as the selection of a governance structure put into use operating the business abroad. Erramilli and Rao (1993) refer to the "choice of the correct entry mode [. . .] as one of the most critical decisions" (p. 19). Thus, the answer to the question 'What is a correct entry mode' lies in the problem of determining the most appropriate mode to control operations abroad (ibid: 20).

The Limits of Extensive Planning

Edith Penrose summarized these problems in the following quote: "Extensive planning requires co-operation of many individuals who have confidence in each other, and this, in general, requires knowledge of each other," and she continues to claim that "it follows, therefore, that if a firm is deliberately or inadvertently expanding its organization more rapidly than the individuals in the expanding organization can obtain the experience with each other and with the firm that is necessary for the effective operation of the group, the efficiency of the firm will suffer, even if optimum adjustments are made in the administrative structure; in extreme cases, this may lead to such disorganization that the firm will be unable to compete efficiently in the market with other firms, and a period of 'stagnation' may follow" (Penrose, 1959: 47).

Although a great majority of entry mode studies use transaction cost approaches (Morschett et al., 2010; Puck et al., 2009; Zhao et al., 2017), we know surprisingly little about actual decision making in real entry mode choices (Schellenberg et al., 2017), and we know even less about how firms adapt to the foreign environment after entry (Coviello et al., 2017; Fuchs & Horn, 2019).

4.4.2 Product Readiness

Two main questions concern management dealing with the intention to enter a foreign market: which product and which country to choose? Neither question has a simple answer. There are many internal (firm-specific) and external factors (domestic and foreign environment) that affect the outcome of this managerial decision-making process (Welch & Wiedersheim-Paul, 1979; Wiedersheim-Paul et al., 1978). The selection of a feasible product is fundamentally connected with the question of which country market may be appropriate. Both questions arise at the same time. Choosing a possible product is deeply related to the selection of a target country and vice versa. Firms prepare to make a decision by screening possible country markets. The purpose of provisional screening is preliminary. Management all too often commits too early on a set of countries, often due to personal biases. Screening for potential markets and opportunities narrows the number of possible countries. A set of potential markets, usually much smaller at the end of this screening procedure, will be more carefully explored. Choosing a market is motivated by the search for opportunities to expand abroad but often ignores the search for assets and resources needed to become more efficient (Cuervo-Cazurra et al., 2015; Dunning & Lundan, 2008).

A systematic entry mode choice focuses on the question of how much a product or service is 'ready' for the chosen market. Readiness may require adaptation. One of the key aspects of market entry strategies is the selection of the right product or service for the target country. The question is then boiled down to how much adaptation the product or service actually needs to be successful in the foreign market. Products can be categorized in terms of their differentiation. A high degree of product differentiation can be a source of competitive advantage. Product differentiation is a key feature in generating a unique selling position. Product differentiation can be based on an exclusive design of a product or a reputable brand name. Products are classified according to the required level of service support, both before, during and after the point of sale. These distinctions create additional expense and often a sophisticated distribution structure in a foreign market. Therefore, the question becomes what distribution channel fits the product in a foreign market. Products may require a considerable degree of adaptation after entry in a new foreign market that will affect all the properties of the product or service (Root, 1994: 45). Adaptation requires the allocation of additional resources and further effort and commitment.

One of the first discussions of the specificity of product features and how they might matter for internationalization was made by Paul-Wiedersheim, Hans Olson and Lawrence

C Welch. These authors referred to products, which go largely unchanged into the export and referred to the service-intensive proportion of products that often needed adaptation and incurred higher costs. The extent to which management devotes attention to these product-specific factors, along with other factors, is outlined as the driving force that affects awareness and export orientation (Wiedersheim-Paul et al., 1978).

Levitt on Globalization

Levitt (1983) argued in the early 1990s that globalization will contribute to an increasingly homogeneous world. Although his prudent description of the global economy is still doubted, at that time, it was a great and influential debate. Levitt was convinced and convinced many others that tastes will become more similar and cultural differences less meaningful, preparing the ground and markets for making it necessary to design global products. Although there are a few strong and exceptionally global brands and products, more than ever, international firms need to adapt to different cultural, social, political and economic contexts and differentiate products for various customer segments in multiple countries across the globe. However, Levitt strongly believed in global products and the "Globalization of Markets". The result, he argued, "is a new commercial reality—the emergence of global markets for standardized consumer products on a previously unimagined scale of magnitude. Corporations geared to this new reality benefit from enormous economies of scale in production, distribution, marketing, and management. By translating these benefits into reduced world prices, they can decimate competitors that still live in the disabling grip of old assumptions about how the world works" (Levitt, 1983: 92).

Subsequently, the extant literature has focused on globalization as one of the core drivers of the convergence of income, products, consumer preferences, media and cultural patterns (Boczkowski et al., 2011; Czinkota & Ronkainen, 1989). However, international consumer research increasingly questioned the validity of this so-called convergence thesis (de Mooij, 2000, 2013, 2015). The widespread appeal of the convergence that came with the advent of globalization caused almost a euphoric appeal for global products and product standardization. However, multinational firms soon learned a more balanced view and became concerned about how to balance business activities between forces that ask for standardization and other drivers that require a greater local responsiveness (Segal-Horn, 1996).

Practitioners follow all-too-often routine approaches and are accustomed to replicating what has been done in the past. They rely on habitual routines and past experiences. Many decisions are embedded in these organizational routines and are carried out without much awareness as long as no severe crises arise. Changing routines is less common or difficult (Kano & Verbeke, 2015; Whittington, 2008). This is another reason why decision makers often assume that they intuitively know what to do, thus using gut feelings to make a final decision. Many of them are confronted day after day with a complex and uncertain reality, which is highly reduced and filtered by existing habits. A new reality is perceived only selectively and distortedly. Practitioners are not used to reflecting much about how to interpret something new; they are accustomed to solving daily problems, reacting immediately, and making decisions without spending much effort on in-depth analyzes. Indeed, it is one thing to make a reasonable choice about the mode of entry and then to enact this entry mode, to shape changes, to implement modifications and to analyze these changes and dig into the factors that affect adaptation. Each decision made implies allocating scarce resources, mobilizing extra commitment, and often motivating staff to put extra effort into matching the additional workload produced by internationalizing.

Firms mostly accommodate current operations and resources, capabilities and people to take on the workload of growing abroad and slowly and gradually acquire additional resources to complement these efforts. Most often, management is aware of many of these implications and can respond to existing constraints but often negates and defers necessary decisions to act upon these challenges (Cohen et al., 1972; Takanobu, 2015).

Therefore, the question remains how much a systematic and rational approach to entry mode choice is really a *rational* approach, considering a firm's limited resources and constraints as it enters a new, unfamiliar and complex, ever-changing environment. Many firms suffer because of ambiguous and poorly defined problems that must be dealt with; they are prone to having incomplete information about possible alternatives and the potential consequences of the chosen mode of entry, and they suffer from fairly limited knowledge of their preferences, values and interests (Forester, 1984: 24).

Welch et al. (2018) explicitly emphasize that the entry mode and foreign operation mode or method are not the same. The key point of their argument is that there is an elementary difference between the decision to select a market entry mode and the capability of the firm to manage a successful operation in a foreign market (Welch et al., 2018).

Often, practitioners make market selection decisions in a biased way, driven by images about fantastic opportunities. They design their ad hoc strategies with arbitrary perceptions about potential sales. Very often, the psychological and physical distance to the foreign market is underestimated. The lack of language proficiency and miscommunication caused by differences in cultural values are frequently underestimated. Selective perception coupled with the adverse effects of hubris and insistence on the importance of one's own beliefs can lead to serious mistakes in decision making (Gigerenzer, 1996; Kahneman & Tversky, 1996).

4.4.3 Assessing Risks with PESTEL

Firms can apply approaches to become acquainted with an unfamiliar foreign environment using models such as PESTEL. PESTEL is the acronym for political, economic, social, technological, environmental and legal dimensions that are used to categorize and analyze the impact of a macro-environmental framework for a country that a firm seeks to enter. The output of the analyzes is used to find an entry mode that is capable of dealing with the proposed potential risk and uncertainty in a given target market (Balasopoulou et al., 2016; Ghotge et al., 2020; Marinović-Matović & Arsić, 2020; Schomaker & Sitter, 2020; Thakur, 2021; Wu, 2020).

Calculating the risk using the different categories offers a practical tool to evaluate the probability of success or failure. The analyzes are used to keep firms from choosing supposedly risky environments. However, the overall goal of a Pestel analysis is to identify the environment in which the company is capable of operating. Importantly, all the analyzes are carried out ex ante. It is used to reduce a broad selection of targets to a few feasible country markets. However, the Pestel model assumes that the results of the analyzes enable the firm to deal with the identified risks. Factors describing potential risks are a mixture of objective and subjective data. Political stability can be high or low, and institutional infrastructure that affects the protection of investments can be highly complex and difficult to grasp. The outcome of these approaches can provide the firm with a general impression about how several markets can be compared, but it does not account for emerging contingencies that will surface later in a risky or non-risky environment or for any missed opportunity by not entering a risky market or losing growth generated because a firm decides to choose a more convenient or less risky target.

4.4.4 Maximizing Profits and the Rational Entry Mode Choice

All approaches that are developed to help firms prepare and plan for a sound entry mode assume that more information, motivation, commitment, resources and a concrete strategy are better than any ad hoc market entry. All these approaches assume that firm management is rational, aiming to maximize profits and to choose entry strategies that will result in better performance. A core assumption is that management is capable of identifying those factors that affect the performance of the firm. Theory and entry mode studies are straightforward in that respect. Entry mode choice is supposed to maximize expected profits using those entry modes that offer the best revenue options minus the cost of operating (governance) and the cost of production. Welch, Benito and Petersen provide a simple formalized equation (Welch et al., 2018: 31)

$$(S) : R(S) - [c(S) + g(S)]$$

S is the entry mode, R is the revenue, c is the cost of production of S, and g is the cost of the governance of the chosen entry mode. Assuming all the information for a particular entry mode choice is available, the formalization offers a clear cut and precise statement of how the entry mode is related to the income it generates. Taking this information about the generated income, the cost of operating the entry mode and producing the products and services is a transparent statement about potential profits and how to calculate them. Note, firms are assumed to choose those modes of entry that maximize expected profits, denoted as

$$\max E\left[(\mathrm{S})\right]$$

Firms will choose those entry modes that maximize expected profit E(S). Welch et al. assumed that firms select exports (arm's length trade) or use another firm, making a contract about sharing the profits or costs of trading, and a firm may decide to make a foreign direct investment (FDI) by establishing a subsidiary and directly selling the product in the foreign market. FDI is held as the entry mode that maximizes the profit options compared to other entry modes (exporting and contracting). What follows is obvious, and the expected rational decisions will be based on the following calculation (Welch et al., 2018: 31):

$$R\left(S_{(FDI)}\right) > \left[R\left(S_{export}\right), R\left(S_{contract}\right)\right]$$

Therefore, if all the assumptions are correct, then it is reasonable and understandable that a firm would choose FDI as entry mode if the earnings are greater than the earnings for alternative entry modes, for example in exporting or choosing a contract. Every rational agent would follow the calculation to make a sound entry mode decision.

The major objection is that many firms do not have information about the actual costs of a chosen entry mode option; they rarely calculate exactly the governance costs, and the expected profit cannot be traced back in detail to the respective entry mode choice. There are problems in cost accounting and the fact that investments are made during different time periods that generate profits (or losses) much later and earnings can be the outcome of unobserved residual effects.

4.4.5 Managerial Experience and Export Orientation

Early empirical research identified factors that separated exporting from non-exporting firms and aimed to explain how a firm is blocked from initiating exporting (Luostarinen, 1989; Welch & Luostarinen, 1988). In general, studies have identified a lack of language proficiency and qualified personnel as impediments in non-exporting firms (Dichtl et al., 1990). All these impediments seem to be linked with the presence or absence of an overall export inclination in the management of these firms. One insight of these early empirical studies on exporting was that although firms did have some export potential, they were unaware of the benefits of exporting.

Importantly, this research was specifically embedded in a postwar context and therefore concentrated on factors that assisted non-exporting firms in starting to export (Dichtl et al., 1990: 26). Not unexpectedly, researchers assumed that the management of non-exporters was less experienced; being on average older, with a lower educational level and lacking language proficiency. Additionally, non-exporting firm management was characterized as "risk averse, [more] rigid and unwilling to change" compared to exporters (Dichtl et al., 1990).

Wiedersheim-Paul et al. (1978) characterized the influences on internationalizing decision-makers in firms on two levels. On one level, the authors isolated the influence by analyzing how the manager's personal characteristics affected his or her perceptions. Specifically, they argued that the manager's value system and the experiences he or she had in the past influenced behavior substantially. Analyzing this effect, the authors concentrated on actual information seeking, information acquisition, and how these activities were assessed by management (1978: 48). They identified information seeking as an activity that is rated as nonexistent, low, medium, or high in their firm sample.

The key question in their study was how firms started an export activity. The authors identified several key variables that affected firms starting to export. The three dimensions—the decision-maker, the firm environment, and the firm—are interdependent; that is, each dimension is affected by the two others. The argument is simple but important. A decision-maker is affected by his or her environment, which can either produce pressure to internationalize or may generate information that does not require a change. The firm, although embedded in the same environment, is characterized by a set of factors such as knowledge, resources, and culture. Information generated by the environment depends on the capability of the firm's sensitivity to acknowledge this noise. The decision-maker can block, maintain, or nurture this sensitivity. The outcome of this interdependent and mutual context produced what the authors coined as "attention-evoking" factors. The central message is that the awareness produced by early pre-export information activities initiates or promotes the start of an export activity ((Wiedersheim-Paul et al., 1978).

4.4.6 Motives to Internationalize

Consequently, many models implicitly assumed that "systematic market entry decisions" would overcome most if not all of these impediments and facilitate internationalization as a top priority. Motives are coined differently as "Readiness to Export" (Miller & Weigel, 1972) or "International Readiness" (Tan & Sousa, 2018). Generally, motives are conceptualized as important triggers to enable the firm to successfully manage its internationalizing (Cuervo-Cazurra et al., 2015; Hennart et al., 2019). It seems obvious that every action is driven by motives (Anscombe, 2016). A motive or motivation is defined as a cause for doing something. The motive or motivation is the driver for a specific action. The behavior is a means to a motive, defined as the primary impact on human behavior. Motives can operate at a conscious or unconscious level. However, we are not fully aware to what degree a mélange of motivation controls or regulates our behavior. In economics, humans are described as a robotlike homo economicus, who act rational when seeking to maximize utility. The sources and drivers of personal preferences are somewhat an anathema. In that context, the literature differentiates 'right' from 'false' motivation (Baz, 2016).

The management of a firm may perceive a foreign market as an option to grow or sustain its viability and competitive position. However, it may be largely unaware of the underlying motives. Often, motives are mixed with an intended outcome (growth or increasing sales). The manager may experience a strong motivation to enter a promising target market, but the direct link between the motivation as a driver and the expected outcome is often left open. Thus, a firm can be motivated to grow by increasing sales abroad, with the intention of increasing its profitability.

The extent literature observes a variety of reasons that attract companies to foreign markets (Benito, 2015; Crick & Chaudhry, 1997). Motives are recognized as the impetus that stimulates companies to start or intensify business activities abroad. Studies in IB have classified these motives into four categories. Early research termed these factors "initiating and auxiliary forces" (Aharoni, 1966), others coined the phrase "triggering cues" (Wiedersheim-Paul et al., 1978), and later literature focused on "antecedents" (Kim & Hemmert, 2016).

All these motivational aspects can be separated between "push" and "pull" forces but are not explicitly called motives—more often, they are called catalysts that initiate internationalization. Although there is no clear definition, 'pull' factors imply a much more active behavior, while 'push' factors may indicate a less active character; both terms are transitive verbs, indicating that something is at play here.

The separation and simultaneously unclear delineation between the two "effects" is echoed in a wide range of internationalization frameworks (Andersen & Strandskov, 1997; Calabretta et al., 2017; Erramilli, 1990; Erramilli et al., 2002; Erramilli & D'Souza, 1993; Johanson & Vahlne, 1977).

In the literature, motives are metaphorically summarized as "sell more, buy better, upgrade and escape" (Cuervo-Cazurra et al., 2015). The essence of these studies is recapitulated in a pointed way. Drivers and motives focus on four major triggers for internationalizing: (1) *sell more*, which is based on exploiting more efficiently existing resources; (2) *buying better* is characterized as "exploit existing resources and avoid poor" home market locations, to look for better opportunities abroad; (3) *upgrading* is defined as the exploration of "new resources in better host country" locations; and (4) *escaping* is used to describe activities seeking to "explore new resources and avoid poor home country conditions" (Cuervo-Cazurra et al., 2015: 26). All four drivers are related to a particular weakness diagnosed in the home market. In all four motives, seeking a better opportunity abroad is predominant.

The lines drawn along how each classification of motive is set up can be questioned, but the study tried to summarize existing literature more systematically. The authors' synopsis is based on a review of earlier research on motives to internationalize. The categorization of the apparent drivers to internationalize includes the intent to scale, focusing on the commercialization (exploiting) of existing assets and products, the search for a better (more efficient) position, and the accomplishment of better access to new resources, markets, and assets (Behrman, 1982). For example, Dunning categorized motives as resource seeking, market seeking, efficiency seeking and asset seeking (Dunning, 1993).

Although these motives are repeated in many studies and used in surveys frequently, they seem to be more the objectives or strategic goals of internationalization and less the underlying motive.

4.4.7 The Pattern and Scope of Internationalization

What empirical research in general shares is the recognition that "entry into and operation in overseas markets is not easily achieved" (Katsikeas & Leonidou, 2000: 122). Other studies point to the complex difficulty of selecting an appropriate entry mode (Erramilli et al., 2002). Early research focused on the problem that firms lack the knowledge and experience to enter markets (Johanson & Vahlne, 1977). One focus is to explain the decision-making process as a problem of sampling, collecting and processing information about unfamiliar and uncertain foreign markets. In addition, the lack of information and knowledge, although still important, was equally treated as a problem of managerial cognition, and firms were scrutinized as to how management approached, perceived and treated available information (Andersen & Strandskov, 1997; Calabretta et al., 2017; Inkpen & Crossan, 1995; Maitland & Sammartino, 2015). Activities such as exporting are actually considered by many firms as an attractive economic activity for several reasons: companies can make better use of idle production facilities and improve overall production and existing technology, quality and service standards, strengthen sources of competitiveness; expand the profit base; create funds for new investments and growth; and diversify business risk by enabling companies to be active in multiple markets (Leonidou et al., 2010).

The important question, however, is how are these objectives carried out successfully? In addressing such a question, it is particularly interesting to look at studies in the extant literature that have identified a cause-effect relationship between the scope and pattern of internationalization and firm performance (Glaum & Oesterle, 2007; Kahiya & Dean, 2014; Lu & Beamish, 2001; Mol et al., 2005; Nguyen & Kim, 2020; Zhou & Wu, 2014).

4.4.8 Liability of Foreignness

Firms entering a new foreign market are confronted by the liability of foreignness (Gorostidi-Martinez & Zhao, 2017; Nachum et al., 2008; Nachum & Zaheer, 2005). These firms need to learn to navigate in a new and unfamiliar environment. Most, if not all, firms are forced to change habitual perceptions and routine practices that have worked well in home markets. Firms that increase the scope of international exposure are confronted with additional and unexpected costs caused by the liability of foreignness (Hymer, 1976). In addition, the firm's management often underestimates the additional costs imposed by the different cultural and regulatory frameworks in the potential host countries. Not surprisingly, early internationalization was characterized by its expansion into familiar and neighboring foreign markets in many firms, a feasible strategy to keep risks low and unforeseen costs down. Thus it is argued that the liability of foreignness is increasing proportionally with the geographical, cultural, and/or institutional distance. The simple truth is that the greater the distance between the home and host country, the more difficult and complex foreign market entry.

Stephen Hymer defined the concept of liability of foreignness (LOF) as the disadvantages of foreignness. Although not defined in detail by Hymer, the primary notion was in the early 1970s that enhanced control exercised by the internationalizing firm is keeping LOF lower. The increasing unfamiliarity in foreign markets causes LOF. The general unfamiliarity abroad highly correlates with the degree of uncertainty resulting from host economies' unique legal and institutional environments (Luo & Mezias, 2002). However, as a concept that can be precisely measured, LOF remains ambiguous. The multiple sources of LOF seem to be responsible for the difficulty of operationalizing LOF. For example, lack of knowledge can be a source of LOF, an obvious disadvantage for the newly internationalizing firm. However, the lack of knowledge is caused by multiple dimensions (limited resources, biased information, and inability to deal with the foreign environmental rules and laws). But this lack of knowledge vanishes if the firm is capable of learning in these new environments. Then, LOF is associated with the higher (expected) transaction costs arising from foreign expansion. For example, is information asymmetry the outcome or cause of LOF?

Liabilities of foreignness are defined as additional costs that nonresident firms face when operating abroad. Four types of costs can be identified: (1) costs directly related to the geographical distance between home and host location; (2) costs caused by the unfamiliar country environment; (3) costs incurred for the foreign firm from nationalistic economic policies and the lack of legitimacy; and (4) risks due to sales compliance rules enforced by the home country (Mezias, 2002; Zaheer, 1995).

However, the question is not only how companies learn during internationalization, a central topic in IB research (Coviello, 2015; Madsen & Servais, 1997; Zander et al., 2015), but also how new knowledge is created on the basis of pre-existing knowledge, how it corresponds with it, and how this existing stock of knowledge is replaced. The core idea of "Born Globals" is that these companies operate successfully in international markets at early stages (Autio, 2005; Oviatt & McDougall, 2005; Zahra, 2005). The major assumption is that early internationalizers do something substantially different, but what? What are the effects of early internationalization? Do these firms have access to different and more international experiences? Do they have access to a different and more valuable network of social ties? Is their learning rate better?

The management of an internationalizing firm must not only decide how to enter a market but also ensure that the chosen market entry is feasible. The extent to which a selected entry mode works in a new and unknown market environment depends on several factors. Some of these factors are discussed below. However, the focus is on a discussion and presentation on the specific advantages and disadvantages of the particular market entry modes. Whether an individual market entry mode creates a specific fit with the actual environment after the initial market entry also strongly depends on the extent to which a company is capable of adapting itself to the existing environment and to what extent a chosen market entry mode is adjusted to the existing environment in the course of time.

The actual selection of an appealing and promising foreign market is supposed to be a conscious decision, although this may not always hold true. Once a company has chosen a foreign market, a key decision that is often complex, particularly for companies internationalizing for the first time, is to decide which mode of market entry to adopt. In principle, a company has several alternatives at its disposal, differing in terms of the chosen product and the chosen target market and the requirements that arise from them. From the outset, however, there is one notion that is all too common: companies make a market entry mode decision under uncertainty, but by and large, they make a rational decision. They choose a possible form of market entry, which they believe is viable from past experience and can be implemented. It should be kept in mind that in principle, it is possible to compare all alternatives, to evaluate advantages and disadvantages, and to evaluate one's own resources, but this decision is not an either-or decision, a decision for an export venture versus a joint venture, or a decision for a joint venture versus a wholly owned subsidiary. It is a decision that depends on a number of known and unknown premises, decisions that are at times made on the basis of existing biases, or false information. At other times, a decision must be made quickly, even though it might have been wise to have waited longer to make it.

Not accidentally, researchers criticize that entry mode decisions are myopic, often erratic; others refer to the decision process as 'muddling through', while others refer to it as 'trial and error'. All these references demonstrate that decision making itself is an ongoing process and not simply a matter of rationality.

Choices are generated before actual market entry. When carrying out market entry, a continuous process is set in motion in which the entry mode, once chosen, has to demonstrate its feasibility in a contingent environment. After actual market entry, the true nature of a previous decision becomes apparent slowly, and the feedback gradually allows firms to identify how wise the initial market entry decision was and how it will work in the future.

(continued)

Thus, for now, we should be modest about the question of the "right market entry decision", for it refers to a complex and demanding upfront choice. New entrant firms may not have access to information that enables them to know whether their initial choice was right or wrong. Moreover, they will have to tackle the cost of suboptimal choices that were made long before they entered the market. They will painfully realize how often their decisions were based on idiosyncratic biases. Many practitioners will have to learn during the internationalization process that decisions not only grow out of normative and prescriptive decision theory but also emerge from contingent environments.

Furthermore, let us not forget that the human actors, managers, are not making decisions in a vacuum but deliberate choices on their own embedded in a social reality, a composite mixture of a past, a present and a future reality.

It is reasonable to plan market entry in a systematic and structured way and not to take every opportunity head over heels. However, it is equally important to recognize that any structured and systematic plan will have its limits, limitations that exist due to the finite cognitive abilities of the actors. Boundaries are also imposed by the limited information given to the decision makers. Additional limitations are placed on large and small firms that lack resources, and management is never omniscient or omnipotent. However, knowing the cognitive limits and human weaknesses makes principals adaptable and capable of learning, some more than others.

Study Questions

1. How does uncertainty and the sequential nature of the process of internationalization affect entry mode choices?
2. Think about the concept of rationality in the process of decision making and describe how the different concepts of rationality affect the entry mode choice.
3. Describe the five stages of planning in the process of entry mode choice.
4. How do transaction costs affect the choice of entry modes?
5. How does the concept of distance determine an optimal entry mode choice?
6. Think about the difference between uncertainty and risk. How does uncertainty relate to the process of internationalization?

References

Aharoni, Y. (1966). *Foreign investment decision profess.* Harvard Business School Press.

Aharoni, Y. (2010). *Foreign direct investments from emerging markets* (pp. 37–60). OECD.

Aharoni, Y., & Brock, D. M. (2010). 50 years of IB research: What have we achieved, and what have we not yet achieved? *Journal of International Management, 16*(1), 3–4.

Aharoni, Y., Tihanyi, L., & Connelly, B. L. (2011). Managerial decision-making in international business: A forty-five-year retrospective. *Journal of World Business, 46*(2), 135–142.

Ahi, A., Baronchelli, G., Kuivalainen, O., & Piantoni, M. (2016). International market entry: How do SMEs make decisions? *Journal of International Marketing, 25*(1), 1–21.

Ahi, A., Baronchelli, G., Kuivalainen, O., & Piantoni, M. (2017). International market entry: How do small and medium-sized enterprises make decisions? *Journal of International Marketing, 25*(1), 1–21.

Andersen, P. H., & Strandskov, J. (1997). International market selection. *Journal of Global Marketing, 11*(3), 65–84.

Anderson, E., & Gatignon, H. (1986). Modes of foreign entry: A transaction cost analysis and propositions. *Journal of International Business Studies, 17*(3), 1–26.

Anscombe, G. E. M. (2016). Truth, sense and assertion. *Philosophy, 91*(1), 3–14.

Aulakh, P. S., & Kotabe, M. (1997). Antecedents and performance implications of channel integration in foreign markets. *Journal of International Business Studies, 28*(1), 145–175.

Autio, E. (2005). Creative tension: The significance of Ben Oviatt's and Patricia McDougall's article 'toward a theory of international new ventures'. *Journal of International Business Studies, 36*(1), 9–19.

Balasopoulou, A., Latsou, D., Kousoulakou, H., Michael, N., Kenzie, D. M., et al. (2016). The use of PESTEL as a change management tool to inform change management of polypharmacy and adherence within SIMPATHY program. *International Journal of Integrated Care, 16*(6), 52.

Baz, A. (2016). Motivational indeterminacy: Motivational indeterminacy. *European Journal of Philosophy, 25*(2), 336–357.

Behrman, J. N. (1982). *The role of international companies in Latin America: Autos and petrochemicals*. Lexington Books.

Benassy, J.-P. (1992). Are rational expectations really rational? *Economics Letters, 40*(1), 125.

Benhabib, J., & Day, R. H. (1981). Rational choice and erratic behaviour. *The Review of Economic Studies, 48*(3), 459–471.

Benito, G. R. G. (2015). Why and how motives (still) matter. *The Multinational Business Review, 23*(1), 15–24.

Benito, G., & Welch, L. S. (1993). Foreign market servicing: Beyond choice of entry mode. *Journal of International Marketing, 2*(2), 7–27.

Benito, G. R., Petersen, B., & Welch, L. S. (2009). Towards more realistic conceptualisations of foreign operation modes. *Journal of International Business Studies, 40*(9), 1455–1470.

Beugelsdijk, S., Maseland, R., Onrust, M., van Hoorn, A., & Slangen, A. (2014). Cultural distance in international business and management: From mean-based to variance-based measures. *The International Journal of Human Resource Management, 26*(2), 165–191.

Bilkey, W., & Tesar, G. (1977). *The export behavior of smaller-sized Wisconsin manufacturing firms*. Springer. https://doi.org/10.2307/254403

Binmore, K., & Samuelson, L. (1997). Muddling through: Noisy equilibrium selection. *Journal of Economic Theory, 74*(2), 235–265.

Blomstermo, A., Sharma, D. D., & Sallis, J. (2006). Choice of foreign market entry mode in service firms. *International Marketing Review, 23*(2), 211–229.

Boczkowski, P. J., Mitchelstein, E., & Walter, M. (2011). Convergence across divergence: Understanding the gap in the online news choices of journalists and consumers in Western Europe and Latin America. *Communication Research, 38*(3), 376–396.

Boisot, M. (2013). *Information space (RLE: Organizations)* (pp. 445–462). Routledge.

Brouthers, K. D. (2002). Institutional, cultural and transaction cost influences on entry mode choice and performance. *Journal of International Business Studies, 33*(2), 203–221.

Brouthers, K. D. (2013). A retrospective on: Institutional, cultural and transaction cost influences on entry mode choice and performance. *Journal of International Business Studies, 44*(1), 14–22.

Brouthers, K. D., & Hennart, J.-F. (2007). Boundaries of the firm: Insights from international entry mode research. *Journal of Management, 33*(3), 395–425.

Brouthers, K. D., & Nakos, G. (2004). SME entry mode choice and performance: A transaction cost perspective. *Entrepreneurship Theory and Practice, 28*(3), 229–247.

Brouthers, L. E., Mukhopadhyay, S., Wilkinson, T. J., & Brouthers, K. D. (2009a). International market selection and subsidiary performance: A neural network approach. *Journal of World Business, 44*(3), 262–273.

Brouthers, L. E., Nakos, G., Hadjimarcou, J., & Brouthers, K. D. (2009b). Key factors for successful export performance for small firms. *Journal of International Marketing, 17*(3), 21–38.

Brown, M. B. (1975). The asymptotic standard errors of some estimates of uncertainty in the two-way contingency table. *Psychometrika, 40*(3), 291–296.

Brown, J., & Duguid, P. (2001). Knowledge and organization: A social-practice perspective. *Organization Science, 12*(2), 198–213.

Buckley, P. J., Devinney, T. M., & Louviere, J. J. (2007). Do managers behave the way theory suggests? A choice-theoretic examination of foreign direct investment location decision-making. *Journal of International Business Studies, 38*(7), 1069–1094.

Calabretta, G., Gemser, G., & Wijnberg, N. M. (2017). The interplay between intuition and rationality in strategic decision making: A paradox perspective. *Organization Studies, 38*(3–4), 365–401.

Canabal, A., & White, G. O. (2008). Entry mode research: Past and future. *International Business Review, 17*(3), 267–284.

Chandler, A. (1962). *Strategy and structure. Chapter in the history of the industrial enterprise*. MIT Press.

Chen, M.-Y., & Chang, J.-Y. (2011). The choice of foreign market entry mode: An analysis of the dynamic probit model. *Economic Modelling, 28*(1–2), 439–450.

Chia, R. C. H., & Holt, R. (2009). *Strategy without design*. Cambridge University Press. https://doi.org/10.1017/cbo9780511642234.001

Child, J., Ihrig, M., & Merali, Y. (2014). Organization as information – A space odyssey. *Organization Studies, 35*(6), 801–824.

Chung, H. F. L., Wang, C. L., & Huang, P. (2012). A contingency approach to international marketing strategy and decision-making structure among exporting firms. *International Marketing Review, 29*(1), 54–87.

Cohen, M. D., March, J. G., & Olsen, J. P. (1972). A garbage can model of organizational choice. *Administrative Science Quarterly, 17*(1), 1.

Coviello, N. (2015). Re-thinking research on born globals. *Journal of International Business Studies, 46*(1), 17–26.

Coviello, N., Kano, L., & Liesch, P. W. (2017). Adapting the Uppsala model to a modern world: Macro-context and microfoundations. *Journal of International Business Studies, 48*(9), 1151–1164.

Crick, D., & Chaudhry, S. (1997). Small businesses' motives: For exporting the effect of internationalization. *Journal of Marketing Practice: Applied Marketing Science, 3*(3), 156–170.

Cristofaro, M. (2017). Herbert Simon's bounded rationality. *Journal of Management History, 23*(2), 170–190.

Cuervo-Cazurra, A., & Narula, R. (2015). A set of motives to unite them all? Revisiting the principles and typology of internationalization motives. *The Multinational Business Review, 23*(1), 2–14.

Cuervo-Cazurra, A., Maloney, M., & Manrakhan, S. (2007). Causes of the difficulties in internationalization. *Journal of International Business Studies, 38*, 709–725. https://doi.org/10.1057/palgrave.jibs.8400295

Cuervo-Cazurra, A., Narula, R., & Un, C. A. (2015). Internationalization motives: Sell more, buy better, upgrade and escape. *Multinational Business Review, 23*(1), 25–35. https://doi.org/10.1108/MBR-02-2015-0009

Cyert, R. M., & March, J. G. (1963). *A behavioral theory of the firm*. Prentice Hall.

Czinkota, M., & Ronkainen, I. (1989). Global business linkages. *Journal of Business Research, 18*(3), 268.

Damnjanović, K., & Janković, I. (2014). Normative and descriptive theories of decision making under risk. *Theoria Beograd, 57*(4), 25–50.

Davis, P. S., Desai, A. B., & Francis, J. D. (2000). Mode of international entry: An isomorphism perspective. *Journal of International Business Studies, 31*(2), 239–258.

de Mooij, M. (2000). *International advertising: Realities and myths* (pp. 77–102). Sage.

de Mooij, M. (2013). On the misuse and misinterpretation of dimensions of national culture. *International Marketing Review, 30*(3), 253–261.

de Mooij, M. (2015). Convergence and divergence in consumer behaviour: Implications for global advertising. *International Journal of Advertising, 22*(2), 183–202.

de Ven, A. H. V., & Poole, M. S. (1995). Explaining development and change in organizations. *Academy of Management Review, 20*(3), 510–540.

Delios, A., & Beamish, P. W. (1999). Ownership strategy of Japanese firms: Transactional, institutional, and experience influences. *Strategic Management Journal, 20*(10), 915–933.

Devinney, T. M. (2011). *Bringing managers' decision models into FDI research* (p. 15). Emerald Publishing Group.

Dichtl, E., Koeglmayr, H.-G., & Mueller, S. (1990). International orientation as a precondition for export success. *Journal of International Business Studies, 21*(1), 23–40.

Donaldson, L. (1987). Strategy and Structural adjustment to regain fit and performance: In defence of contingency theory. *Journal of Management Studies, 24*(1), 1–24.

Donaldson, L. (2001). *The contingency theory of organizations*. Sage.

Dow, D., & Larimo, J. (2009). Challenging the conceptualization and measurement of distance and international experience in entry mode choice research. *Journal of International Marketing, 17*(2), 74–98.

Drazin, R., & de Ven, A. H. (1985). Alternative forms of fit in contingency theory. *Administrative Science Quarterly, 30*(4), 514.

Dunning, J. H. (1988). *Explaining international production (Routledge Revivals)* (1st ed.). Routledge. https://doi.org/10.4324/9781315739250

Dunning, J. H. (1993). *Multinational enterprise and the global economy*. Addison-Wesley.

Dunning, J., & Lundan, S. M. (2008). *Multinational enterprises and the global economy*. Edward Elgar Publisher. https://doi.org/10.18356/43ce1fe7-en

Elia, S., Larsen, M. M., & Piscitello, L. (2019a). Entry mode deviation: A behavioral approach to internalization theory. *Journal of International Business Studies, 50*(8), 1359–1371.

Elia, S., Massini, S., & Narula, R. (2019b). Disintegration, modularity and entry mode choice: Mirroring technical and organizational architectures in business functions offshoring. *Journal of Business Research, 103*, 417–431.

Ellis, P. D. (2010). Is market orientation affected by the size and diversity of customer networks? *Management International Review, 50*(3), 325–345. https://doi.org/10.1007/s11575-010-0037-0

Ellis, V., & Taylor, P. (2006). 'You don't know what you've got till it's gone': Re-contextualising the origins development and impact of the call centre. *New Technology Work and Employment, 21*(2), 107–122. https://doi.org/10.1111/j.1468-005X.2006.00167.x

Erramilli, M. K. (1990). Entry mode choice in service industries. *International Marketing Review, 7*, 5. https://doi.org/10.1108/eum0000000001535

Erramilli, M. K., & D'Souza, D. E. (1993). Venturing into foreign markets: The case of the small service firm. *Entrepreneurship Theory and Practice, 17*(4), 29–41.

Erramilli, M. K., & Rao, C. P. (1993). Service firms' international entry-mode choice: A modified transaction-cost analysis approach. *Journal of Marketing, 57*(3), 19–38.

Erramilli, M., Agarwal, S., & Dev, C. (2002). Choice between non-equity entry modes: An organizational capability perspective. *Journal of International Business Studies, 33*(2), 223–242.

Fligstein, N. (2001). Social skill and the theory of fields. *Sociological Theory, 19*(2), 105–125.

Fligstein, N. (2018). *The architecture of markets* (pp. 223–238). Springer.

Fligstein, N., & White, H. C. (2003). Markets from networks: Socioeconomic models of production. *Contemporary Sociology, 32*(6), 673.

Forester, J. (1984). Bounded rationality and the politics of muddling through. *Public Administration Review, 44*(1), 23.

Forsgren, M. (2016). A note on the revisited Uppsala internationalization process model – The implications of business networks and entrepreneurship. *Journal of International Business Studies, 47*(9), 1135–1144.

Fry, L. W., & Smith, D. A. (1987). Congruence, contingency, and theory building. *Academy of Management Review, 12*(1), 117–132.

Fuchs, M. (2011). *Export performance and managerial capabilities in German SMEs*. Springer.

Fuchs, M., & Horn, S. (2019). Managerial decision making and the evolutionary process of internationalization. *Academy of Management Proceedings, 2019*(1), 14801.

Fuchs, M., & Köstner, M. (2014). Export performance and contingency theory. In *AIB Annual Conference 2014 Proceedings*. Springer.

Fuchs, M., & Köstner, M. (2015). Standardisation and adaptation of firms' export marketing strategies in familiar European and non-familiar non-European markets. *European Journal of International Management, 9*(3), 306.

Fuchs, M., & Köstner, M. (2016). Antecedents and consequences of firm's export marketing strategy. *Management Research Review, 39*(3), 329–355.

Ghotge, R., van Wijk, A, Vandeventer, E., & Álvarez, J. S. (2020). A global analysis on microgrids through the PESTEL framework. In *2020 IEEE International Conference on Power Electronics, Smart Grid and Renewable Energy (PESGRE2020)*, pp. 1–5.

Giachetti, C., Manzi, G., & Colapinto, C. (2019). Entry mode degree of control, firm performance and host country institutional development: A meta-analysis. *Management International Review, 59*(1), 3–39.

Gigerenzer, G. (1996). On narrow norms and vague heuristics: A reply to Kahneman and Tversky (1996). *Psychological Review, 103*(3), 592–596.

Gigerenzer, G., & Gaissmaier, W. (2011). Heuristic decision making. *Annual Review of Psychology, 62*(1), 451–482.

Gigerenzer, G., & Selten, R. (2002). *Bounded rationality: The adaptive toolbox*. Springer.

Glaum, M., & Oesterle, M.-J. (2007). 40 years of research on internationalization and firm performance: More questions than answers? *Management International Review, 47*(3), 307–317.

Gold, N., Colman, A. M., & Pulford, B. D. (2011). Normative theory in decision making and moral reasoning. *Behavioral and Brain Sciences, 34*(5), 256–257.

Gorostidi-Martinez, H., & Zhao, X. (2017). Strategies to avoid liability of foreignness when entering a new market. *Journal of Advances in Management Research, 14*(1), 46–68. https://doi.org/10.1108/JAMR-09-2016-0067

Hennart, J. F. (2007). The theoretical rationale for a multinationality-performance relationship. *Management International Review, 47*, 423–452. https://doi.org/10.1007/s11575-007-0023-3

Hennart, J.-F., & Slangen, A. H. (2015). Yes, we really do need more entry mode studies! A commentary on Shaver. *Journal of International Business Studies, 46*(1), 114–122.

Hennart, J.-F., Majocchi, A., & Forlani, E. (2019). The myth of the stay-at-home family firm: How family-managed SMEs can overcome their internationalization limitations. *Journal of International Business Studies, 50*(5), 758–782.

Hong, S. J. (2016). When do MNCs fail to learn from prior failure experience? *Canadian Journal of Administrative Sciences/Revue Canadienne Des Sciences de l'Administration, 33*(1), 7–20.

Hult, G. T. M., Gonzalez-Perez, M. A., & Lagerström, K. (2020). The theoretical evolution and use of the Uppsala model of internationalization in the international business ecosystem. *Journal of International Business Studies, 51*(1), 38–49.

Hultman, M., Robson, M. J., & Katsikeas, C. S. (2009). Export product strategy fit and performance: An empirical investigation. *Journal of International Marketing, 17*(4). https://doi.org/10.1509/jimk.17.4.1

Hutzschenreuter, T., Pedersen, T., & Volberda, H. W. (2007). The role of path dependency and managerial intentionality: A perspective on international business research. *Journal of International Business Studies, 38*(7), 1055–1068. https://doi.org/10.1057/palgrave.jibs.8400326

Hymer, S. (1976). *The international operation of national firms: A study of direct foreign investment.* MIT Press.

Inkpen, A. C., & Crossan, M. M. (1995). Believing is seeing: Joint ventures and organization learning*. *Journal of Management Studies, 32*(5), 595–618.

Javalgi, R. G., Todd, P. R., Johnston, W. J., & Granot, E. (2012). Entrepreneurship, muddling through, and Indian Internet-enabled SMEs. *Journal of Business Research, 65*(6), 740–744.

Johanson, J., & Vahlne, J.-E. (1977). The internationalization process of the firm—A model of knowledge development and increasing foreign market commitments. *Journal of International Business Studies, 8*(1), 23–32.

Johanson, J., & Wiedersheim-Paul, F. 2007. The internationalization of the firm - Four Swedish cases, Wiley 12: 305 323.

Jones, M. V., & Coviello, N. E. (2005). Internationalisation: Conceptualising an entrepreneurial process of behaviour in time. *Journal of International Business Studies, 36*(3), 284–303.

Kabongo, J. D., & Okpara, J. O. (2019). Timing and speed of internationalization: Evidence from African banks. *Journal of Business Research, 102*, 12–20.

Kahiya, E., & Dean, D. L. (2014). Export performance: Multiple predictors and multiple measures approach. *Asia Pacific Journal of Marketing and Logistics, 26*(3), 378–407.

Kahneman, D., & Thaler, R. H. (2005). Anomalies: Utility maximization and experienced utility. *SSRN Electronic Journal.* https://doi.org/10.2139/ssrn.870494

Kahneman, D., & Tversky, A. (1996). On the reality of cognitive illusions. *Psychological Review, 103*(3), 582–591.

Kano, L., & Verbeke, A. (2015). The three faces of bounded reliability: Alfred Chandler and the micro-foundations of management theory. *California Management Review, 58*(1), 97–122.

Katsikeas, C., & Leonidou, L. (2000). *Firm-level export performance assessment: Review, evaluation, and development.* Springer. https://doi.org/10.1177/0092070300284003

Khan, K. U., Atlas, F., Ghani, U., Akhtar, S., & Khan, F. (2020). Impact of intangible resources (dominant logic) on SMEs innovation performance, the mediating role of dynamic managerial capabilities: Evidence from China. *European Journal of Innovation Management.* https://doi.org/10.1108/ejim-07-2020-0276

Kim, J., & Hemmert, M. (2016). What drives the export performance of small and medium-sized subcontracting firms? A study of Korean manufacturers. *International Business Review, 25*(2), 511–521.

Knight, F. F. (1921). *Risk.* Hart, Schaffner, and Marx.

Kogut, B., & Singh, H. (1988). The effect of national culture on the choice of entry mode. *Journal of International Business Studies, 19*(3), 411–432.

Kogut, B., & Zander, U. (1993). Knowledge of the firm and the evolutionary theory of the multinational corporation. *Journal of International Business Studies, 24*(4), 625–645.

Krugman, P., & Wells, R. (2006). *Economics*. https://doi.org/10.1007/978-1-349-91968-0

Kutschker, M., & Schmid, S. (2011). *Internationales management* (7th ed.). Oldenburg Wissenschaftsverlag.

Langley, A., Smallman, C., Tsoukas, H., & de Ven, A. H. V. (2013). Process studies of change in organization and management: Unveiling temporality, activity, and flow. *Academy of Management Journal, 56*(1), 1–13.

Leonidou, L. C., Katsikeas, C. S., & Coudounaris, D. N. (2010). Five decades of business research into exporting: A bibliographic analysis. *Journal of International Management, 16*(1), 78–91.

Levitt, T. (1983). The globalization of markets. *Harvard Business Review, 1983*, 92–102.

Liesch, P. W., Welch, L. S., & Buckley, P. J. (2011). Risk and uncertainty in internationalisation and international entrepreneurship studies. *Management International Review, 51*(6), 851–873.

Lindblom, C. E. (1979). Still muddling, not yet through. *Public Administration Review, 39*(6), 517–526.

Lu, J. W., & Beamish, P. W. (2001). The internationalization and performance of SMEs. *Strategic Management Journal, 22*(6–7), 565–586.

Lundan, S. M., & Li, J. (2019). Adjusting to and learning from institutional diversity: Toward a capability-building perspective. *Journal of International Business Studies, 50*(1), 36–47.

Luo, Y., & Mezias, J. M. (2002). Liabilities of foreignness: Concepts, constructs, and consequences. *Journal of International Management, 8*, 217–221.

Luostarinen, R. (1989). *Internationalization of the firm: An empirical study of the internationalization of firms with small and open domestic markets with special emphasis on lateral rigidity as a behavioral characteristic in strategic decision making*. Helsinki School of Economics.

Madsen, T., & Servais, P. (1997). *The internationalization of born globals: An evolutionary process?* Springer.

Maitland, E., & Sammartino, A. (2015). Managerial cognition and internationalization. *Journal of International Business Studies, 46*(7), 733–760.

Makino, S., & Delios, A. (1996). Local knowledge transfer and performance: Implications for alliance formation in Asia. *Journal of International Business Studies, 27*(5), 905–927.

Makkonen, H., Olkkonen, R., & Halinen, A. (2012). Organizational buying as muddling through: A practice–theory approach. *Journal of Business Research, 65*(6), 773–780.

Mantere, S., & Sillince, J. A. A. (2007). Strategic intent as a rhetorical device. *Scandinavian Journal of Management, 23*(4), 406–423.

March, J. G. (1978). Bounded rationality, ambiguity, and the engineering of choice. *Bell Journal of Economics, 9*(2), 587.

March, J. G. (1991). How decisions happen in organizations. *Human-Computer Interaction, 6*(2), 95–117.

March, J. G., Sproull, L. S., & Tamuz, M. (1991). Learning from samples of one or fewer. *Organization Science, 2*(1), 1.

Marinović-Matović, I., & Arsić, L. (2020). Ecological dimension of PESTEL analysis in small enterprises in the Republic of Serbia. *Recycling and Sustainable Development, 13*(1), 63–71.

Maseland, R., Dow, D., & Steel, P. (2018). The Kogut and Singh national cultural distance index: Time to start using it as a springboard rather than a crutch. *Journal of International Business Studies, 49*(9), 1154–1166.

Mellers, B. A. (2006). *Encyclopedia of cognitive science*. Springer. https://doi.org/10.1002/0470018860.s00511

Mezias, J. M. (2002). How to identify liabilities of foreignness and assess their effects on multinational corporations. *Journal of International Management, 8*(3), 265–282. S1075425302000698. https://doi.org/10.1016/S1075-4253(02)00069-8

Miller, R. R., & Weigel, D. R. (1972). The motivation for foreign direct investment. *Journal of International Business Studies, 3*(2), 67–79.
Mol, M. J., van Tulder, R. J. M., & Beije, P. R. (2005). Antecedents and performance consequences of international outsourcing. *International Business Review, 14*(5), 599–617.
Morschett, D., Schramm-Klein, H., & Swoboda, B. (2010). Decades of research on market entry modes: What do we really know about external antecedents of entry mode choice? *Journal of International Management, 16*(1), 60–77.
Mousavi, S., & Gigerenzer, G. (2014). Risk, uncertainty, and heuristics. *Journal of Business Research, 67*(8). https://doi.org/10.1016/j.jbusres.2014.02.013
Mousavi, S., & Gigerenzer, G. (2017). Heuristics are tools for uncertainty. *Homo Oeconomicus, 34*(4), 361–379.
Nachum, L., & Zaheer, S. (2005). The persistence of distance? The impact of technology on MNE motivations for foreign investment. *Strategic Management Journal, 26*(8), 747–767. https://doi.org/10.1002/smj.472
Nachum, L., Zaheer, S., & Gross, S. (2008). Does it matter where countries are? Proximity to knowledge markets and resources and MNE location choices. *SSRN Electronic Journal*. https://doi.org/10.2139/ssrn.1134422
Nakos, G., & Brouthers, K. D. (2002). Entry mode choice of SMEs in Central and Eastern Europe. *Entrepreneurship Theory and Practice, 27*(1), 47–63.
Nguyen, Q. T. K., & Kim, S. (2020). The multinationality and performance relationship: Revisiting the literature and exploring the implications. *International Business Review, 29*(2), 101670.
North, D. C. (1990). *Institutions, institutional change and economic performance*. Cambridge University Press. https://doi.org/10.1017/cbo9780511808678.010
Nowak, J. (1997). International market selection. *Journal of Transnational Management Development, 3*(1), 93–110.
Oliver, D., & Roos, J. (2005). Decision-making in high-velocity environments: The importance of guiding principles. *Organization Studies, 26*(6), 889–913.
Oviatt, B. M., & McDougall, P. P. (2005). Defining international entrepreneurship and modeling the speed of internationalization. *Entrepreneurship Theory and Practice, 29*(5), 537–554.
Papadopoulos, N., & Martín, O. M. (2011). International market selection and segmentation: Perspectives and challenges. *International Marketing Review, 28*(2), 132–149.
Patterson, P. G., Cicic, M., & Shoham, A. (1997). A temporal sequence model of satisfaction and export intentions of service firms. *Journal of Global Marketing, 10*(4), 23–43.
Penrose, E. T. (1959). *The theory of the growth of the firm*. Blackwell Publisher.
Pitelis, C. N. (2004). Edith Penrose and the resource-based view of (international) business strategy. *International Business Review, 13*(4), 523–532.
Pla-Barber, J., Villar, C., & León-Darder, F. (2014). Augmenting versus exploiting entry modes in soft services. *International Marketing Review, 31*(Issue 6), 621–636.
Puck, J. F., Holtbrügge, D., & Mohr, A. T. (2009). Beyond entry mode choice: Explaining the conversion of joint ventures into wholly owned subsidiaries in the People's republic of China. *Journal of International Business Studies, 40*(3), 388–404.
Puranam, P., Stieglitz, N., Osman, M., & Pillutla, M. M. (2015). Modelling bounded rationality in organizations: Progress and prospects. *The Academy of Management Annals, 9*(1), 337–392.
Qiu, J., Donaldson, L., & Luo, B. (2012). The benefits of persisting with paradigms in organizational research. *Academy of Management Perspectives, 26*(1), 93–104.
Root, F. R. (1964). Strategic planning for export marketing. *The International Executive, 6*(4), 17–17.
Root, F. R. (1968). The expropriation experience of American companies what happened to 38 companies. *Business Horizons, 11*(2), 69–74.

Root, F. R. (1988). Managing export entry and expansion. *Journal of International Business Studies, 19*(1), 149–151.

Root, F. R. (1994). *Entry strategies for international markets*. Lexington Books.

Sakarya, S., Eckman, M., & Hyllegard, K. H. (2007). Market selection for international expansion. *International Marketing Review, 24*(2), 208–238.

Sanchez-Peinado, E., & Pla-Barber, J. (2006). A multidimensional concept of uncertainty and its influence on the entry mode choice: An empirical analysis in the service sector. *International Business Review, 15*(3), 215–232.

Sarasvathy, S. D. (2001). Causation and effectuation: Toward a theoretical shift from economic inevitability to entrepreneurial contingency. *Academy of Management Review, 26*(2), 243–263.

Schellenberg, M., Harker, M. J., & Jafari, A. (2017). International market entry mode – A systematic literature review. *Journal of Strategic Marketing, 26*(7), 1–27.

Schmid, S. (2018). Internationalization of business, cases on strategy formulation and implementation. *MIR Series in International Business, 2018*, 1–25.

Schomaker, R. M., & Sitter, A. (2020). Die PESTEL-Analyse – Status quo und innovative Anpassungen. *Der Betriebswirt, 61*(1), 3–21.

Schweizer, R. (2012). The internationalization process of SMEs: A muddling-through process. *Journal of Business Research, 65*(6), 745–751.

Segal-Horn, S. (1996). The limits of global strategy. *Strategy & Leadership, 24*(6), 12–17.

Sent, E.-M. (2005). Simplifying Herbert Simon. *History of Political Economy, 37*(2), 227–232.

Shaver, J. M. (1998). Accounting for endogeneity when assessing strategy performance: Does entry mode choice affect FDI survival? *Management Science, 44*(4), 571–585.

Shaver, J. M. (2013). Do we really need more entry mode studies? *Journal of International Business Studies, 44*(1), 23–27.

Shoham, A. (1999). Bounded rationality, planning, standardization of international strategy, and export performance: A structural model examination. *Journal of International Marketing, 7*(2), 24–50.

Slick, J. F. (2001). Measuring corporate readiness to implement distance education. *Performance Improvement, 40*(10), 39–42.

Szulanski, G. (1996). Exploring internal stickiness: Impediments to the transfer of best practice within the firm. *Strategic Management Journal, 17*(S2). https://doi.org/10.1002/smj.4250171105

Szulanski, G. (2000). The process of knowledge transfer: A diachronic analysis of stickiness. *Organizational Behavior and Human Decision Processes, 82*, 9–27.

Szulanski, G., & Jensen, R. J. (2006). Presumptive adaptation and the effectiveness of knowledge transfer. *Strategic Management Journal, 27*(10), 937–957.

Takanobu, M. (2015). *A study of institutional research: The garbage can model perspective* (pp. 441–442).

Taliman, S. (2003). The significance of Bruce Kogut's and Udo Zander's article, "Knowledge of the firm and the evolutionary theory of the multinational corporation". *Journal of International Business Studies, 34*(6). https://doi.org/10.1057/palgrave.jibs.8400061

Tan, Q., & Sousa, C. M. (2018). Performance and business relatedness as drivers of exit decision: A study of MNCs from an emerging country. *Global Strategy Journal, 8*(4), 612–634.

Taylor, C. R., Zou, S., & Osland, G. E. (2000). Foreign market entry strategies of Japanese MNCs. *International Marketing Review, 17*(Issue 2), 146–163.

Thakur, V. (2021). Framework for PESTEL dimensions of sustainable healthcare waste management: Learnings from COVID-19 outbreak. *Journal of Cleaner Production, 287*, 125562.

Tuppura, A., Saarenketo, S., Puumalainen, K., Jantunen, A., & Kyläheiko, K. (2008). Linking knowledge, entry timing and internationalization strategy. *International Business Review, 17*(4), 473–487.

Uli, V. (2018). A co-evolutionary perspective on business processes. *Business Process Management Journal, 24*(3), 00–00.

Vahlne, J.-E., & Johanson, J. (2013). The Uppsala model on evolution of the multinational business enterprise – From internalization to coordination of networks. *International Marketing Review, 30*(3), 189–210.

Vuori, N., & Vuori, T. (2014). Comment on "Heuristics in the strategy context" by Bingham and Eisenhardt (2011). *Strategic Management Journal, 35*(11), 1689–1697.

Welch, L. S., & Luostarinen, R. (1988). Internationalization: Evolution of a concept. *Journal of General Management, 14*(2), 34–55.

Welch, L. S., & Luostarinen, R. K. (1990). Inward-outward connections in internationalization. *Journal of International Marketing, 1*(1), 44–56.

Welch, L., & Luostarinen, R. (1993). Inward-outward connections in internationalization. *Journal of International Marketing, 1*(1), 13.

Welch, L. S., & Wiedersheim-Paul, F. (1979). Export promotion policy-a new approach. *Australian Journal of Management, 4*(2), 165–177.

Welch, L. S., Benito, G. R. G., & Petersen, B. (2018). *Foreign operation methods: Theory, analysis, strategy*. Edward Elgar.

Whittington, R. (2008). Alfred Chandler, founder of strategy: Lost tradition and renewed inspiration. *Business History Review, 82*(2), 267–277.

Wiedersheim-Paul, F., Olson, H. C., & Welch, L. S. (1978). Pre-export activity: The first step in internationalization. *Journal of International Business Studies, 9*(1), 47–58.

Wilkinson, B., Cohen, R. B., Felton, N., Nkosi, M., & van Liere, J. (1980). The multinational corporation: A radical approach: Papers by Stephen Herbert Hymer. *The Canadian Journal of Economics, 13*(4), 738.

Williams, D. A. (2014). Resources and other failures of SMEs. *Journal of Developmental Entrepreneurship, 19*(01), 1450007.

Williamson, O. E. (2002). The theory of the firm as governance structure: From choice to contract. *Journal of Economic Perspectives, 16*(3), 171–195.

Wrona, T., & Trąpczyński, P. (2012). Markteintrittsstrategien. *Dynamik und Komplexität, 2012*, 123–152.

Wu, Y. (2020). The marketing strategies of IKEA in China using tools of PESTEL. *Five Forces Model and SWOT Analysis, 2020*, 348–355.

Yan, W. M. (2014). Reliability and external validity of neurobiological experiments. *International Studies in the Philosophy of Science, 27*(4), 429–446.

Yip, G. S., Biscarri, J. G., & Monti, J. A. (2000). The role of the internationalization process in the performance of newly internationalizing firms. *Journal of International Marketing, 8*(3), 10–35.

Zaheer, S. (1995). Overcoming the liability of foreignness. *Academy of Management Journal, 38*(2), 341–363. https://doi.org/10.5465/256683

Zahra, S. A. (2005). A theory of international new ventures: A decade of research. *Journal of International Business Studies, 36*(1), 20–28.

Zander, I., McDougall-Covin, P., & Rose, E. L. (2015). Born globals and international business: Evolution of a field of research. *Journal of International Business Studies, 46*(1), 27–35.

Zhao, H., Ma, J., & Yang, J. (2017). 30 years of research on entry mode and performance relationship: A meta-analytical review. *Management International Review, 57*(5), 653–682.

Zhou, L., & Wu, A. (2014). Earliness of internationalization and performance outcomes: Exploring the moderating effects of venture age and international commitment. *Journal of World Business, 49*(1), 132–142.

Market Entry Modes

5

As discussed in the preceding chapter, entry mode choice is seen as "a critical component" in the process of internationalization (Morschett et al., 2010: 60). The question about the right international strategy is often divided into five major subjects: (1) Market entry as part of a general strategy, (2) the selection of target markets, (3) choosing the right time to enter a foreign market, (4) making a choice to allocate firm resources between markets, and (5) deciding how to coordinate business activities (Schmid, 2018).

Market entry modes are divided into functional market entry modes, which are prepared and conducted mainly from the home country location, and institutional market entry modes, which are accomplished and operated in the host country locations. The success of so-called functional market entry forms is highly dependent on the commitment of a sales agent, intermediaries, licensees, or franchisees (Coviello et al., 2017). Although the proposed dependency is not one-sided, a significant effect on the success rests on the capabilities and effort provided by local partners in host countries. In all functional market entry modes, the primary leverage of control is limited by the ability to bridge the gap between home and host location while operating exclusively from the home location to serve markets abroad. Thus, functional or institutional market entry strategies can be adopted to fit different needs and capabilities for controlling international activities. The desired operative control can be carried out by relying on exports, licensing, franchising, or forming an international joint venture, and setting up a wholly-owned subsidiary (WOS) in a host location abroad.

Generally, market entry modes are portrayed as market entry strategies, although this definition can be confusing because the choice of market entry strategy is more than an elaborated long-term objective, but also a means of how to operate in the foreign market to achieve the projected objectives.

M. Fuchs, *International Management*,
https://doi.org/10.1007/978-3-662-65870-3_5

Market entry strategies and the entry mode decision are a core topic in international management. Efforts to systematize market entry strategies rely on various aspects.

But the list of criteria can be long, so control is one aspect to systematically define entry mode strategies but this dimension needs to be balanced with the subsequent resource commitment to exercise and operate the entry mode by the firm, often restricted by the lack of resources and information (Anderson & Gatignon, 1986). Other approaches highlight the impact of managerial experience required to operate entry modes in unfamiliar and distance markets (Johanson & Vahlne, 1977; Johanson & Wiedersheim-Paul, 2007; Vahlne & Johanson, 2017).

Yet, in the IB literature there are many more prevalent categorizations applied to describe entry modes (Kutschker & Schmid, 2011: 853f). While the literature identifies the merits and drawbacks of different entry options, there is no ready-made recipe for assessing risks and weighing trade-offs.

In order to assess the benefits and weaknesses of the various entry modes, it will be necessary to explain in detail the main features of each entry mode. However, we have to limit the discussion to a few central aspects. The following overview should also help to compare the different market entry modes with each other. It should furthermore be noted that often particular descriptions focus on a choice between discrete market entry modes, which is often not practical in actual business practices. Thus, it is true that particular entry modes require lower effort and less international experience in implementing the selected mode successfully, but these criteria themselves are not static states, but change through the process of applying the selected entry mode and evolve through the experience firms gain in the process of internationalization. The decision between several possible entry modes is never clear-cut choice. Very often, firms use a mix of different entry modes, combine similar modes, and switch from one to the other over time as states and environments, like firms, evolve.

5.1 Export

Exporting is a widely used foreign market entry strategy for all types of business firms, but especially for small and medium-sized enterprises (SMEs). Especially for the SMEs, exporting can be a significant success. One reason is that export consumes considerably fewer resources than other entry modes. In addition, export exposes the firm to substantially lower risks (Hultman et al., 2009; Leonidou & Katsikeas, 1996; Sousa & Lengler, 2009). The relative low commitment of resources and the limited exposure to potential risk are major motives for choosing exporting as an entry mode strategy.

While there is an ample body of research on how different factors affect export performance (Brouthers et al., 2009; Cavusgil & Zou, 1994; Lages et al., 2008), several weaknesses have been identified in analyzing performance in export ventures (Lages et al., 2008; Morgan et al., 2004). Morgan et al. argue that the export performance literature is fraught with three problems. A weakness of export performance studies is that they mostly remain descriptive and lack a robust theoretical grounding. It is also criticized that they rely on many, often diverging theoretical assumptions. Several authors regret that most studies neglect the multidimensionality of export performance (Morgan et al., 2004).

In addition, another almost undisputed assumption dealing with export is that management in SMEs is held to be more risk-averse than managers of larger firms and thus tends to choose exports (Erramilli & D'Souza, 1993).

Not surprisingly, drivers of export success have attracted most attention from researchers, although empirical results are generally mixed, sometimes inconclusive, and contradictory (Calof, 1994; Katsikeas et al., 2006). This is due mainly to the fact that measures differ substantially across export performance studies (Diamantopoulos & Kakkos, 2007).

In international business, early research focused on exporting because in the 1950s and early 1960s, domestic firms struggled to rebuild their manufacturing facilities and started slowly to expand selling products and services into adjacent markets abroad (Axinn, 1988; Buckley & Casson, 1998; Crick & Czinkota, 1995; Dow, 2000; Fuchs & Köstner, 2016; Hultman et al., 2011; Katsikeas, 1994; Katsikeas et al., 1996; Styles et al., 2008).

In the 1970s, the growing trade liberalization and rising consumer demand soon became a major trigger for increasing exports (McDowell, 1997; Raut, 2017; UNCTAD, 1992).

In general, export is a viable growth strategy for many firms (Knudsen & Madsen, 2002), as it requires fewer resources compared to other entry modes, such as equity-based entry modes (Chen et al., 2016; Hultman et al., 2009, 2011).

5.1.1 Export Pattern and Trade

The share of the value of exports related to the value of the gross domestic product (GDP) varies considerably across countries. The value of exports, merchandise goods and services include the value of freight, insurance, transport, travel, royalties, and licensing fees are typically included in the value of exports of goods and services (World Bank, 2021). Looking at the Eurostat data, in 2020, the value of exports as a percentage of the GDP ranged from 30% in the UK to 210% in Luxembourg, while 56% was reported for Austria, 47% for Germany, and 85% for Slovakia. By and large exports are a major component of the GDP. The value of export indicate how vital exports are to a nation's economy. The abovementioned figures consider intra- and extra-EU trade, i.e., trade with countries outside the EU and between member states (Eurostat, 2020).

However, many firms export only to a small number of countries, mostly neighbors, replicating a widely identified pattern (Coviello et al., 2017; Leonidou & Katsikeas, 1996).

Moreover, EU data on firm size show that the number of export markets for smaller companies is quite limited, while only a small percentage of larger firms export to more than 10, or more than 20 countries. Accordingly, the distribution of shares by value is very disproportionate. For Austria, the figures are presented in Table 5.1.

Table 5.1 Trade by number of partner countries in 2018 (Austria)

Trade by number of partner countries in 2018 for imports and exports and in % of total number of enterprises and in % of value traded (Data from Statistics Austria, NACE, 2020)

Number of partner countries	Imports		Exports		Trade intensity			
	Enterprises	Value in Euro (mill)	Enterprises	Value in Euro (mill)	Enterprises	in %	Value in Euro (mill)	Value in %
1	147 518	10 773	27 519	4 288	147 118	83.4	9 421	3.1
2	9 603	4 177	4 714	2 347	11 047	6.3	6 220	2.1
3 to 5	6 151	10 627	3 381	4 965	7 520	4.3	11 689	3.9
6 to 9	2 683	9 866	1 598	5 732	3 106	1.8	11 745	3.9
10 to 14	1 927	12 234	1 170	12 937	2 122	1.2	13 127	4.4
15 to 19	1 250	13 119	740	9 890	1 454	0.8	14 505	4.8
20 or more	2 412	92 758	1 777	107 190	3 951	2.2	234 198	77.8
Total	171 544	153 557	40 899	147 352	176 318	100	300 909	100

Source: Statistics Austria. Compiled on 30 November 2020. The compilation "TEC—Trade by Enterprise Characteristics" is based on a linkage of the Austrian international trade in goods statistics (ITGS; national concept) on microdata level with enterprise characteristics of the business register and Foreign Affiliates Statistics (FATS); Source: Statistics Austria, TEC data, 2021

As can be seen from Table 5.1, a highly unequal distribution of trade activity is reported. According to the Austrian Central Statistical Office, 83.4% of all Austrian enterprises (171,544) conduct foreign trade with only one country. Although it is the great majority of firms, the value of exports for this category account if or only 3.1% of the total merchandise trade. In contrast, only 2.2% of the total number of enterprises carry out trade with more than 20 countries, amounting to 77.8% of Austria's total foreign trade (Statistik Austrian, Außenhandelsstatistik, 2020).

The picture does not look much different if we look at the firm size and the pertinent export/import pattern. Usually, firm size classes are based on the number of employees. Figures shown in Table 5.2 relate to the share of different firm size classes separated between exports and imports (measured in Euro) in Austria for 2018. Exports and imports are added to the total trade intensity. Each column shows the number of enterprises in each size class and the value of imports, exports, and trade intensity for each class size. The largest class size are micro firms, employing up to nine personnel, but usually not more than one or two, which constitute 67% of all firms, but these firms account for only 12% of all export trade. The next size class (ranging from 10 to 49 employees) accounts for 23% of all firms and carries out 10.5% of the total export value. The next firm size class, with 50 to 249 staff, accounts for only 7% of the total number of firms but accounts for 19% of total exports. The last firm size class (comprising of firms with more than 250 employees), accounts for 3% of the total number of firms. However, it was responsible for almost 62% of the total exports in 2018.

Most studies on export focus on small and medium-sized firms (SMEs). However, the data presented in Table 5.1 reveal significant differences among firm size classes. Looking at EU data relating firm sizes and export shares shown in Table 5.2, the pattern is fairly similar. Large firms which employ more than 250 staff account for 40–77% of all exports whereas small micro firms account for only 4–16% of total export trade.

Firm Size and Export Shares

In 2018, SMEs were responsible for a major part of all imports and exports. However, if we take a closer look at the prevalent data, in the 27 EU member states, SMEs also account for 98% of all firms. Yet, they contribute to not more than 48% of all export trade. Micro-firms, which constitute 68% of the total number of firms, are responsible for only 7% of total exports. The next firm size class, ranging from 10 to 49 employees, accounts for 10% and the size class ranging from 50 to 250 employees account for a share of 21 % of total exports. Large firms employing more than 250 people account for the lion's share, 62% of export trade, but only represent 2% of the total number of firms recorded.

Hence, if exporting is seen as a viable growth strategy, this message needs to be significantly rectified in terms of company size.

Table 5.2 Share of firm size class related to the total value of exports in EU countries for the year 2018

Share of firm size class related to the total value of exports for EU Member countries for the year 2018

		Number of employees				Value of total exports				
Country	0–9	10–49	50–249	Large	nk	0–9	10–49	50–249	Large	nk
		Share of firm class size in %				Share of firm class size in %				
EU-27	68	23	7	2	5	7	10	21	62	3
Belgium	67	25	6	2	44	9	15	28	47	3
Bulgaria	66	24	9	2	1	14	11	22	53	0
Czech Rep.	37	34	22	7	7	4	8	20	68	2
Denmark	61	27	9	2	15	6	16	27	52	5
Germany	66	22	9	3	0	5	6	13	77	0
Estonia	76	18	5	1	18	18	18	40	24	10
Ireland	59	27	10	3	0	6	4	19	71	0
Greece	62	28	8	2	0	9	12	23	56	0
Spain	73	20	6	2	0	13	14	24	49	0
France	62	25	9	4	17	4	7	11	78	2
Croatia	59	27	10	3	18	15	15	26	44	16
Italy	65	28	6	1	0	5	17	29	48	0
Cyprus	69	23	7	2	25	45	28	18	9	4
Latvia	66	25	7	1	0	15	22	34	39	4
Lithuania	63	28	8	2	0	11	16	24	50	0
Luxembourg	46	30	18	6	16	8	12	37	42	11
Hungary	68	24	7	2	0	6	7	19	67	0
Malta	48	32	15	5	0	13	15	23	49	0
Netherlands	79	15	5	1	0	11	17	36	36	0
Austria	67	23	7	3	0	12	8	19	62	0
Poland	70	20	7	2	1	6	9	18	67	0
Portugal	67	25	7	1	1	6	13	27	51	0
Romania	48	32	15	4	0	4	8	18	71	0
Slovenia	81	14	4	1	0	13	14	22	52	0
Slovakia	74	18	6	2	2	7	8	13	72	1
Finland	68	21	8	3	0	3	8	24	65	0
Sweden	72	20	6	2	0	15	9	18	58	0
UK	66	24	8	3	0	17	9	16	58	0
Iceland	56	25	13	5	16	16	15	15	53	3
Switzerland	68	22	8	2	0	7	6	32	55	0

Estimate based on all Member States latest year available
Source: Eurostat (online data code: ext_tec01)

For example, in Hungary, only 2% of firms in the largest size class (>250 employees) account for 67% of all export trade. In Germany, 33% of the largest size class makes up 77% of the total export trade. In Slovakia, a mere 2% of firms in the size class with more than 250 employees take 72% of the total share of the country's exports. Although firm size had been the focus of numerous empirical studies, the analyses tend to be overly generic and pertain to the entire SME category.

Thus, if these different size classes were taken into account, the conclusions of a large number of these studies would probably have to be corrected considerably (Dhanaraj & Beamish, 2003; Francis & Collins-Dodd, 2004; Fuchs & Köstner, 2016; Morgan et al., 2004; Reddy & Naik, 2011; Serra et al., 2012).

In addition, we need to note that mostly small firms serve only a small number of export markets, and the value of their exports is pretty limited (EUSTAT, 2020). Although across all 27 EU members, the exports of goods and services accounted for 49% of the GDP in 2019, ranging from about 30% in France to 82% in Belgium (EUSTAT, 2021). It seems true that export and import trade significantly contributes to the GDP in many countries, but many small firms serve only a very limited number of export markets, and important, less than 2 %, the largest firm size account for the lion's share (exemplified in Fig. 5.2).

5.1.2 How to Define Exports

Export is defined as the cross-border sale of goods and services from one country (the home of the exporting entity) to another country (home of the importing entity). Export is a transfer of goods or services delivered by a business unit, the seller (located in the home country) to an entity, the buyer at a foreign location. The products or services are either for final consumption or as an intermediary input in a production line. The entity receiving the exported product or service can be a legally independent business or subsidiary of the exporting business unit.

The parent firm can ship exports to a foreign subsidiary, and equally, the subsidiary can export to the parent firm located at home, giving rise to intra-firm trade (Bernard et al., 2010; Lanz & Miroudot, 2011; OECD, 2010).

Firms are engaged in foreign markets by exporting or selling their products, manufactured or bought in the domestic markets, through their foreign subsidiaries. However, cross-border export or import data does not reveal the actual degree of value-added through exports or imports.

Exports and Value Added by Imports

Considering the import value of exports, Germany was the most important export market for Austria in 2020. However, the USA is more important than Italy and

(continued)

imports from Russia are considerably higher than those from Switzerland and France (OECD, 2017: 6). Looking in detail at cross-border export and import data reveals a much more extra-regional trade pattern for Austria than the cross-border export values suggest (OECD-WTO TiVA data, 2017, 2020). Focusing on these export figures, most countries show how deeply their economies are embedded and as well as dependent on the prevalent pattern of global value chains (GVCs). For smaller EU economies, value-added (by imports) in exports range from 40% to 75%.

Moreover, these figures tend to be higher in smaller economies than in large ones (OECD, 2018: 8). An analysis of the content of cross-border export shows how much value-added in an export goods is sourced from other countries through imported values added before exporting. For example, the value-added content of Chinese exports declined by about 19% between 2005 and 2016, illustrating that the Chinese economy became more self-sufficient or independent from foreign suppliers (OECD TiVA data, 2018).

5.1.3 Inter-firm and Intra-firm Trade

A major component of total exports and imports is generated by cross border inter- and intra-firm trade. The value of intra-firm trade for exports shipped to the US parent by its foreign affiliates, increased within ten years from 32.4% in 1979 to 89.2% in 1989 (Bonturi & Fukasaku, 1993: 150). These numbers indicate the early heyday of globalization. Cross border intra- and inter-firm trade is measured as exports and imports, it is aggregated at the country level, but carried out by a network of firm affiliates operated by multinational firms. Studying intra-firm trade allows us to examine the export and import activities between firms, which is defined as inter-firm trade and trade within firms, which is intra-firm trade. These figures demonstrate that international trade, measured in exports and imports in goods and services, is in fact not trade carried out by a country or a region but by the firms located in home and host countries or regions.

Exporting is considered an attractive entry mode to foreign markets, and it is treated in the literature as the most straightforward approach to penetrate a foreign market. However, while it seems easy to start, i.e., with ad hoc exports after receiving a random request from a firm or customer abroad, the control and management of export markets in multiple countries, serving different market segments can be very challenging. Although SMEs are attracted to exporting, firm size is a significant limiting factor for growth via exports.

5.1.4 How Do Firms Export

An exporting firm has to decide whether to use an intermediary or sell directly to a foreign customer, both options are defined as direct or indirect export. As shown in Fig. 5.1, generally, there are three options available to the exporting firm. An exporter can sell a product directly or indirectly to the final customer in the host country. Using the option of exporting indirectly, the exporter can cooperate with an intermediary located in its home market or use an intermediary in the host market.

When choosing to export indirectly (options two and three), the company is deciding not directly to manage the export activities. Conversely, opting for direct exports (option one) offers a closer contact to customers in host countries, but the firm needs to handle export documents, manage product pricing for different markets, and may organize the physical transport of the exported goods to the customer. Option one allows the manufacturer to deliver to a customer abroad products without much more effort compared to domestic sales. Selecting option two or three requires establishing a sustainable cooperation with an intermediary, which constitutes an agency relationship between the manufacturer (principal) and the intermediary (agent). Agency relationships are prone to information asymmetry between the principal and the agent, which affects the efficiency of the relationship. Exporting is a low-risk and relatively flexible entry mode but offers low control (Michael, 2019).

Generally, entry modes literature assume that risk-averse managers prefer to export (Hollensen, 2010: 326), but this also limits the level of control of firm's international operations. However, export requires fewer firm resources and offers more flexibility, as

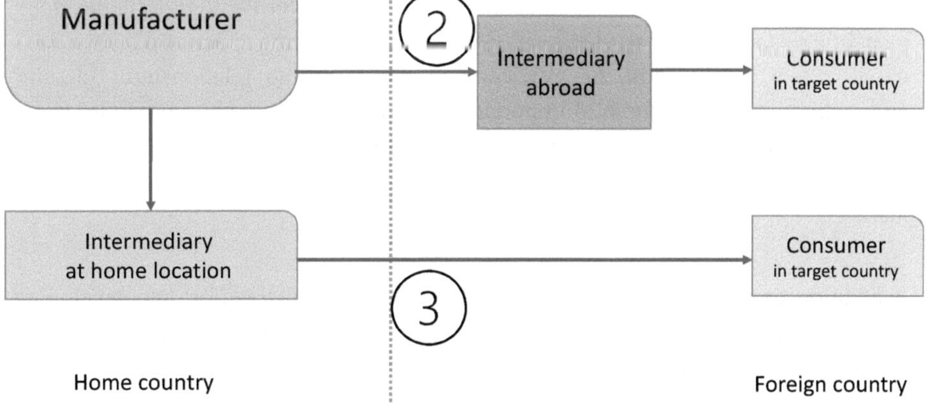

Fig. 5.1 Direct and indirect export as entry mode (author's own compilation)

switching between export markets or ceasing operations in less attractive markets is easier (Diamantopoulos et al., 2014; Pedersen et al., 2002; Raut, 2017; Serra et al., 2012).

Intermediaries can have multiple customers and may sell similar products from competitors (Bello et al., 1991). The advantage of an intermediary acting at the home location of the manufacturer is that it can be much easier to establish a closer relationship. Still, establishing a reliable network of international intermediaries can be costly and will take time, and requires more resources to control and monitor the efforts of sales agents.

In addition, as exporting firms may not have direct and immediate access to foreign markets, exchanging information about foreign markets may suffer prototypical problems generated by an asymmetric relationship between the firm (principal) and the intermediary (agent). The agent will not pass over all knowledge acquired about the costs of selling abroad, and the exporting firm cannot fully control the apparent negative effects of adverse selection. However, an exporting firm can mitigate losses caused by information asymmetry by implementing an incentive mechanism that aims to realign information asymmetries. An incentive mechanism is an effort to control the disadvantages arising from information asymmetries in agency relations. Managing successfully the relationship with intermediaries requires that both parties invest extra efforts in trust building, and dedicate more time to communication to strengthen the mutual collaboration and ensure that the common purpose of both the exporting firm and the intermediary is maintained.

Still, it is worth noting that an intermediary can support significantly smaller enterprises in organizing exports and can offer specialized knowledge about foreign markets as well as provide the services on an established distribution channel. However, in later stages of exporting, intermediaries can become a critical bottleneck limiting further sales growth.

A reliance on the intermediaries may save time and resources. But intermediaries may block the acquisition of the knowledge about unfamiliar export markets, while they allow to reducing the risk associated with direct exports.

Exporters need to negotiate and reach an agreement with the intermediary to let both sides share proper profits. Each agreement is constitutive for the long-term development of a sustainable and trusted relationship and, considering apparent agency costs, it will affect significantly the efficiency of the exporting relationship. But, the intermediary can be a source of important disadvantages if the chosen partner lacks incentives selling a discrete product or service. Less motivated intermediaries with exclusive distribution rights may eventually block the expansion in other export markets.

In addition, an intermediary does not automatically put an extra effort into developing or maintaining a positive image for a particular export product if the sales volume of the respective product is marginal and the profit margin low.

In most cases, finding a suitable partner to manage exports is the first step toward successful export activities (Ju & Gao, 2017). For firms seeking a partner for distribution abroad, comprehensive negotiations are vital. Negotiating an agreement may be carried out in person to make a first hand assessment of a future partner; it will permit both sides an opportunity to articulate more directly apparent expectations and weigh the feasibility of their respective stakes. In any negotiation, exporters should focus on the required resources and capabilities a potential partner must bring into a relationship (Root, 1994).

Exporters may decide to start selling products and services directly to foreign customers, but they can also rely on distributors in the host countries (importers). Apart from ad hoc export activities, growing sales through exports will depend on safeguarding close, sustainable and trusted ties with apparent customers in a target foreign market and will require adapting a product marketing mix that fits several customer segments in a foreign market.

5.2 Licensing

Licensing is a widely used entry mode and an attractive mechanism for granting a controlled access to proprietary knowledge. A licensing agreement can be used to exploit commercially firm specific advantages in a foreign market.

Licensing has become more attractive since the 1990s as the international regulatory environment has improved considerably (Cross, 2000). However, a large proportion of licensing agreements is used to organize intrafirm trade of IP rights, but it is also used to repatriate firm profits to attractive tax regimes offered by a number of countries.

License

A license is defined as an agreement between the licensor, the owner of a technology and the licensee, who leases the right to use a legally protected intellectual property (IP) from the licensor. A licensing agreement is a contract specifying the scope and extent of the use of property rights between the owner (licensor) and the party (licensee) which will be entitled by the agreement to use these property rights.

Empirical research demonstrates that licensing has emerged as a viable alternative for FDI or export as a market entry mode for firms seeking to service distant markets that are fragmented, volatile, or to small (Clegg & Cross, 2000; Contractor, 1984). Firm can choose to serve foreign markets using affiliate and non-affiliate licensing. Affiliate licensing is a prevalent practice dominant in developed countries (Clegg & Cross, 2000). Licensing is different from franchising, but both are used as a common method to internationally transfer IP rights and both can be a viable strategy for firms aiming to grow in international markets. Usually, licensing is regarded as a non-equity form of IP rights transfer. It is often viewed as a substitute for horizontal and vertical FDIs which require substantially more investment to control and organize business operations abroad (Contractor, 1984).

However, enforcing control on a licensee can be more challenging than exerting hierarchical control. Therefore, a licensor needs to ensure that the licensee maintains the quality of the product or service by stipulating that key inputs are sourced by the licensee from the licensor (Hennart, 1977: 111). Licensing as an entry mode strategy can augment the scope of exploiting existing firm-specific advantages (Pla-Barber et al., 2014). Licensing is also an important strategy for firms developing, designing, and manufacturing high-tech products. Research demonstrates that patent royalties (licensing fees) for a smartphone account for almost 30% of the sales prices (Chen et al., 2017: 502).

5.2.1 Licensing and Agency Problems

Licensing as an entry strategy is frequently bundled with other entry modes (Contractor, 1984; Yasar & Paul, 2007). John Dunning argued in his celebrated OLI paradigm that entry mode decisions are based on the reciprocity between (O) ownership advantages and the realization of (I) internalization advantages and the exploitation of (L) location advantages. A firm which only leverages firm-specific advantages abroad, but is incapable of exploiting internalization and locational benefits, can still exploit attractive export markets by licensing out parts of its firm-specific advantages to other firms (Dunning, 1995b; Dunning & Lundan, 2008; Rugman, 2010).

Several aspects of firm-specific advantages, such as trademarks, patents, and industrial design, can be sold or leased to other parties. Although in IB, licensing is sometimes treated as a simple 'indirect' entry mode, it is in fact a complex arrangement between two mutually dependent parties. Licensing is combined increasingly with other entry modes, such as sharing IP rights in international joint ventures (IJVs) or used in strategic alliances.

In such cases, licensing fees can be based on sharing earnings, direct payment of royalty fees, or cash payments for inputs provided by the parent company for the IJV (Contractor, 1985). Licensing is an instrument for the owner of IP rights to commercialize the intellectual property in different market segments and across geographical regions s/he does not intend to exploit directly. License is the right to use technological capabilities in a specific geographical region. Licensing agreements can be one-way agreements between a licensor and a licensee to use IP rights related to a single patent (brand, industrial design, trademark, patent) or it can be part of cross-licensing agreement between two or more firms to use several patents from a pool of jointly owned patents (Grindley & Teece, 1997). Licensing can be used as a core entry mode strategy or as a supplement to existing entry modes (Grindley, 2018). Typically, the relationship between a licensor (the seller of the IP right) and the licensee (buyer) is affected by agency problems, such as hidden action and hidden information.

> Difficulties arise from the fact that a licensor cannot fully control and monitor the licensee. The opportunism of the licensee can be an issue for the licensor, because it

(continued)

may harm the image of a licensed product/service/technology in the particular market in the long term. Parallel imports from products sold by a licensee can mutilate other markets (Agrawal, 2007; Ishikawa et al., 2020; Tan et al., 1997).

A licensor usually requires an up-front payment and royalties on sales. The licensor is in fact selling for a given period an intangible right with the intention to receive royalties for the sales in the target market.

Licensing is a technology sharing agreement, where the owner of the IP rights intends to share the potential value (using either a fixed fee or royalty payments) with the licensee. The licensee is paying for the use of the technology (or trademark or design) (Nguyen et al., 2017).

In the 1980s, Chinese government supported domestic car industry to acquire key technology with licensing agreements (Glass & Saggi, 2002). Multinational firms are often confronted with compulsory licensing policies, such as those in place in India, which force the management to balance the need for IP protection with the aim of developing foreign markets (Baten et al., 2017; Frankel & Lai, 2014; Kaszubska, 2017). Without or under the restriction of compulsory licensing, contracting and enforcement is conceived as an agency problem.

Hidden action refers to a scenario in which the licensee operates with a license in a way that benefits the licensee at the expense of the licensor. For example, the licensee can use the license to develop a product or service that substitutes the original product or service that is the subject of a licensing agreement, or actual sales figures are underreported. These problems arise because a licensor can only imperfectly monitor and control the licensee's intentions. Hidden information, on the other hand, relates to the gap between licensor's and licensee's ability to measure the value of the technology that will be sold in a license agreement to use in the prospective geographical territory. Hidden information problems are caused by information asymmetries that do not allow both parties to negotiate an efficient contract, because either the needed information is not available or cannot or will not be provided.

Agency problems that arise from apparently incomplete or asymmetric information concern both the licensor and the licensee as they result from conflicting intentions caused by missing or unequal access to critical information and lead to limited control of prevalent opportunistic behavior caused by the intangible properties of IP goods. It is generally assumed by agency theories that the principal (licensor in this context) can motivate the agent (licensee) not to harm the interests of the principal.

However agency problems, described as moral hazard, hidden action and hidden information, that lead to adverse selections will considerably affect the efficiency of contracting between a licensor and a licensee (Zenger & Gubler, 2018). How much signaling can reduce agency problems in a licensing agreement depends on finding a trusted licensee, and is also affected by the degree to which both parties can adapt the situational context evolving over the lifetime of an agreement.

Although a license agreement can be terminated, intangible intellectual property and technology rights already transferred cannot be blocked against further unauthorized exploitation (Gifford, 1999; Schmitz, 2007; Shapiro, 1986). These hazards arise especially where it is difficult to enforce IP infringements.

A high degree of uncertainty in the enforcement of legal resolutions in cases of IP infringement can, in effect, turn a contractual licensing agreement into a costly liability (Chen et al., 2017). Infringement disputes drag on for many years, often without a straightforward resolution, while incurring astronomical costs (lawyer fees, court costs, compensation for damages, etc.). The high costs and the long-term uncertainty are illustrated by patent infringement litigation between rival firms that collaborate on many fronts, such as Apple and Samsung, but also by many others (ITC, 2004).

Thomas and D'Aveni demonstrated that large firms spam small firms with petitions and complaints in patent infringement disputes, which can prolong the cases and exacerbate the costs for small clients (Thomas & D'Aveni, 2009).

Further, Arijit Mukherjee argues that licensing agreements with more than three licensees with a mix of fixed fee and output royalty payment is preferred in industries with a declining return to scale. Pertinent literature further reveals that the possibility of imitation, the number of firms, product differentiation, and diminishing returns to scale are significant determinants of the coexistence of fixed fee and royalty in licensing contracts. Mukherjee convincingly demonstrated how market size affects licensing contracts, as the stronger the potential expansion effect (defined as the rate of growth in a licensee's sales in a selected product market), the greater the incentive effect on output-related royalties' payments (Mukherjee, 2020)

In the extant licensing literature, it is generally assumed that licensing promotes technology transfer and innovation within and between business firms, but weak enforcement in cases of adverse selection problems increases the volatility of licensing. In all cases where a firm develops a technology and has licensed that technology to downstream firms for a fixed fee and a per-unit royalty, strict execution per-unit royalties maximizes the licensor's profit when there is effective competition between individual licensees. If competition is imperfect, the licensor has the option to increase its revenue by reducing variable (outcome-based) royalties to minimize fraud, where fraud is defined as misrepresentation of sales revenue (Gilbert & Kristiansen, 2017).

5.2.2 Licensing Mixed with Other Entry Modes

Multinational firms employ licensing strategies as alternative entry modes to grow in small and volatile markets. IB research suggests that a firm possessing propriety advantages will expand into foreign markets either by using FDI or licensing (Hymer, 1976).

FDI and licensing differ greatly and the entrepreneurial decision should focus on comparing the risk-adjusted net present value of the expected return from an FDI with that from a licensing agreement. The difficulty seems to directly compare FDI and the licensing. FDI and licensing may be exposed to different kinds of uncertainty implementing rights and exercising control. Yet, the main argument comparing these two different entry modes may be flawed, because it rests on the expected value that will be appropriated in an uncertain future period, at a time, where those who need to make the choice, lack much of the information about the contingent future (Contractor, 1984).

Research in IB on licensing conducted in the 1990s revealed a higher prevalence of licensing in countries where licensee demonstrate a greater capability to exploit the technology transferred than the licensor. Conversely, the relative level of licensing decreases in countries with where the licensor can better operate and control firm specific advantages (FSA) in a more appropriate institutional setting (Contractor, 1984: 182). Studies suggest that the greater the international experience of a business firm the lower the propensity to license firm-specific technology, concluding that firms that have higher learning rates and thus more experience prefer a FDI compared to licensing. Whereas inexperienced firms resort to licensing because their somewhat poorer capability to learn in distant markets is preventing them to seek other entry modes (Arora & Fosfuri, 2000).

5.2.3 Compulsory Licensing

Compulsory licensing (CL) is a policy tool often applied in developing regions to grant access to life-saving pharmaceutical technologies. Research on this topic primarily focuses on the regulatory impact on innovating firms and the influence that the market entry of the imitator (equipped with a compulsory license) exerts on product price and the impaired innovation rate of innovating market participants (Frankel & Lai, 2014; Sarmah et al., 2020; Sarmah & Hoang, 2017). Studies suggest that the effect of compulsory licensing is neutral or positive if the products manufactured with the licensee are sold only in the licensed sales market. If compulsory licensing is used to establish gray markets for parallel imports, the effect on the rate of innovation is generally negative (Autrey et al., 2015; Fu et al., 2015).

While patents typically grant protection for 20 years, they can be a costly strategy in industries where the rate of technological change and the pace of change are high.

Patent or License?

For example, the patent for the CD player was filed in 1987 by Blaupunkt Werke GmbH in Germany and was published in 1987. In 1993, the first worldwide litigation was filed. In 2007, the property rights expired. Blaupunkt was founded in 1924 and

(continued)

initially manufactured radio receivers and sold more than one million car radios in 1959. In 1996, the firm expanded into car multimedia. In 1982, Blaupunkt developed the first prototype for car navigation, and in 2010 it relaunched into consumer electronics. Currently, hardly any vehicles need CD players, as most drivers rely on streaming services and other storage systems. Blaupunkt continues to sell car audio but licenses its brand. Among other things, Blaupunkt TVs are manufactured by competitors in Slovenia and are sold throughout Europe.

Compared to a license a patent provides some protection, for a limited time, but it does not protect the firm from being overtaken by radically new generations of a specific technology while filing patents to protect proprietary technologies. Within a few years, technologies and products protected by patents can become obsolete. Selling a license early, especially in rapidly changing technologies, will help increase revenue and will allow broader use of IP rights. Thus, licensing agreements allow other companies to sell the protected technologies to licensees, but they do not protect the firm from being overtaken by radically new generations of a specific technology while preserving its own technology. The extended use of the technology can generate licensing income. In general, licensing as a mode of market entry is only applied when either exports or institutional market entry is not possible (Kollmer & Dowling, 2004).

5.2.4 Licensing and Learning Attributes

Licensing may be beneficial if, in the absence of a license, the related market development would not be undertaken by the licensor. Licensing can also be advantageous if the licensor lacks the resources required to exploit a possible market potential through stand-alone market exploitation.

However, the exploitation of the licensing-related benefits always depends on the internal firm capabilities and external (contextual) environmental conditions, as well as on the licensor's capacity to realistically assesses the existing conditions. Licenses may be omitted due to excessive caution; whereby potential additional revenues may be missed. Likewise, licenses may be granted too generously, thereby blocking the company's own future market development. A licensor may lose control over the product, its reputation, packaging, price, and promotion mechanisms in a specific licensed market abroad. Due to licensing, intangible areas of knowledge are always passed onto potential competitors who may become competitors in the future.

Although licensing is often treated as an easy approach to exploit the potential of foreign markets by the licensor, it is a complex arrangement between one licensor and one or more licensees. Cross-licensing is part of an elaborate IP strategy, which SMEs often underestimate, and often lack personnel resources and legal expertise to deal with appropriately

(Kaszubska, 2017; "WTO | intellectual property (TRIPS) - TRIPS and public health: Compulsory licensing of pharmaceuticals and TRIPS", n.d.). In extant studies, patents are often seen as bargaining tool for the negotiation of balanced deals in cross-licensing (Contractor & Kundu, 1998; Davis, 2006). Cross-licensing as a strategy is prevalent in industries with high R&D expenditures, like the chemical industry, which use patents, trade secrecy, and licensing to block rivals' entry into established markets (Arora, 1997). On the other hand, cross-licensing strategies with non-affiliate rivals are prevalent in high-tech industries, where the innovation and production of new high-tech goods and services (software, mobile phone technologies, pharmaceuticals) requires multiple licenses acquired from collaborating and competing rivals (Aulakh et al., 2010; Choi & Gerlach, 2019; Davis, 2006).

5.2.5 Factors Affecting the Licensing Choice

The choice whether or not to pursue licensing as an entry strategy may be based on genuine reasons why a potential market is not exploited through other entry modes.

In the early literature on market entry modes, the holder of IP rights that is not willing or capable to exploit potential target markets is assumed to prefer licensing (Root, 1994: 108). This view is not wrong, but it implies that licensing is the easiest option if the firm is not considering export or other entry options. Research further shows that licensing is used as a strategy in fragmented and small markets (Gleason et al., 2000, 2006). The licensing strategy is also affected by the internal firm capabilities of the licensor, characteristics of the product market, and industry parameters (Kotabe et al., 1996). In other words, licensing is much more complex than often assumed. It is also used as a steppingstone into volatile and fragmented markets (Welch et al., 2018). Many authors view it as a proactive strategy in high-tech markets as it allows firms to align with rapidly changing technologies to exploit network externalities in highly interdependent industries by co-aligning with competing and complementing product development (Banerji & Dutta, 2009; Liebowitz & Margolis, 2017). If a particular product rises in popularity, and a licensor has licensed a key technology for that product, it can share the rent on increased value generated by network externalities. In sum, it is a viable strategy for achieving firm growth (Buckley & Casson, 1998; Kotabe et al., 1996; Mottner & Johnson, 2000). However, making a decision to license firm-specific IP rights to other non-affiliate firms seems far less a choice between competing options, such as export or licensing, licensing or FDI, but more as one option within a whole set of other chosen entry modes.

Luostarinen and Welch (1990: 41) illustrate how licensing as entry mode may be used as an alternative to other entry modes, or in combination with exports, IJV, WOS, or other contractual forms of cooperation. Licensing can emerge as a viable strategy after entry, but implementing a licensing agreement, finding a suitable licensee, and managing the tacit relationship between licensor and licensee can be tricky (Welch et al., 2018). A licensor must be clear about the scope of the license agreement and needs to define the geographic region in which the license will apply. An agreement on the prevention of parallel imports should also be made. Negotiations with a licensee will indicate how trustworthy the planned relationship will be, but managing this relationship is an ongoing process that requires commitment from both sides and does not stop when the license agreement is signed. It is also important to know how changes to a license agreement, if they become necessary, can be implemented, what terms the license agreement will have, and how a license agreement can be terminated. Negotiations will usually allow the licensor to assess the suitability of the licensee, but the relationships will change after signing the agreement.

After the contract is signed, it often becomes clear whether the effort, the necessary personnel, and the communication channels committed to the relationship are sufficient to ensure an effective transfer of the intellectual property. The success of a licensing agreement is thus dependent on the commitment and trust invested by both parties in that long-term relationship (Welch et al., 2018: 142).

Existing contractual partners, such as importers, distributors, or sales agents, might be feasible candidates for licensees. The advantage they bring into that tacit relationship is that both parties know each other and the past experience indicates much better the goodwill necessary for an effective licensing agreement (Mottner & Johnson, 2000).

5.3 Franchising

In many countries, franchising is seen as an inevitable component of the business landscape (Czinkota et al., 2021: 221f.). Franchising was popularized in the 1970s first in the USA, where it was used to organize the rapid growth of retailing concepts. The concept of franchising used to internationalize demonstrated a high growth potential in the last decade (Fladmoe-Lindquist & Jacque, 1995; Robins et al., 2002).

Franchising shares some similarities with licensing. For example, McDonald's, Burger King, Pizza Hut, Hertz, Body Shop, Midas, and many other not so well-known businesses use franchising as profitable internationalization strategy and entry mode to international markets. The concept is prevalent in many regions and industries. In retailing franchising accounts for as much as 50 % (Welch et al., 2018: 57). Business firms using franchise concepts operate in almost all industries and in almost all regions across the globe. But the concept is most prevalent in business that depend for success on a profound designed concept (business model) for distributing a product or service.

These firms usually sell their well-established and well-proven business model to an owner-operator for a fee. Franchising is not limited to well-known brand names in the fast-food industry, a great number of service companies and several higher educational institutions apply franchise concepts all over the world. Not surprisingly, franchising has become one of the major and rapidly growing international market entry strategies (Alon, 2001; Elango, 2019).

Franchising is a special form of cooperation between two or more independent firms, as the franchisor and franchisees negotiate the scope of their relationship in the form of a licensing agreement (Gillis & Castrogiovanni, 2012).

Franchise System

A **franchise system** is based on a bargain about the distribution of product or service in a selected geographical area. The franchise agreement is a contract about the right to use an approved, well-established and successfully tested business format, that may include a shop design, the service, branded products served for example in a fast-food restaurant or the services offered in a car repair shops. The core of the franchise agreement involves the transfer of tangible and intangible knowledge, marketing, training embedded and delivered in the business concept, which typically includes the rights to use trademarks, brands, store or industrial design, product design, as well as trade secrets in an agreed manner within a restricted geographically area.

Franchising and licensing as an international market entry mode share several similarities. In both cases, motives overlap and intangible rights are transferred in return for payment. Usually, the franchise contract specifies the scale and scope of the business format and how additional training, or services are delivered to guarantee the implementation of the franchised business format. The franchisor receives from the franchisee often an up-front payment, royalties, calculated as a % of sales.

5.3.1 The Pros and Cons of Franchising

The advantage of a franchise system lies in the sharing of risk among the franchise partners. Franchisees benefit from the ability to implement a proven business concept. The franchisor profits from the franchisee's entrepreneurial effort and the more profound market knowledge (Combs et al., 2011a; Dada & Watson, 2013; Rosado-Serrano et al., 2018).

In general, franchising is chosen when a franchisor wants to increase its presence but does not want to invest additional capital in a market that tends to be less attractive. As a result, franchisors often subcontract franchise concepts to locations that are less profitable and operate attractive and profitable locations by themselves. The franchisee enjoys the brand awareness and strongly developed and tested marketing concepts.

Disadvantages of franchising tend to arise from poor implementation of the concept by franchisees and can cause a lasting loss of image or a damage of reputation in the respective market. There are also both pre- and post-contractual agency problems between franchisor and franchisee. Only ex-post can the franchisor see whether the franchisee was actually capable of effectively implementing the franchise concept. Ensuring a high standard is one of the mutual interests of a franchise system, but the reputational damage for the franchisor is usually higher than for the franchisee.

A disadvantage for the franchisee is that the expected probability of success of a 'rather' less common concept is at the expense of the franchisee. Successful franchise concepts sometimes require substantial financial outlays before the franchise concept is launched (Kehoe, 1996; Lee et al., 2015b).

Franchisor use often IJV or WOS to manage their franchising agreements with franchisee in foreign markets. McDonalds approached the Japanese market establishing a Joint Venture for master franchising, which developed a highly successful mechanism to penetrate the local market (Welch et al., 2018: 63). Franchisors operating with a large number of franchisees in a foreign market may leverage potential spill over effects (ibid, 66). For many firms using a franchising system to expand internationally it can be a low cost and more rapid alternative compared to other entry modes.

5.3.2 Performance, Learning and Productivity in Franchising

The performance of franchising is explained by several theories. Most studies use resource based theories of the firm and institutional theories (Combs et al., 2004, 2011a; Kidwell et al., 2007). Efforts to understand franchising suggest that a franchisee will choose franchising to gain access to critical resources needed for growth (Combs et al., 2009).

Research on franchising is very diverse and comprehensive; it often addresses very specific franchise problems, such as the structure of franchising systems, its strategy, the reputation of the franchise system (Clegg & Cross, 2000; Combs et al., 2011a; Elango, 2019; Kidwell et al., 2007; Rosado-Serrano & Paul, 2018). Theories that focus on particular problems implementing a franchise system rely often on agency theories, elaborating the information asymmetry between the franchisor and the franchisee (Kehoe, 1996).

Applying these specific theories to explain discrete cause-and-effect relationships is common and help to understand prevalent problems arising in managing franchising (Doherty et al., 2014; Garg & Rasheed, 2003; Kehoe, 1996; Michael, 2019). Generally, the resource-based theory of the firm is focused on the lack of resources for exploitation firm-specific technologies and consequently is concentrating on questions how a franchisor and a franchisee can complement each other, exploiting possible common synergies. Institutional theories are used to explain the effect of institutions, constituted by norms, rules, values apparent in different cultures, and ask how franchising will be affected by these institutional differences in foreign markets (Combs et al., 2011a, b; Elango, 2019; Elango & Fried, 1993).

Research conducted by Darr et al. (1995) on a sample of 46 franchise outlets demonstrated that productivity gains translate effectively to per-unit cost reduction, but this requires effective transfer of experiential knowledge to the managers and staff of franchise units. Knowledge transfer was also found to be enhanced through face-to-face meetings and conferences (Darr et al., 1995: 1756ff).

Factors Affecting the Performance of Franchising

In extant literature about franchising, four theoretical perspectives are typically adopted to determine the drivers of successful inter-organizational relationship performance, and can thus be applied to a franchise relationship, focusing respectively on (1) commitment and trust, (2) dependency between contracting parties, (3) transaction costs resulting from contracting, and (4) culture-dependent rules and norms, all of which are found to affect the functioning of inter-firm or inter-organizational relationships (Palmatier et al., 2007).

Kalnins and Mayer contributed similar evidence on the relationship between franchising, ownership, and experience on restaurant survival. They concluded that the probability of failure decreases with the local experience, whereas the transfer between affiliate franchisees increases the value of local experience of owners. Although the meaning of local experience is a broad concept, it denotes acquaintance with culture-specific norms and rules, as well as institutional characteristics. Studies indicate that the success of a franchise relationship depends on the extent to which the franchisee is able to navigate or adapt to the local working environment. Hence, local owners' experience significantly contributes to the survival rate of their business units (Kalnins & Mayer, 2004).

However, that assumed closeness and intimacy of franchise relationships points to another problem related to growth of a franchise system, as in a rapidly expanding spatially dispersed system, more time and effort is needed to control and manage franchisees (Fladmoe-Lindquist, 1996). Yet, managerial capabilities can be another limitation if inadequate (Penrose, 1959; Mahoney, 1995; Pitelis, 2004; Rugman & Verbeke, 2004), suggesting that greater entrepreneurial effort should be invested by the franchisees to bridge this gap (Gillis & Castrogiovanni, 2012; Rachlin et al., 1987).

In many entry modes, not only in franchising and licensing, it matters how intellectual property rights are transferred and controlled between and within firm boundaries. There are several distinct differences that affect the sharing, transfer, co-ownership or sale of intellectual property (IP) rights. In this subsection, a brief description of the specific features of intellectual property rights is provided.

5.3.3 Why Do Intellectual Property Rights Matter?

Intellectual property (IP) rights are categorized as copyrights, patents, trademarks, industrial design, geographical indications, and brand names provided for the design of a product. A business firm, who uses licensing as the entry mode grants to one or more other firms the exclusive right to produce a product or a service in a specified foreign market using the licensed technologies, brands or other intellectual properties. Granting a license to use a firm's proprietary knowledge generates income in markets that the owner is not serving or is not capable to enter. Licensing is used between independent contracting parties, but also within a firm between headquarters and subsidiaries, often for tax reasons. But licensing is based on selling the IP rights granted, for example by a patent.

The International Patent Classification

Filing an application with the International Patent Classification (IPC) system, instead of a national patent application, may be preferable as this ensures that the IPC rules will be followed from the outset (see the IPC System at the WIPO in Genf).

The WIPO (World Intellectual Property Organisation) is an international organization within the United Nations Systems, founded in 1967. In 2021, it had 193 member states and about 250 non-governmental organizations with official observer status. The organization is headquartered in Geneva, Switzerland, and is the most important international organization managing the international IP system. The WIPO is also the administrative body for the PCT (Patent Cooperation Treaty), which allows inventors to apply for international patents. The application is usually filed at the national patent office, which will transmit it to the WIPO and to the ISA (International Searching Authority), SISA (Supplementary International Searching Authority), and IPEA (International Preliminary Examining Authority). The three international bodies carry out research related to the application, prepare an opinion, and report to the WIPO. The WIPO reports and communicates with the (designated) national or regional patent offices, which grant the patents. The so-called PCT system is used by many large multinational firms, but also by individual inventors and SMEs to receive protection for their inventions.

The WIPO IP Portal grants easy access to global patents granted. A patent is the right to use an invention for a limited time (usually for 20 years) to exclusively exploit the invention in a patented product or process.

In international business a number of intellectual property rights matter and influence how the owner can control and operate exploiting these IP rights abroad. A major question is also how to protect the infringement of these IP rights by other parties. There are different categories of IP rights, which need to be distinguished.

5.3.3.1 Copyright

A copyright is the right of an author over his/her literary and artistic work, such as books, paintings, sculpture, films, software, databases, maps, technical drawings, or advertisements (Norman, 2001). It is applied to the expression of literary and art work, which can also be a logo, slogan, or similar. The copyright allows the owner to get a financial remuneration for the use of his/her work by others. According to the Berne Convention, copyright protects the literary and artistic work automatically (Emruli et al., 2016; Sterling, 2004). However, replication of daily news and the provision of accessible formats for disabled people are exempted from the copyright protection (WIPO, 2021, Copyrights).

5.3.3.2 Patents

A patent is the exclusive right granted for an invention (related to a product or a process). The invention needs to be new, and the inventor has to prove the novelty and originality of his/her work (such as a technical solution). The exclusive right granted and all the information describing the invention provided as a part of the patent application is publicly disclosed to enhance the rate of innovation in a society, while the exclusiveness of rights granted aims for strengthening the incentive to invest in R&D. The inventor has to prove that the inventions is (a) novel, (b) is a non-obvious improvement of an existing technology (invention), and (c) is feasible for an industrial application (Petruzzelli et al., 2015).

The exclusiveness of the IP rights allows the IP holder to prevent any other party from exploiting commercially the technology or process patented. In other words, no one is allowed without owner's consent to manufacture or distribute (including importing or exporting) products containing the protected technology, or products using part of that technology. These rights are guaranteed in all the countries (territories) in which the patent has been filed. A patent protection is generally granted for 20 years (from the start of filling the application). There are many benefits of patented IP, but also many drawbacks. As large multinationals rely on the continuation of patents to extend the period in which the invention remains private (Graham & Mowrey, 2004, 2005; Risch, 2013; Singh, 2019), protection of IP rights is often seen as a constraint to the free flow of scientific knowledge (Murray & Stern, 2007) On the other hand, studies on patent citations suggest that the emerging new technologies based on existing patents are actually accelerating the rate of inventions (Lee et al., 2015a).

5.3.3.3 Trademarks

The main purpose of a trademark is to distinguish goods and services provided by one enterprise from those of other enterprises. Trademark is a protected IP right obtained through the registration administered by the WIPO, using the Madrid System designated for registering and managing existing trademarks. After registration and fee payment, the trademark can be protected in 124 countries using the Madrid System (Madrid System, WIPO). A trademark right does not have a limited life, but can be renewed. A renewal of an expired trademark is not possible.

5.3.3.4 Industrial Designs

Product design can be protected if it "constitute[s] the ornamental aspects of an article" (WIPO, Industrial Designs, 2021). An industrial design is a three-dimensional feature, like the shape of a bottle or mobile phone, or a two-dimensional feature like the pattern of a fabric, or its color. The contour of the Coke bottle, the mini cooper, Piaggio's Vespa, or Dyson's cyclone vacuum cleaner are examples of protected industrial design, for which the IP rights are indefinite. The owner of a patented design is entitled to block third parties from using the designed product feature. The design patent is a viable substitute for patents granted for an innovative product or process, as the protection for a design is granted for an unlimited period of time.

Samsung Electronics, headquartered in the Rep. Korea headed the list of top applicants consecutively within the last three years until 2019, with 929 designs registered for protection. Fonkel, a Dutch retailer of furniture followed next with 859 designs registered, next followed by LG Electronics, Korea Republic, with 598, Volkswagen AG, Germany for 536 and Procter & Gamble (P&G), USA with 410 applications.

The top ten applicants were from the automotive, electronics, furnishings, and household/consumer goods industries (WIPO, 2021).

5.3.3.5 Trade Secrets

A trade secret is an IP based on confidential information about a production process or technology that is not disclosed to the public. The holder of a trade secret may commercialize the intellectual property contained in the "trade secret" by licensing or selling it to a limited number of users. Trade secrets can be sold, legally held by the owner, or given to a licensee for use for a limited time under a license agreement. The problem with commercialization of trade secrets is that the contractual part of the sale or licensing should be closed from the moment the trade secret is disclosed because, upon disclosure, the trade secret can be misused. In these cases, the contractual relationships show the classic characteristics of an agency problem. The value of trade secrets is substantially damaged by industrial espionage, violation of negotiated agreements, and in the absence of trusted relationship between owner, the licensor, and licensee. Post-contract shirking may be prevalent in any agreement between an owner and a licensee. The problem of post-contract shirking can be avoided by selling the trade secret for a fixed price (Depken et al., 2001; Marburger, 2003).

A technology can be patented, a product name, logo, or brand name trademarked and the design of a product, its appearance, and haptic properties can be legally protected. All these IP rights are the outcome of firm-specific advantages. A company that has no manufacturing facilities abroad can sell its technology to existing local manufacturers.

The Use of IP Rights in International Business

Nestlé India Ltd (the licensee), pays to Société des Produits Nestlé S.A. as the licensor 4.5% of net sales of products sold (Company Information, Nestle, 2021). Coca-Cola company licenses the right to bottle its soft drinks to Ferrero Group, an Italian multinational, but also the right to sell the Tic-Tac mint candy with Coca-Cola flavor in 70 countries (Coca Cola, company data, 2021).

Angelo Trocchia, CEO of Safilo, sold in the last two decades more than 30 million Dior sunglasses and eyeglass frames. Safilo paid 13% of its total sales as licensing fee

(continued)

to Dior, but lost the license in 2020. Salfino Group is an Italian eyeglass manufacturer and licenses over 25 brands, including Moschino, Missoni, Givenchy, and Fendi. In 2018, it generated net sales of 780 million €, making a gross profit of 362.5 million €. Safilo group produced eyewear in six plants, three of which were located in Italy, with the remaining three in Ormoz, Slovenia, Salt Lake City, USA, and Suzhou, China. It operates three distribution centers in Padua, Italy, Denver, Colorado, and Hong Kong. Safilo sells eyewear and sunglasses in more than 40 countries. To operate in these markets it owns licenses from 67 licensors, all of which are well-known brands (Safilo, Annual Report, 2019).

5.4 Entry Modes and Asset Commitment

One of the key issues that characterize a market entry mode is the commitment and control of resources. Although some market entry modes can be implemented effectively with few resources and limited experience, others, like foreign direct investment, mergers and acquisitions (M&A) or international joint ventures require more commitment, time, resources, and experience for an effective implementation in an unfamiliar foreign environment. There are internal and external factors, two broad categories, sometimes overlapping, that affect significantly the performance of a selected entry mode (Brouthers, 2013; Dhanaraj & Beamish, 2003; Glaum & Oesterle, 2007; Styles et al., 2008; Zhao et al., 2017). Generally, foreign direct investment and international joint ventures are considered more elaborate than export, licensing and franchising, but each entry mode is not simply dependent on an increasing linear level of managerial know-how or commitment. In fact, each mode needs to fit an unfamiliar institutional environment, a fit that requires efforts to adapt or change according to a co-evolving and contingent situational context.

Mixing Entry Modes

The use of FDI as entry mode is generally characterized as complex. It requires the transfer of firm assets, particularly managerial knowledge, continuous effort, the transfer of technologies, human resources, and other form of tangible and intangible firm assets. FDI is particularly applied to exercise a more direct and ideally efficient control in foreign operated business activities. A higher degree of assets transferred usually correlate to a greater exposure to risks and increase the volatility in often unfamiliar environments. More or stouter control over the prevalent foreign business do not automatically endorse more flexibility and reliability managing business operations in a contingent foreign market. The greater exposure of FDI, which is often discussed as a problem, can be eventually become an opportunity. However, it is a challenge to find the balance between a desired level of control and the exposure to a risky and uncertain foreign environment.

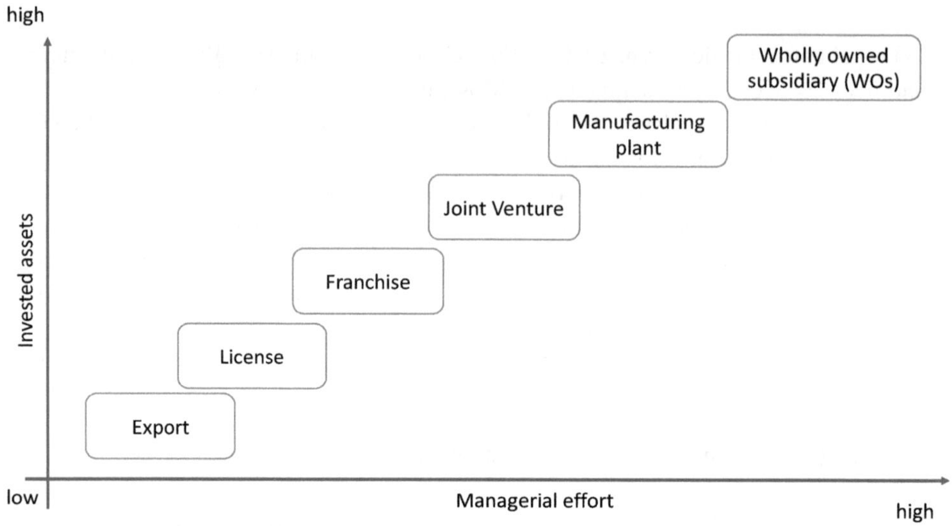

Fig. 5.2 Entry modes categorized along supposed commitment, managerial control and needed market knowledge

A common categorization of the scale and scope of entry modes is illustrated in Fig. 5.2. In the graph the exemplified entry modes are classified according to two dimensions that affect the control of firm operations in foreign markets. Firm management selecting a market entry mode will seek to balance the obvious strengths and weaknesses of the chosen market entry mode to gain a fit in the prevalent foreign market environment. The overall argument illustrated in Fig. 5.2 is based on the conception of internationalization as a gradual process. The assumed incremental and gradual stages in the process of internationalizing led to a particular categorization of entry modes two dimensions. Market knowledge and managerial experience (managerial effort) are defined on the horizontal axis and commitment (invested assets) on the vertical axis as key attributes related to the success for the selection of a particular mode of market entry.

The general implication of this gradual progression of entry modes with respect to invested assets and managerial effort conveys the prevalent view that firms in their initial stage of internationalization will typically choose export because it requires only limited resources and low market knowledge and experience. That contention is associated with the assumption that firms in this initial stage seek to keep apparent risks low and therefore enter familiar markets, typically by exporting to nearby countries. In later stages, firms may apply entry modes, such as licensing, franchising, or seek to establish IJVs, all of which involve contract negotiations, and all require a higher degree of managerial experience and more effort and commitment of resources. Although contracting is susceptible to problems arising from information asymmetries, it is widely assumed that both the internationalizing firm and the cooperating (usually) host-country partner will share the risks and effort to serve the selected target markets.

The entry modes that are adopted in more advanced stages, especially FDI, needed for example, to establish a foreign sales subsidiary, a foreign manufacturing plant, or a wholly owned subsidiary entail even more commitment and managerial effort.

The entry forms in the lower left panel on the graph are characterized by low or no ownership ratio, whereas those in the upper right are associated with high ownership ratio. Figure 5.2 is an illustration of the two drivers in the process of internationalization that influence entry mode choice. One widely discussed driver is (a) the increasing scope of ownership-based control exercised by a higher managerial commitment abroad, and (b) the assumption that a higher scale of investment allows for more control. The two dimensions interact, but they moreover illustrate different levels of risk, ascending from low levels associated with exporting to a much higher exposure in a wholly owned foreign production plant.

These two dimensions are not the only factors that need to be considered when selecting an entry mode, as the relationship between the two variables is more complex and their effects are highly interdependent.

Example

An international joint venture (IJV) with a majority stake does not necessarily imply greater control for the majority owner in the joint management, and a sales subsidiary will not automatically lead to greater control in an unfamiliar environment. In both cases, other internal (firm specific) and external (host environmental) factors are equally important in co-determining the outcome.

The characterization of the entry modes as an incremental and organic approach is at the same time right and wrong. It is correct because firms acquire new knowledge and experience from previous entry modes which can enhance the skills and capability to manage subsequent, more demanding entry modes. It is wrong, as it implies that firms mechanically follow the incremental escalation of entry modes—an assumption that is critiqued in several studies (Dzikowski, 2018; Efrat & Shoham, 2012; Fletcher, 2001; Hennart, 2014; Rennie, 1993). The incremental and gradual character of the escalating entry modes shown in Fig. 5.2 is based on the premise that, in the early stage of internationalization, firms need to learn how to operate a chosen entry mode in an unfamiliar foreign market. This argument point at the fact, that firms experientially learn from current activities and thereby expand their knowledge and augment capabilities (Björkman & Eklund, 1996; Childs & Jin, 2014; Dominguez, 2018; Hult et al., 2020; Steen & Liesch, 2007). But in many cases, firms operate simultaneously several entry modes in foreign markets (Welch et al., 2018).

For example, firm A may carry out export, franchising and an IJV, while Firm B focuses on exporting, operating two IJVs, and a subsidiary for managing sales and production in the chosen foreign market. It is important to note that the gradual learning process does not imply that a firm that is moving on to negotiate a licensing agreement for a country market and is setting up a foreign sales subsidiary in another market will cease its exporting activities. A firm making an entry mode choice needs to balance the stock of resources and its commitment among several entry modes in different markets.

By experientially learning in a particular market, a firm can attempt to transfer the new knowledge and capabilities to other current international markets (Freeman et al., 2010). Entry modes related with equity based FDI require establishment of IJVs and wholly owned foreign subsidiaries. All these entry modes are initiated with the goal of gaining a greater influence over the foreign investment being made. The influence is then defined as the exertion of intentional control over managerial responsibilities and other essential operative activities. These entry modes are thus selected to control and to exploit firm-specific advantages in the host market (Hymer, 1976; Teece, 2006).

5.5 International Joint Ventures

The international joint venture (IJV) is a widely used entry mode. It is defined as a collaboration between two or more enterprises. The international joint venture is organized by a common governance structure. It is a common structure designed with the intention to use in a joint effort resources and capabilities brought into the joint venture (Inkpen, 2000; Inkpen & Crossan, 1995). A common assumption is that the IJV provide a successful platform for organizational learning (Inkpen, 2000: 1019). They are described as an efficient vehicle to exploit the competence of partnering firms (Lane et al., 2001).

But IJVs also require joint efforts to develop new technologies and capabilities. The basic philosophy behind a joint venture strategy is to exploit synergies from the joint use of shared resources (Contractor & Lorange, 2002). However, IJVs are difficult to manage, especially in unfamiliar institutional environments (Geringer & Hebert, 1989). A joint venture is a legal agreement, mostly based on making a direct investment by venture partners to set up a formally independent business entity. The joint venture is based on an agreement between two or more partner firms who agree to share common assets, information, and technologies in order to achieve a common goal. Compared to other entry modes an International Joint Venture requires a significant effort by all cooperating parties, from the initial idea to establish an IJV, to the operation of the venture. An IJV requires a continuous commitment to manage common interests, especially during difficult periods in the lifetime of the IJV.

International Joint Venture (IJV)
An international joint venture (IJV) is characterized by the intended collaboration between two or more enterprises, whereas at least on joining enterprise is from a foreign country. The IJV is managed by a common governance structure designed with the intention to use jointly the invested collection of resources and capabilities. The joint venture is an outcome of a deliberate decision to contribute complementary resources, skills, and expertise. The primary goal is sharing these common resources.

5.5.1 Joint Venture Goals

The primary goal of an IJV is sharing common resources, skills, and capabilities, but this necessitates sharing likewise risks and costs. IJVs are an entry mode strategy to access foreign markets by creating a joint entity, assuming that both partners are willing and capable to contribute complementing skills and expertise. But complementing these resources, an antecedent for joint venture success is not easily accomplished (Bener & Glaister, 2010; Geringer & Hebert, 1989; Luo, 2002a). Sharing common resources is not achieved automatically once initiated.

Operating a joint venture is based on an intricate reciprocal and interdependent relationship evolving by exercising efforts to cooperate in the IJV (Parkhe, 1993). A smooth cooperation in a IJV is dependent on a co-evolving subtle social dynamics that determine the ability to achieve jointly the intended outcome (Agrawal & Hollensen, 2002; Meschi & Wassmer, 2013).

5.5.2 High Failure Rates in IJVs

The apparent high failure rate of IJVs can be substantially reduced if negotiated agreements allow partners to adapt to emerging contingencies (Luo, 2002a). IJV failure can occur if partnering firms' IJV goals are vague or imprecise with respect to the contracting period, capitalization, and/or how and when capital is provided. IJV agreements are often unclear on how specific projects are carried out, or fail to regulate the terms of termination. Thus, to avoid such pitfalls, partnering firms need to be clear about how to operate and who will manage the venture (Farrell et al., 2011; Geringer & Hebert, 1989; Nisar et al., 2012; Puck et al., 2009; Shu et al., 2017). The majority of the problems that arise during the IJV operation stem from the fact that the IJV motives are often inconclusive, which in turn affects negotiating the scale and scope of the partnership (Nisar et al., 2012).

In addition, an indeterminate consensus about how to measure the performance can also increase the risk of failure (Geringer & Hebert, 1991; Jain & Jain, 2004; Kwok et al., 2019;

Ozorhon et al., 2010). All these aspects add to a potential instability in IJVs (Barkema et al., 1996, 1997; Geringer & Hebert, 1991; Reuer & Koza, 1998).

5.5.3 Major Motives for IJVs

Major motives often labeled as objectives of IJVs are the exchange of technologies, attaining economies of scale, sharing risks and assets to finance R&D, or operate in difficult competitive foreign environments (Welch et al., 2018). The motives typically discussed in the extant literature include the intention to (a) exchange of technologies, (b) reduce risks, by sharing it, (c) sharing the costs of research and development (R&D), dividing unforeseen costs, (d) creating better value than acting alone, (e) combining, supplementing, or complementing capabilities and resources, (f) pooling activities and resources to realize economies of scale, and (g) reducing risks in large international projects (Beamish & Berdrow, 2003; Benito & Welch, 1993; Boateng & Glaister, 2002; Glaister et al., 2005; Idris & Tey, 2011; Larimo et al., 2016; Li et al., 2009; Pak et al., 2009; Si & Bruton, 2005; Welch et al., 2018; Zhang & Li, 2001).

A joint venture is a strategic alliance between two or more business entities. It is an international joint venture (IJV) when at least one foreign entity is part of the joint venture. An IJV is set up as a separate (legally independent) business unit. It can be based either on a formal contractual agreement (non-equity based) or, in most cases, on capital and resources (equity) brought into the joint venture. A major goal of an IJV is its intention to share a common pool of assets.

If an IJV is established as a legally independent unit by two parent firms located in the domestic market, they may jointly set up a JV in the target foreign locations, whereby Firm A depends on an existing subsidiary in the foreign location and Firm B may opt for establishing a new entry with the common JV.

A simplified example for an IJV is shown in Fig. 5.3, where a business firm X headquartered in country A is setting up an IJV with another parent firm Y located in country B. The Joint Venture is established in country A. The IJV is established as a separate legal entity serving markets in country A and market in other locations. But IJV goals do not exist independently from Firm X and Firm Y. Thus, the success of the IJV in country A is affected by the effort of firm X and Y to organize the sharing common resources. The compatibility and complementarity of the objectives of the partnering business firms are a major antecedent that determine IJV performance (Pak et al., 2009).

Figure 5.3 illustrates a typical international set up of an IJV, established by two parent firms. By definition, the IJV does not need to operate in a particular host market, but many international JVs are established with a foreign parent firm to allow easier access to resources in that market, which may be difficult for the parent firm Y without firm X. In an IJV, parent firms use common resources to serve foreign markets and agree to share tangible and intangible resources, for example machinery, firm-specific technologies,

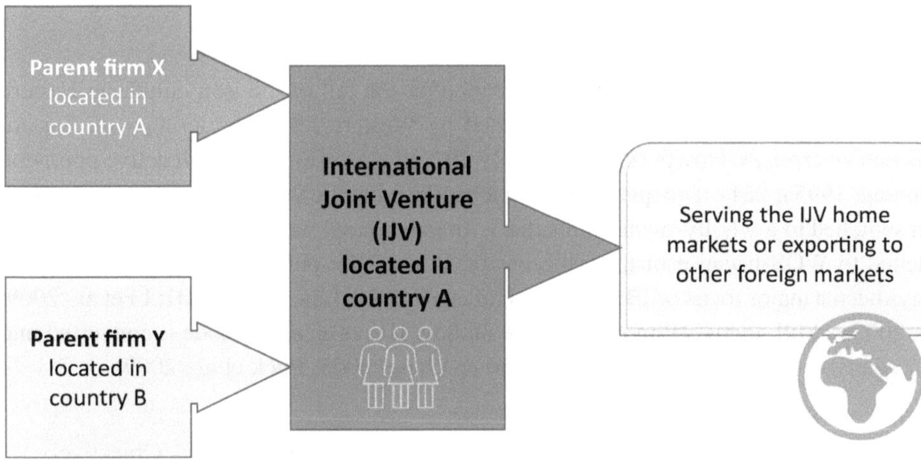

Fig. 5.3 International joint venture

managerial know how and experience, human resources and locally developed routines and skills, or IP rights owned by one of the partner firms.

The IJV strategy is focused on bundling these resources for a common objective. The difficulty is not only the willingness to share fully firm-specific advantages contributed but to manage a IJV being capable to exploit these common resources. This objective is mostly dependent on informal and formal social relations. These relations need to be established among the IJV personnel.

From a legal point of view, IJVs are established as separate legal business unit, but all too often parent firms exert a great deal of ad hoc or permanent control over the joint venture management.

The choice of IJV as an entry strategy is based on the premise that the newly established IJV in the host country is capable of productively utilizing the joint resources to serve the market in the IJV locations. The core purpose of IJVs is the efficient use of these jointly provided resources and/or capabilities. By pursuing a common strategy in the host market, the IJV partners can exploit several resources provided by parent firm A and B, ideally complementing existing managerial know-how and technologies. However, many IJVs are not as successful as originally intended, because partnering firms missed to

- define the contribution and responsibility of each IJV partner
- describe the criteria how to measure performance and distribute profits among partners (Mohr & Puck, 2007)
- specify who is operating and managing the IJV (Dhanaraj & Beamish, 2004; Lu & Beamish, 2001)
- agree on how contributed IP rights are shared when IJV is terminated (Bao et al., 2006; Chaudhry & Zimmerman, 2012; Luo, 2002b; Yuan et al., 1998).

5.5.4 Performance and IJV Stability

John Dunning reported that, within four years after the fall of the iron curtain in Eastern Europe, almost 25,000 IJVs were established by Western firms partnering with Eastern European enterprises. However, in 1991 only 10% of these IJVs were still active operation (Dunning, 1995a: 221). The question is what happened to the 90 %, a proportion may have been switched to a wholly-owned subsidiary. In either case, were these IJVs terminated or switched to WOS because of their success or failure? IJV performance and stability has always been a major focus of IB research (Hui et al., 2020; Lane et al., 2001; Li et al., 2009; Luo, 2002a). Still, there is limited evidence on how IJV as an entry mode is converted into other equity or non-equity entry modes (Lin & Wang, 2008; Puck et al., 2009).

Joint venture stability is determined by objective and subjective criteria. Objectively, IJV stability can be measured by its duration and survival rate. Conversely, change of ownership or early termination does not necessarily indicate instability. Subjective measures can substantially change over the life time of a IJV.

Control is often viewed as a critical dimension of IJV success (Geringer, 1998; Geringer & Hebert, 1989; Parks, 1984). However, control can mean different things. Joint venture partners may seek to exercise more control to ensure that common goals are met. This may raise by the partner the perception of not having an equal role and responsibility. In many cases, control is more predominant in IJVs with majority ownership, intended to protect incorporated property rights. A biased perception often expresses a lack of trust, which may push the other party to safeguard more its own interests while neglecting common benefits.

But control exercised straightforwardly destroys trust between IJV partners, and the inherent objective of control is actually nullified. However, the level of satisfaction with IJV performance is often subjective, even though in practice it is typically operationalized as the degree to which the common operational goals are met, including sales growth, sales volume, or profitability. These factors highlight the intricate and dynamic interaction between control, the enactment of mutual trust, and the scope of common objectives, which affect cooperation in IJVs (Alexander & Wilkins, 1982; Parks, 1984). But measuring performance in IJVs is difficult, because often partnering firms agree on common objectives although they often nurture their diverging interests (Geringer & Hebert, 1989; Geringer, 1998).

Not surprisingly, IJV research concentrated on apparent sources of conflict, such as unequal or contradicting firm cultures and their effect on the scope of cooperation. But are conflicting IJV cultures and a low level of cooperation the source or outcome of conflicts? In most studies, cooperation is the prevalent issue. The pertaining analyses are typically based on the assumption that the common management of an IJV may mitigate the negative effects of opportunism (Inkpen, 1998a, b). In practice, it is difficult to suppress or overcome partner opportunism (Huang et al., 2015; Luo, 2007) and the quality and content of research on cooperation in IJVs has been described as messy research, providing often contradicting evidence, based on ambiguous results.

5.5.5 Messy Research

Existing IJV research is described as "theory thin and method-driven" (Parkhe, 1993: 231). Arvind Parkhe labels almost 80% of IJV research with that tag, criticizing the lack of nomological validity. The crux of success in IJVs is about mutual forbearance (Parkhe, 1993), defined as self-control and tolerance, as well as willingness to refrain from exercising control over someone dependent on one's actions or assets. Forbearance is formally defined as "refraining from the enforcement of something, such as a debt, right, or obligation" (Merriam-Webster, n.d.). It is assumed the outcome of sustainable reciprocal relations. Parkhe (1993) describes forbearance as one of four key triggers of IJV stability and performance, along with reciprocity, trust, and opportunism. All these dimensions are conceptualized as interrelated, mutually reciprocating in determining the success of an IJV. These four dimensions are the building blocks for a more systematic theory that help to explain the evolutionary character of cooperation and control in an IJV.

5.5.5.1 Reciprocity

Reciprocity in the IJV motives of partnering firms should be established during the process of IJV formation (while negotiating and establishing the joint venture). However, reciprocity is more than the mere pooling of common goals, raw materials, supplies, manufacturing resources, marketing, or distribution capabilities. Reciprocity is a bond between two or more acting partners and is in practice very fragile. The fragility is caused by the threat of opportunism prevalent in many social relations. In joint ventures, reciprocity is viewed as a tacit property that develops slowly and is thus a key ingredient for attaining potential synergies between partnering entities. Consequently, it has to be maintained and developed continually.

5.5.5.2 Trust

Trust is an essential aspect of any relationship, and thus affects the IJV success (Parkhe, 1993). As a result, the formation of trust is a commonly discussed topic in IJV research (Ali & Khalid, 2017; Ando & Rhee, 2009; Lin & Wang, 2008; On et al., 2013; Svejenova, 2006; Wang et al., 2020). In two somewhat conflicting streams of research, the focus is given to (1) the formation and evolution of trust in IJV, and (2) a potentially damaging effect of opportunism in intra- and inter-organizational entities, supported by the theory of transaction costs (Ali & Larimo, 2016; Larimo et al., 2016; Owens et al., 2018).

5.5.5.3 Opportunism

Opportunism is the quest for self-interest with the use of guile or deliberate deception (Williamson, 1985). As opportunism is a major source of uncertainty in the assessment of an actor's actual purposes, it gives rise to behavioral problems, such as hold-up, adverse selection, and moral hazards (Zenger & Gubler, 2018). Ex post opportunism is seen as particularly harmful to the relationship if no protective measures are in place to prevent it. Consequently, governance mechanisms need to be put in place to avoid or minimize opportunism (Mahoney, 2016). But opportunism is based on a narrow behavioral model of human agency (Ghoshal & Moran, 1996). In this context, hold-up is defined as a behavior of a contracting partner narrowly aimed at appropriating gains that are supposed to be shared among all involved entities. Likewise, adverse selection is damaging as it indicates low-quality performance because of an existing information asymmetry between parties. Moral hazard occurs when agents pursue risky actions because the partner or others are sharing potential losses (Landes, 2013). Although transaction costs economics assumed that an organization can design appropriate governance structures to minimize losses caused by hold-up, information asymmetry, or moral hazard, trust will be difficult to establish in such circumstances (Gifford, 1999; Shapiro, 1986).

5.5.5.4 Forbearance

Trust is closely related to partner selection and partner characteristic. Consequently, IJVs tend to be more stable when firms partner with familiar entities, as this helps with establishing closer and more intimate social ties. Forbearance is assumed to have a direct effect on IJV stability (Brown et al., 1989) as does opportunism (Parhke, 1993: 231). These factors are typically incorporated into conceptual models aiming to identify their influence on IJV formation and success (Contractor & Lorange, 2002; Gomes-Casseres, 2003; Kutschker, 2003).

5.6 Wholly Owned Subsidiary as Entry Mode Strategy

A wholly owned foreign subsidiary (WOS) established for the purpose of operating directly in a foreign market is part of a complex structure organized and maintained by a multinational firm. A WOS is a preferred entry mode in contrast to possible other entry modes, because it offers assumably the highest level of control. Most importantly, the management of WOS do not need to arbitrate between conflicting interests or potential IP infringements caused by other parties (Welch et al., 2018: 351). The major leverage to manage a WOS is based on hierarchy as governance mechanism. The assumption that the WOS offers the highest level of control is based on the conviction that the control is easier to exercise within the boundaries of the firm, using an established hierarchy (Finkelstein, 2018; Hennart, 1993).

5.6.1 WOS and Control

WOS are not prone to conflicts arising from sharing control, like in IJVs, but it is a challenge to coordinate the different roles of subsidiaries across several affiliates (Barnard, 2011; Birkinshaw et al., 1998). By and large, WOS offer a more responsive operative control. However, several factors are used to "differentiate between high and low-contributing subisidiaries", which is a major topic in the IB literature (Birkinshaw et al., 1998). Compared to other entry modes based on cooperation with external firms they allow the parent firm to repatriate the return on assets invested in a subsidiary (Welch et al., 2018: 328). In entry mode studies a major question remains what determines the choice between WOS and other entry modes (Jung et al., 2008; Jung & Suh, 2013; Puck et al., 2016).

However, establishing a feasible control is a major issue (Hedlund, 1986, 1993). Much of the discussion in IB concentrating on WOS as an entry mode is mixed with the perspective which roles the foreign subsidiaries have been ascribed in the multinational enterprise.

Control is still an ambiguous concept. The idea that headquarters' control of subsidiaries is easier to achieve because there are no external partners or other affiliates seems straightforward, but several issues caused by the geographical, cultural, or psychic distances between the home and host location affect the implementation of an effective and uniform control (Ha et al., 2020; Puck et al., 2016; Wang & Larimo, 2017). Control requires a clear-cut and relatively static strategic concept, a common goal between HQ and WOS (Egelhoff & Wolf, 2017). But exercising control in subsidiaries can be a paradox because management is neither omnipotent nor omniscient (Mousavi & Gigerenzer, 2014; Simon, 1986).

Essentially different perspectives between HQ and subsidiary make it a challenge to align these different roles across a common governance structure. Moreover, the top management of multinational firms tends misconstrue the roles of subsidiaries (Birkinshaw et al., 2000: 322). The arguments about the misconception of the role of subsidiaries are partially the outcome of classical theories of FDI and the MNC, where FDI is primarily explained by the intention to control and exploit firm-specific advantages abroad (Hymer, 1970, 1976).

Thus, the overall purpose of strategic control is left to a one-sided incentive model developed for the senior management who determines the level of performance of a subsidiary by monitoring and providing feedback to business units. In theory, the headquarter monitors performance of several fairly different WOS, operating in idiosyncratic contexts by carrying out a formal and informal control system intended to coordinate misaligned efforts between and within subsidiaries (Goold & Quinn, 1990).

Example

"The control system, [. . .] is the process which allows senior management to determine whether a business unit is performing satisfactorily, and which provides motivation for business unit management to see that it continues to do so. It therefore normally involves the agreement of objectives for the business between different levels of management; monitoring of performance against these objectives; and feedback on results achieved, together with incentives and sanctions for business management" (Goold & Quinn, 1990: 43).

The prevalent argument in support of WOS is that a fully-owned subsidiary allows the most direct control operated in a decentralized and internationally dispersed business operation (Birkinshaw et al., 1998). That immediate relation between control and ownership is analyzed in several studies (Anderson & Gatignon, 1986; Zhao et al., 2017). However, the complexity of the relationship between ownership and control is not always operationalized.

In addition, the question of control is a challenge in many multinational firms with a widespread subisidary network (Brouthers & Hennart, 2007). Thus, the issue of selecting the mode of entry with a focus on WOS can rest on a fairly narrow vision limited to the immediate relationship between the headquarter and its subsidiaries, or it could be a more holistic perspective that abandons this narrow focus on isolating the governance issue as one that is only relevant within the corporate boundaries.

Wholly Owned Subsidiary (WOS)

The wholly owned subsidiary (WOS) is defined as a business unit carrying out value adding activities outside the home location of the parent organization. Full ownership enables the parent multinational to control, coordinate, and manage several stages of value-adding activities conducted by different subsidiaries (Birkinshaw & Pedersen, 2009).

It is important to acknowledge that subsidiary establishment is usually not a single and isolated decision, but a choice rather embedded in an ongoing evolving process (Johanson & Vahlne, 1977, 2006, 2009; Johanson & Wiedersheim-Paul, 2007; Vahlne & Johanson, 2017). The overall argument about using WOS relies on the proposition that the bundling resources within the boundaries of a international firm is more efficient than exploiting resources provided in a business network of interdependent and independent firms. Note, the proposition rest of a sound measurement of efficiency. Not surprisingly, this logic has been criticized because the argument is based on the belief that the actual cost of bundling and the actual outcome must be known at all times (Pitelis & Teece, 2018; Schuster & Holtbrügge, 2012; Vahlne & Johanson, 2021).

5.6.2 The WOS and Liability of Foreignness (LoF)

Stephen Herbert Hymer (1976: 34) observed that firms entering a foreign market are faced with the disadvantage of liability of foreignness (LoF). The liability of foreignness is a challenge for the entrant firm, because it has access only to limited and biased information compared to the incumbent local firm. The subsidiary of a foreign firm is not only compelled to operate in a more complex, and unfamiliar environment, it is further exposed to discriminatory policies by the host government, while facing the risk of volatile exchange rates. However, the exposure to greater risk is balanced by the seemingly greater control maintained in a WOS in the host environment. The assumption is that a wholly owned subsidiary permits more efficient coordination and enhanced control, which both compensate for the additional costs caused by LoF (Zaheer, 1995). Westney (1993) applied institutionalized theory (Scott, 1983; Zucker, 1987) to demonstrate that the lack of knowledge about the local environment can lead to maladaptive practices (Mezias, 2002a, b; Westney, 1993). However, a WOS is not confronted with the same level of LoF over time, as learning capability allows the subsidiary to adopt practices that increase conformity in the foreign environment (Zaheer & Mosakowski, 1997). Although theoretically sound, the operationalization of the concept of LoF remains ambiguous (Mezias & Mezias, 2007). While the concept LoF focuses on the disadvantages foreign firms face when operating in an unfamiliar location, it also illustrates the capacity of subsidiaries to learn and adapt to dynamically changing environments abroad. Thus, whether foreignness is an asset or liability is not easy to establish (Gorostidi-Martinez & Zhao, 2017; Hayter et al., 2021).

5.6.3 The Role of MNE Subsidiaries

Research dealing with wholly owned foreign subsidiary (WOS) and the relationship between HQ and subsidiaries is embedded in a more general interest in strategies of multinational firms (Bouquet & Birkinshaw, 2011; Raisch & Birkinshaw, 2008). A firm may enter a foreign market by establishing a wholly owned subsidiary abroad because it can control the business activities more directly. In strategy research, the subsidiary role is an assigned role or task, designed by the HQ. The use of the term subsidiary strategy assumes some level of choice made by the subsidiary management (Birkinshaw & Pedersen, 2009). The focus on the role of the subsidiary is related to a more substantially changing perspective in which the subsidiary is conceived no longer an almost passive implementer of parent technologies, but as an active contributor to firm-specific advantages (Birkinshaw et al., 1998). That view alters the prior perspective that MNEs can compensate for the higher costs of operating in foreign locations through the advantages generated almost exclusively in the headquarters home locations. In fact, when subsidiaries are selected as the preferred entry mode, the multinational firm explores and exploits capabilities generated in home and host locations (Barnard, 2011; Figueiredo et al., 2020; Riviere et al., 2020).

The general debate on how to manage WOS and how to define the strategic role of WOS is differentiated into four streams. The first focus was basically oriented on the relation between the design of structure and strategy in the multinational firms, also called the classical hierarchical approach (Egelhoff, 1988; Stopford & Wells, 1972). The core question in that stream was how firms develop a fit between global strategies and their organizational design. This stream was followed by a concern about how apparent value adding activities can be organized more efficiently by questioning the degree of centralization and decentralization and searching for an efficient mechanism to integrate and coordinate the increasingly fragmented intrafirm division of labor (Hedlund, 1986; Hennart, 1993; Schmid & Maurer, 2011). The third stream approached the WOS asking what managerial mentality is more appropriate to set up an effective governance mode organzing the complex relations between HQ and subsidiaries, whereas the overall focus remained on how to control an increasing number of subsidiaries (Dearlove, 2004; Doz, 2006, 2016; Inkpen, 2004; Prahalad, 1990, 1999). The last stream dealing with the role of subsidiaries discussed how knowledge generated in an existing subsidiary network can be more efficiently exploited across the whole multinational firm. This perspective also discussed an increasingly more independent role of subsidiaries in extent HQ subsidiary relations (Birkinshaw et al., 2000; Raisch & Birkinshaw, 2008).

The role of the subsidiary as an entry mode choice has changed considerably in the last four decades. The rise of offshoring, global sourcing, the conception of the MNE as a global factory, and the impact of fragmented and spatially dispersed global value chains exemplify the underlying forces of change (Ambos et al., 2021; Contractor et al., 2021; Pham & Petersen, 2021; Sinkovics et al., 2021; Wang et al., 2021). Today, many firms struggle to find a feasible mix of entry modes. These firms invest considerable efforts to adapt existing entry modes. They think about switching between entry modes. These firms need to find a feasible fit, despite continuously changing, replacing, and reorganizing their cross border business activities (Gereffi, 2019; Gereffi et al., 2021; Gereffi & Wu, 2020; McWilliam & Nielsen, 2020). It is a common argument that foreign direct investment is a strategy used to establish a foreign subsidiary made primarily to establish a sustaining and effective managerial control (Buckley & Casson, 2010; Finkelstein, 2018; Pearce, 2017). FDI was defined by its capability to exercise control in an unfamiliar environment (Goold & Quinn, 1990). It is further assumed that the management, characterized as a rational agent prefer more control in unfamiliar foreign environments. But unfamiliarity is also a source of learning and change, not always a threat (Fuchs & Horn, 2019).

Hence, whether a high degree of unfamiliarity leads to a greater desire for control remains disputed in the literature (Hennart et al., 2002; Luo & Mezias, 2002; Luo et al., 2002; Mezias, 2002a, b; Wu & Salomon, 2017).

(continued)

Likewise, only few studies exist about how firms actually are switching and mixing entry modes (Puck et al., 2009; Putzhammer et al., 2020; Welch et al., 2018). However, the important point is that a WOS, like any other entry mode, is actually not some static structural design, but continuously evolving in the course of mandatory change and adaptations in a co-evolving dynamic environment (Birkinshaw & Pedersen, 2009). Given this complexity of the entry mode choice, it is no surprise that a large body of empirical research on this topic offers mixed or inconsistent results about factors affecting performance (Bae et al., 2008; Kirca et al., 2010; Powell, 2014; Thomas & Eden, 2004).

Study Questions

1. How can we define exports? Discuss how important this entry mode strategy is for small and medium sized firms. Think about the core reasons to choose exports as entry mode strategy.
2. How does licensing differ from franchising as entry mode choice? Think about the main pro and cons of these two entry mode choices.
3. Why do intellectual property (IP) rights matter in choosing an appropriate entry mode?
4. Discuss benefits and challenges of an international joint venture (IJV). How do you explain the high failure rate in international joint ventures?
5. How do you define a wholly owned subsidiary? How does the effort to control affect the relationship between headquarter and subsidiary?

References

Agrawal, D. K. (2007). Combating parallel import in India. *SSRN Electronic Journal*. https://doi.org/10.2139/ssrn.997270

Agrawal, M. L., & Hollensen, S. (2002). Failure of an international joint venture: Implications for the India enthusiasts. *Metamorphosis: A Journal of Management Research, 1*(1), 35–51.

Alexander, E. R., & Wilkins, R. D. (1982). Performance rating validity: The relationship of objective and subjective measures of performance. *Group & Organization Management, 7*(4), 485–496.

Ali, T., & Khalid, S. (2017). Trust-performance relationship in international joint ventures: The moderating roles of structural mechanisms. *Journal of Business & Industrial Marketing, 32*(7), 962–973.

Ali, T., & Larimo, J. (2016). Managing opportunism in international joint ventures: The role of structural and social mechanisms. *Scandinavian Journal of Management, 32*(2), 86–96.

Alon, I. (2001). The use of franchising by U.S.-based retailers. *Journal of Small Business Management, 39*(2), 111–122.

Ambos, B., Brandl, K., Perri, A., Scalera, V. G., & Assche, A. V. (2021). The nature of innovation in global value chains. *Journal of World Business, 56*(4), 101221.

Anderson, E., & Gatignon, H. (1986). Modes of foreign entry: A transaction cost analysis and propositions. *Journal of International Business Studies, 17*(3), 1–26.

Ando, N., & Rhee, D. K. (2009). Antecedents of interorganizational trust: Joint decision-making, cultural adaptation, and bargaining power. *Journal of Asia Business Studies, 3*(2), 16–28.

Arora, A. (1997). Patents, licensing, and market structure in the chemical industry. *Research Policy, 26*(4–5), 391–403.

Arora, A., & Fosfuri, A. (2000). Wholly owned subsidiary versus technology licensing in the worldwide chemical industry. *Journal of International Business Studies, 31*(4), 555–572.

Aulakh, P. S., Jiang, M. S., & Pan, Y. (2010). International technology licensing: Monopoly rents, transaction costs and exclusive rights. *Journal of International Business Studies, 41*(4), 587–605.

Autrey, R. L., Bova, F., & Soberman, D. A. (2015). When gray is good: Gray markets and market-creating investments. *Production and Operations Management, 24*(4), 547–559.

Axinn, C. N. (1988). Export performance: Do managerial perception make a difference? *International Marketing Review, 5*(2), 61–71. https://doi.org/10.1108/eb008353

Bae, S. C., Park, B. J. C., & Wang, X. (2008). Multinationality, R&D intensity, and firm performance: Evidence from U.S. manufacturing firms. *Multinational Business Review, 16*(1), 53–78.

Banerji, A., & Dutta, B. (2009). Local network externalities and market segmentation. *International Journal of Industrial Organization, 27*(5), 605–614.

Bao, H., Xu, M., & Gu, S. (2006). 'Patent pool' initiatives in manufacturing clusters in Zhejiang. *Innovation: Management, Policy & Practice, 8*(1–2), 153–159.

Barkema, H. G., Bell, J. H., & Pennings, J. M. (1996). Foreign entry, cultural barriers, and learning. *Strategic Management Journal, 17*(2), 151–166.

Barkema, H. G., Shenkar, O., Vermeulen, F., & Bell, J. H. J. (1997). Working abroad, working with others: how firms learn to operate international joint ventures. *Academy of Management Journal, 40*(2), 426–442.

Barnard, H. (2011). Emerging multinationals benefiting from subsidiaries located in more developed countries: Drivers for the sharing of capabilities. *Innovation and Development, 1*(2), 187–203.

Baten, J., Bianchi, N., & Moser, P. (2017). Compulsory licensing and innovation – Historical evidence from German patents after WWI. *Journal of Development Economics, 126*, 231–242.

Beamish, P., & Berdrow, I. (2003). Learning from IJVs: The unintended outcome. *Long Range Planning, 36*(3), 285–303.

Bello, D. C., Urban, D. J., & Verhage, B. J. (1991). Evaluating export middlemen in alternative channel structures. *International Marketing Review, 8*, 5.

Bener, M., & Glaister, K. W. (2010). Determinants of performance in international joint ventures. *Journal of Strategy and Management, 3*(3), 188–214.

Benito, G., & Welch, L. S. (1993). Foreign market servicing: Beyond choice of entry mode. *Journal of International Marketing, 2*(2), 7–27.

Bernard, A. B., Jensen, J. B., Schott, P. K., & Redding, S. J. (2010). Intra-firm trade and product contractibility. *SSRN Electronic Journal*. https://doi.org/10.2139/ssrn.1602026

Birkinshaw, J., & Pedersen, T. (2009). Strategy and management in MNE subsidiaries. In A. M. Rugman (Ed.), *The Oxford handbook of international business* (2nd ed., pp. 367–388). Oxford University Press.

Birkinshaw, J., Hood, N., & Jonsson, S. (1998). Building firm-specific advantages in multinational corporations: The role of subsidiary initiative. *Strategic Management Journal, 19*(3), 221–242.

Birkinshaw, J., Holm, U., Thilenius, P., & Arvidsson, N. (2000). Consequences of perception gaps in the headquarters–subsidiary relationship. *International Business Review, 9*(3), 321–344.

Björkman, I., & Eklund, M. (1996). The sequence of operational modes used by Finnish investors in Germany. *Journal of International Marketing, 4*(1), 33–55.
Boateng, A., & Glaister, K. W. (2002). Performance of international joint ventures: Evidence for West Africa. *International Business Review, 11*(5), 523–541.
Bonturi, M., & Fukasaku, K. (1993). Globalisation and intra-firm trade: An empirical note. *OECD Economic Studies, 20*, 145–159.
Bouquet, C., & Birkinshaw, J. (2011). How global strategies emerge: An attention perspective. *Global Strategy Journal, 1*(3-4), 243–262.
Brouthers, K. D. (2013). A retrospective on: Institutional, cultural and transaction cost influences on entry mode choice and performance. *Journal of International Business Studies, 44*(1), 14–22.
Brouthers, K. D., & Hennart, J.-F. (2007). Boundaries of the firm: Insights from international entry mode research. *Journal of Management, 33*(3), 395–425.
Brouthers, L. E., Nakos, G., Hadjimarcou, J., & Brouthers, K. D. (2009). Key factors for successful export performance for small firms. *Journal of International Marketing, 17*(3), 21–38. http://www.jstor.org/stable/27755606
Brown, L. T., Rugman, A. M., & Verbeke, A. (1989). Japanese joint ventures with western multinationals: Synthesising the economic and cultural explanations of failure. *Asia Pacific Journal of Management, 6*(2), 225–242.
Buckley, P. J., & Casson, M. C. (1998). Analyzing foreign market entry strategies: Extending the internalization approach. *Journal of International Business Studies, 29*(3), 539–561. https://doi.org/10.1057/palgrave.jibs.8490006
Buckley, P. J., & Casson, M. (2010). The multinational enterprise revisited. *The Essential Buckley and Casson, 2010*, 177–204.
Calof, J. L. (1994). The relationship between firm size and export behavior revisited. *Journal of International Business Studies, 25*(2), 367–387. http://www.jstor.org/stable/155394
Cavusgil, S. T., & Zou, S. (1994). Marketing strategy-performance relationship: An investigation of the empirical link in export market ventures. *Journal of Marketing, 58*(1), 1–21. https://doi.org/10.2307/1252247
Chaudhry, P., & Zimmerman, A. (2012). *Protecting your intellectual property rights, understanding the role of management, governments, consumers and pirates* (pp. 125–140). Springer.
Chen, J., Sousa, C. M. P., & He, X. (2016). The determinants of export performance: a review of the literature 2006-2014. *International Marketing Review, 33*(5), 626–670.
Chen, J., Liang, L., & Yao, D. (2017). An analysis of intellectual property licensing strategy under duopoly competition: Component or product-based? *International Journal of Production Economics, 193*, 502–513.
Childs, M. L., & Jin, B. (2014). Is Uppsala model valid to fashion retailers? An analysis from internationalisation patterns of fast fashion retailers. *Journal of Fashion Marketing and Management, 18*(1), 36–51.
Choi, J. P., & Gerlach, H. (2019). Optimal cross-licensing arrangements: Collusion versus entry deterrence. *European Economic Review, 120*, 103315.
Clegg, J., & Cross, A. R. (2000). Affiliate and non-affiliate intellectual property transactions in international business: an empirical overview of the UK and USA. *International Business Review, 9*(4), 407–430.
Combs, J. G., Ketchen, D. J., & Hoover, V. L. (2004). A strategic groups approach to the franchising–performance relationship. *Journal of Business Venturing, 19*(6), 877–897.
Combs, J. G., Michael, S. C., & Castrogiovanni, G. J. (2009). Institutional influences on the choice of organizational form: The case of franchising. *Journal of Management, 35*(5), 1268–1290.
Combs, J. G., Ketchen, D. J., Shook, C. L., & Short, J. C. (2011a). Antecedents and consequences of franchising: Past accomplishments and future challenges. *Journal of Management, 37*(1), 99–126.

Combs, J. G., Ketchen, D. J., & Short, J. C. (2011b). Franchising research: Major milestones, new directions, and its future within entrepreneurship. *Entrepreneurship Theory and Practice, 35*(3), 413–425.
Contractor, F. J. (1984). Choosing between direct investment and licensing: Theoretical considerations and empirical tests. *Journal of International Business Studies, 15*(3), 167–188.
Contractor, F. J. (1985). A generalized theorem for joint-ventures and licensing negotiations. *Journal of International Business Studies, 16*(2), 23–50.
Contractor, F. J., & Kundu, S. K. (1998). Modal choice in a world of alliances: Analyzing organizational forms in the international hotel sector. *Journal of International Business Studies, 29*(2), 325–356.
Contractor, F. J., & Lorange, P. (2002). The growth of alliances in the knowledge-based economy. *International Business Review, 11*(4), 485–502.
Contractor, F. J., Nuruzzaman, N., Dangol, R., & Raghunath, S. (2021). How FDI inflows to emerging markets are influenced by country regulatory factors: An exploratory study. *Journal of International Management, 27*(1), 100834.
Coviello, N., Kano, L., & Liesch, P. W. (2017). Adapting the Uppsala model to a modern world: Macro-context and microfoundations. *Journal of International Business Studies, 48*(9), 1151–1164.
Crick, D., & Czinkota, M. R. (1995). Export assistance. *International Marketing Review, 12*(3), 61–72. https://doi.org/10.1108/02651339510091708
Cross, A. R. (2000). Licensing and franchising across borders: Theory, management and strategies for the 21st century. *International Business Review, 9*(4), 403–406.
Czinkota, M., Ronkainen, I., & Gupta, S. (2021). *International Business* (9th ed.). Cambridge University Press. https://doi.org/10.1017/9781108667487
Dada, O., & Watson, A. (2013). Entrepreneurial orientation and the franchise system. *European Journal of Marketing, 47*(5/6), 790–812.
Darr, E. D., Argote, L., & Epple, D. (1995). The acquisition, transfer, and depreciation of knowledge in service organizations: Productivity in franchises. *Management Science, 41*(11), 1750–1762. http://www.jstor.org/stable/2632871
Davis, L. (2006). *Contemporary management of innovation, are we asking the right questions?* (pp. 248–263).
Dearlove, D. (2004). Interview: C. K. Prahalad. *Business Strategy Review, 15*(2), 13–16.
Depken, C. A., II, Redmount, E., & Snow, A. (2001). Shirking and the choice of technology: A theory of production inefficiency with an empirical application. *Journal of Economic Behavior & Organization, 44*(4), 383–402.
Dhanaraj, C., & Beamish, P. W. (2003). A resource-based approach to the study of export performance. *Journal of Small Business Management, 41*(3), 242–261.
Dhanaraj, C., & Beamish, P. W. (2004). Effect of equity ownership on the survival of international joint ventures. *Strategic Management Journal, 25*(3), 295–305.
Diamantopoulos, A., & Kakkos, N. (2007). Managerial assessments of export performance: Conceptual framework and empirical illustration. *Journal of International Marketing, 15*(3), 1–31. http://www.jstor.org/stable/25049089
Diamantopoulos, A., Ring, A., Schlegelmilch, B. B., & Doberer, E. (2014). Drivers of export segmentation effectiveness and their impact on export performance. *Journal of International Marketing, 22*(1), 39–61.
Doherty, A. M., Chen, X., & Alexander, N. (2014). The franchise relationship in China: Agency and institutional theory perspectives. *European Journal of Marketing, 48*(9/10), 1664–1689.
Dominguez, N. (2018). *SME Internationalization Strategies* (pp. 5–27). Wiley.

Dow, D. (2000). A note on psychological distance and export market selection. *Journal of International Marketing, 8*(1), 51–64. https://doi.org/10.1509/jimk.8.1.51.19563

Doz, Y. (2006). Knowledge creation, knowledge sharing and organizational structures and processes in MNCs: A commentary on Foss N. "Knowledge and organization in the theory of the MNC.". *Journal of Management & Governance, 10*(1), 29–33.

Doz, Y. (2016). Managing multinational operations: From organisational structures to mental structures and from operations to innovations. *European Journal of International Management, 10*(1), 10.

Dunning, J. (1995a). *The globalization of business*. Routledge.

Dunning, J. H. (1995b). Reappraising the eclectic paradigm in an age of Alliance Capitalism. *Journal of International Business Studies, 26*(3), 461–491.

Dunning, J. H., & Lundan, S. M. (2008). Institutions and the OLI paradigm of the multinational enterprise. *Asia Pacific Journal of Management, 25*(4), 573–593.

Dzikowski, P. (2018). A bibliometric analysis of born global firms. *Journal of Business Research, 85*, 281–294.

Efrat, K., & Shoham, A. (2012). Born global firms: The differences between their short- and long-term performance drivers. *Journal of World Business, 47*(4), 675–685.

Egelhoff, W. G. (1988). Strategy and structure in multinational corporations: A revision of the Stopford and Wells model. *Strategic Management Journal, 9*(1), 1–14.

Egelhoff, W. G., & Wolf, J. (2017). *Understanding matrix structures and their alternatives, the key to designing and managing large, complex organizations* (pp. 43–74). Springer.

Elango, B. (2019). A bibliometric analysis of franchising research (1988–2017). *The Journal of Entrepreneurship, 28*(2), 223–249.

Elango, B., & Fried, V. H. (1993). Flexible manufacturing technologies: Implications for competition between small and large firms. *The Journal of High Technology Management Research, 4*(2), 241–254.

Emruli, S., Nuhiu, A., & Kadriu, B. (2016). Copyright and copyright protection. *European Journal of Interdisciplinary Studies, 2*(4), 36–40.

Erramilli, M. K., & D'Souza, D. E. (1993). Venturing into foreign markets: The case of the small service firm. *Entrepreneurship Theory and Practice, 17*(4), 29–41.

Farrell, M. A., Oczkowski, E., & Kharabsheh, R. (2011). Antecedents and performance consequences of learning success in international joint ventures. *Industrial Marketing Management, 40*(3), 479–488.

Figueiredo, P. N., Larsen, H., & Hansen, U. E. (2020). The role of interactive learning in innovation capability building in multinational subsidiaries: A micro-level study of biotechnology in Brazil. *Research Policy, 49*(6), 103995.

Finkelstein, S. (2018). *The Palgrave Encyclopedia of strategic management* (pp. 655–656). Palgrave.

Fladmoe-Lindquist, K. (1996). International franchising: Capabilities and development. *Journal of Business Venturing, 11*(5), 419–438.

Fladmoe-Lindquist, K., & Jacque, L. L. (1995). Control modes in international service operations: The propensity to franchise. *Management Science, 41*(7), 1238–1249.

Fletcher, R. (2001). A holistic approach to internationalisation. *International Business Review, 10*(1), 25–49.

Francis, J., & Collins-Dodd, C. (2004). Impact of export promotion programs on firm competencies, strategies and performance. *International Marketing Review, 21*(4/5), 474–495.

Frankel, S., & Lai, J. C. (2014). Compulsory licensing. *MPI Studies on Intellectual Property and Competition Law*, 149–164.

Freeman, S., Hutchings, K., Lazaris, M., & Zyngier, S. (2010). A model of rapid knowledge development: The smaller born-global firm. *International Business Review, 19*(1), 70–84.

Fu, Z., He, J., Xiang, Y., Cui, R., & Yi, S. (2015). Image segmentation based on gray-level spatial correlation maximum between-cluster variance. *PLoS One, 15*(3), e0229651. https://doi.org/10.2991/isci-15.2015.28

Fuchs, M., & Horn, S. (2019). Managerial decision making and the evolutionary process of internationalization. *Academy of Management Proceedings, 2019*(1), 14801.

Fuchs, M., & Köstner, M. (2016). Antecedents and consequences of firm's export marketing strategy. *Management Research Review, 39*(Issue 3), 329–355.

Garg, V. K., & Rasheed, A. A. (2003). International multi-unit franchising: An agency theoretic explanation. *International Business Review, 12*(3), 329–348.

Gereffi, G. (2019). Global value chains and international development policy: Bringing firms, networks and policy-engaged scholarship back in. *Journal of International Business Policy, 2*(3), 195–210.

Gereffi, G., & Wu, X. (2020). *The Oxford handbook of industrial hubs and economic development* (pp. 1048–1068). Oxford University Press.

Gereffi, G., Lim, H.-C., & Lee, J. (2021). Trade policies, firm strategies, and adaptive reconfigurations of global value chains. *Journal of International Business Policy, 2021*, 1–17.

Geringer, J. M. (1998). Assessing replication and extension. A commentary on Glaister and Buckley: Measures of performance in UK International Alliances. *Organization Studies, 19*(1), 119–138.

Geringer, J. M., & Hebert, L. (1989). Control and performance of international joint ventures. *Journal of International Business Studies, 20*(2), 235–254.

Geringer, J. M., & Hebert, L. (1991). Measuring performance of international joint ventures. *Journal of International Business Studies, 22*(2), 249–263.

Ghoshal, S., & Moran, P. (1996). Bad for practice: A critique of the transaction cost theory. *Academy of Management Review, 21*(1), 13–47.

Gifford, S. (1999). Efficient moral hazard. *Journal of Economic Behavior & Organization, 40*(4), 427–442.

Gilbert, R., & Kristiansen, E. G. 2017. *Licensing and innovation with imperfect contract enforcement by Richard Gilbert, Eirik Gaard Kristiansen*, SSRN. Retrieved from https://papers.ssrn.com/sol3/papers.cfm?abstract_id=2585999

Gillis, W., & Castrogiovanni, G. J. (2012). The franchising business model: An entrepreneurial growth alternative. *International Entrepreneurship and Management Journal, 8*(1), 75–98.

Glaister, K. W., Husan, R., & Buckley, P. J. (2005). International joint ventures: An examination of the core dimensions. *Journal of General Management, 30*(4), 43–72.

Glass, A. J., & Saggi, K. (2002). Licensing versus direct investment: Implications for economic growth. *Journal of International Economics, 56*(1), 131–153.

Glaum, M., & Oesterle, M.-J. (2007). 40 years of research on internationalization and firm performance: More questions than answers? *Management International Review, 47*(3), 307–317.

Gleason, K. C., Mathur, I., & Singh, M. (2000). Operational characteristics and performance gains associated with international licensing agreements: the US evidence. *International Business Review, 9*(4), 431–452.

Gleason, K. C., Madura, J., & Wiggenhorn, J. (2006). Operating characteristics, risk, and performance of born-global firms. *International Journal of Managerial Finance, 2*(2), 96–120.

Gomes-Casseres, B. (2003). Competitive advantage in alliance constellations. *Strategic Organization, 1*(3), 327–335.

Goold, M., & Quinn, J. J. (1990). The paradox of strategic controls. *Strategic Management Journal, 11*(1), 43–57.

Gorostidi-Martinez, H., & Zhao, X. (2017). Strategies to avoid liability of foreignness when entering a new market. *Journal of Advances in Management Research, 14*(1), 46–68.

Graham, S. J. H., & Mowery, D. C. (2005). The use of USPTO "continuation" applications in the patenting of software: Implications for free and open source. *Law & Policy, 27*(1), 128–151.

Graham, S. J. H., & Mowrey, D. C. (2004). Submarines in software? Continuations in US software patenting in the 1980s and 1990s. *Economics of Innovation and New Technology, 13*(5), 443–456.

Grindley, P. (2018). *The Palgrave encyclopedia of strategic management* (pp. 897–898). Palgrave.

Grindley, P. C., & Teece, D. J. (1997). Managing intellectual capital: Licensing and cross-licensing in semiconductors and electronics. *California Management Review, 39*(2), 8–41.

Ha, N. M., Binh, Q. M. Q., & Dang, P. P. (2020). Cultural distance and entry modes in emerging markets: Empirical evidence in Vietnam. *Journal of Risk and Financial Management, 13*(1), 14.

Hayter, R., Edgington, D., & W. (2021). Panasonic in China: A search to overcome the liability of foreignness. *Journal of Asia-Pacific Business, 22*(1), 1–26.

Hedlund, G. (1986). The hypermodern MNC—A heterarchy? *Human Resource Management, 25*(1), 9–35.

Hedlund, G. (1993). *Organization theory and the multinational corporation* (pp. 211–236). Springer.

Hennart, J.-F. (1977). *A theory of foreign direct investment*. University of Maryland, Doctoral thesis.

Hennart, J.-F. (1993). *Organization theory and the multinational corporation* (pp. 157–181). Springer.

Hennart, J. (2014). The accidental internationalists: A theory of born globals. *Entrepreneurship Theory and Practice, 38*(1), 117–135.

Hennart, J.-F., Roehl, T., & Zeng, M. (2002). Do exits proxy a liability of foreignness? The case of Japanese exits from the US. *Journal of International Management, 8*(3), 241–264.

Hollensen, S. (2010). *Global marketing. A decision-oriented approach*. Prentice Hall.

Huang, M.-C., Hsiung, H.-H., & Lu, T.-C. (2015). Reexamining the relationship between control mechanisms and international joint venture performance: The mediating roles of perceived value gap and information asymmetry. *Asia Pacific Management Review, 20*(1), 32–43.

Hui, K. N., Hult, G. T. M., & Ketchen, D. J. (2020). Causal attribution for peer performance and international joint venture divestment. *Journal of International Management, 26*(2), 100754.

Hult, G. T. M., Gonzalez-Perez, M. A., & Lagerström, K. (2020). The theoretical evolution and use of the Uppsala Model of internationalization in the international business ecosystem. *Journal of International Business Studies, 51*(1), 38–49.

Hultman, M., Robson, M. J., & Katsikeas, C. S. (2009). Export product strategy fit and performance: An empirical investigation. *Journal of International Marketing, 17*(4).

Hultman, M., Katsikeas, C. S., & Robson, M. J. (2011). Export promotion strategy and performance: The role of international experience. *Journal of International Marketing, 19*(4), 1739.

Hymer, S. (1970). The efficiency (contradictions) of multinational corporations. *American Economic Review, 60*, 441–444. https://doi.org/10.2307/1815843

Hymer, S. H. (1976). *The international operations of national firms: A study of direct foreign investment*. The MIT Press.

Idris, A., & Tey, L. S. (2011). Exploring the motives and determinants of innovation performance of Malaysian offshore international joint ventures. *Management Decision, 49*(10), 1623–1641.

Inkpen, A. (1998a). Learning, knowledge acquisition, and strategic alliances. *European Management Journal, 16*(2), 223–229.

Inkpen, A. (1998b). Knowledge works: Managing intellectual capital at Toshiba. *Journal of International Business Studies, 29*(3), 643–646.

Inkpen, A. C. (2000). Learning through joint ventures: A framework of knowledge acquisition. *Journal of Management Studies, 37*(7), 1019–1044.

Inkpen, A. C. (2004). Theories of the multinational enterprise: Diversity, complexity and relevance. *Advances in International Management, 2004*, 43–52.

Inkpen, A. C., & Crossan, M. M. (1995). Believing is seeing: Joint ventures and organization learning. *Journal of Management Studies, 32*(5), 595–618.

Ishikawa, J., Morita, H., & Mukunoki, H. (2020). Parallel imports and repair services. *Journal of Economic Behavior & Organization, 172*, 137–160.

ITC. (2004). *Why should I enforce my intellectual property rights? Who is responsible for enforcing them if they are infringed?* UN iLibrary. https://doi.org/10.18356/58f6be38-en

Jain, K., & Jain, S. (2004). Performance evaluation criteria for international joint venture. *Journal of International Business and Economy, 5*(1), 53–76.

Johanson, J., & Vahlne, J.-E. (1977). The internationalization process of the firm—A model of knowledge development and increasing foreign market commitments. *Journal of International Business Studies, 8*(1), 23–32.

Johanson, J., & Vahlne, J.-E. (2006). Commitment and opportunity development in the internationalization process: A note on the Uppsala internationalization process model. *Management International Review, 46*(2), 165–178.

Johanson, J., & Vahlne, J.-E. (2009). The Uppsala internationalization process model revisited: From liability of foreignness to liability of outsidership. *Journal of International Business Studies, 40*(9), 1411–1431.

Johanson, J., & Wiedersheim-Paul, F. (2007). The internationalization of the firm - Four Swedish cases. *Journal of Management Studies, 12*(305), 323.

Ju, M., & Gao, G. Y. (2017). Relational governance and control mechanisms of export ventures: An examination across relationship length. *Journal of International Marketing, 25*(2), 72–87. http://www.jstor.org/stable/44873452

Jung, J. C., & Suh, T. (2013). Why IJV over WOS? Home country effect on the US and Japanese MNEs. *Journal of Asia Business Studies, 7*(2), 153–170.

Jung, J. C., Beamish, P. W., & Goerzen, A. (2008). FDI ownership strategy: A Japanese-US MNE comparison. *Management International Review, 48*(5), 491–524.

Kalnins, A., & Mayer, K. J. (2004). Franchising, ownership, and experience: A study of Pizza restaurant survival. *Management Science, 50*(12), 1716–1728.

Kaszubska, K. (2017). Compulsory licensing under India's new model bilateral investment treaty. *Review of Market Integration, 9*(3), 139–154.

Katsikeas, C. S. (1994). Export competitive advantages: The relevance of firm characteristics. *International Marketing Review, 11*(3), 33–53.

Katsikeas, C. S., Piercy, N. F., & Ioannidis, C. (1996). Determinants of export performance in a European context. *European Journal of Marketing, 30*(6), 6–35. https://doi.org/10.1108/03090569610121656

Katsikeas, C. S., Samiee, S., & Theodosiou, M. (2006). Strategy fit and performance consequences of international marketing standardization. *Strategic Management Journal, 27*(9), 867–890. http://www.jstor.org/stable/20142381

Kehoe, M. R. (1996). Franchising, agency problems, and the cost of capital. *Applied Economics, 28*(11), 1485–1493.

Kidwell, R. E., Nygaard, A., & Silkoset, R. (2007). Antecedents and effects of free riding in the franchisor–franchisee relationship. *Journal of Business Venturing, 22*(4), 522–544.

Kirca, A. H., Hult, G. T. M., Roth, K., Cavusgil, S. T., Perryy, M., Akdeniz, M. B., et al. (2010). Firm-specific assets, multinationality, and financial performance: A meta-analytic review and theoretical integration. *SSRN Electronic Journal*. https://doi.org/10.2139/ssrn.1672973

Kollmer, H. K., & Dowling, M. (2004). Licensing as a commercialisation strategy for new technology-based firms. *Research Policy, 33*(8), 1141–1151. S0048733304000708. https://doi.org/10.1016/j.respol.2004.04.005

Knudsen, T., & Madsen, T. K. (2002). Export strategy. *Scandinavian Journal of Management, 18*(4), 475–502.

Kotabe, M., Sahay, A., & Aulakh, P. S. (1996). Emerging role of technology licensing in the development of global product strategy: Conceptual framework and research propositions. *Journal of Marketing, 60*(1), 73.

Kutschker, M. (2003). *Kooperationen, Allianzen und Netzwerke, Grundlagen — Ansätze — Perspektiven* (pp. 235–254). Springer.

Kutschker, M., & Schmid, S. (2011). *Internationales management* (7th ed.). Oldenburg Wissenschaftsverlag.

Kwok, F., Sharma, P., Gaur, S. S., & Ueno, A. (2019). Interactive effects of information exchange, relationship capital and environmental uncertainty on international joint venture (IJV) performance: An emerging markets perspective. *International Business Review, 28*(5), 101481.

Lages, L. F., Jap, S. D., & Griffith, D. A. (2008). The role of past performance in export ventures: A short-term reactive approach. *Journal of International Business Studies, 39*(2), 304–325. https://doi.org/10.1057/palgrave.jibs.8400339

Landes, X. (2013). Moral hazard. In S. O. Idowu, N. Capaldi, L. Zu, & A. D. Gupta (Eds.), *Encyclopedia of corporate social responsibility* (pp. 1715–1722). Springer. https://doi.org/10.1007/978-3-642-28036-8_47

Lane, P. J., Salk, J. E., & Lyles, M. A. (2001). Absorptive capacity, learning, and performance in international joint ventures. *Strategic Management Journal, 22*(12), 1139–1161.

Lanz, R., & Miroudot, S. (2011). *Intra-firm trade*. OECD. https://doi.org/10.1787/5kg9p39lrwnn-en

Larimo, J., Nguyen, H. L., & Ali, T. (2016). Performance measurement choices in international joint ventures: What factors drive them? *Journal of Business Research, 69*(2), 877–887.

Lee, W. S., Han, E. J., & Sohn, S. Y. (2015a). Predicting the pattern of technology convergence using big-data technology on large-scale triadic patents. *Technological Forecasting and Social Change, 100*, 317–329.

Lee, Y.-K., Kim, S.-H., Seo, M.-K., & Hight, S. K. (2015b). Market orientation and business performance: Evidence from franchising industry. *International Journal of Hospitality Management, 44*, 28–37.

Leonidou, L., & Katsikeas, C. (1996). The export development process: An integrative review of empirical models. *Journal of International Business Studies*. https://doi.org/10.2307/155437

Li, J., Zhou, C., & Zajac, E. J. (2009). Control, collaboration, and productivity in international joint ventures: Theory and evidence. *Strategic Management Journal, 30*(8), 865–884.

Liebowitz, S. J., & Margolis, S. E. (2017). *The new Palgrave dictionary of economics and the law, Volume 1–3: A-Z, 1329–1333*. Palgrave.

Lin, X., & Wang, C. L. (2008). Enforcement and performance: The role of ownership, legalism and trust in international joint ventures. *Journal of World Business, 43*(3), 340–351.

Lu, J. W., & Beamish, P. W. (2001). The internationalization and performance of SMEs. *Strategic Management Journal, 22*(6–7), 565–586.

Luo, Y. (2002a). Contract, cooperation, and performance in international joint ventures. *Strategic Management Journal, 23*(10), 903–919.

Luo, Y. (2002b). Partnering with foreign firms: How do Chinese managers view the governance and importance of contracts? *Asia Pacific Journal of Management, 19*(1), 127–151.

Luo, Y. (2007). Private control and collective control in international joint ventures. *Management International Review, 47*(4), 531–566.

Luo, Y., & Mezias, J. M. (2002). Liabilities of foreignness. *Journal of International Management, 8*(3), 217–221.

Luo, Y., Shenkar, O., & Nyaw, M.-K. (2002). Mitigating liabilities of foreignness. *Journal of International Management, 8*(3), 283–300.

Luostarinen, R., & Welch, L. (1990). *International business operations*. Helsinki.
Mahoney, J. T. (1995). The management of resources and the resource of management. *Journal of Business Research, 33*(2), 91–101.
Mahoney, J. (2016). *The Palgrave encyclopedia of strategic management*. Palgrave.
Marburger, D. R. (2003). Does the assignment of property rights encourage or discourage shirking? Evidence from major league baseball. *Journal of Sports Economics, 4*(1), 19–34.
McDowell, S. D. (1997). *Globalization, liberalization and policy change, a political economy of India's communications sector* (pp. 123–166). Springer.
McWilliam, S. E., & Nielsen, B. B. (2020). Global value chains and development: Redefining the contours of 21st century capitalism: Gary Gereffi Cambridge University Press, Cambridge, 2018, 494 pp. ISBN: 978-1108458863. *Journal of International Business Studies, 51*(8), 1347–1350.
Merriam-Webster. (n.d.). *Forbearance. Merriam-Webster.com dictionary*. Retrieved April 15, 2022, from https://www.merriam-webster.com/dictionary/forbearance
Meschi, P.-X., & Wassmer, U. (2013). The effect of foreign partner network embeddedness on international joint venture failure: Evidence from European firms' investments in emerging economies. *International Business Review, 22*(4), 713–724.
Mezias, J. M. (2002a). Identifying liabilities of foreignness and strategies to minimize their effects: The case of labor lawsuit judgments in the United States. *Strategic Management Journal, 23*(3), 229–244.
Mezias, J. M. (2002b). How to identify liabilities of foreignness and assess their effects on multinational corporations. *Journal of International Management, 8*(3), 265–282.
Mezias, J. M., & Mezias, S. J. (2007). *Man without a country: Is there a liability of foreignness in individual outcomes?* Retrieved from http://citeseerx.ist.psu.edu/viewdoc/download?doi=10.1.1.535.816&rep=rep1&type=pdf
Michael, S. C. (2019). Dual agency in retail chains. *Journal of Marketing Channels, 2019*, 1–14.
Mohr, A. T., & Puck, J. F. (2007). Role conflict, general manager job satisfaction and stress and the performance of IJVs. *European Management Journal, 25*(1), 25–35.
Morgan, N. A., Kaleka, A., & Katsikeas, C. S. (2004). Antecedents of export venture performance: A theoretical model and empirical assessment. *Journal of Marketing, 68*(1), 90–108.
Morschett, D., Schramm-Klein, H., & Swoboda, B. (2010). Decades of research on market entry modes: What do we really know about external antecedents of entry mode choice? *Journal of International Management, 16*(1), 60–77.
Mottner, S., & Johnson, J. P. (2000). Motivations and risks in international licensing: a review and implications for licensing to transitional and emerging economies. *Journal of World Business, 35*(2), 171–188.
Mousavi, S., & Gigerenzer, G. (2014). Risk, uncertainty, and heuristics. *Journal of Business Research, 67*(8).
Mukherjee, A. (2020). Optimal licensing contract: The implications of preference function. *Journal of Economic Theory and Practice, 19*(1), 61–67.
Murray, F., & Stern, S. (2007). Do formal intellectual property rights hinder the free flow of scientific knowledge? An empirical test of the anti-commons hypothesis. *Journal of Economic Behavior & Organization, 63*(4), 648–687.
Nguyen, X., Sgro, P., & Nabin, M. (2017). Optimal licensing policy under vertical product differentiation. *Review of Development Economics, 21*(3), 497–510.
Nisar, S., Boateng, A., Wu, J., & Leung, M. (2012). Understanding the motives for SMEs entry choice of international entry mode. *Marketing Intelligence & Planning, 30*(7), 717–739.
Norman, S. (2001). What's your (current copyright) problem? *Legal Information Management, 1*(2), 14–16.

OECD. (2010). *Intra-firm trade in selected OECD countries*. OECD. https://doi.org/10.1787/9789264084360-74-en

OECD. (2017). Skills and global value chains: What are the stakes? In *OECD skills outlook 2017: Skills and global value chains*. OECD Publishing. https://doi.org/10.1787/9789264273351-5-en

On, L. W., Liang, X., Priem, R., & Shaffer, M. (2013). Top management team trust, behavioral integration and the performance of international joint ventures. *Journal of Asia Business Studies, 7*(2), 99–122.

Owens, M., Ramsey, E., & Loane, S. (2018). Resolving post-formation challenges in shared IJVs: The impact of shared IJV structure on inter-partner relationships. *International Business Review, 27*(3), 584–593.

Ozorhon, B., Arditi, D., Dikmen, I., & Birgonul, M. T. (2010). Performance of international joint ventures in construction. *Journal of Management in Engineering, 26*(4), 209–222.

Pak, Y. S., Ra, W., & Park, Y.-R. (2009). Understanding IJV performance in a learning and conflict mediated context. *International Business Review, 18*(5), 470–480.

Palmatier, R. W., Dant, R. P., & Grewal, D. (2007). A comparative longitudinal analysis of theoretical perspectives of interorganizational relationship performance. *Journal of Marketing, 71*(4), 172–194.

Parkhe, A. (1993). "Messy" research, methodological predispositions, and theory development in international joint ventures. *Academy of Management Review, 18*(2), 227–268.

Parks, R. B. (1984). Linking objective and subjective measures of performance. *Public Administration Review, 44*(2), 118.

Pearce, R. (2017). *The development of international business* (pp. 13–25). Springer.

Pedersen, T., Petersen, B., & Benito, G. R. G. (2002). Change of foreign operation method: Impetus and switching costs. *International Business Review, 11*(3), 325–345.

Penrose, E. T. (1959). *The theory of the growth of the firm*. Blackwell Publisher.

Petruzzelli, A. M., Rotolo, D., & Albino, V. (2015). Determinants of patent citations in biotechnology: An analysis of patent influence across the industrial and organizational boundaries. *Technological Forecasting and Social Change, 91*, 208–221.

Pham, H. S. T., & Petersen, B. (2021). The bargaining power, value capture, and export performance of Vietnamese manufacturers in global value chains. *International Business Review, 101829*.

Pitelis, C. N. (2004). Edith Penrose and the resource-based view of (international) business strategy. *International Business Review, 13*(4), 523–532.

Pitelis, C. N., & Teece, D. J. (2018). The new MNE: 'Orchestration' theory as envelope of 'Internalisation' theory. *Management International Review, 58*(4), 523–539.

Pla-Barber, J., Villar, C., & León-Darder, F. (2014). Augmenting versus exploiting entry modes in soft services. *International Marketing Review, 31*(6), 621–636.

Powell, K. S. (2014). From M–P to MA–P: Multinationality alignment and performance. *Journal of International Business Studies, 45*(2), 211–226.

Prahalad, C. K. (1990). Globalization: The intellectual and managerial challenges. *Human Resource Management, 29*(1), 27–37.

Prahalad, C. (1999). *Knowledge and strategy* (pp. 41–59). Butterworth Heinemann.

Puck, J. F., Holtbrügge, D., & Mohr, A. T. (2009). Beyond entry mode choice: Explaining the conversion of joint ventures into wholly owned subsidiaries in the People's Republic of China. *Journal of International Business Studies, 40*(3), 388–404.

Puck, J., Hödl, M. K., Filatotchev, I., Wolff, H.-G., & Bader, B. (2016). Ownership mode, cultural distance, and the extent of parent firms' strategic control over subsidiaries in the PRC. *Asia Pacific Journal of Management, 33*(4), 1075–1105.

Putzhammer, M., Puck, J., & Lindner, T. (2020). Changes in foreign operation modes: A review and research agenda. *International Business Review, 29*(1), 101619.

Rachlin, H., Castrogiovanni, A., & Cross, D. (1987). Probability and delay in commitment. *Journal of the experimental analysis of behavior, 48*(3), 347–353.
Raisch, S., & Birkinshaw, J. (2008). Organizational ambidexterity: Antecedents, outcomes, and moderators. *Journal of Management, 34*(3), 375–409.
Raut, L. K. (2017). Cost-effectiveness, competitiveness and export performance of Indian private firms. *SSRN Electronic Journal*. https://doi.org/10.2139/ssrn.3013752
Reddy, Y. V., & Naik, S. S. (2011). Determinants of Goan SME firms going global: Theoretical and empirical approach. *Vikalpa: The Journal for Decision Makers, 36*(2), 45–58.
Rennie, M. W. (1993). Born global. *The McKinsey Quarterly, 4*, 45–52.
Reuer, J., & Koza, M. (1998). *International joint venture instability and corporate strategy*. Springer.
Risch, M. (2013). Framing the patent troll debate. *Expert Opinion on Therapeutic Patents, 24*(2), 127–130.
Riviere, M., Bass, A. E., & Andersson, U. (2020). Dynamic capability development in multinational enterprises: Reconciling routine reconfiguration between the headquarters and subsidiaries. *Global Strategy Journal*. https://doi.org/10.1002/gsj.1389
Robins, J. A., Tallman, S., & Fladmoe-Lindquist, K. (2002). Autonomy and dependence of international cooperative ventures: An exploration of the strategic performance of U.S. ventures in Mexico. *Strategic Management Journal, 23*(10), 881–901.
Root, F. (1994). *Entry strategies for international markets*. Lexington Books.
Rosado-Serrano, A., & Paul, J. (2018). A new conceptual model for international franchising. *International Journal of Hospitality Management, 75*, 179–188.
Rosado-Serrano, A., Paul, J., & Dikova, D. (2018). International franchising: A literature review and research agenda. *Journal of Business Research, 85*, 238–257.
Rugman, A. M. (2010). Reconciling internalization theory and the eclectic paradigm. *Multinational Business Review, 18*(2), 1–12.
Rugman, A. M., & Verbeke, A. (2004). A final word on Edith Penrose. *Journal of Management Studies, 41*(1), 205–217.
Sarmah, A., & Hoang, H. (2017). Allying with a prospective rival: New entrant-incumbent R&D alliance formation. *Academy of Management Proceedings, 2017*(1), 15461.
Sarmah, A., Giovanni, D. D., & Giovanni, P. D. (2020). Compulsory licenses in the pharmaceutical industry: Pricing and R&D strategies. *European Journal of Operational Research, 282*(3), 1053–1069.
Schmid, S. (2018). Internationalization of business, cases on strategy formulation and implementation. *MIR Series in International Business, 2018*, 1–25.
Schmid, S., & Maurer, J. (2011). *Internationale Unternehmungen und das Management ausländischer Tochtergesellschaften* (pp. 53–83). Springer.
Schmitz, P. W. (2007). Exclusive versus non-exclusive licensing strategies and moral hazard. *Economics Letters, 97*(3), 208–214.
Schuster, T., & Holtbrügge, D. (2012). Market entry of multinational companies in markets at the bottom of the pyramid: A learning perspective. *International Business Review, 21*(5), 817–830.
Scott, R. W. (1983). *Institutions and organizations. Ideas, interests, and identities*. Sage.
Serra, F., Pointon, J., & Abdou, H. (2012). Factors influencing the propensity to export: A study of UK and Portuguese textile firms. *International Business Review, 21*(2), 210–224.
Shapiro, C. (1986). Investment, moral hazard, and occupational licensing. *The Review of Economic Studies, 53*(5), 843.
Shu, C., Jin, J. L., & Zhou, K. Z. (2017). A contingent view of partner coopetition in international joint ventures. *Journal of International Marketing, 25*(3), 42–60.
Si, S. X., & Bruton, G. D. (2005). Knowledge acquisition, cost savings, and strategic positioning: Effects on Sino-American IJV performance. *Journal of Business Research, 58*(11), 1465–1473.

Simon, H. (1986). *Rationality in psychology and economics*. Springer.
Singh, P. (2019). Patent trolls: Nature and legal issues. *SSRN Electronic Journal*. https://doi.org/10.2139/ssrn.3485981
Sinkovics, N., Liu, C.-L., Sinkovics, R. R., & Mudambi, R. (2021). The dark side of trust in global value chains: Taiwan's electronics and IT hardware industries. *Journal of World Business, 56*(4), 101195.
Sousa, C. M. P., & Lengler, J. (2009). Psychic distance, marketing strategy and performance in export ventures of Brazilian firms. *Journal of Marketing Management, 25*(5–6), 591–610.
Steen, J. T., & Liesch, P. W. (2007). A note on Penrosean growth, resource bundles and the Uppsala model of internationalisation. *Management International Review, 47*(2), 193–206.
Sterling, J. A. L. (2004). Copyright law: World copyright law. *Computer Law & Security Review, 20*(6), 511.
Stopford, J. M., & Wells, L. T. (1972). *Managing the multinational enterprise: Organization of the firm and ownership of the subsidiaries*. Longman, Basic Books.
Styles, C., Patterson, P. G., & Ahmed, F. (2008). A relational model of export performance. *Journal of International Business Studies, 39*(5), 880 900.
Svejenova, S. (2006). How much does trust really matter? Some reflections on the significance and implications of Madhok's trust-based approach. *Journal of International Business Studies, 37*(1), 12–20.
Tan, S. J., Lim, G. H., & Lee, K. S. (1997). Strategic responses to parallel importing. *Journal of Global Marketing, 10*(4), 45–66.
Teece, D. J. (2006). Reflections on the Hymer thesis and the multinational enterprise. *International Business Review, 15*(2), 124–139.
Thomas, L. G., & D'Aveni, R. (2009). The changing nature of competition in the US manufacturing sector, 1950–2002. *Strategic Organization, 7*(4), 387–431.
Thomas, D. E., & Eden, L. (2004). What is the shape of the multinationality-performance relationship? *Multinational Business Review, 12*(Issue 1), 89–110.
UNCTAD. (1992). *Reforming trade policies*. UNCTAD. https://doi.org/10.18356/d92cb17c-en
Vahlne, J.-E., & Johanson, J. (2017). From internationalization to evolution: The Uppsala model at 40 years. *Journal of International Business Studies, 48*(9), 1087–1102.
Vahlne, J.-E., & Johanson, J. (2021). Coping with complexity by making trust an important dimension in governance and coordination. *International Business Review, 30*(2), 101798.
Wang, Y., & Larimo, J. (2017). *Distance in international business: Concept, cost and value* (Vol. 12, pp. 157–182). Emerald Publishing.
Wang, L., Jin, J. L., Yang, D., & Zhou, K. Z. (2020). Inter-partner control, trust, and radical innovation of IJVs in China: A contingent governance perspective. *Industrial Marketing Management, 88*, 70–83.
Wang, W., Thangavelu, S., & Lin, F. (2021). Global value chains, firms, and wage inequality: Evidence from China. *China Economic Review, 66*, 101585.
Welch, L. S., Benito, G. R. G., & Petersen, B. (2018). *Foreign operation methods: Theory, analysis, strategy*. Edward Elgar.
Westney, D. E. (1993). *Organization theory and the multinational corporation* (pp. 53–76). Springer.
Williamson, O. E. (1985). *The economic institutions of capitalism*. Free Press.
WIPO. (2021). *Hague yearly review 2020: International registrations of industrial design*. WIPO.
WTO | intellectual property (TRIPS) - TRIPS and public health: Compulsory licensing of pharmaceuticals and TRIPS. (n.d.). Retrieved April 1, 2021, from https://www.wto.org/english/tratop_e/trips_e/public_health_faq_e.htm
Wu, Z., & Salomon, R. (2017). Deconstructing the liability of foreignness: Regulatory enforcement actions against foreign banks. *Journal of International Business Studies, 48*(7), 837–861.

Yasar, M., & Paul, C. J. M. (2007). International linkages and productivity at the plant level: Foreign direct investment, exports, imports and licensing. *Journal of International Economics, 71*(2), 373–388.

Yuan, B. J. C., Chang, C.-Y., & Lo, M. C. (1998). Strategies of semiconductor industry in Taiwan. In *IEMC'98 Proceedings. International Conference on Engineering and Technology Management. Pioneering New Technologies: Management Issues and Challenges in the Third Millennium (Cat. No. 98CH36266)* (pp. 541–545). IEEE.

Zaheer, S. (1995). Overcoming the liability of foreignness. *Academy of Management Journal, 38*(2), 341–363. https://doi.org/10.5465/256683

Zaheer, S., & Mosakowski, E. (1997). The dynamics of the liability of foreignness: A global study of survival in financial services. *Strategic Management Journal, 18*(6), 439–463.

Zenger, T., & Gubler, T. (2018). *The Palgrave Encyclopedia of strategic management* (pp. 25–27). Palgrave.

Zhang, Y., & Li, H. (2001). The control design and performance in international joint ventures: A dynamic evolution perspective. *International Business Review, 10*(3), 341–362.

Zhao, H., Ma, J., & Yang, J. (2017). 30 years of research on entry mode and performance relationship: A meta-analytical review. *Management International Review, 57*(5), 653–682.

Zucker, L. G. (1987). Institutional theories of organization. *Annual Review of Sociology, 13*, 443–464. http://www.jstor.org/stable/2083256

The Coordination and Configuration of Global Value Chains (GVCs) 6

Multinational firms struggle to balance the degree of integration and standardization of internally and externally organized cross-border value creation activities. Thus, a significant question in managing international business activities remains: what are the gains of internalizing discrete stages of value-adding activities organized by a lead firm? Considering the scale and scope of global production networks, the multinational firm has been a significant nexus in studying international business. A vital part of the study of the strategies and structures of multinational firms was the question of how to manage and organize multiple cross-border business activities within the boundaries of the firm (Birkinshaw & Terjesen, 2003; Doz & Prahalad, 1993; Fitzgerald, 2015; Ramstetter, 1992; Stopford, 2005; Stopford & Wells, 1972). This perspective of how to organize value-adding activities within the international firm was narrowed down to focus on intrafirm governance problems, which was the prevailing emphasis for a long time in IB research (Birkinshaw et al., 2000; Hennart, 1993; Raisch & Birkinshaw, 2008; Wolf & Egelhoff, 2002, 2013).

Nevertheless, the encompassing and likewise fragmented global division of labor of value creation processes revealed this limited scope of a somewhat deluded approach (Casson, 2013; Ernst, 2009; Fernandez-Stark & Gereffi, 2019; Fröbel et al., 1978).

The study of the strategies of the multinational firm remains an important subject matter in international business, and is largely embedded in the question of how to structure the international scope of value-adding activities. These activities are spatially dispersed and highly fragmented across multiple foreign locations. These global value activities have been organized both within and between firms, transcending the supposed boundaries of the firm substantially. It is this radical transformation of a perspective, not neglecting firm boundaries but adding a critical new viewpoint, that demonstrate the strength and the weakness of multinational firms in global production networks (Cooper & Yoshikawa,

M. Fuchs, *International Management*,
https://doi.org/10.1007/978-3-662-65870-3_6

1994; Humphrey & Schmitz, 2008; Palomino-Tamayo & Timaná, 2021; Sapukotanage et al., 2016; Sinkovics et al., 2021).

There are two seminal theories of the firm. One is the view that the enterprise is a production function in which the source of its superior efficiency is the optimum sequence of combining input factors (Alchian & Demsetz, 1972; Foley, 1997; Holmstrom & Tirole, 2020). The other theory assumes that the hierarchical management structure of the enterprise can be more efficient than the market mechanism (Buckley, 2009; Buckley & Casson, 2009; Coase, 1937; Williamson, 2005). In both branches, the business firm's value-adding activities are managed, organized, coordinated, and integrated within its boundaries. The source of the firm's superior efficiency is generated within the firm boundaries.

6.1 Coordination and Control Between and Within Firm Boundaries

Although control and coordination have long been considered a neglected and vaguely understood area of management (Dauten et al., 1958), the meaning of control is still regarded as ambiguous (Zahra, 2003). One of the earliest interpretations of control focused on methods applied by the executive management to exercise their authority to ensure that organizational members carry out their activities by the existing rules and laws embedded in a corporate structure (Diemer, 1912). Subsequently, the meaning of control was equated with its function, performed by several layers of management to guarantee the execution of a thorough, designed plan. A plan was generated intentionally to be carried out in a controlled environment, thereby endorsing a predictable outcome. Control included determining how to measure the output (Weick, 1991, 2010; Gillespie, 1938; Hoskisson et al., 1999; Whittington, 2008).

Applying that logic, the standard definition of the multinational firm is "an enterprise that engages in foreign direct investment (FDI) [which] owns or, in some way, controls value-added activities in more than one country." A perspective which is still an almost undisputed "threshold definition" (Dunning & Lundan, 2008: 3).

However, identifying the determining factors of the actual boundaries of the multinational firm is a complex and almost impossible effort within the logic of this orthodox perspective.

The dominant body of theories about the multinational firm is based on transaction costs economics (Tallman, 2004; Verbeke & Kano, 2016) or the internalization paradigm (Buckley, 2009, 2011; Buckley & Casson, 2009, 2010). Endorsing these perspectives, the firm is treated as a mechanism capable of handling discrete transactions more efficiently than the market in the context of high uncertainty and asset specificity. This perspective explains the behavior of the multinational firm, which is assumed to be the outcome of a series of rational decisions to improve the efficiency within and across several business activities, supposing the superior efficiency is realized primarily within firm boundaries (Benito et al., 2019; Clougherty & Skousen, 2019; Enderwick & Buckley, 2019; Perelman, 2011).

Efficiency gains effectuated by the multinationality are assumed to serve as the primary trigger for the existence of multinational firms (Buckley, 1989; Buckley & Casson, 2010). However, the core of the argument that efficiency is the outcome of a superior capability of organizing transactions defined by its asset specificity and the power of controlling opportunism rests on the assumption that internalizing will not only mitigate costs caused by the liability of foreignness but that the marginal costs of internalizing offset the cost of alternative market transactions (Buckley & Casson, 2009, 2010; Hennart, 1977; Williamson, 1979, 1998, 2005).

Yet, almost no firm chooses to internalize all possible value-adding activities. Most stay embedded in an extensive network of suppliers and subcontractors, contributing value adding activities carried out by many large and small firms located in multiple different countries. And yet, large multinationals are key and leading actors in global trade (Aghion & Holden, 2011; Ruhl, 2015).

6.2 Coordination and Configuration

Firms coordinate and configure cross-border value-adding activities for several reasons. One is to ensure an efficient integration across a wide range of upstream and downstream value-adding activities within the firm boundaries. The primary outcome of coordination is assumed to be a more efficient integration of previously separated activities, an immediate outcome of a highly specialized division of labor within and between the multinational firm (Buckley, 2014; Fitzgerald, 2015; Jones, 2003; Wilkins, 2008).

However, the goal of coordination of value-adding activities that extent firm boundaries, that is, coordination of activities carried out in inter-organizational networks, is likewise challenging and has been substantially growing for decades.

Thus, addressing how value-adding activities are configurated and coordinated in a highly fragmented and dispersed network of inter-firm relationships is increasingly more complex than the coordination and configuration of cross-border activities within the firm. Thus, the coordination and configuration of multilayered inter-and intra-firm relations include managing sustainable, trusted, and economically efficient ties with suppliers, subcontractors, licensees, franchisees, alliances, IJVs, and WOS.

The Manufacturing Map of Two Large Multinational Firms

Two examples illustrate the extensive range of relations operated within and beyond firm boundaries, orchestrated or led by the large multinational firms. One example is Adidas, a global firm based in Germany, which generated 2020 net sales of almost 20 billion EUR primarily by outsourcing most of its production, which is built around a network of more than 500 legally independent firms, operating factories in more than 55 countries (adidas, 2022). Similarly, Nike, the US-based multinational firm, sources its finished products from 458 factories located in 36 countries while sourcing materials from 147 suppliers located in 18 countries. In 2021, Nike generated net sales of 44,53 billion USD (Nike, 2022). Nike sources its products from 144 factories located in mainland China, 44 factories are based in Indonesia, and 138 factories are sited in Viet Nam (Nike, 2022).

Against this background, the management of the multinational firm departs radically from the somewhat narrow conception of operating a firm within its so-called own legally instituted boundaries. A look beyond those categories reveals a profound shift in the global division of labor. It discloses how inter-and intra-firm relationships are organized, including the coordination of suppliers and contractors, in an extended global production network.

From that point of view, Oliver Williamson's notion of the firm as a nexus of contracts can be extended and applied to analyze the governance mechanisms within and beyond firm boundaries (Williamson, 1979, 1985).

Thus, we need to acknowledge that the prevalent global division of labor in multilayered international production networks is extremely differentiated. The interdependency between and within firms is growing, extremely fragile, and susceptible to economic and political frictions. Moreover, the geographical, cultural, and psychic distance between these fragmented but highly interdependent value-adding activities is an essential trigger for the increasing complexity.

6.2.1 Hierarchy and Control

Within the multinational firm, hierarchy is used to control highly specialized and fragmented activities. Across firm boundaries, the major mechanism of control is dependence. Thus, the notion of coordination goes far beyond simply managing value-adding activities situated within the boundaries of wholly-owned production facilities.

Coordination is the effort to bring two or more different activities carried out by several agents into a common ground. Coordination is intended to match or harmonize activities performed in various functional departments and locations. Control implies a particular notion of coordination, a coordination designed to direct, supervise, or monitor organizational activity, enabling people with different interests to keep a previously designed course of objectives. Hence, coordination includes action designed and maintained in advance to keep an intended system or to react to an unintended departure from once established objectives (Langlois, 1995, 2019).

Coordination is about control and is intended to guide a system or direct the course of action (Giglioni & Bedeian, 1974). Control is about establishing order and maintaining predictability; control is achieved by centralizing or decentralizing responsibilities (Tannenbaum, 1956). A dominant interpretation of control in organizations was that a higher level of control could be implemented by increasing participation, thus resulting in a better integration (Tannenbaum, 1962).

Within the boundaries of a firm, coordination of different specialized activities is a permanent issue, and integration is necessary to coordinate these highly specialized activities carried out in often independent organizational units (Langlois, 2007, 2016).

Neoclassical economics assumed that a market's price information was a sufficient means to match supply with demand. Within organizations, coordination is exercised by an elaborated multilayered hierarchy enabling the firm to operate these in fact disjoint activities more efficiently than the market mechanism (Alchian & Demsetz, 1972; Coase, 1937; Foss, 2002). The most basic meaning of hierarchy is derived from the superiority of someone or something supernatural (*hieros*) or the ruler (*archos*). Thus, coordination is characterized by establishing and maintaining an organizational order between superior and subordinate layers, including people and functions. It is related to the need to integrate differentiated activities, which have branched out due to a highly specialized division of labor practiced within and between firms.

Differentiation is based on apportioning specific activities to exploit the benefits of specialization (Babbage, 1835). Each specialized activity or task is grouped into departments, where similar functions are located or grouped into a common organizational unit. Although all these specialized work units generate synergies by becoming increasingly separated, the benefits derived from each work unit need to be integrated within and across each specialized unit. Despite integration, each specialized work unit develops a somewhat autonomous and unique mentality, as their identity is defined by the prime activities carried out in the work units. However, they still depend on effective linkages to one or more other work units within the organization (Dougherty, 2018: 1668). However, increasingly an ever more significant portion of international business activities are carried out between independent business firms.

6.2.2 The Boundaries of the Firm and Value-Adding Activities

Economists often ask two questions: One focuses on the firm's purpose, the other on what, in fact, determines its scale and scope of the firm (Holmstrom & Tirole, 2020: 65). These two questions are held as the essential core for any theory of the firm.

The Firm Is a Complex of Joint Sequential Decision Processes
In industrial economics, the business firm is the result of a series of "complex joint decision processes" that are performed or generated "within a network of agency relations" (Holmstrom & Tirole, 2020: 63). Holmstrom and Tirole emphasize that firm behavior is the outcome of a collaborative decision-making process comprising a series of sequential decisions. They assume that firm behavior stems from an aggregate of several decision-making processes of agents that act for "their superiors rather than for themselves" (Holmstrom & Tirole, 1989: 63).

This notion of the argument is essential, not because agents often do not do precisely what their superiors want, but because the firm's behavior is affected by joint decision-making processes that do not stop at the firm boundaries but include and are affected by the firm's extended network of agency relations. Still, originally the approach does not specify whether joint decisions are carried out within or between firms. Suppose a firm organizes its production processes by integrating upstream and downstream value-adding activities to accomplish more control over these activities. In that case, it is assumed that the integration is preferred over non-integration because of efficiency gains (Williamson, 1979).

Alchian and Demsetz contributed to this debate by arguing: "resource owners [firms] increase productivity through cooperative specialization" and assume that "cooperation between specialists is achieved within the firm" if the gains of cooperation and specialized production within-firm are greater than relying on market transactions (Alchian & Demsetz, 1972: 777). However, Alchian and Demsetz contend that "if the organization meters poorly, with rewards and productivity only loosely correlated, then productivity [gains] will be smaller; but if the economic organization meters well, productivity will be greater" (Alchian & Demsetz, 1972: 779).

Thus, it is presumed that firms are better at reducing the negative outcomes caused by shirking and adverse selection problems. However, a firm cannot address every issue "by authority, or by disciplinary action" because it is impossible to directly measure the marginal productivity or output of every economic activity (Alchian & Demsetz, 1972: 777). Considering the costs of monitoring and the prevalence of shirking within firm boundaries, we need to acknowledge that "the lower the costs of managing [. . .] the greater will be the comparative advantage of organizing resources within the firm" (Alchian & Demsetz, 1972: 783). The implication of this argument for managerial behavior in a multinational firm seems obvious.

If organizing value-adding activities within the firm are more productive than organizing the same value-adding activities using the market, management will opt for expanding the size of the firm. But, if the control of a firm cannot measure the output directly, the governance mode employing hierarchy has its limits. A famous quote epitomizes the real problem: "Two men jointly lift heavy cargo into trucks. Solely by observing the total weight loaded per day, it is impossible to determine each person's marginal productivity" (Alchian & Demsetz, 1972: 779). Thus, within a large organization with its multiple teams, it is almost impossible to measure precisely the contribution of each organizational member. Yet, if firms do have difficulties measuring productivity gains from merging upstream and downstream activities, the expansion of the international firm network cannot be exclusively legitimized by efficiency gains and superior capabilities.

Figure 6.1 shows a typical aggregation of value-adding activities organized within and beyond firm boundaries. The supply of raw materials and the provision of intermediary products is organized outside firm boundaries basically by using market mechanism according to the theory of the firm, but these markets can be replaced by establishing none-equity cooperation (contracting) with various subfirms (Gudergan et al., 2016; Wong, 2017; WTO, 2019). Inbound logistics, assembling and manufacturing and sales and marketing is managed within the firm, but each of these activities, or particular parts, can be outsourced. In Fig. 6.1 the retailing of products and after sales service are organized outside the firm boundaries. The prototypical firm, exemplified in Fig. 6.1 may expand its size by internalizing suppliers of intermediary products (or producers of critical raw materials). Expanding the internal organization of activities can be defined as upstream vertical expansion (see the left side of Fig. 6.1) if the integrated activity is going backward along the same production line. If the internalization is moving forward (extending into retailing) the manufactured products and services (see the right side) the integration of value adding processes is defined as downstream integration.

Each value activity as illustrated, is describing a value adding process, i.e., provision of raw materials, production of intermediary products, inbound logistics, assembling and manufacturing the products and services, marketing and sales, and retailing. All these value adding activities can be either organized as a joint effort within the boundaries of the firm or may be sourced in from or out to other firms (subcontractors and suppliers) or markets.

Value-adding activities are organizational tasks that involve mechanical processing ranging from highly automated production steps (up to full robotization) or they rely on labor-intensive manual processing of material components, described as grinding, filing, turning in and out single components (Langlois & Foss, 1999). Each work task can potentially include one or more value-adding activities that can be either organized as a joint effort by a team within the firm as the core organizational unit, where resources and

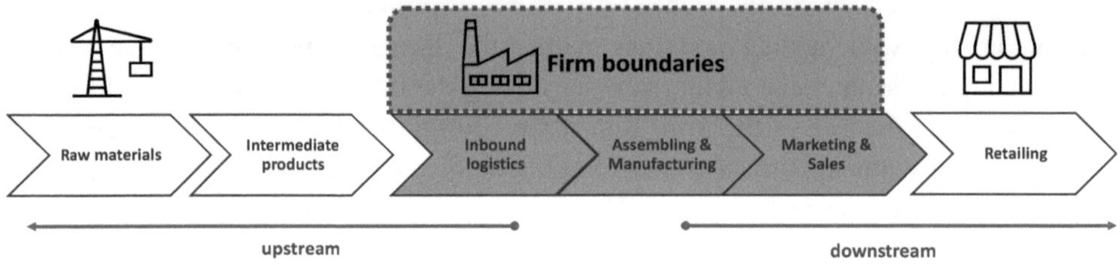

Fig. 6.1 The traditional view of the boundaries of the firm

specialized skills and capabilities are jointly pooled to carry out a common activity (Kogut, 1985: 15).

The effective control and configuration—within and across firm boundaries– of these value activities is a major objective of managing any international firm. As the name suggests, value-adding activities are about generating added value in the processing, manufacturing, transformation of raw materials, intermediate products and other tangible and intangible factors of production (Adner & Helfat, 2003; Helfat & Raubitschek, 2000; Langlois & Foss, 1999: 204ff). Note, this process of value creation is something that can take place both inside and outside the traditional conception of firm boundaries.

In fact, several value-adding activities contribute to a final product or service, as well as the exchange of (intermediary or semi-finished) goods and services within and between companies.

For example, the design and conception for an advertising campaign for a given product, the production of advertising, and the adaptation of an advertising campaign for a product, all that can be organized by in-house value-adding activities, or as joint efforts in cooperation with an external independent firm or the whole service may be sourced from a reputed external provider of marketing services.

From a close perspective, the control and coordination of a discrete value-adding activity may be the focus of an elaborate but manageable and feasible managerial task. Each task can be located (configurated) within a particular functional or divisional responsibility. Each task can be carried out independently by exploiting resources and capabilities available in-house or the task can be operated jointly with other affiliated firms.

But from a bird's eye view, it becomes apparent that a single product is made up of many interrelated value-adding tasks, accomplished by many different processes, implemented by a variety of firms in multiple locations.

These complex and highly fragmented production relationships are likewise organized, controlled and configured by individual leading firms and the design and control of an extended value chain can be a viable and unique firm strategy (Kogut, 1985).

Arndt and Kierzkowski describe these global production networks as "fragmented" because single value-adding activities in a production process are "physically separated" and scattered across different locations worldwide (Arndt & Kierzkowski, 2001; Gereffi et al., 2005: 79). The way an elaborated value chain is organized, as a separate or joint activity (Coase, 1937), by a firm or the market, depends (among others) on the gains and trade-offs between joint and separate production activities.

Economists argued that the "rising integration of world markets has brought with it a disintegration of the production process, in which manufacturing or services activities done abroad are combined with those performed at home. Companies are now finding it profitable to outsource increasing amounts of the production process, a process which can happen either domestically or abroad. This represents a breakdown in the vertically-integrated mode of production–the so-called—'Fordist' production, exemplified by the automobile industry—on which American manufacturing was built" (Feenstra, 1998: 31).

6.2.3 Value-Adding Activities as a Chain of Interrelated Activities

A second focus to analyze the extent and scope of value adding activities is still Michael Porter's classical account of a value chain illustrated in Fig. 6.2, which illustrates, albeit crudely, a typified configuration of major functional and cross-functional value adding activities. Originally, these value added activities were designated according to their functional and their cross-functional focus. The concept of a value chain shown in Fig. 6.2 was used by Michael Porter to elaborate the essence of his proposed generic strategies (Porter, 2008). He argued that a value chain is constituted by its *primary* and *supplementing activities*. Primary activities are directly accountable for a particular function of added value in the provision of a service or product.

For example, under the heading inbound logistics all activities are summarized, which are needed to manage incoming supplies, storage, distribution, and timely delivery to other units for further processing. Operations are characterized by those activities that transform supplied inputs into a finished or semi-finished product or service, for example a particular set of assembling processes.

Outbound logistics deliver the manufactured product or service to the customer, and may include packaging, storage, warehousing, and dispatching the product. Value adding activities described as marketing and sales comprise several efforts to sell a product, using special advertising, training and managing sales people, and developing a promotional campaign.

Service activities are adding value in this overall process by maintaining the quality of the product or service after sales, services offered for repairing and supplying spare parts, or assisting and training users to operate the product.

The supplementing value activities are described as supporting the primary activities, they provide the backup and add value across several activities. Supporting activities are essentially designed to organize primary activities. Activities such as accounting, financing, monitoring, etc. produce, handle, and provide information across the primary activities that are required to maintain and improve the efficiency of the primary activities. Human resource management organizes the recruiting, training, and rewarding of staff employed in primary and supporting activities. Technology management is organizing the

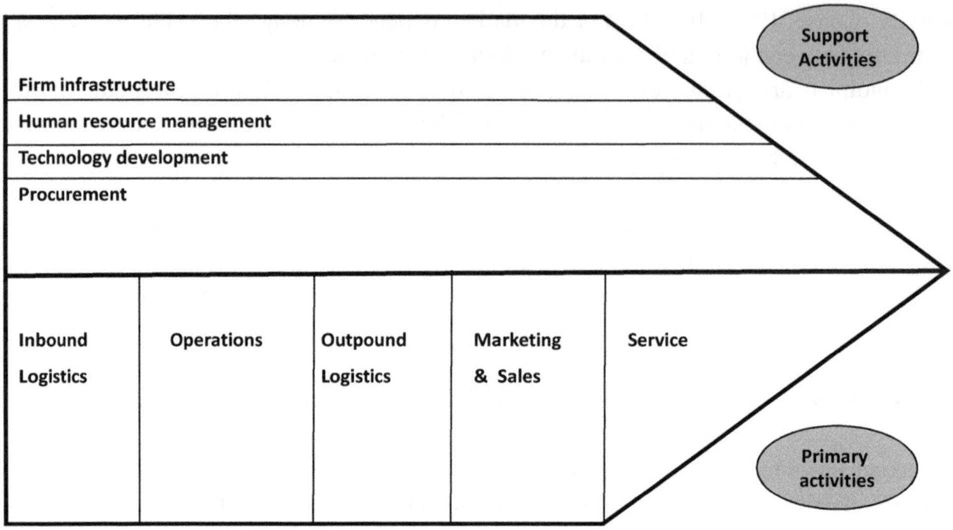

Fig. 6.2 A basic value chain (Porter, 1980: 26)

development of the technologies used to produce goods and services. Procurement is accountable for managing and providing the resources required in primary activities.

Defining the Value Chain

Bruce Kogut originally described a value chain as a "process by which technology is combined with material and labor inputs, and then processed inputs are assembled, marketed, and distributed" (Kogut, 1985: 15). This definition sounds technically and abstract, but it describes how a firm is transforming tangible and intangible resources into a valuable product or service. Yet, the term technology can be misleading, it is not a static concept or simply a tangible asset, it as well is about applying and implanting technologies. Combining technologies is about the know-how, based on several capabilities, a skill how to apply technologies or technological processes. The exploitation of technologies is itself an organizational capability and an essential value-creation activity. Eventually, technology is not only about the management of technological capabilities, but includes organizing the "entire dynamics of how innovation comes about and the speeds of both invention and diffusion" (Mokyr, 2010).

6.2.4 Coordination and Configuration of Cross-Border Value Activities

The major question related to the need to coordinate and configure a value chain is then twofold, (1) how it is allocated efficiently across several locations, and (2) on what value activities a firm should concentrate its own resources and competencies (Kogut, 1985). The answer to these two questions affects significantly how an international firm generates its competitive advantages and has become a major technique of analyzing the competitiveness of industries (Brown & Duguid, 2001; Kogut, 1985: 16, 1991; Verbeke, 2003).

Although primary activities (as illustrated in Fig. 6.2) are conceptualized around functional units, the actual organization of value-adding activities remains a cross-functional challenge. Value adding activities cannot readily be isolated or fragmented into any possible single sequential activity, overall, the entire value adding chain remains a fragile holistic process in organizing cross border production.

For example, R&D activities are often located in several departments, at different locations. They are implemented effectively in close cooperation with a number of other functions exploiting synergies within and across specific functions. R&D is categorized as a supporting activity, because it generates essential inputs for several value adding activities. A supporting activity is not always a one-way provision of a critical input, it can equally receive significant inputs from so-called *inter* dependent functional activities. Quite often, skills and knowledge gained through a primary activity cross over into another activity (Porter, 2008).

The primary value-adding activity, inbound logistics are responsible for organizing and maintaining a repository of incoming and warehoused materials. Operations are value-adding activities that manufacture and assemble products or services, which may include quality management. Outbound logistics is the activity that is concerned with the organization of the distribution of final goods and services to customers.

How to control and configurate value adding activities within and beyond firm boundaries remains a core question of international management. The challenge is whether to manage several cross-border business operations more integrated, more decentralized or both, balancing integration and decentralization needs. Seeking a balance between integration or decentralization may affect the management of value adding activities within firm boundaries, for example the coordination between subsidiaries, or coordinating activities across firm boundaries, for example managing multiple outsourced and offshored value activities (Prahalad, 1995; Prahalad & Dearlove, 2009).

All these approaches identified a real challenge rooted in finding a fit between the conflicting demands of integration and decentralization across core value-adding activities (see the next chapter). Efforts have been made to find an elaborate answer how a discrete value-adding activity should be organized within and across boundaries of the multinational firm, based on the need to be more local responsive or to exploit the synergies of standardizing products and services. Understandably, it is impossible to produce a simple recipe for these complex tasks.

6.2.5 Managing Interlocked Patterns of Cross-Border Value Adding Activities

A central problem in the coordination and control of complex value creation processes lies in the limited access to and the insufficient information about the quality of the performance of individual value creation activities in a corporate network. No manager has complete or sufficiently qualified information to make an optimal decision (Gigerenzer & Selten, 2002; Kahneman & Tversky, 1996; Vuori & Vuori, 2014). In any organization, access to and meaning of information is distorted, filtered and manipulated - both consciously and unconsciously. Perfect rationality is often just a wish that cannot be fulfilled (Cyert & March, 1963).

Nevertheless, in multinational firms, there is the constant need to coordinate and control various value creation activities as complexity increases. The management of the multinational firm is confronted by the task to coordinate highly fragmented and dispersed functions across several locations established in various country environments (Luo & Mezias, 2002; Petersen & Pedersen, 2002). The larger the scope and scale of multinationality the more complex the tasks either to increase integration or decentralization of core business operation. However, this debate seems largely disconnected from the need to arrange global value chains within and between companies.

6.3 Global Value Chains and Firm Networks

For decades, the literature on global value chains (GVCs) has been growing rapidly (Ashenbaum, 2018; Gereffi, 1984a, 1989a, 2019; Gupta, 2016; Humphrey & Schmitz, 2008; Kano et al., 2020; McWilliam et al., 2019; Sinkovics et al., 2021; UNCTAD, 2011; WTO, 2019). In international business the multinational firm was conceived as the primary mechanism efficiently internalizing uncertainty. The massive growth of large multinational firms was consequently explained by its superior efficiency resulting from vertical and horizontal integration, establishing and managing ever more multiple "geographically dispersed economic activities" (McWilliam et al., 2019: 1). In the effort to explain the huge growth of global value chains the nexus of the firm as the major mechanism and focus demonstrated also its weakness.

A number of studies aiming to develop an in-depth understanding of the scope and pattern of global value chains shifted the perspective from inside the firm to what is actually emerging outside the firm. And increasingly a perspective emerged to analyze how a network of multiple firms contributed to the extensive pattern of global value chains (McWilliam & Nielsen, 2020). In contrast to a more traditional international business perspective, the global value chains approach is often embedded in a more systemic and holistic analysis of the interrelated parts that make up the global economy (Davis, 2019; Gidengil, 1978; Hornborg, 1998; Wallerstein, 2000, 2005).

Global Value Chains (GVCs)

The Global Value Chains (GVCs) approach radically extends the prevailing focus on the multinational firm as the most important link to explain cross-border value-adding activities that are deployed within and beyond firm boundaries.

In general, global value chains (GVCs) are first and foremost highly fragmented. Multiple parts of the value adding activities are embedded in a global network, characterized by intricate and unequal relationships (Casson, 2013; Fernandez-Stark et al., 2014; Gereffi, 2018; Gereffi & Fernandez-Stark, 2018).

Studying GVCs and the role of multinational firms can be split between deploying a focus on the firm, conceptualized as an entity confined by its boundaries, or focusing on how the multinational firms organize a highly fragmented and geographically dispersed chain of production processes of goods and services. This perspective of analyzing the scope and pattern of international production conceives each firm, whether small or large, as embedded in a specific hierarchical network of activities constituting the intricate structure of a global value chain.

These networks are dominated by large producers or by large sellers, in both cases large multinational firms (Dicken, 2017; Gereffi, 2018). Although the multinational firm is a key part of these networks, a major player in organizing these elaborated stages in highly dispersed manufacturing processes, ranging from the design of a product to the final distribution and after-sales services (Hassler, 2003, 2012), it is still only one part of a complex whole, albeit an influential and powerful. Each contributor firm is an additional, and different part of that fragmented network scattered across dispersed geographies. Located in diverse and heterogenous geographies, locations spanning core, semi-peripheral, and peripheral regions.

The purchase of a product such as a pair of shoes or a bouquet of roses in a grocery store is often the end of a long journey made possible by formal and informal labor relations organized by small and large firms, employing people supplying different skills, collecting laborers from all over the globe, organized in often disparate and unequal production relationships, build around a network of transactions feeding into a global value chain (Gereffi, 2019; Gupta, 2016; Kano et al., 2020; Sinkovics et al., 2021).

For a large number of participant firms embedded in a GVC, the intricate relationships are characterized by unequal position. While the choice to make or buy is based on the assumption that in a particular context it is more efficient to organize (make) a value-adding activity within the firm than to depend on likely uncertain market transactions, in reality, major value chains are organized by lead multinational firms.

In the following section, the perspective on global value chains (GVCs) is adopted to examine the phenomenon of globally dispersed interdependent stages of production processes. The GVC is shifting the somewhat traditional and narrow focus to analyze the structure and pattern of global trade. It is also introducing a new question, namely how the

GVCs are affecting behavior, the strategy and structure the global economy. Still, the study of the multinational enterprise remains a formative and major focus. But, the multinational enterprise, although conceived as a core constituent, is only one of several drivers in this complex system of highly fragmented value activities operating in very unique geographic locations and influenced by multiple sets of institutional, social and economic contexts.

The main advantage of this new look at the global economy is to include social, political and economic forces that shape the dynamic growth of GVCs. If research on GVCs were limited to the narrow boundaries of the lead firms, their strategies, and the means by which they organize this extensive network of business relations, it would remain blind to the social, political, and environmental consequences of GVCs. Thus, GVCs analyses can significantly contribute to a re-evalution of the responsibility and role of the multinational firm (Gupta, 2016; Nathan et al., 2018).

6.4 GVC Analytical Framework

A fairly small group of scholars, located somewhat outside the core subjects of international business developed an approach to analyze prevalent global value chains (Dicken, 2017; Ernst, 2009; Fröbel et al., 1978, 1980; Gereffi, 1989b; Gereffi & Fernandez-Stark, 2018; Sturgeon et al., 2008). This perspective structured its approach around six basic interdependent sets of questions. These questions focus on major dimensions that characterize the scope and dynamics of global value chains. The first dimension of a GVC is described by its idiosyncratic input-output relations. The second feature describes the geographical scope of value adding activities. The third aspect focus on the analyses of the governance structure prevalent in different types of GVCs. The fourth aspect is dedicated to a discussion about the possibility how a particular value adding activity performed in a global value chain can be upgraded in order to augment the local economic benefits. The fifth feature is about how the institutions affect the apparent position of an activity in a global value adding chain. The six dimension looks at the power, the weakness and strength of supplier-buyer interaction predominant in particular industries, discussed also as the stakeholder relations in particular global value chains (Fernandez-Stark & Gereffi, 2019).

The governance mechanisms tell us how a global value chain is managed. Governance mechanisms fall between two dichotomous poles, markets and hierarchies. In between, there are other governance modes that indicate how a value created at one location is transferred to another stage in GVCs, it tells us how value is appropriated across the whole range of value adding activities.

Each of these perspectives sheds a particular light on a specific problem or a defining feature of global value chains. These different perspectives can be used on their own to explore specific GVCs in greater depth or to ask how several dimensions complement each other.

The first three dimensions relate to the pattern and structure of GVCs, from a perspective directed at the macro-level. The other three dimensions that characterize GVCs look at aspects defining the role and scope of activities and how they are performed in a specific local environment (looking at the micro-structures). The first three dimensions are constituted by a perspective which can be defined as top down view, whereas the latter three dimensions describe a perspective that looks at GVCs from the bottom up.

The bottom up focus looks at the regional and country level, tries to understand the division of labour between different geographies where sequential stages of a global production is carried out, it analyzes the different, and unequal labor relations and focuses on the working conditions, the risk and inequality existing within the many modes of the global value chain (Gupta, 2016; Nathan et al., 2018), and it asks how these aspects influence the pattern and structure of GVCs. This bottom up approach questions how people and places participate in and how they can improve their position in the prevalent hierarchy of GVCs (Fernandez-Stark & Gereffi, 2019).

Global value chain (GVC) analyzes the outcome of a radical change in the global production, coordinated and controlled by multinational firms which evolved throughout the last four decades (Contractor et al., 2009; Fengru & Guitang, 2019; Kano et al., 2020).

The same analyses are sometimes carried out under a different name and from a different point of view in order to criticize the persisting inequality and exploitation, for example by Immanuel Wallerstein (Wallerstein, 2005, 2004), who uses the term global commodity chain (GCC) to examine the unequal relations of dependency between core and periphery within the world economy. An additional focus independently was developed by Dieter Ernst who employs the term global production networks (GPN) to refer to the fundamental shift in the international division of labor between the West and the East in the last decades (Ernst, 2009). Others point at the transformations which emerged in the early 1960s analyzed as a shift from the structure of an old international division of labor between industrialized and developing economies to the emergence and manifestation of a "New International Division of Labour" (Fröbel et al., 1978; Schmidt, 1990).

In international business research, global value chains have always been a core topic, but rather indirectly using detours, although isolated studies appeared as early as the 1980s (Dam, 1978; Kogut, 1984). But it is only recently that the topic of global value chains has undergone a renaissance in IB (Casson, 2013; McWilliam et al., 2019; Rugman et al., 2009). A major trigger for this resurgence is the acknowledgement of the conceptional analyzes offered by Gary Gereffi, who has been working on this central theme since the 1960s (Gereffi, 1984b, 1989b, 1995, 2018; Gereffi et al., 2005).

Charles Babbage as the Originator of GVCs

It seems odd to mention that the global economy is organized around global value chains, but how each industry sectors is in fact organized may differ substantially,

(continued)

although a prevalent pattern is mostly shared. Global value chains are the actual result of a distinct international division of labour maintained at several locations, linking rich and poor economies together. Charles Babbage (1762–1871) professor of mathematics at Cambridge University described the division of labour "the most important principle on which the economy of a manufacture depends" (Babbage, 1835: 21). The division of labour is conceived of an almost unlimited source of efficiency, resting on the division of "work to be executed into different processes, each requiring different skill or of force" which allows the manufacturer, who organizes and control this process to "purchase exactly that precise quantity of both which is necessary for each process; whereas, if the whole work were executed by one workman, that person must possess sufficient skill to perform the most difficult, and sufficient strength to execute the most laborious, of the operations into which the art is divided" (Babbage, 1835: 25).

The idea and principle described here by the ingenious Charles Babbage revolutionized the organization of industrial work and led to a sophisticated separation of tasks into the smallest component parts needed for making a product. Not only did this separation lead to the repeatedly cited efficiency gain, but it also permitted in the organization of this process the acquisition of only the amount of skill necessary for the minute task. The key message here, however, is that the principle has set in motion a fully-fledged fragmentation of a complex division of labor, breaking up a complicated process that consisted of a medley of highly skilled, less skilled and unskilled work force, ultimately, leading to a relocation (decoupling) of single value adding activities wherever the corresponding supply of labour skills needed can be sourced most cheaply. Each global value chain contains value adding activities ranging from research and development (R&D), the design of a product, its production, marketing and distribution. These activities are operated within the boundary of a single firm or coordinated and operated between many highly and unequal but different firms. The scale and scope of these inter- and intrafirm division of labor is a major question in International Business.

The following section, which briefly discusses the six dimensions of a GVC analysis, is based on a conception of GVCs developed by Gary Gereffi and his many coauthors over the last decade, that offer an established methodological tool for analyzing different patterns of GVCs (Fernandez-Stark et al., 2013, 2014; Fernandez-Stark & Gereffi, 2019). It should be noted, this is not the dominant perspective used in IB research (Buckley & Casson, 2014; Devinney et al., 2001; Girod & Rugman, 2005; Rugman & D'Cruz, 1997).

6.4.1 Input–Output Structure of GVCs

The first level relates to estimating the impact of GVCs by using the input–output analysis to map the existing supply and demand relations characterizing an industry. The input-output analysis is a tool to measure the interdependent relations within an economy and allows the drawing of a fairly detailed picture of the proportion of input to outputs in a given system of production. The input-output structure of a GVCs is the description how inputted value adding activities relate to the output of value created in other sectors. Ideally, the input-output pattern fully documents the process line of manufacturing a product or service, including all supporting and related activities, from the first idea (the design of a product) to the final consumption. The input-output analysis is presented in a table, where the horizontal lines designate the value of the total product or service in an industry, whereas the vertical column denotes the list of inputs processed in the product line. The Input–output analysis, developed by Nobel laureate Wassily Leontief, rely on data that calculate in detail how a value adding activities contributes in an industry manufacturing the final output (product or service) which can be used as an input for another industry. The input–output analysis in its tabular form account for all transactions between and within households and business firms within and between a region. It measures exactly how the value of an input is used to produce the value of an output, and how that value of the output is further processed or used as input for the subsequent production processes in other stages for other outputs (services or goods).

The input-output approach allows us to identify the core stages of a value chain and how these different stages relate to each other. Thus, the value chain of a product is characterized by the totality of its related interdependent ties to in and outputs in the overall production processes.

A GVCs approach does not usually document every detail in a value chain, but restricts its analysis to the major, most significant stages. In general, it is a specification how raw materials are produced, how these raw materials are traded, it is about the production and procurement of these raw materials. A GVCs analysis describes how these raw materials are processed, subsequently becoming further inputs and intermediary goods and services that enter later production processes. How these inputs and outputs in a full production line are organized, whether they are dominated by a few large firms or powerful traders, what role and responsibility smaller or medium-sized enterprises assume is the core objective of an input-output approach applied in a GVC analysis.

The value chain then describes how the production is organized within and between firms mapping exactly the input output relations. But in a GVCs analysis the exact input output relation between discrete value adding activities is often highly aggregated, usually the most basic activities aggregated in boxes (see Fig. 6.3) representing a particular but crudely aggregated bundle of values, such as the production of raw materials, the number of producers at several stages, their function being exporters, responsible for packaging and storage, or processing, and how distribution and sale is organized (Gereffi, 2018: 308).

Fig. 6.3 Fruit and vegetables GVC segments (Gereffi, 2018: 308, reproduced with permission of Cambridge University Press)

The value chain at that level is used to describe how a product is designed, assembled or manufactured, and distributed. A more in-depth analysis of each stage of the value chain is intended to reveal who is dominating the GVCs, typically a number of firms (small, medium-sized, or large). Each stage itself is characterized by an idiosyncratic division of labour (comprising a wide range of possible labour relations, from permanent well-paid full time employment to insecure, unhealthy or even illegal occupations).

The input–output analysis is capable of providing a picture of the consumption pattern of households and describes the inter-industry relationship of an interdependent system of input and outputs. The input output relations can be aggregated on the product level or on the firm level. It shows how the output from one stage of production carried out by a firm enter the production process of another firm. The input output analyses provide the picture how industry sectors of an economy depend on the input of other sectors (e.g. agriculture, banking services, energy supply).

The input output analysis allows us to identify the key segments, which vary from industry to industry, in a given GVC. Major segments constitute the R&D processes, the design of a product, the provision and manufacturing of inputs, the production and assembling processes, the distribution and marketing of goods using different channels, and sales (Gereffi & Fernandez-Stark, 2018).

Each industry has evolved industry-specific patterns of fragmentation related to how particular goods and services are produced. The highly segmented and dispersed division of labor between and within firms that operate along a value-adding chain exhibits a unique dynamic and structural pattern. Any GVC exemplifies how the activities of a business firm is split into a large number of discrete value adding activities. The major objective of breaking up a process into several discrete steps is to optimize the configuration of the overall process of production, an idea invented by Charles Babbage in the early nineteenth century (Babbage, 1835). The ever increasing division of labor, an augmented specialization in each production stage, made it possible to outsource (or offshore) particular activities, which has been called an "increasingly finer micro-dissection of company functions" (Contractor et al., 2009: 3) which allowed the management of the multinational firm to intensify the geographical relocation and offshoring of value adding activities previously operated in-house.

The so-called dissection of functions performed within firm boundaries, its geographical relocation, the rise of an ever increasing proportion of outsourcing and offshoring in the management of value adding activities can be documented in almost all industries (Beaverstock, 2009; Dicken, 2017; Faulconbridge, 2007; Zhang, 2012).

The last decades have seen a substantial transformation, for instance, of the global food industry. For a host of reasons, the global food industry is an outstanding example that portrays the strengths and weaknesses, the benefits and drawbacks of a global food production system. While most food is still locally produced, both the globally and locally food producers, small and large ones, are embedded in a sensitive and fragile ecosystem. The production of livestock and vegetable food using tons of fertilizers, herbicides, pesticides and fast growing breeds (both in animal and plant production) have a lasting impact on the local environment. Existing global food value chain systems increase water scarcity, pollution, and huge monocultures not only destroy the production bases of local producers, but also imperil the entire planet.

In many global food production chains high value food is exported to consumer markets, primarily in the EU, USA and partly to East Asia. Many products, if not all, leave the local geographies where they have been produced. Although the value chain in food production has become a truly global industry, its major feature is that it is primarily produced locally, relying on a specific fragile soil and climatic environment.

Global Poultry Farms

Poultry farms operate in a sophisticated highly integrated industry, dominated by very few large producers, especially in the USA and in Asia (Dastagiri, 2017). The integration of several production stages allow large producers to control product quality and food safety closer throughout the entire production cycle (Ariyawardana & Collins, 2013; Burnham & Epperson, 1998; Li et al., 2013). The largest producers of poultry are the USA, followed by China and Brazil accounting for about 50% of the total world markets. The US poultry industry was the largest exporter of poultry meat, but has been overtaken by Brazil recently (Dastagiri, 2017; Dicken, 2017: 425ff).

Another exemplary case is the production of fresh fruits and vegetables.

Fresh Fruits and Vegetables

The industries' value chains are made up either (a) by large contract farmers, or agro-industrial plantations, and outgrowers, or (b) smaller farms or small-holders. The size of the small producer varies from country to country and from product to product (Náglová & Rudinskaya, 2021). The size of farms producing fresh vegetables or dairy products can range from less than one hectare to several thousands. Producers are highly-profitable enterprises, or subsistence family-farmers selling only a fraction of their produce, often forced into market production, by a circle that severely kept them indebted. Small producers sell their produce to local or regional small

(continued)

exporters, or to larger independent traders who export the products in other markets. The independent traders and importers distribute products to wholesalers, who sell to supermarkets or small grocery stores. Fresh vegetables sold in a neighborhood market can be produced by large plantations and contract farmers in Kenya, which sell their produce to large exporting firms in Kenya or Zimbabwe, who resell the food to large importers in the UK, for instance, who supply supermarkets or wholesalers. The agro-industry growing fresh fruits and vegetables is dominated by large producers from China, accounting for a bit more than 30%, followed by India producing 10% of world output. The paradox in this market is that a large number of poor countries produce food for the affluent consumers, primarily for the EU, the USA and East Asia (Dicken, 2017: 431).

A major impact in the organization of the global food industry has been the transformation of the global transporting systems. Today, long-distance trade in fresh fruits and other food products is based on sophisticated and permanent cooling systems for air, sea and road logistics. Another major trigger impacting the global value chain in food production comes from advances in biotechnologies that supply engineered breeding variants for the food industry that promise more resistance to environmental degradation, hazards and increase still the output. In addition, the food industry is highly regulated and governments heavily subsidize their own producers and try to protect domestic markets from food imports especially in high income economies (Cammies et al., 2021; Dicken, 2017: 437; Erklavec et al., 2021).

Food production (fruits and vegetables) is dominated by a mix of small, medium, and large multinationals, including large corporations such as Dole or Del Monte. Farming the products like coffee, cocoa beans, pineapples, or bananas rely on local or seasonal immigrant labor. Large multinationals which dominate the global food industry are Monsanto, Du Pont, Syngenta, Bayer, Nestlé, Kraft Foods, Unilever, Dow AgroSciences, Walmart, Carrefour, Tesco, Aldi, and Rewe (Dicken, 2017: 441).

The produce of large contract farmers is divided among large plantations and outgrowers, who plant fruits and vegetables for large exporters located in or near the producing countries, like Kenya or Zimbabwe (illustrated in Fig. 6.4). In that figure each arrow indicates the dominant governance mechanism used in a particular production stage prevalent in organizing relations between different groups of producers and buyers. As illustrated in Fig. 6.4 the large contract farmers and outgrowers are organized around captive governance modes. Large plantations and exporters in Zimbabwe and Kenya are organized hierarchically. Exporters in Kenya and Zimbabwe are connected by relational governance modes to large UK importers, responsible for the wholesale and quality control. These UK importers are embedded using modular governance modes with UK supermarkets, selling the food products to end consumers responsible for marketing, monitoring and specifying product categories. This entire food global value chain is

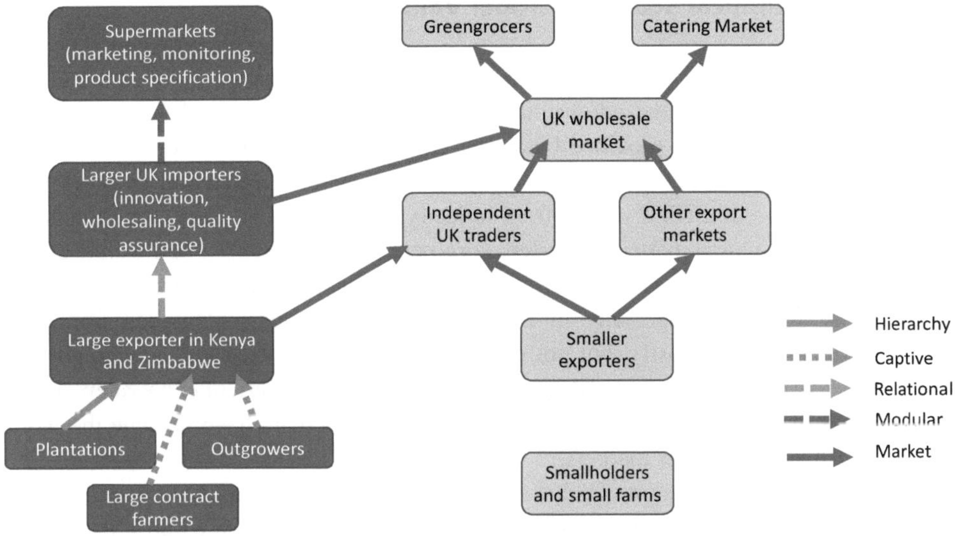

Fig. 6.4 The Fresh vegetable value chain (source: Dolan and Humphrey, 2004: 496)

organized using market transaction with small and large exporters, dependent UK traders or other UK wholesale chains that deliver the product to greengrocers and small neighborhood markets.

At the final stage, the large supermarkets buy the fresh food from large UK importers. Their relation is coined modular, because the large UK importers carry out testing product quality and package products according to safety specifications required by supermarket chains. On the right side at the bottom of the global value chain in fresh foods are situated the smallholders and small farmers producing food for the affluent consumer markets in Europe and the US and Japan. These small farmers sell their harvested produce to smaller exporters who sell the food to either smaller independent traders located in the UK or to other export markets. These independent traders sell the food to small grocery stores and smaller neighborhood markets. Additionally, large exporters in Kenya and Zimbabwe sell to independent UK traders and large UK importers and supply food to UK wholesalers. On the left side of the exemplified food value chain are all relations between seller and buyer organized either (but only at the bottom) as captive, hierarchical, or relational or modular, depending on the value generated or exploited throughout the trade pattern. Not surprisingly on the right side, smaller units, starting with small farmers, transaction are organized by markets (Dicken, 2017: 427; Fernandez-Stark & Gereffi, 2019; Gereffi & Fernandez-Stark, 2010).

6.4.2 Geographical Scope of Global Value Chains

The second dimension characterizing GVCs is the geographical scope of value adding activities. Today, most value adding activities are scattered across different locations. Value adding activities are provided by a great pool of heterogenous labor, defined by its formal and informal labor relation at different stages in a production network. The geographical scope of a GVC differs from industry to industry but shows a pertinent and often unequal structural pattern between core-periphery locations. High value adding activities tend to be concentrated in high-income urban regions or core cities. Lower value-adding activities, especially in labor-intensive industries, outsourced from high income economies, are mostly, but not exclusively located in periphery regions attract a wide range of low paid value adding activities. A pattern, particular prevalent in the clothing industry, where countries like Bangladesh and Vietnam have become the work-bench for affluent consumer markets.

The geographical dispersion of value-adding activities is demonstrated by the increasing value of intra-firm and inter-firm trade, which contribute to as much as 80% to the final value of a product or service (Lanz & Miroudot, 2011; OECD, 2010). Advanced information technology, new production technologies, computer applied and computer aided design, are supporting the fragmentation of the manufacturing process, moving partly finished across several locations adding often only a small fraction to the total value of the final product. Additionally, new technologies and still cheap transport systems triggered the spatial distribution of value-adding activities across the globe (Fitzgerald, 2015; Hassler, 2003; Hodgson & Knudsen, 2004).

Currently, almost no firm is capable or willing to operate the entire production process for finishing a product in-house without substantially relying on outsourcing and offshoring a wide array of inputs and services.

The geographical scope of that highly fragmented and specialized division of labor is based on a huge pool of cheap and disciplined labor, which is a vital component of the current scale and scope of the geographical dispersion of GVCs.

The geographical patterns of GVCs have substantially changed during the last five decades. A change that is the outcome of a no less comprehensive transformation how the lead firms operate, control and structure their production processes (Casson, 2013; Frobel et al., 1978; Haakonsson, 2009; Kreye et al., 1980; Snidal, 1982).

The data about the global trade flows during these last decades offers an initial insight into the structural pattern of intra- and inter-firm trade. However, it was only in the early 1970s, prototypically studied in the transformation of the clothing industry that systematically outsourced production to cheap and convenient manufacturing sites offered in numerous new export processing zones and special economic sites set up by developing economies to attract foreign direct investment (Fröbel et al., 1978).

6.4.3 Governance Structure of the Global Value Chains

Across different stages in the production process, various intricate and vital agency relations constitute the management of GVCs. A value chain is coordinated and controlled by a particular governance mechanism. The governance mode can range from applying hierarchy deployed by a particular powerful actor, using an explicit authority exercised over subordinate contractors to somewhat pure market relations, where only the market price is coordinating the relationship between buyer and seller. In between these two options a range of three other agency relations are possible, called modular, captive and relational governance modes that control, coordinate, and integrate heterogeneous activities. Governance is described by GVC analysts as "the authority and power relationship that determine how financial, material and human resources are allocated, and flow within a [global value] chain" (Gereffi, 2018: 310). But how exactly the governance is performed depends on basically three triggers: One is the complexity of information needed to organize the exchange between buyer and seller. The other is the degree of codification of information transmitted to organize the activity. And the third aspect is the needed competence, skill or capabilities of the supplier to produce the product or service for the buyer (Gereffi, 2018: 310). All three factors affect the prevalence of asymmetry in existing agency relations between the contracting parties.

An agency relationship is defined by its frequent information asymmetry between principal and agent affecting significantly the efficiency and possibility to control, monitor and operate the relation across several contributing entities in a GVC.

Governance refers to an institutionalized regulatory framework available for directing and controlling an organizational unit. But the source of control in the case of GVCs is transcending the so-called dominating lead firms. In complex GVCs numerous firms contribute value activities performed in a particular geographical location, that will be shipped after finishing the discrete stage in a fragmented production stage to another site for adding other process activities, which is repeated for different particular stages in the whole production circuit of a product or service. A subcontractor in the garment industry performs numerous operations to produce a garment. Significant activities include cutting, sewing, and finishing, but these stages are broken up into sub-operations categorized as pre-production, production planning, cutting process, manufacturing, and quality control and delivery. Pre-production activities include sourcing the material. Production is about managing that all necessary production steps are carried out in time. All these production stages are offshored or outsourced. Cutting is most highly automatized using CAD machines to avoid unnecessary wastage of expensive fabrics. At the bottom of these GVCs the manual labor force is still needed for labor-intensive sewing and trimming (Boggis, 2003; Taplin et al., 2003). At that stage of the GVCs, the prevalent production system is called piece rate production, where operators are paid according to how many pieces of work (often discrete activities) they finish (Chi & Kilduff, 2010; Gereffi, 2018; Gereffi et al., 2021; Pangsapa & Smith, 2008; Sakarya et al., 2007; Yasar & Paul, 2007).

Either buyer-driven or producer-driven governance structures are a distinguishable trait of GVCs (Gereffi, 2018: 310). In buyer-driven GVCs, one or more lead firms, large retailers, or big merchandising firms, such as Walmart, Tesco, H&M, Nike, or Adidas, dominate the entire production circle. In producer-driven GVCs, the lead firms are large integrated producers, often large multinational firms, that leverage their firm-specific advantages and exploit scale economies across all significant stages in a production line.

In analyzing a particular governance structure, it is essential to focus on how value-adding activities are carried out by the different actors and what governance mode is predominant making the whole product circle efficiently work throughout its other geographical locations and various stages of production. Gereffi, Humbphrey, and Sturgeon identified five governance modes of GVCs. A critical aspect that differentiates the five types is the *relationship* between the lead firms with their suppliers (contractors and subcontractors). In an entire production circuit, there may be one or a combination of several types of governance, depending on the status of suppliers and also depending on their ability to affect the structure of the relationship (Gereffi et al., 2005). Each of these five governance modes is defined by the specificity of information exchanged to fulfill a discrete value-adding activity (Fig. 6.5).

1. Markets as governance structures are basically defined by the fact that the price of a product or service is assumed to hold all the information needed to establish a transaction between buyer and seller. Transactions exchanged using the market mechanism are mostly standardized and easy to specify goods or services. Governance relationships operated via markets are affected by a low need to coordinate the relationship between the principal (lead firm) and agent (contractor). The designation as a market assumes easily accessible information to organize the exchange relationship effectively. Market transactions are defined as arms-length exchanges between buyers and sellers because presumably little or no coordination is needed. The price information is essentially sufficient and the only needed governance structure. Essential is that markets usually signify low switching costs for both seller and buyer (Gereffi et al., 2005: 83).
2. The modular governance structure is designated as modular because the value-adding activity is made of an interchangeable, compact component in a complete device, appliance, or machine that represents a self-contained functional unit. For example, a module is a separate unit of software or hardware. A typical feature of a modular component is its portability, permitting a module to be used in various system environments. A module is also defined by its interoperability, which allows it to function with other system components without further adaptation. The organizational form (sustaining the governance mode) for the modular exchange relationships in a GVC refers to the fact that the exchange relationships themselves are simple to design (Gereffi, 2018: 311). The manufacturer independently produces a technically complex product that meets the buyer's requirements. The supplier of modular components or

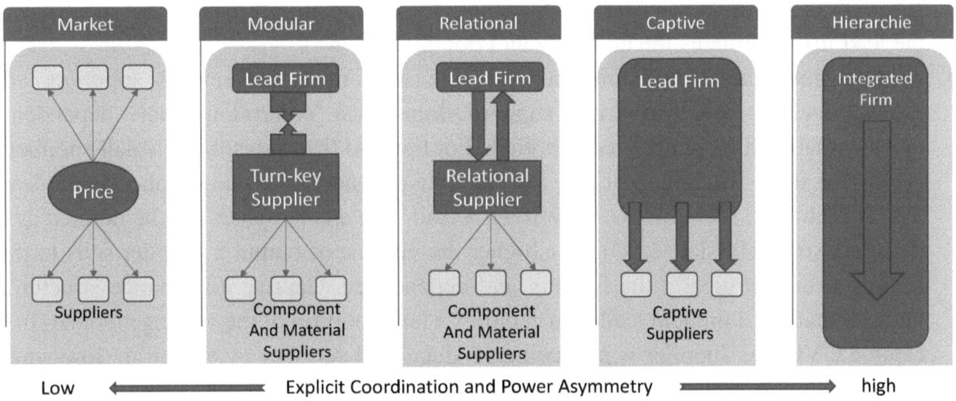

Fig. 6.5 Governance modes of GVC (Gereffi 2018: 85, reproduced with permission of Cambridge University Press)

services is a specialized firm with its own know-how and expertise in manufacturing the components and delivering ready-to-assemble items for the client. Codification of the product is usually not an issue, but the switching costs for suppliers between component manufacturers can be low if competition between component manufacturers is high. The modular suppliers manufacture products according to the more or less detailed specifications the lead firm provides. However, in giving these ready-to-install modular components, they are responsible for developing necessary process technologies and complementary competences on their own. Suppliers of modular components are, in turn dependent on several other suppliers who are not directly linked to the buyers (the lead firm).

3. Relational governance structure. Core suppliers act as essential mediators between the lead firms. These core suppliers manufacture essential components and materials and are embedded in a strong, long enduring, and trusted relationship with the lead firms. The relationship is described as complex, relying on intense communication to enact an effective exchange of more complex products and services that require an extensive transmission of codified and uncodified knowledge. Relational governance forms are typified because they require comprehensive effort to develop an effective and efficient relationship. The outcome is a dense network structure. These dense social ties between lead firms and core suppliers are based on trusted relationships and greater geographical proximity. The lead firm still dominates the relationship; however, the suppliers provide relationship-specific and highly differentiated products and services that have co-developed and grown from a closer relationship. The high specificity of the relationship in this governance mode has also been defined as bounded reliability in a different context (Kano & Verbeke, 2015, 2019). For the lead firm, switching costs are much higher for differentiated suppliers, and building a strong and effective relationship

requires considerable time and effort. Although closer relationships increase reciprocity, the lead firm maintains the authority and dominance.

4. Captive governance structures between the lead firm and several suppliers are characterized by the lead firm's superior dominance, controlling many dependent, mostly small and medium sized suppliers. For the lead firm substituting small suppliers is easy because switching costs are low, and the dependency of the supplier on the lead firm is high. The social network between a lead firm and suppliers can be defined as a loose network (Hassler, 2003). The higher the volume of output a supplier sells to the leading firm, the greater the liability and dependence. Captive governance structures indicate that the dominant lead firm captures a large portion of the value generated. In a captive GVC, the supplier is producing products and services by exploiting low-wage unskilled labor in labour-intensive industries typified in the clothing industry. In contrast, the lead firm is specialized in design, marketing, and retailing which represent the most significant part to capture value added in a GVC. At the bottom of these GVCs are textile workers in Bangladesh or Vietnam, where wages are meager (Amadeo & Pero, 2000; Ormerod, 1999; Pacheco & Naiker, 2006; Tripathi & Mishra, 2021). Asset-specificity of goods and services exchanged between the lead firm, and suppliers are low, but the frequency of exchange is high. The governance mode is called captive because the lead firm is in the privileged position to appropriate the significant share of the value-added in the whole circuit of the global production chain (Gonzalez et al., 2015; Nikulin et al., 2021; OECD, 2017; Sproll, 2022).
5. Hierarchy is the governance type placed at the opposite end of the spectrum in relation to market transactions. The core dimension defining hierarchy is that the relation between principal and agent, or employer and employee is determined by the established hierarchical ties, embedded in a firm structure, based on a clear-cut design, which is elaborated in explicit roles and responsibilities prescribed by the central authorities. The somewhat traditional description of hierarchical relations defines the integrated firm, usually a large multinational enterprise (Li et al., 2009; Qiu & Donaldson, 2012; Tallman, 2004). The internal relations in the integrated firm are subject to strict and explicit control and coordination. The existing asymmetry between principals and agents in the integrated firm is managed by the hierarchical organization among several entities in the firm, from the top, each other unit being a subordinate (Ashenbaum, 2018; Chandler, 1962, 1977). Hierarchy is usually associated with high asset specificity and uncertain intermediary markets, making it almost impossible to efficiently organize a transaction between independent contractors. The lead firm relying on the hierarchy is assumed to be the best option to manufacture complex products that depend on intricate and intangible firm-specific knowledge and know-how that cannot or won't be communicated with independent suppliers.

6.4.4 Upgrading Within a GVC

The fourth dimension characterizes the GVCs by the opportunity of firms, countries, or regions—that occupy a unique role in global value-adding networks—to move a step ahead, improving their position in the current value of their performed activities. Upgrading is about the capability to develop an activity further to increase the potential benefits arising from being embedded in the overall structure of a global production circuit (Gereffi & Fernandez-Stark, 2018: 313). The primary idea behind the characteristic of this fourth dimension to capture the nature of GVCs is that each participant embedded in a global value is confined by its discrete contribution. The concept assumes that the capability to acquire a higher value-adding position is affected by several constraints, either caused by internal or external limitations. The idea that value-adding activities can be upgraded is based equally on the notion that a supplier, in principle, can escape or transform limits and exigencies of the production at any stage of the GVC (see Fig. 6.6) process that inherently characterizes that particular stage. However, the employed logic implies upgrading a position in the overall added value process, as indicated by Fig. 6.6, moving away from pure manufacturing jobs into more intangible task on both sides in the pre- and post-production stages of a value chain. If one follows this reasoning, upgrading a production stage remains a zero-sum game, because if one supplier leaves a lower graded position it must be filled by someone else.

The concept of upgrading is not necessarily a positive one. In a system where contractors are fiercely competing for orders, the outcome can be a race to the bottom (Latimer, 2021; Willborn, 2013). The idea of upgrading within an existing GVC also needs to address whether change is possible from the perspective of a single contributing but minor subcontracting firm or if change is dependent on the pervasiveness of a basic systemic change.

An important question is how much a participant firm in a lower graded value chain activity can improve, maintain, or stop worsening its relative position. However, probably more critical will be how each stage will be transformed into more sustainable and less environmentally degrading stage of processing. Changing the structure of a GVC by participants may move beyond the individual focus of the firm and seek how to stop the most devastating and exploitative, non-sustainable work and environmental conditions still existing in developing countries that do the manufacturing of the goods and services for the affluent economies. Thus, it will be more than merely upgrading or catching up, or acquiring a better position in GVCs. While Gereffi defines an overall improvement in value-adding as upgrading processes related to products or functions (Gereffi, 2018: 312), which is essential for many developing countries, the discussion must not end here but focus on the inherent sustainability of these global, highly fragmented and geographically dispersed GVCs.

The U-shaped curve depicting the different stages in the production process of a GVC, documented originally by Baldwin et al. (2003), exemplifies a conventional perspective of how much value is added by subsequent activities (e.g., in R&D, Design, Purchasing,

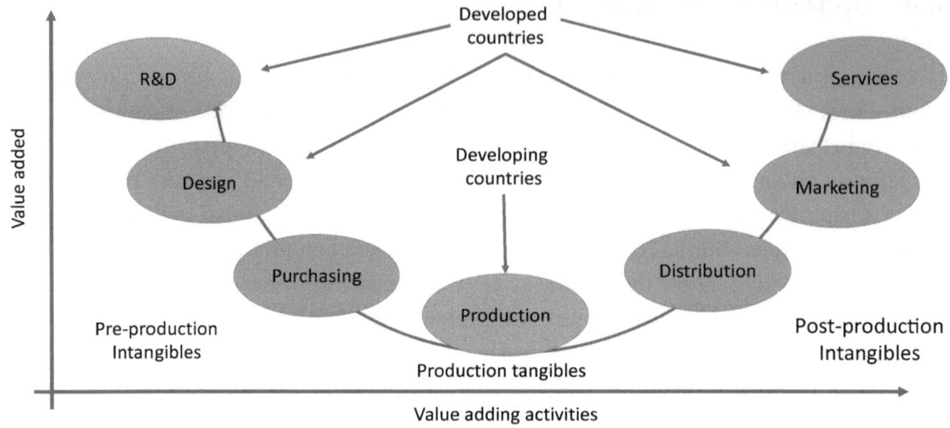

Fig. 6.6 The smile curve of value-adding in GVCs (Gereffi, 2018: 315, reproduced with permission of Cambridge University Press)

Production, Distribution, Marketing, and Services). The graph in Fig. 6.6 assumes that R&D, design and marketing, and services are carried out by firms located in the so-called developed countries, which acquire the most significant share of the value added. Whereas activities described as production activities carried out by suppliers in so-called developing countries receive a much smaller percentage. Categorizing segments in the GVCs as pre-production intangible and post-production intangible activity and, at the bottom, production as tangible action implies that the knowledge content embedded in an activity is automatically responsible for higher returns.

Mexican Apparel Industry

The rationale for the overall arguments follows the story of the development of the Mexican apparel industry, which is a well-documented empirical example of how upgrading across different stages in a GVC took place. In 1993, the Mexican blue jeans industry was carrying out sewing, a labor-intensive input, low-wage activity, while importing cut pieces of material from the U.S. lead firms, such as Farha, Sun Apparel, Wrangler, and Levi Strauss. These lead firms pushed Mexican contractors that did the sewing to move into higher value-adding activities, including cutting, sewing, washing and finishing, and distribution.

Studies about the impact of the expansion into these higher graded value-adding activities argued that this resulted in an increase in employment from 12,000 in 1993 to 75,000 in 2000. But the employment figures soon declined to 40,000 in 2002, indicating the fragility of upgrading in the apparel industry that relies on low-cost and unskilled labor (Bair & Gereffi, 2003).

The issue of upgrading low-skilled value-adding activities is twofold. On the micro-level, the challenge is how low-skilled and low-cost labor, which is the pull factor for lead firms and local suppliers to enter the GVCs at the bottom, can be shifted into medium- or high-skilled and medium- or high-cost labor without destroying the apparent rationale for the supply of these activities. At the macro level, the challenge is for local and national governments to invest in infrastructure that allows a more significant share of the GVCs in each region to be captured.

6.4.5 Local Institutional Context of a GVC

The fifth dimension of GVCs focuses on how local institutions affect the position of a firm, in a particular GVC. At the macro level, the challenge is for local and federal governments to invest in infrastructure that allows reaching a more significant share of value in a prevalent GVC. Since the Second World War, many poor countries have succeeded in establishing better positions in a dynamically developing world economy by their special economic policies attracting foreign direct investment. Prominent examples, widely referred to, are the South-East Asian four tiger economies, which have developed successfully. Moreover, specific industries, such as the apparel industry, which grew in countries such as Japan, Taiwan, and Korea have successfully progressed to more advanced stages in the value chain. Activities carried out in Taiwan and Korea in the early 1960s are now undertaken mainly by China, Thailand, Vietnam, and Bangladesh. How much and what institutional factors had been a significant trigger in this upgrading process still is a debate (Acemoglu & Robinson, 2012; Cornell, 1987; Harms, 2000; Motyl, 1992; Sekhon, 2004). For example, cheap labor costs still attract stages in the value-adding chain that are sourced by industries depending on labor-intensive and relatively low-skilled activities (Gonzalez et al., 2015).

6.4.6 Industry Stakeholders

The sixth dimension focuses on the power of stakeholders across the entire structure of GVCs. A significant question is how much single, powerful stakeholders affect and impact the evolution of global value chains. Major stakeholders are firms, industry associations, worker associations, consumer associations, governments, and many others (Gereffi, 2018: 316). Peter Dicken from the University of Manchester, a pioneer in global value chain analyses, demonstrated how the role of multinational firms has changed in several studies. The question of how lead firms transformed the privileged status they have enjoyed in the past into a more moderate form, orchestrating the structure of GVCs aiming at a more sustainable and more equal pattern remains a pertinent issue. However, multinational firms may need to substantially change their role as leading actors embedded in network buyer-supplier relations, focusing on the need to introduce much more societal and environmentally sustainable value chains.

For decades, the literature on global value chains (GVCs) has been growing. However, in international business the multinational firm is still conceived as the primary and most efficient player in the global economy. The massive growth of large multinational firms is still explained by its superior efficiency resulting from vertical and horizontal integration, establishing and managing multiple "geographically dispersed economic activities" (McWilliam et al., 2019: 1). In the effort to explain the huge growth of global value chains the nexus of the firm as its major mechanism proved also its weakness. A number of studies aiming to develop an in-depth understanding of the scope and pattern of global value chains shifted the perspective from ***inside the firm*** to what is actually emerging ***outside the firm***. And more and more a perspective emerged to analyze how a network of multiple firms contributed to the extensive pattern of global value chains (McWilliam & Nielsen, 2020). This view became somewhat a contrasting perspective to a still more traditional international business perspective how global value chains are organized. To some degree a GVCs approach may allow to start a more systemic and holistic analysis of the global economy (Davis, 2019; Gidengil, 1978; Hornborg, 1998; Wallerstein, 2000, 2005).

Study Questions

1. Discuss the differences between the theory of the firm widely accepted in IB studies with the global value chain approach. What is the key difference?
2. Discuss how the global value chain analysis is affecting the structure and strategies of the multinational firm.
3. Take a piece of apparel you have recently bought and try to analyze the stages of its global value-adding activities. Try to analyze the degree of fragmentation and geographical dispersion of the global production chain of the apparel you bought. Start with the production of the raw materials and continue until the final selling point of the product.
4. Think about the sustainability of global production networks.

References

Acemoglu, D., & Robinson, J. A. (2012). Is this time different? Capture and anti-capture of US politics. *The Economists' Voice, 9*(3). https://doi.org/10.1515/1553-3832.1902

adidas. (2022). *Adidas network of subscontractors and supply chain structure*. Retrieved from https://www.adidas-group.com/en/sustainability/managing-sustainability/human-rights/supply-chain-structure/

Adner, R., & Helfat, C. E. (2003). Corporate effects and dynamic managerial capabilities. *Strategic Management Journal, 24*(10), 1011–1025.

Aghion, P., & Holden, R. (2011). Incomplete contracts and the theory of the firm: What have we learned over the past 25 years? *Journal of Economic Perspectives, 25*(2), 181–197.

Alchian, A. A., & Demsetz, H. (1972). *Production, information costs, and economic organization*. Springer. https://doi.org/10.2307/1815199

Amadeo, E. J., & Pero, V. (2000). Adjustment, stabilisation and the structure of employment in Brazil. *Journal of Development Studies, 36*(4), 120–148.

Ariyawardana, A., & Collins, R. (2013). Balancing industry needs against global competitiveness: A challenge for the Australian vegetable industry. *Outlook on Agriculture, 42*(3), 155–161.

Arndt, S., & Kierzkowski, H. (2001). *Fragmentation: New production patterns in the world economy*. Oxford University Press.

Ashenbaum, B. (2018). From market to hierarchy: An empirical assessment of a supply chain governance typology. *Journal of Purchasing and Supply Management, 24*(1), 59–67.

Babbage, C. (1835). *On the economy of machinery and manufactures*. Charles Knight.

Bair, J., & Gereffi, G. (2003). Upgrading, uneven development, and jobs in the North American apparel industry. *Global Networks, 3*(2), 143–169.

Baldwin, R., Forslid, R., Martin, P., Ottaviano, G., & Robert-Nicoud, F. (2003). *Economic geography and public policy*. Princeton University Press.

Beaverstock, J. V. (2009). International Encyclopedia of human geography. *Transactions of the Institute of British Geographers, 29*(2004), 162–163.

Benito, G. R. G., Petersen, B., & Welch, L. S. (2019). The global value chain and internalization theory. *Journal of International Business Studies, 50*(8), 1414–1423.

Birkinshaw, J., & Terjesen, S. (2003). The customer-focused multinational: Revisiting the Stopford and Wells Model in an era of global customers. In J. Birkinshaw, S. Ghoshal, C. Markides, J. Stopford, & G. Yip (Eds.), *The future of the multinational company* (pp. 115–127). Wiley.

Birkinshaw, J., Holm, U., Thilenius, P., & Arvidsson, N. (2000). Consequences of perception gaps in the headquarters–subsidiary relationship. *International Business Review, 9*(3), 321–344.

Boggis, J. J. (2003). "On the shopfloor" with clothing workers in the 1990s. *Employee Relations, 25*(2), 168–181.

Brown, J., & Duguid, P. (2001). Knowledge and organization: A social-practice perspective. *Organization Science, 12*(2), 198–213.

Buckley, P. J. (1989). The multinational enterprise. *Theory and Applications, 1989*, 3–23.

Buckley, P. J. (2009). Internalisation thinking: From the multinational enterprise to the global factory. *International Business Review, 18*(3), 224–235.

Buckley, P. J. (2011). International integration and coordination in the global factory. *Management International Review, 51*(2), 269.

Buckley, P. J. (2014). Adam Smith's theory of knowledge and international business theory and practice. *Journal of International Business Studies, 45*(1), 102–109.

Buckley, P. J., & Casson, M. C. (2009). The internalisation theory of the multinational enterprise: A review of the progress of a research agenda after 30 years. *Journal of International Business Studies, 40*(9), 1563–1580.

Buckley, P. J., & Casson, M. (2010). The multinational enterprise revisited. *The Essential Buckley and Casson, 2010*, 177–204.

Buckley, P. J., & Casson, M. (2014). *The multinational enterprise and the emergence of the global factory* (pp. 20–51). Springer.

Burnham, J. C., & Epperson, J. E. (1998). A profile of foreign direct investment by the US fruit and vegetable industry. *Agribusiness, 14*(5), 379–388.

Cammies, C., Mytton, D., & Crichton, R. (2021). Exploring economic and legal barriers to commercial aquaponics in the EU through the lens of the UK and policy proposals to address them. *Aquaculture International, 29*(3), 1245–1263.

Casson, M. (2013). Economic analysis of international supply chains: An internalization perspective. *Journal of Supply Chain Management, 49*(2), 8–13.

Chandler, A. E. (1962). *Strategy and structure: Chapters in the history of the industrial enterprise*. MIT Press.

Chandler, A. D. (1977). *The visible hand. The managerial revolution in American business*. Belknap Press of Harvard University Press.

Chi, T., & Kilduff, P. P. D. (2010). An empirical investigation of the determinants and shifting patterns of US apparel imports using a gravity model framework. *Journal of Fashion Marketing and Management: An International Journal, 14*(3), 501–520.

Clougherty, J. A., & Skousen, B. R. (2019). The efficiency and market-power interpretations of the multinational enterprise: Two out of three ain't bad. *Global Strategy Journal, 11*(3), 356–379.

Coase, R. (1937). The nature of the firm. *Economica, 4*(16), 386–405.

Contractor, F. J., Kumar, V., Kundu, S., & Pedersen, T. (2009). *Global outsourcing and offshoring* (pp. 3–47). Springer.

Cooper, R., & Yoshikawa, T. (1994). Inter-organizational cost management systems: The case of the Tokyo-Yokohama-Kamakura supplier chain. *International Journal of Production Economics, 37*(1), 51–62.

Cornell, L. L. (1987). Reproduction, production, social science, and the past: A dissenting review. *Social Science History, 11*(1), 43–52.

Cyert, R. M., & March, J. G. (1963). *A behavioral theory of the firm*. Prentice Hall.

Dam, A. V. (1978). Toward a different role for multinationals in the third world. *Journal of International Business Studies, 9*(3), 125–128.

Dastagiri, M. B. (2017). Global agriculture: Vision and approaches. *European Scientific Journal, ESJ, 13*(21), 312.

Dauten, P. M., Gammill, H. L., & Robinson, S. C. (1958). Our concepts of controlling need re-thinking. *Academy of Management Journal, 1*(3), 41–55.

Davis, J. B. (2019). Economics and economic methodology in a core-periphery economic world. *SSRN Electronic Journal*. https://doi.org/10.2139/ssrn.3324569

Devinney, T. M., Rugman, A. M., & D'Cruz, J. R. (2001). Multinationals as flagship firms. *The Academy of Management Review, 26*(3), 462.

Dicken, P. (2017). *Global shift. Mapping the changing contours of the world economy*. Sage.

Diemer, H. (1912). Factory organization in relation to industrial education. *The Annals of the American Academy of Political and Social Science, 44*(1), 130–140.

Dolan, C., & Humphrey, J. (2004). Changing governance patterns in the trade in fresh vegetables between Africa and the United Kingdom. *Environment and Planning A: Economy and Space, 36* (3), 491–509. https://doi.org/10.1068/a35281

Dougherty, D. (2018). *The Palgrave encyclopedia of strategic management* (pp. 1668–1671). Palgrave.

Doz, Y., & Prahalad, C. K. (1993). *Organization theory and the multinational corporation* (pp. 24–50). Springer.

Dunning, J., & Lundan, S. M. (2008). *Multinational enterprises and the global economy*. Edward Elgar. https://doi.org/10.18356/43ce1fe7-en

Weick, K. E. (1991). The nontraditional quality of organizational learning. *Organization Science, 2*(1), 116.

Enderwick, P., & Buckley, P. J. (2019). Beyond supply and assembly relations: Collaborative innovation in global factory systems. *Journal of Business Research, 103*, 547–556.

Erklavec, U., Birt, C., & Pushkarev, N. (2021). Common agricultural policy (CAP) from a public health perspective. *European Journal of Public Health, 31*(Suppl 3), ckab164.188.

Ernst, D. (2009). A new geography of knowledge in the electronics industry? Asia's role in global innovation networks. *SSRN Electronic Journal*. https://doi.org/10.2139/ssrn.2742923

Faulconbridge, J. (2007). Global shift, fifth edition: Mapping the changing contours of the world economy. *Journal of Economic Geography, 7*(6), 777–779.

Feenstra, R. C. (1998). Integration of trade and disintegration of production in the global economy. *Journal of Economic Perspectives, 12*(4), 31–50.

Fengru, C., & Guitang, L. (2019). *Global value chains and production networks* (pp. 3–25). Springer.

Fernandez-Stark, K., & Gereffi, G. (2019). *Global value chain analysis: A primer* (2nd ed.). Duke University. https://doi.org/10.4337/9781788113779.00008

Fernandez-Stark, K., Bamber, P., & Gereffi, G. (2013). *Oxford handbooks online*. Oxford University Press. https://doi.org/10.1093/oxfordhb/9780199765904.013.0021

Fernandez-Stark, K., Hernández, R. A., Mulder, N., & Sauvé, P. (2014). *Introduction*. United Nation iLibrary. https://doi.org/10.18356/b9138ae4-en

Fitzgerald, R. (2015). *The rise of the global company*. Cambridge University Press. https://doi.org/10.1017/cbo9781139029209.002

Foley, D. K. (1997). Theory of production. *Journal of Economic Behavior & Organization, 32*(2), 321–324.

Foss, N. J. (2002). "Coase vs Hayek": Economic organization and the knowledge economy. *International Journal of the Economics of Business, 9*(1), 9–35.

Fröbel, F., Heinrichs, J., & Kreye, O. (1978). The world market for labor and the world market for industrial sites. *Journal of Economic Issues, 12*(4), 843–858.

Frobel, F., Heinrichs, J., & Kreye, O. (1978). Export-oriented industrialization of underdeveloped countries. *Monthly Review, 30*(6), 22–27.

Fröbel, F., Heinrichs, J., & Kreye, O. (1980). *The new international division of labour*. Cambridge University Press.

Gereffi, G. (1984a). Power and dependency in an interdependent world: A guide to understanding the contemporary global crisis. *International Journal of Comparative Sociology, 25*(1–2), 91–113.

Gereffi, G. (1984b). Power and dependency in an interdependent world: A guide to understanding the contemporary global crisis. *Comparative Sociology, 25*(1), 91–113.

Gereffi, G. (1989a). Rethinking development theory: Insights from East Asia and Latin America. *Sociological Forum, 4*(4), 505–533.

Gereffi, G. (1989b). Development strategies and the global factory. *The Annals of the American Academy of Political and Social Science, 505*(1), 92–104.

Gereffi, G. (1995). Winners and losers: How sectors shape the developmental prospects of states. D. Michael Shafer. *American Journal of Sociology, 101*(2), 506–508.

Gereffi, G. (2018). *Global value chains and development: Redefining the contours of 21st century capitalism* (Development trajectories in global value chains). Cambridge University Press. https://doi.org/10.1017/9781108559423

Gereffi, G. (2019). Global value chains and international development policy: Bringing firms, networks and policy-engaged scholarship back in. *Journal of International Business Policy, 2*(3), 195–210.

Gereffi, G., & Fernandez-Stark, K. (2010). The offshore services value chain: Developing countries and the crisis. *Policy Research Working Papers*. https://doi.org/10.1596/1813-9450-5262

Gereffi, G., & Fernandez-Stark, K. (2018). Global value chain analysis: A primer. In G. Gereffi (Ed.), *Global value chains and development: Redefining the contours of 21st century capitalism*

(Development trajectories in global value chains) (2nd ed., pp. 305–342). Cambridge University Press. https://doi.org/10.1017/9781108559423.012

Gereffi, G., Humbphrey, J., & Sturgeon, T. (2005). The governance of global value chains. *Review of International Political Evonomy, 1*, 78–104.

Gereffi, G., Lim, H.-C., & Lee, J. (2021). Trade policies, firm strategies, and adaptive reconfigurations of global value chains. *Journal of International Business Policy, 2021*, 1–17.

Gidengil, E. L. (1978). Centres and peripheries: An empirical test of Galtung's theory of imperialism. *Journal of Peace Research, 15*(1), 51–66.

Gigerenzer, G., & Selten, R. (2002). *Bounded rationality: The adaptive toolbox*. The MIT Press.

Giglioni, G. B., & Bedeian, A. G. (1974). A conspectus of management control theory: 1900-1972. *Academy of Management Journal, 17*(2), 292–305.

Gillespie, C. (1938). Managerial control: Instruments and methods in industry. *Journal of Political Economy, 46*(5), 749–750.

Girod, S. J. G., & Rugman, A. M. (2005). Regional business networks and the multinational retail sector. *Long Range Planning, 38*(4), 335–357.

Gonzalez, J. L., Kowalski, P., & Achard, P. (2015). *Trade, global value chains and wage-income inequality*. OECD. https://doi.org/10.1787/5js009mzrqd4-en

Gudergan, S. P., Devinney, T. M., & Ellis, R. S. (2016). Cooperation and compliance in non-equity alliances. *Journal of Business Research, 69*(5), 1759–1764.

Gupta, N. (2016). Domestic value-added growth is vital. *South Asia Economic Journal, 17*(2), 271–294.

Haakonsson, S. J. (2009). Transnational corporations and development policy. *Critical Perspectives, 2009*, 274–301.

Harms, P. (2000). International investment. *Political Risk, and Growth, 2000*, 25–56.

Hassler, M. (2003). The global clothing production system: Commodity chains and business networks. *Global Networks, 3*(4), 513–531.

Hassler, M. (2012). Macroregional economic integration in Southeast Asia: AFTA and the automobile industry from a Thai perspective. *Singapore Journal of Tropical Geography, 33*(1), 124–136.

Helfat, C. E., & Raubitschek, R. S. (2000). Product sequencing: Co-evolution of knowledge, capabilities and products. *Strategic Management Journal, 21*(10–11), 961–979.

Hennart, J.-F. (1977). *A theory of foreign direct investment*. University of Maryland, Doctoral thesis.

Hennart, J.-F. (1993). *Organization theory and the multinational corporation* (pp. 157–181). Springer.

Hodgson, G. M., & Knudsen, T. (2004). The firm as an interactor: Firms as vehicles for habits and routines. *Journal of Evolutionary Economics, 14*(3), 281–307.

Holmstrom, B., & Tirole, J. (1989). The theory of the firm. In R. Schmalensee & R. Willig (Eds.), *Handbook of industrial organization* (pp. 61–133). Elsevier.

Holmstrom, B. R., & Tirole, J. (2020). *Chapter 2. The theory of the firm* (Vol. 1). Cambridge University Press. https://doi.org/10.1016/s1573-448x(89)01005-8

Hornborg, A. (1998). Towards an ecological theory of unequal exchange: Articulating world system theory and ecological economics. *Ecological Economics, 25*(1), 127–136.

Hoskisson, R. E., Hitt, M. A., Wan, W. P., & Yiu, D. (1999). Theory and research in strategic management: Swings of a pendulum. *Journal of Management, 25*(3), 417–456.

Humphrey, J., & Schmitz, H. (2008). Inter-firm relationships in global value chains: Trends in chain governance and their policy implications. *International Journal of Technological Learning, Innovation and Development, 1*(3), 258.

Jones, G. (2003). *Business history around the world*. Cambridge University Press. https://doi.org/10.1017/cbo9780511512100.018

Kahneman, D., & Tversky, A. (1996). On the reality of cognitive illusions. *Psychological Review, 103*(3), 582–591.
Kano, L., & Verbeke, A. (2015). The three faces of bounded reliability: Alfred Chandler and the micro-foundations of management theory. *California Management Review, 58*(1), 97–122.
Kano, L., & Verbeke, A. (2019). Theories of the multinational firm: A microfoundational perspective. *Global Strategy Journal, 9*(1), 117–147.
Kano, L., Tsang, E. W. K., & Yeung, H. W. (2020). Global value chains: A review of the multi-disciplinary literature. *Journal of International Business Studies, 51*(4), 577–622.
Kogut, B. (1984). Normative observations on the international value-added chain and strategic groups. *Journal of International Business Studies, 15*(2), 151–167.
Kogut, B. (1985). Designing global strategies: Comparative and competitive value-added chains. *Sloan Management Review, 26*(4), 15–28.
Kogut, B. (1991). Country capabilities and the permeability of borders. *Strategic Management Journal, 12*(S1), 33–47.
Kreye, O., Frobel, V., & Heinrichs, J. (1980). *The new international divison of labour*. Cambridge University Press.
Langlois, R. N. (1995). Do firms plan? *Constitutional Political Economy, 6*(3), 247–261.
Langlois, R. N. (2007). *Dynamics of industrial capitalism* (pp. 36–51).
Langlois, R. N. (2016). The corporation is not a nexus of contracts. It's an iPhone. *SSRN Electronic Journal*. https://doi.org/10.2139/ssrn.2856631
Langlois, R. N. (2019). *The corporation is not a nexus of contracts: It's an iPhone*. https://doi.org/10.4337/9781785365003.00019.
Langlois, R. N., & Foss, N. J. (1999). Capabilities and governance: The rebirth of production in the theory of economic organization. *Kyklos, 52*(2), 201–218.
Lanz, R., & Miroudot, S. (2011). *Intra-firm trade*. OECD. https://doi.org/10.1787/5kg9p39lrwnn-en
Latimer, A. (2021). *The Palgrave encyclopedia of imperialism and anti-imperialism* (pp. 2546–2561). Palgrave.
Li, J., Zhou, C., & Zajac, E. J. (2009). Control, collaboration, and productivity in international joint ventures: Theory and evidence. *Strategic Management Journal, 30*(8), 865–884.
Li, J., Ma, C., Liu, L. H., & Guo, M. R. (2013). The integration mode and evaluation on vegetables quality and safety supervision automatic control system. *Applied Mechanics and Materials, 373–375*, 1304–1311.
Luo, Y., & Mezias, J. M. (2002). Liabilities of foreignness. *Journal of International Management, 8*(3), 217–221.
McWilliam, S. E., & Nielsen, B. B. (2020). Global value chains and development: Redefining the contours of 21st century capitalism: Gary Gereffi Cambridge University Press, Cambridge, 2018, 494 pp. ISBN: 978-1108458863. *Journal of International Business Studies, 51*(8), 1347–1350.
McWilliam, S. E., Kim, J. K., Mudambi, R., & Nielsen, B. B. (2019). Global value chain governance: Intersections with international business. *Journal of World Business, 55*, 101067.
Mokyr, J. (2010). The contribution of economic history to the study of innovation and change: 1750–1914. In *Handbook of the economics of innovation* (Vol. 1, pp. 11–50). Elsevier. https://doi.org/10.1016/S0169-7218(10)01002-6
Motyl, A. J. (1992). Concepts and Skocpol: Ambiguity and vagueness in the study of revolution. *Journal of Theoretical Politics, 4*(1), 93–112.
Náglová, Z., & Rudinskaya, T. (2021). Factors influencing technical efficiency in the EU dairy farms. *Agriculture, 11*(11), 1114.
Nathan, D., Tewari, M., & Sarkar, S. (2018). *Development with global value chains*. Cambridge University Press. https://doi.org/10.1017/9781316221730
Nike. (2022). *Nike manufacturing map*. Retrieved from https://manufacturingmap.nikeinc.com

Nikulin, D., Wolszczak-Derlacz, J., & Parteka, A. (2021). GVC and wage dispersion. Firm-level evidence from employee? Employer database. *Equilibrium, 16*(2), 357–375.

OECD. (2010). *Intra-firm trade in selected OECD countries*. OECD. https://doi.org/10.1787/9789264084360-74-en

OECD. (2017). *Skills and global value chains: What are the stakes?* (pp. 37–72). OECD.

Ormerod, A. (1999). Textile manufacturing: Smokestack industry or an essential sector of the National Economy? *Journal of the Textile Institute, 90*(2), 93–103.

Pacheco, G., & Naiker, V. (2006). Impact of the minimum wage on expected profits. *International Review of Applied Economics, 20*(4), 469–490.

Palomino-Tamayo, W., & Timaná, J. S. (2021). Creating firm value, overcoming organizational inertia through the marketing value chain. *Academia Revista Latinoamericana de Administración*. https://doi.org/10.1108/arla-06-2021-0119

Pangsapa, P., & Smith, M. J. (2008). Political economy of southeast Asian borderlands: Migration, environment, and developing country firms. *Journal of Contemporary Asia, 38*(4), 485–514.

Perelman, M. (2011). Retrospectives: X-efficiency. *Journal of Economic Perspectives, 25*(4), 211–222.

Petersen, B., & Pedersen, T. (2002). Coping with liability of foreignness. *Journal of International Management, 8*(3), 339–350.

Porter, M. E. (1980). *Competitive strategy. Techniques for analyzing industries and competitors*. Free Press.

Porter, M. E. (2008). The five competitive forces that shape strategy. *Harvard Business Review, 86*(1), 78–93.

Prahalad, C. K. (1995). New view of strategy: An interview with C.K. Prahalad. *European Management Journal, 13*(2), 131–138.

Prahalad, C. K., & Dearlove, D. (2009). On the verge of something extraordinary. *Business Strategy Review, 20*(1), 16–20.

Qiu, J. X., & Donaldson, L. (2012). Stopford and Wells were right! MNC matrix structures do fit a "high-high" strategy. *Management International Review, 52*(5), 671–689.

Raisch, S., & Birkinshaw, J. (2008). Organizational ambidexterity: Antecedents, outcomes, and moderators. *Journal of Management, 34*(3), 375–409.

Ramstetter, E. D. (1992). Rival states, rival firms: Competition for world market shares. *The Journal of Asian Studies, 51*(3), 632–633.

Rugman, A., & D'Cruz, J. (1997). The theory of the flagship firm. *European Management Journal, 15*(4), 403–412.

Rugman, A. M., Li, J., & Oh, C. H. (2009). Are supply chains global or regional? *International Marketing Review, 26*(4/5), 384–395.

Ruhl, K. J. (2015). How well is US intrafirm trade measured? *American Economic Review, 105*(5), 524–529.

Sakarya, S., Eckman, M., & Hyllegard, K. H. (2007). Market selection for international expansion. *International Marketing Review, 24*(2), 208–238.

Sapukotanage, S., Warnakulasuriya, B. N. F., & Yapa, S. T. W. S. (2016). A conceptual model for understanding the outcomes of buyer-supplier relationships in supply chains. *International Business Research, 9*(8), 72.

Schmidt, W. (1990). Umbruch in der Weltwirtschaft (upheaval in the global economy). *Jahrbuch Für Wirtschaftsgeschichte/Economic History Yearbook, 31*(1), 196–197.

Sekhon, J. S. (2004). Quality meets quantity: Case studies, conditional probability, and counterfactuals. *Perspectives on Politics, 2*(2), 281–293.

Sinkovics, N., Liu, C.-L., Sinkovics, R. R., & Mudambi, R. (2021). The dark side of trust in global value chains: Taiwan's electronics and IT hardware industries. *Journal of World Business, 56*(4), 101195.

Snidal, D. (1982). The new international division of labour: Structural unemployment in industrialized countries and industrialization in developing countries. *American Journal of Sociology, 87*(5), 1218–1220.

Sproll, M. (2022). *Economic and social upgrading in global value chains, comparative analyses, macroeconomic effects, the role of institutions and strategies for the global south* (pp. 145–169). Wiley.

Stopford, J. (2005). *International business and government relations in the 21st century* (pp. 103–116). Cambridge University Press.

Stopford, J. M., & Wells, L. T. (1972). *Managing the multinational enterprise: Organization of the firm and ownership of the subsidiaries*. Longman, Basic Books.

Sturgeon, T., Biesebroeck, J. V., & Gereffi, G. (2008). Value chains, networks and clusters: Reframing the global automotive industry. *Journal of Economic Geography, 8*(3), 297–321.

Tallman, S. (2004). *Theories of the multinational enterprise: Diversity, complexity and relevance* (pp. 53–64). Wiley.

Tannenbaum, A. S. (1956). The concept of organizational control. *Journal of Social Issues, 12*(2), 50–60.

Tannenbaum, A. S. (1962). Control in organizations: Individual adjustment and organizational performance. *Administrative Science Quarterly, 7*(2), 236.

Taplin, I. M., Winterton, J., & Winterton, R. (2003). Understanding labour turnover in a labour intensive industry: Evidence from the British Clothing Industry. *Journal of Management Studies, 40*(4), 1021–1046.

Tripathi, T., & Mishra, N. K. (2021). Precarious self-employment in India: A case of home-based own account enterprises. *Journal of Labor and Society, 24*(1), 133–162.

UNCTAD. (2011). *World investment report 2011*. UNCTAD. https://doi.org/10.18356/6c9c5276-en

Verbeke, A. (2003). The evolutionary view of the MNE and the future of internalization theory. *Journal of International Business Studies, 34*(6), 498–504.

Verbeke, A., & Kano, L. (2016). An internalization theory perspective on the global and regional strategies of multinational enterprises. *Journal of World Business, 51*(1), 83–92.

Vuori, N., & Vuori, T. (2014). Comment on "Heuristics in the strategy context" by Bingham and Eisenhardt (2011). *Strategic Management Journal, 35*(11), 1689–1697.

Wallerstein, I. (2000). Globalization or the age of transition? *International Sociology, 15*(2), 249–265.

Wallerstein, I. (2005). The actor and world-systems analysis. *Contemporary Sociology: A Journal of Reviews, 34*(1), 9–10.

Wallerstein, I. (2004). *World-systems analysis. An introduction*. Duke University Press.

Weick, K. E. (2010). Reflections on enacted sensemaking in the Bhopal disaster. *Journal of Management Studies, 47*(3), 537–550.

Whittington, R. (2008). Alfred Chandler, founder of strategy: Lost tradition and renewed inspiration. *Business History Review, 82*(2), 267–277.

Wilkins, M. (2008). The European Enterprise. *Historical Investigation into a Future Species, 2008*, 37–50.

Willborn, S. L. (2013). Labor law and the race to the bottom. *SSRN Electronic Journal*. https://doi.org/10.2139/ssrn.2339274

Williamson, O. E. (1979). Transaction-cost economics: The governance of contractual relations. *The Journal of Law and Economics, 22*(2), 233–261.

Williamson, O. E. (1985). *The economic institutions of capitalism*. Free Press.

Williamson, O. E. (1998). Transaction cost economics: How it works; where it is headed. *De Economist, 146*(1), 23–58.

Williamson, O. E. (2005). *The economics of governance*. AEA Papers and Proceedings.

Wolf, J., & Egelhoff, W. G. (2002). A reexamination and extension of international strategy–structure theory. *Strategic Management Journal, 23*(2), 181–189.

Wolf, J., & Egelhoff, W. G. (2013). An empirical evaluation of conflict in MNC matrix structure firms. *International Business Review, 22*(3), 591–601.

Wong, W. K. O. (2017). *Automotive global value chain* (pp. 1–12). Cambridge University Press.

WTO. (2019). *Footloose global value chains*. WTO. https://doi.org/10.30875/e94585be-en

Yasar, M., & Paul, C. J. M. (2007). International linkages and productivity at the plant level: Foreign direct investment, exports, imports and licensing. *Journal of International Economics, 71*(2), 373–388.

Zahra, S. A. (2003). The practice of management: Reflections on Peter F. Drucker's landmark book. *Academy of Management Perspectives, 17*(3), 16–23.

Zhang, J. (2012). Global shift: Mapping the changing contours of the world economy. *Economic Geography, 88*(3), 337–338.

The Management of the Multinational Firm 7

7.1 The Early Focus on Managing Large Industrial Enterprises

At the age of 19, Henri Fayol (1841–1925), a French mining engineer and practitioner, began to work for an international company that he later managed until his retirement. He categorized management as a process entailing five complementary but differing tasks: forecasting and planning, organizing, commanding, coordinating, and controlling (Wilson & Thomson, 2006: 9). His conception of the essence of management was guided by his education as a mining engineer and was deeply affected by his practical experiences. Fayol's approach to effective management became an early, highly systematic, and rational approach to managing the modern business firm. Fayol was first and foremost a practitioner; he conceived the five above-mentioned tasks as specialized functions necessary for the successful operations of a business enterprise. To establish the effective governance of a large organization, he recognized that all these functions produced and required multiple layers of administrative personnel.

The impact of Fayol's approach was ubiquitous, particularly in the 1950s and 1960s when ever-larger planning departments emerged from elaborated task strategies, thereby intentionally supporting the top tiers of management with an ever-growing body of detailed information. This was information produced and processed in order to generate numerous budgeting and auditing tools. These increasingly sophisticated tools were introduced to reduce the apparent uncertainties that arose within the corporate world and provide practical means for the controlled and proper handling of large and complex industrial organizations (Peaucelle, 2016; Peaucelle & Guthrie, 2015).

Not surprisingly, Henry Mintzberg categorized several "strategic management" approaches into schools, denoted as the design, planning, or positioning schools. These

M. Fuchs, *International Management*,
https://doi.org/10.1007/978-3-662-65870-3_7

terms signified what concepts seemed to be at the core of the significant objectives of managing a business enterprise.

The planning approach was characterized by a select number of individuals in large organizations that are responsible for "planning for the future"; they are, in turn, supported by a large number of others. Increasingly, a large portion of organizational efforts in a firm was "inexorably intertwined with planning," which later became the "integrated [part] of decision making" (Mintzberg, 1994: 10f).

Management turned out to be highly reliable on—or perhaps even addicted to—information that was collected and prepared by subordinate positions and fed by heterogeneous managerial roles. Huge chunks of data were generated by formal and informal mechanisms within all units in an organization. The growing amount of increasingly sophisticated information was compiled to enable management to make decisions that would ultimately affect the performance of the whole organization. However, this meant that top management became dependent on the efforts of many different organization members (Kano & Verbeke, 2019).

A **plan is the outcome of a distinct hierarchical organization**. Planning as "a formalized procedure to produce an articulate result" had its heydays in the 1960s, when it "became not just an approach to managing the organization's future but the only conceivable one, [virtually a] religion (Mintzberg, 1994: 13). From this perspective, the need to control "became a touchy subject." Planning was defined as a rational activity directed at formalizing behavior; however, at the same time, the process of planning became "institutionalized" and embedded in a formal system that was primarily separated from the management that actually operated a firm (Mintzberg, 1994: 23).

Although management is primarily associated with top management, particularly the role of chief executives in formulating a firm's core strategies, the departments responsible for the planning process became somewhat independent and self-referential entities; planning thus came to be characterized as something different from managing (Chia & Holt, 2009; Mintzberg, 1994: 29).

7.2 The Meaning of Management

The etymological roots of the word "management" originate from the fifteenth-century practice of handling a horse; in other words, being able to direct and train a horse. The meaning of management, arising from the Latin word *manus* (hand), implies having a "good hand," but the term also includes the implicit idea of being motivated to put on a hand to fix something. Later, in the early eighteenth century, "management" came to refer to the governance of a collective body. However, "to manage" is a transitive verb that implies an active action for an authorized person to do something. Fayol's five dimensions of management emerge from this original meaning, indicating that the managerial activity had gradually matured into an established role model for managers.

> Management is not restricted to designing measures and receiving information prepared elsewhere; instead, it involves enacting measures to monitor and control intended actions.

The principal merit of Fayol's approach to management was that he was the first to elaborate on these critical functions that became the requisite tasks in managing a firm (Parker & Ritson, 2005; Peaucelle, 2016). In modern, large industrial firms, most of these functions developed into clearly elaborated activities framed by the needs of single departments and specialized functions embedded in well-defined organizational roles equipped with distinct authorities (Neuberger, 1995: 83). In small-sized firms, especially those led by owner-entrepreneurs, these functional activities were often exercised and executed by a single idiosyncratic personality, one that often tends to be biased and overconfident.

Therefore, effective management cannot be accomplished without a well-defined strategy, which relies for its implementation on a robust organizational structure. The structure of an organization (be it formal or informal) sustains the efforts exercised by the management. Because it is hard to build, a structural design usually evolves to maturity slowly. Strategies based on ideas built around concise objectives are more often easier to grasp; however, they do not always necessarily fit into the more profane organizational structure. Therefore, an important assumption grounded in contingency theory is how a successful approach to management depends on a good fit between structure and its presumed strategic content.

7.3 The Rise and Success of the Multidivisional Structure

Harvard historian Alfred D. Chandler Jr. is credited for initiating an in-depth analysis of how large-scale industrial enterprises developed their organizational structure and how they adjusted their strategies. A significant upshot from his many in-depth clinical studies on the structural transformations of large industrial firms is that, by and large, changes to an inefficient organizational structure are primarily engendered by internal and external pressures to address the inefficiencies of an outdated structural design. In his famous study titled "Strategy and structure: Chapters in the history of the industrial enterprise" (1962), he demonstrated how large industrial firms such as Du Pont, General Motors, Jersey Standard, and Sears independently developed "brand new ways of administering [these] great industrial enterprises" (Chandler, 1962: 3). His well-known dictum was "structure follows strategy," which means that the purpose of an organizational structure is to implement and accomplish a prescribed corporate strategy.

Chandler studied almost fifty large US enterprises and questioned how these firms had successfully designed and implemented an administrative structure to efficiently manage their highly diversified business operations.

The great challenge was transforming an administrative structure built around functions into an organizational design that supported decentralized and largely independent divisions.

The first two large industrial enterprises that introduced a decentralized structure were Du Pont and General Motors. Pressured by a severe crisis caused by the radically changing market environment, both industrial giants began reforming their highly centralized administrative systems soon after the First World War. Thereafter, Standard Oil and Sears began in the late 1920s to modify their inefficient centralized management systems. In his analyses of the history of organizational change in these four large industrial firms, Chandler described why the needed changes evolved from each firm's particular growth pattern in a distinct environment (Chandler, 1962: 3). The designs of the necessary changes were deeply grounded in the fundamental transformation of the American economy, mainly induced by the cyclical demand for the products these companies manufactured. Chandler witnessed how the decentralized firm structure became a necessity for overcoming the in-built inefficiencies of the old centralized system. They accomplished this by focusing on the roles and responsibilities of four fundamental management functions.

The first top executive position in a firm was situated in what is known as the "General Office," in which the "general executives and staff specialists coordinate, appraise, and plan"—the three core managerial functions. The success of the new multidivisional structure depended on establishing effective management strategies performed by a small group of top executives that set the overall strategic "goals and policies" for the newly established "quasi-autonomous [and] fairly self-contained divisions" (Chandler, 1962: 9ff). They were ultimately responsible for deciding on how to "allocate resources" to these divisions.

It is important to note that these top executives needed the assistance of specialized staff that organized how essential information was received and how it was uniformly produced to get a precise picture of the different firm-wide activities across several business units. Establishing a new information system and determining how to audit and measure performance in these diverse divisions were essential elements to managing these large industrial firms effectively.

The second management role was associated with the tasks of the newly established central office, which was responsible for coordinating the different business divisions that autonomously manage several functional departments (e.g., sales, engineering, research, manufacturing, purchasing, and finance).

The third essential management layer was associated with the organization within each department, which became responsible for managing its respective functional activities (i.e., sales or research) on its own. These departmental managerial functions were situated in the departmental headquarters; their focus was on coordinating related efforts, appraising, and planning activities within the departments.

Finally, the fourth level of responsibility was established at the lowest level: these were "field units" responsible for managing multiple units, production plants, laboratories, and so forth. These were the only units where the management would personally carry out the control and monitoring (i.e., "supervision") of their respective departments (cf. Chandler, 1962: 9–11).

These radical shifts in structure were based on a new perspective on managing a large, diversified, and multidivisional enterprise. The executive committee relied on individual departments to obtain the correct information that would facilitate making a practical decision. It was acknowledged that the answer to the problem was not simply a new structure but rather how to get better information and knowledge across the fragmented functions throughout such a large organization. It became clear that it was necessary to implement more effective control over, for example, the inventory, and it was evident that the existing system of communication between and within firms did not work (Chandler, 1962: 99). It slowly became acknowledged that managing firms meant managing products, not functions.

However, as Chandler demonstrated, change does not occur automatically but is instigated by external pressure caused, in turn, by a radical crisis. His case studies showed that management often organizes "old and new activities with the same personnel, using the same channels of communication and authority and the same type of information" (Chandler, 1962: 15). A certain structure does not automatically follow a projected change in strategy. Most firms are prone to a management style that is change-averse. A successful organization cannot be transformed easily and so management processes tend to remain caged in well-established routines. However, the inefficiency of the centralized structure in large industrial enterprises resulted in massive integration and consolidation at the turn of the nineteenth century. The management of these corporations relied on countless "informal personal contacts" (Chandler, 1962: 37).

As noted above, the core responsibilities of management are, according to Chandler, to coordinate, appraise, and plan (1962: 8). However, in order to carry out these core functions, management needed accurate information on their firm's functional activities. This was "usually left to such employees as salesmen, buyers, production supervisors and foremen, technicians, and designers" and so management first needed to generate a system to collect this information, which would entail the effective organization of subordinate managers to carry out the tasks (Chandler, 1962: 8). As Chandler concedes, in small firms, all these activities can be executed by one person, usually the owner or owner-entrepreneur who is responsible for the coordinating the buying of materials, selling finished goods, and supervising the manufacturing process. In larger firms, however, the planning and coordination processes are increasingly separated from the daily operations. The following section describes how a difficult but successful transformation eventually occurred; this is exemplified in how General Motors (GM) changed its centralized structure to a decentralized multidivisional organizational form.

7.3.1 General Motors' Transformation from the U-Form to the M-Form

Alfred Sloan Jr. was appointed CEO of GM by Pierre du Pont (1870–1954) in 1921 when the company was in a severe crisis. During the recession of the 1930s, the demand for automobiles declined sharply. GM had extremely high inventories of produced and unsold vehicles, yet continued to manufacture cars at full speed in its factories.

Ford Motor Company, a direct competitor, faced similar problems but conceded by cutting the price of its only model, the Ford Model T, by over 25%. GM could not afford such price cuts because it faced much higher production costs. In 1921, Ford had a market share of 55% with the Model T, Chevrolet had a market share of 4% with another GM brand, and GM's total market share at the time was 11%, although GM produced several vehicles and model lines rather than just the one.

Regardless of its sales problems and small market share, GM was not capable of producing vehicles at a lower price and lacked the optimal operating size, which caused higher than average long-term fixed costs, primarily due to the affluent segment of model lines such as the Cadillac, Buick, Oakland, Oldsmobile, and Chevrolet. All the cars produced by GM competed with the Ford Model T and its own brands.

The top tier of management at the company was aware that these problems needed to be addressed. Therefore, it was decided that a brand strategy had to be devised to compete with Henry Ford's successful Model T ("the car for every purse and purpose").

Alfred Sloan Jr. came up with several ideas. Cadillac was to be an exclusive brand, affordable only to the highest income segments. The other car brands were to target progressively less demanding customer segments. Chevrolet thus produced more affordable vehicles than Ford. In their purchasing decisions, Sloan was firmly convinced that most consumers would choose either a more expensive or a cheaper vehicle than Ford Model T, reflecting his strategy for selling cars in a growing and more competitive market.

However, implementing this plan (i.e., strategy) was a challenging task. On the one hand, the individual product divisions had to remain specialized in order to implement distinct advantages over competing vehicle models from other manufacturers. On the other hand, the respective business areas (product divisions) had to be coordinated with each other (i.e., coordinated according to explicit rules), a procedure that had hitherto never been practiced in the automobile industry (Chandler, 1962).

Specialization was justified and considered necessary because each product division had to create its own distinctive product design. In addition, a separate dealer network had to be established for each vehicle of a brand as Sloan was aware that customer-specific information was necessary for each market segment. For each type of vehicle and production plant, the respective relationships with suppliers had to be coordinated accordingly. It was also deemed appropriate that the individual vehicle types produced in GM factories should not compete too strongly with GM's other vehicles. In addition, many suppliers had to be brought together to the extent that common ideas (i.e., requirements) could be exchanged to improve production.

While Ford was able to realize fixed cost-reduction advantages in its one-product strategy (precisely because they sold only one model meant that only one kind of engine, clutch, gearbox, tires, suspension, seats, steering, etc. had to be produced), GM was confronted with other challenges.

At GM, each location (series and brand) had to conduct its own negotiations with suppliers. Each site developed its own sales strategies geared to each specific customer segment. Business operations were conducted independently without any central coordination. This organizational model was born out of necessity considering the requirements of individual operating divisions. However, it meant that information on what costs the respective divisions incurred was not available to GM: "At General Motors, the problem had been the integration and coordination of many almost completely independent divisions" (Chandler, 1962: 115). William C. Durant, who had founded GM in 1908 as a holding company, was by 1920 in a severe crisis and "[u]nless some action was taken quickly, [GM] would be forced in bankruptcy" (Chandler, 1962: 114). After a meeting with JP Morgan and other investors, Durant resigned as the president of GM. Within a few weeks, the new executive committee had begun adopting the new organizational design developed by Sloan. What had caused this severe crisis?

As a pioneering giant in the automobile industry, Durant was convinced that "moderately priced cars" had enormous market potential. While Ford was essentially an engineer who focused on optimizing car production, Durant was a salesman who focused on selling cars. Durant built a large conglomerate of several manufacturing plants that produced in different locations with many individual parts being assembled in scattered facilities. Durant did not have the motivation to invest much effort in organizing the overall structure and neglected the potential to integrate the separated plants. However, General Motors grew rapidly because Durant was convinced that more segmented car markets would offer more significant profits. Since its foundation in 1885, Durant, a young salesman at the time, had acquired a patent to manufacture two-wheel cars for 50 USD (Chandler, 1962: 116).

His enormous skills in marketing increased the demand for these cars dramatically, and soon Durant acquired other suppliers and plants because he recognized the great potential that lay in automobiles. Seemingly aiming to internalize insecure supplies for his many scattered car manufacturing plants, he was involved in the process of empire-building with all its negative aspects. Four years later, he took over the failed Buick Motor Company in Flint, redesigned the cars, and put most of his energy into establishing a nationwide distribution deal with dealers. At first, he granted franchises to sell his cars. Sales and marketing were organized into district offices. With growing sales, the production of parts was gradually relocated to Flint. However, as noted earlier, his main interest was in selling produced cars and so he did not spend much time organizing an efficient manufacturing structure. As a result, several plants supplying the Flint factory were largely independent. The overall mandate to structuring the car manufacturing process was delegated to a production manager at Buick and Walter Chrysler, who designed a "fairly standard centralized structure, with manufacturing, sales, engineering, purchasing, and financial departments" to manage the "rapidly growing" output (Chandler, 1962: 117). The core focus of these efforts was to develop a more effective organization strategy for the growing output of cars, but—and this is one of the significant inefficiencies that arose—nobody seemed overly concerned "with obtaining [. . .] better costs and other data necessary for the effective administration of manufacturing activities"(Chandler, 1962: 118). Chandler described Durant's strategy as one that expanded production volume and increased vertical integration. Expanding production was carried out by acquiring other car manufacturers such as Cadillac, Oldsmobile, and the McLaughlin Motor Car Company in Canada. Durant's acquisition strategy was thus maintained to guarantee his scattered manufacturing plants' supply. This strategy resulted in a massive increase in sales from 29 million to 49 million USD between 1908 and 1910. Nevertheless, when sales eventually decreased below the actual output of the plants that produced the cars, Durant started facing difficulties financing the supplies for his ever-growing number of plants (cf. Chandler, 1962: 120).

The first setback was external; in other words, it was not caused by internal problems arising from the sheer number of independently operating entities. Nevertheless, a massive drop in sales accelerated the systemic failures of such an unstructured giant. His many affiliate firms produced axles, wheels, bodies, paint, or only whip sockets but lacked coordination or any sound integration to the larger whole. Each entity worked as a somewhat independent supplier but as demand grew, adequate and timely sourcing became "increasingly a serious problem" (Chandler, 1962: 116).

In 1930, Pierre du Pont—a salesman extraordinaire—resigned as chairman of GM due to pressure from the banks who were no longer willing to finance GM's massive losses. Du Pont had rejected an elaborate plan to introduce a multi-divisional organizational structure to GM. The plans drawn up by Sloan were the result of a ruthless analysis of GM's problems. Sloan knew that GM's factories were inefficient and worked in an uncoordinated manner and thus needed to be integrated. The integration process was done through the General Office, which had existed at GM since 1920 but had struggled to hold together the many thousands of departments and several factory locations with hundreds of managers.

Chandler described this setup as "a vast number of men, money, and materials" (1962: 115). The expansion of GM was, in the first stage, based on a rapid growth of sales. To ensure a consistent stream of supplies, Durant strongly moved into forward and backward vertical integration of formerly independent suppliers. Both phases of expansion were driven by Durand's exceptional entrepreneurial spirit. Still, Durant paid "almost no attention to developing [an efficient production] line of cars" and he "gave even less thought" to the development of an effective overall structure to manage his scattered business (Chandler, 1962: 123). After 1919, a year that saw GM massively expand, the management's focus was to enlarge the capacity of the older plants. However, the relations between the numerous operating divisions and general management remained highly uncoordinated, and "major decisions, such as plant expansion, capital investments [and so forth] were decided by Durant" who met somewhat occasionally with "the heads of the operating divisions." In other words, Durant's decisions were made without much consultation with his general managers and were instead based on "casual reference or contact" (Chandler, 1962: 125). This type of decision-making may seem highly entrepreneurial but was, in fact, extremely biased by random and casual information provided by operation managers who had only a narrow focus on their plants. With such ad hoc meetings, Durant bypassed many of his committees such as the Finance Committee, which was established to introduce and formulate a standardized financial policy across the whole company. The Finance Committee "failed to push for organizational improvements" because "Durant continued to make nearly all the important decision concerning the divisions" (Chandler, 1962: 126).

While du Pont, who had made huge investments into GM to save it from bankruptcy, commissioned a number of studies on how to get the needed information required to implement more effective administration and control, Durant continued his "horse trading" (Chandler, 1962: 127) with plant managers.

The crisis of 1920, however, which was at first perceived as only a short intermezzo, drastically interrupted the supply for much longer than expected. In such a situation, the plant managers "stocked up their inventories" and neglected to address the overall problem. During that period, GM spent 79 million USD. The Finance Committee believed there would be no problem in raising the requisite money on the capital market. However, within a few months, at the end of May, the cost of stocking up the inventories skyrocketed to 167 million USD and the production figures over the upcoming years declined. In September 1920, the car market collapsed, and GM struggled to find the cash to finance the immediate costs of maintaining its business. While Durant's competitor Henry Ford "slashed prices" by almost 30% (Chandler, 1962: 129), GM sustained its prices. The GM stock price declined sharply and Durant was forced to hand over the presidency to Pierre du Pont (Chandler, 1962: 129). What is important to note here is that, internally, for a couple of years, managers such as Chrysler, du Pont, and Haskell painstakingly tried to adapt the highly inefficient organizational structure; their efforts largely failed, however, because of the strong influence of Durant. It was thus a severe external crisis that finally prompted the company to pursue fundamental change, making Durant's retreat possible.

The introduction of the General Office was not driven by du Pont but was instead demanded by two influential investors. The Depression of the 1920s and the pressures imposed by investors were why a fundamental "structural [re]design" was finally implemented (Chandler, 1962: 115).

7.3.2 The New Multidivisional Structure of Alfred Sloan Jr.

Sloan had studied electrical engineering at MIT and, after graduating, started working at Hyatt Roller Bearing, a company he later owned and managed. Along with other companies, Hyatt merged into the United Motor Company, which General Motors later acquired. Sloan was appointed Vice-President of GM in 1923. Sloan's plan to transform the structure of GM was finally approved at the end of 1920. Sloan's approach succeeded because it radically changed GM "into a single, coordinated enterprise" (Chandler, 1962: 130).

As President of United Motors, a subsidiary of GM, Sloan was to "coordinate and expand the activities of the different operating units" (Chandler, 1962: 131). Within his area of influence, he set up a standardized accounting system that allowed him to "evaluate the profitability of his operating divisions" (ibid). Although he was reasonably successful in implementing a practical organizational framework to manage United Motors, Sloan was deeply concerned by "the lack of structure and system in [GM's] overall organization" that nearly forced him to resign (Chandler, 1962: 132).

7.3.3 The Fundamental Principles of the Sloan Structure

From the outside, Sloan saw the problem inherent to GM's structure from a new perspective and his experiences at the company were different from that of Durant. He also knew that du Pont and others had tried and failed to implement the General Office to "coordinate, appraise, and plan [. . .] for the divisions" at GM. In analyzing the many failures in the overall structure of GM, Sloan became aware that the different divisions needed to keep their autonomy as this setup would motivate their management and promote innovation. However, Sloan also knew that although these divisions needed full autonomy, they had to be coordinated and controlled from the point of common interests for the overall performance of GM.

Sloan planned to put professional managers in charge of coordinating and supervising the company's business operations in the General Office. However, it must be noted that these managers needed access to certain information to do their job. There was to be no interference in the divisions' operational business practices and Sloan made it clear that the managers would "retain full authority and responsibility" (Chandler, 1962: 135). Each business unit (division) was to organize its production and sales independently. To this end, it was necessary to provide each division with management that was authorized to make proper decisions.

The management staff at the Central Office were no longer to be confronted with operational decisions. The role of the GM board and the Central Office staff was to control the entirety of the corporate body and its independent divisions. Sloan also strengthened the position of the financial and accounting units (Chandler, 1962: 134) as this was needed to implement a standardized and uniform system to evaluate the profitability of the investments and output of each division. Therefore, measuring output became the core purpose of developing effective firm-wide communication. It also seemed essential to develop indicators and measurement tools that reflected the individual performance results of the independent divisions so that the Central Office had the information it needed to coordinate the company at large. The Central Office was also responsible for research and development—the first task to be integrated across all the divisions in those early days (Chandler, 1962: 136). The means of central control was to monitor, assess, and make decisions (and thus authorize) all the financing and investment decisions in the independent decentralized divisions.

Another aspect implemented in the Central Office was the preparation of market studies and generating internal transfer prices that reflected the actual costs. For this purpose, suppliers owned by the company were treated as if they were external firms so that GM could better check the efficiency of their operations.

Resisting Change

Henry Ford, who followed the changes at GM closely, was decidedly skeptical: "To my mind there is no bent of mind more dangerous than that which sometimes is described as the 'genius of organization.' This usually results in the birth of a great big chart showing how authority ramifies after the fashion of a family tree. The tree is heavy, with nice round berries, each of which bears the name of a man or an office ... It takes about six weeks for a message from a man living in one berry at the lower left-hand corner of the chart to reach the chairman of the board" (quoted in Levinson 2013: 71).

However, in a relatively short space of time, Sloan had turned this great big chart of his newly designed organizational structure that Ford had apostrophized as cumbersome and slow into a powerful tool. Ford lost over 200 million USD in sales between 1927 and 1937. While GM's market share increased rapidly (to about 45% by 1940) after introducing the new multi-divisional organizational structure (M-form). Conversely, Ford's market share dropped to 16% in the same period.

The M-form proved to be more successful than the U-form, a design that Ford's mass production system still rigidly applied. In the meantime, Ford had to struggle with the considerable disadvantages engendered by organizational inertia.

Implementing Change

Sloan needed to implement a radically new organizational design, beginning with the following:

(continued)

(a) defined the boundaries of each division more accurately, and
(b) implemented a system to develop "an accurate and effective information to flow through the new structure" (Chandler, 1962: 142).

This information system was based on certain procedures that refined the measurements of each division; these included uniform data on costs as well as a standardized system to account for production costs. However, the management responsible for introducing these measures were not primarily concerned with collecting data about the firm's past performance but were instead focused on how to use the information to forecast future development, envision each division's new needs, and thereby allocate budgets. To this end, the new cost accounting unit implemented "new and uniform accounting procedures" across all the GM divisions (Chandler, 1962: 147). This complete redesign of the company structure could not work without elaborating and developing the role of advisory staff that carried out several specialized services and activities to help executive managers in their effort to "coordinate, appraise, and plan." However, some of this advice was met with open or covert resistance from certain divisions (Chandler, 1962: 154). Moreover, the rising costs of purchasing departments supplemented the effort to introduce a centralized unit for "general purchasing" (Chandler, 1962: 156).

Committees introduced to bridge the gaps in the information flow between independent divisions prepared recommendations for the new "executive committee," which was the core governance body of GM: "The members of this committee had the time and psychological commitment and the necessary information to concentrate on broad strategic matters" and had no operational duties (Chandler, 1962: 157).

The success of GM's new multidivisional organizational structure was clear; within a few years (from 1924 to 1927), the company succeeded in increasing its market share from 18.8% to 43.3% and nearly tripled its vehicle sales. Even upcoming problems were more effectively met within that organizational structure, described as "decentralized operations and responsibilities with coordinated control" (Chandler, 1962: 160–161). Chandler's key argument is that, at each level, the role of management is framed by its "own administrative duties, problems, and needs" (Chandler, 1962: 12). These endogenous factors (i.e., internal firm properties) are significantly affected by the dynamic challenges imposed by the external environment. Organizational structures should work to smooth out tensions across functions and precisely define managerial roles within a firm. However, the need to keep friction low by pooling different activities does not occur automatically.

However, the organizational culture provides a frame for each specialized functional role to sustain itself and facilitate effective and efficient operations at each corporate level. Chandler's work can thus be read as providing a formal solution to the problem of bounded information and inefficiency in uncoordinated specialized departments. Nevertheless, the right structure is more than just the proper design for how to coordinate and integrate scattered activities and business units. The most suitable organizational design also needs to provide the grounds for cooperation beyond the formal structural framework. Chandler eloquently describes the invention of the modern corporate form, developed into a multi-divisional structure from a functional design, and argues that the superior efficiency of this structure contributed to its worldwide expansion. He also purported that such changes are not possible without an apparent crisis and the immediate pressure directed from outside on the management of a firm, which he described in his analysis of four large US business firms that switched from the unitary (U-form) to the multi-divisional structure (M-form). His insights illustrate how slow and difficult it was to establish a more effective formal organization based on business divisions (Novicevic et al., 2009; Whittington, 2008). It is worth noting that Whittington, in homage to Chandler as the founder of the strategy that powerfully inspired research in strategy, indicated that Chandler "stood firmly outside the discipline, working as a business historian, not as a strategist" (Whittington, 2008: 267).

However, it is essential to acknowledge how Edith Penrose in particular conceptualized the core problem of how to organize a "bundle of resources" within existing firms. She argued that "extensive planning requires the cooperation of many individuals who have confidence in each other, in general, requires knowledge of each other" (Penrose, 1959: 47). She pointed to the challenge caused by firms' limited potential to grow by elaborating on the problem fundamentally related to the inherent and tacit resource of cooperation. Such cooperation among many individuals is based on the confidence they have in each other that they "will suffer, even if optimum adjustments are made in the administrative structure," which may lead in "extreme cases [. . .] to such disorganization that the firm will be unable to compete efficiently" (Penrose, 1959: 47) if organizations grow faster than the individuals can adapt their experience.

Implicitly, Penrose argues in the quoted section above that efficiency is dependent on a fit between the capabilities of individuals in a firm—with their tacit experiences and learning capabilities—and the degree of the speed of expansion of the firm. Her key arguments, supplementing in essential aspects the question of finding the right structure, rest on the assumption that the process of "increased experience and knowledge" within a firm is significantly dependent on how "the significance of resources to the firm" may change, and require an alignment and continuous adaptation in a changing external environment (Penrose, 1959: 79). She curiously conceives structure as only one part of this equation but elaborates on how a firm depends on an intricate and "close relation between various kinds of resources [the right structure is only one of them, MF] with which a firm works." Consequently, the primary task of managing a firm is to put those close relationships between various resources to work, thereby enabling "the development of the ideas, experience, and knowledge" (Penrose, 1959: 85). Compared to the question of structure, Penrose clearly sees how the "changing experience and knowledge [within a firm] affect not only the productive services available from resources, [. . .] but also create the special productive opportunity of a given firm" (Penrose, 1959: 85).

Looking briefly at the history of the growth of the firm, we recognize that the traditional organizational structure was primarily geared towards the need to attain functional performance, and specialization in a functional department was assumed to automatically generate increasingly positive effects. But how exactly was efficiency attained? It was achieved at the expense of intrinsic motivation and by accepting autonomy in the execution of individual tasks. Therefore, lack of information was diagnosed as the most critical problem. The necessary ideas and knowledge needed to improve or continuously change production processes were located outside of the actual activities performed in separated and widely scattered departments. Slowly, as Chandler showed, mainly due to severe crises or external pressures, the GM management was forced to accept the need to integrate the centripetal forces emanating from the narrow focus on efficiency within the functional areas of individual departmental structures.

In corporate headquarters, a somewhat rigid but highly elaborated accounting and auditing system emerged to implement more effective control. Nevertheless, centralized control and a standardized system of measuring costs could not resolve the inherent deficiencies of the functional structure in large, highly diversified industrial firms. The management of these large organizations were trained to set course on a journey but lacked the capability to look beyond the narrow functional world; all too often, these proverbial captains were challenged by navigating unchartered and stormy waters. Integrating core cross-functional activities was the first attempt to address these issues. Research and development units were placed under the budgetary responsibility of the head office. Competence centers were set up according to the needs of the overall company, and the purchasing departments of national units were merged to realize cost advantages and market power over suppliers. Many complex tasks were broken down into fractions of smaller production units and outsourced to decentralized locations without, however, implementing uniform and effective controlling systems within the company. Management functions, particularly planning and strategy development, in multinational companies remained centralized.

The organizational structure of these very large firms focused on the immediate realization of the organization's goals.

Formal organizational structure is understood as the conscious and permanent design of interlocking operational units and the integration of associated work processes within an organization. Besides the formal regulation and division of areas of competence, however, there is a plethora of spontaneous, ad hoc, seemingly unplanned, and dynamically interacting processes governed by informal structures. Every organizational structure may serve well the needs of a particular size, but as firms grow, this seemingly efficient structure gets increasingly outdated or inept due to the ongoing expansion.

However, it was not the faulty implementation of functional specialization based on specific tasks, but rather its successful realization coupled with the functional departmentalization's inherent strengths, which made these flaws stand out in clearer relief. The advantages of the functional organizational structure are undisputed in the literature and are summarized as follows (Schreyögg, 1999: 133):

- Learning effects and dexterity arise in the routine performance of the same tasks.
- Fixed cost-degression and synergy effects.
- Exchange of know-how and knowledge between similar but not identical activities.
- Use of interdependencies in multi-product companies.

However, as the company grew, the flaws of the functional structure became apparent. The high number of interfaces between separated functions overloaded the executives (Frese, 1998; Morgan, 1986; Schreyögg, 1999: 133). Communication lines between departments, which were based on inflexible relationships, became time-consuming. The high degree of labor division and the processes associated with the realization of fixed-cost advantages made the allocation of performance results challenging, thereby resulting in a high degree of demotivation within the highly specialized work areas. In such a multinational company, the centripetal driving forces were thus strengthened and the influence of territorially responsible managers of subsidiaries with strong sales records increased considerably.

Divisionalization is a form of departmentalization in which the organizational structure is geared toward markets and products. By formally merging the quotidian activities of manufacturing specific products, greater flexibility is achieved due to smaller operational units. This strategy enabled the organization to align itself more specifically to market requirements. Due to the improved clarity and allocation of the service provision, acquisitions and investments were carried out more efficiently. The enhanced clarity in the individual activities of a business unit resulted in a higher degree of motivation because the responsibility for the provision of services could be assigned more specifically. The disadvantages of this divisional organizational form were, conversely, linked to the causes of the advantages. However, the emerging divisional organizational structure had to accept efficiency losses caused by the increase in managerial roles and positions as the administrative workload increased and the divisions developed a pattern of competing against each other, which reduced prevalent inertia but made the realization of potential synergies much more challenging (Schreyögg, 1999: 133).

In fast-growing multinational firms, the influence of managers with area and product responsibility increased, especially in subsidiaries with high sales and earnings.

The centrifugal forces within the company were encouraged by such influential managers to assert their areas of responsibility. In addition to the formal organizational structure of internationally oriented companies, the management relationships between parent and subsidiary companies in the individual countries started to exhibit significant differences. Due to these challenges, various types of international firms have been identified in the relevant literature discussed below.

7.4 The Tortuous Evolution of the Multinational Firm

The question of firm growth remained a challenge for management, regardless of its size. A severe test for how efficiently a firm is organized came with the advent of internationalization from formerly primarily domestically oriented enterprises that moved on to explore and exploit unknown markets abroad. Managerial skills and challenges and the existing structures of domestically oriented firms that evolved in familiar environments—where most firms learned how to serve their current domestic customers and to produce products and services in a somewhat familiar home location by relying on a network of accustomed suppliers—were confronted with hitherto unknown challenges. Making the decision to move abroad at the early stages of the internationalizing process can be rather simple. Nevertheless, sooner or later, with firms expanding in scope and scale to more unfamiliar foreign markets, the top tiers of management needed to adapt their management and firm structures to an ever-growing diversity of locations and markets.

One of the first discussions on the subject of how difficult such a transformation can be was provided by Howard Perlmutter (1969), an engineer and social psychologist who taught at the Wharton School of Business. The change, which he conceived as an evolution from a purely domestic to multi-domestic set-up in different but clustered regions, was termed a "tortuous evolution" (Perlmutter, 1969). Perlmutter equated the "headquarters-orientation" as ethnocentric, polycentric, and geocentric. Ethnocentricity refers to the headquarters' exercise of authority and power throughout the subsidiaries based on a strict hierarchical order, performed in the headquarters by management socialized by a strong home-country orientation, and deriving its identity from a strong inclination toward the superior home-nationality. The meaning of "ethnocentric" in this context is that the firm's own cultural and social background is the sovereign and single measure to evaluate what is right or wrong. Managers who are sent abroad to lead the foreign subsidiaries are recruited and developed in the headquarters or in strong and influential home-based affiliates. The communication flow is one-sided: from the top (the headquarters) to subsidiaries abroad. Communication is reduced to the passing of orders, advice, and commands. Perlmutter assumed that, while increasing the multinationality of a firm, the organizational framework ideally passes through different organizational evolutionary stages, which he described as a "painful development" (Perlmutter, 1969) process. Perlmutter initially identified the communication practiced between headquarters and subsidiaries as a significant criterion of successful management (Perlmutter, 1969: 12).

Perlmutter focused on the question of structure and aimed to elucidate how its effectivity correlates to an existing organizational culture defining the mentality of management that is often difficult to transform. He was aware that a rigid attachment to a home-oriented management culture has become an inadequate tool for grasping the complexity and heterogeneity of foreign markets. Not surprisingly, the homemade organizational management mentality was incapable of bridging the challenging gap between a home and host culture. It increased the difficulty of the challenges presented by sticking to homemade recipes for how to approach organizational problems and was thus less successful in managing business operations in culturally distant foreign environments.

Perlmutter's core dictum was that success in such a venture depends on comprehensively adapting a firm's extremely homogenous home-grown managerial culture; simply put, its rigid habits and routines are ill-suited to grasping the heterogeneity of foreign environments. As a consequence, firms that failed to heed this advice tended to suffer from growing gaps between their home-grown culture and the complex and unfamiliar realities abroad.

The ability to bridge these gaps generated by severe cultural differences was slowly recognized to depend on the "local people [who] know what is best for them"; all other coordination and integration protocols are generated by "good financial controls" (Perlmutter, 1969: 10ff.). The paradigm shift that Perlmutter introduced initialized a new perspective on how to manage a multinational firm. According to Perlmutter, this shift needed to define the multinational firm as "a loosely connected group with quasi-independent subsidiaries as centers," something he termed "akin to a confederation" (Perlmutter, 1969: 12). However, implementing such a transformation remained a difficult and never-ending challenge. Essentially, because the outcome was significantly dependent on an organizational culture—one that has developed over years and has subsequently entrenched quotidian routines and habits—it can be converted from a predominantly ethnocentric orientation (exercised in many large international firms) to a more polycentric approach. The proposed solution, coined in the phrase "let local people [who] know what is best for them" manage the subsidiary, thereby allowing a "local identity" to grow (Perlmutter, 1969), was, in fact, a radical change.

Credit must be given to Howard Perlmutter for recognizing the need for such a paradigm shift. Perlmutter wrote a famous essay metaphorically entitled "The tortuous evolution of the Multinational Firm" (Perlmutter, 1969). In this short essay, he criticizes that it is hardly sufficient to categorize multinational firms according to the number of subsidiaries they have or the proportion of foreign sales in relation to their domestic turnover. On the surface, large multinationals exhibit similar goals and structures. A closer look behind the surface reveals astonishing and profound differences among these several types of corporate structures. Perlmutter offers a surprisingly up-to-date insight. He used several illustrative accounts to reveal how top CEOs' minds seem to work. To look at the mindset of top executives was a new insight and by adopting this focus, Perlmutter was going much further than merely analyzing the structure of the multinational firms. Reading these accounts today and interpreting his original quotations can be useful for understanding how the habitual mentality of top management tiers deeply affects the structure and actions of the multinational firm.

Perlmutter observed three not necessarily consecutive patterns of how multinational firms are managed, which he denoted as ethnocentric, polycentric, and geocentric. The suffix 'centric' in all three patterns signifies the inner core of management mentality. Table 7.1 summarizes a few quotes from the original in-depth interviews Perlmutter conducted for his early studies on the evolution of management mentality in the

Table 7.1 Comparing different corporate mentalities; Perlmutter's tortuous evolution of the multinational enterprise (1969)

Company A	Company B	Company C	Company D (non-American)
"We are a multinational firm. We distribute our products in about 100 countries. We manufacture in over 17 countries and do research and development in three countries—both domestic and overseas—using exactly the same criteria" (p. 9)	"We are a multinational firm. Only 1% of the personnel in our affiliate companies are non-nationals. Most of these are U.S. executives on temporary assignments. In all major markets, the affiliate's managing director is of the local nationality" (p. 9)	We are a multinational firm. Our product division executives have worldwide profit responsibility. As our organizational chart shows, the United States is just one region on a par with Europe, Latin America, Africa, etc., in each product divisions" (p. 9)	"We are a multinational firm. We have at least 18 nationalities represented at our headquarters. Most senior executives speak at least two languages. About 30% of our staff headquarters are foreigners" (p. 9)
"key post in [our] subsidiaries are held by home-country nationals. Whenever replacements [. . .] are sought, it is practice, if not policy, to 'look next to you at the head office' and 'pick someone [. . .] you know and trust" (p. 10)	"You can't find good foreigners who are willing to live in the United States, where our [HQ] is located. American executives are more mobile. In addition, American executives have the drive and initiative we like." (p. 10)	"senior executives in charge of [. . .] divisions have little overseas experience [and] have been promoted from domestic post and tend to view foreign consumer needs 'as really basically the same as our's "(p. 10)	"We are proud of our nationality; we shouldn't be ashamed of it. [. . .] Our country produces good executives, who tend to stay with us a long time. It is harder to keep executives from the United States" (p. 10)

Source: Perlmutter (1969: 9ff); authors own compilation

multinational firm. In the first column, the original tone of an ethnocentric mindset is portrayed. The mentality in that context is a reference to a mindset prevalent among the top management. A mindset is defined in psychology as a way that human beings develop a meaningful and cognitively consistent system of thoughts and values that guide their actions. In this context, lay theory offers an elaborate explanation for how agents, such as managers, apply cognitively inscribed patterns constructed with and from past and current experiences, which are relatively stable and hard to change, and which frame routine behaviors in the existing value system. With these cognitive structures, human beings examine and narrow down the far too complex body of social information we face each day. In that sense, lay theory explains how human beings construct the meaningfulness of their life-world, how they understand their social environment, and how they predict what may happen, as well as how individuals produce a basic understanding of how to gain control in their social environments (Rattan & Georgeac, 2017). The construction of meaning is based on an unconscious reduction and selection of facts and results from a process wherein individuals seek to better understand the world around them (Heider, 1958; Kelly, 1955; Piaget et al., 1983).

However, an existing belief system "may not be accurate" (Rattan & Georgeac, 2017: 2), as this process of reduction and sorting takes place largely unconsciously. Moreover, belief systems are embedded in and built upon traditional cultural patterns. A pertinent question is then, how easily can these belief systems change? Each mental belief, defined as a mindset, "which may or may not be accurate, are people's nonscientific understandings of the world" which are "developed through experience and interactions with others"(Rattan & Georgeac, 2017: 1). It shapes how humans interpret experiences, construct explanations, and form expectations.

For example, in the first line, a manager from Company A in Table 7.1 eloquently announces, "we are a multinational firm, distributing products in [. . .] 100 countries and we manufacture in 17 countries and do R&D in 3 locations, and (!) both domestic and overseas use [...] the same criteria" (Perlmutter, 1969: 9). The important point to realize here is the following: whether or not a company reproduces its routines at every location in exactly the same way does not matter so much as the belief that produces the sense of control that is built upon their fundamental belief system, which is related to how the world is understood. The top executive in that interview was firmly convinced that their practices are right; because it is successful, why should anything be changed at all?

Company B perhaps provides the best contrast to the seemingly "pure" national headquarters perspective and orientation; the top executive claims: "We are a multinational company. Only 1% of the personnel in our affiliate companies are non-nationals. Most of these [1%] are U.S. executives on temporary assignments." Further, the company endorses the fact that "in all major markets, [. . .] the managing director [is a] local" (Perlmutter, 1969: 9). Their central belief is based on the conviction that locals do not distinguish between what is right or wrong "much better" in foreign locations.

Company D (seemingly the only European multinational), who seem somewhat proud to claim that "30% of the staff in the headquarter are foreigners" (Perlmutter, 1969: 9), is once again different.

It seems evident that Company A is categorized as ethnocentric as the managers believe that what is good at home is also good abroad. Ethnocentrism is a core concept in the social sciences, particularly in anthropology; it characterizes a way of seeing things primarily or exclusively from one's own deeply socialized normative values. An ethnocentric perspective takes the position and views of one's own group as the only valid source by which to consider others. Company B is probably best described as polycentric, as its management sees markets abroad as shaped and determined by its respective heterogeneity; it readily acknowledges that the differences in other cultures should be "managed" by the local people.

Irrespective of whether that perception is correct, it does substantially affect how the multinational firm will organize its headquarters and subsidiary relations. While Company C is geocentric, Company D seems to be already moving beyond that categorization.

Company D also appears to be the most inclusive. It has adopted a view wherein the inclusion of different management *cultures* is an apt strategy to learn in an unfamiliar and uncertain foreign environment.

What particular version of lay theory Perlmutter applied in his analyses is not explicitly clear. Nevertheless, he assumes that management can learn new things, that their belief system is not overly stable, and that the underlying 'mindset' may change (Dweck & Leggett, 1988). He argues that a mindset is not only an outcome based on the company's design as it also affects how a company is capable of changing.

Perlmutter's early approach was based on his analyses of stereotypes that perceived different national groups (French, Americans) and how these implicit assumptions influence the reciprocal perceptions among these groups. However, his early research on stereotypes was based on surveys comprising of items that implied an existing/non-existing dichotomy of characteristics, such as the following statement: "Europeans are warmer and friendlier than Americans" indicating a fairly grounded ethnocentric bias (Perlmutter & Shapiro, 1957: 132). Therefore, the respondents in Perlmutter's paper could either agree or disagree with an already biased item, including statements that already convey a specific stereotyped impression of Europeans or Americans.

Perlmutter's typology of mental topographies is described by the quotes selected in Table 7.1, but he does not explain how these routine behaviors in the firms developed over time; what he suggests is a normative progression along different stages in the development of the multinational firm. The intended process of change moves slowly from a plain and straightforward ethnocentric pattern that rest on a strictly home-grown understanding of headquarters to a more open-minded diverse cultural frame that moves away from a "self-referential" pattern. Foreign affiliates seem to evolve into a relatively more equitable but far from independent or autonomous role, which is a relationship pattern that is prevalent among and between subsidiaries in the third stage. Table 7.2. presents a juxtaposition of several selected attributes of these three organizational mentalities. Authority expressed in the headquarters is identified as high in the ethnocentric version, low in the polycentric, and more collaborative (or moderate) in the geocentric multinational firm.

However, it must be noted that the firms at these different stages still intend to establish a common culture of how things ought to be done. The ethnocentric firm tries to maintain home country standards throughout its structure, while the polycentric firm is more inclined to find a proper adaptation to local markets, recognizing that this is easier to accomplish by integrating locals. The geocentric firm, focusing more on how to balance global standards across the firm against emerging local needs, is still amidst the tension typical for such a diversified multinational firm. The polycentric firm is supposed to have casted off the old mental mindset and is actively trying to adapt to multiple host country environments.

Perlmutter's pattern of the evolving managerial mentality in multinational firms had been examined in several contexts but has also been used to elaborate a more appropriate marketing strategy in unfamiliar markets. Wind et al. applied Perlmutter's concept to 15 international marketing options, depending on which managerial mentality is most prevalent in the multinational firm. According to the authors, a conclusion that can be

Table 7.2 The ethnocentric, polycentric and geocentric orientation in the multinational firm

Design	Ethnocentric	Polycentric	Geocentric
Organization	Complex in HQ but simple in S	Varied and independent	Increasingly complex and interdependent
Authority; Decision Making	High in HQ	Low in HQ	Aiming for a collaboration between HQ and S
Evaluation and Control	Home country standards	Determined locally	Exploring universal and local standards
Rewards and incentives	High in HQ, low in S	Wide variation (low and high for S)	Balanced between worldwide and local objectives
Communication	High frequency to S (orders, commands, advice); unidirectional from HQ to S	Low frequency from and to HQ; low between S	Bidirectional and high frequency between HQ and S
Identification	Home country nationality	Host country nationality	Truly international, but identifying with national interests
Recruiting and Staffing	From HQ for key positions everywhere	Training locals for key position in HQ country	Training professionals at every location for positions in any location

Source: Perlmutter (1969: 12), Authors own compilation

drawn from the study is that the polycentric pattern is preferred when firms are pressured to develop a more direct customer presence; geocentric international firms, conversely, rely more on branding and product quality as marketing strategies. Branding is nevertheless the outcome of more robust ethnocentric characteristics. Wind et al. argued that the strongest and most elaborated applications of *modern* marketing tools (i.e., the measurement and forecast of market demand, market segmentation, sales promotion, and product development) are carried out in multinational firms with a polycentric pattern (Wind et al., 1973: 16f).

Although this perspective was developed as far back as the 1970s and 1980s, it is still a useful approach.

The behavior and actions of management and key personnel are embedded in the explicit and implicit stereotypes in ethnocentric, polycentric, and geocentric firms. Note that the behavior of organizational members, including its management, is not enacted independently from the strategies and pertinent structures of a firm. Rattan and Georgeac (2017) assume a growing propensity for more extreme stereotypes and conclude that mindsets consisting of such stereotypes "exhibit greater satisfaction when minimal information is available" (Rattan & Georgeac, 2017: 3). Further, the fixed mindset seems to have a greater propensity "to endorse the existing stereotypes" as a valid cognitive pattern. Instead, a "growing" mindset allows for a relatively greater proclivity to change and subsequently relates to a "lower propensity and readiness to form extreme stereotypes" (ibid: 3).

It is also worth noting that in ethnocentric multinational firms, staff are recruited and trained by and for key managerial positions and that management is socialized and built in the headquarters. In the polycentric pattern, key personnel are organized by headquarters, while in geocentrically orientated multinationals, human resources are trained, recruited, and kept for critical positions in any location.

In a multinational firm organized around *ethnocentric behavioral patterns*, management measures performance "for men and products" by applying the same criteria at home and in host locations (see Table 7.2). The headquarters staff exert control (i.e., the sales performance of several agents) with uniform standards everywhere, without considering whether the sales staff is based in the US or in the Republic of Congo. This kind of general firm policy ignores the apparent market heterogeneity. However, ethnocentric stereotyping may not only neglect cultural and local heterogeneity as it also generates gross misinterpretations and blocks any emerging awareness that leads to possible location-specific learnings. The ethnocentric pattern of perception limits the development of communication skills necessary for adaptation in both host and home locations. The resulting hierarchy—comprising orders, instructions, and advice—is bound by the limited view based on what management assumes is a feasible policy that is thus accepted as the 'only' good way to manage, even if it has only ever been tested at the home location. Any programmatic change will be flawed, as the stereotypical approach is grounded in the view that what works in the home market must work in the foreign market. The fact that only indigenous personnel are recruited at the headquarters for deployment abroad cements dependency on a narrow focus on how foreign affiliates can meet the performance standards cultivated at home locations (Perlmutter, 1969: 12). From this perspective, it is less a technical problem that causes growing inefficiency than the question of how to change the existing propensity to endorse ethnocentric stereotypes and a distorted awareness that makes them trustworthy. Perlmutter subtly coined this implicit dynamic pattern as a "drama in three acts" (Perlmutter, 1969).

The polycentric orientation is built on the premise that top executives in a multinational firm acknowledge the importance of foreign subsidiaries in achieving joint goals. Indeed, the original text, wherein Perlmutter claims that "top executives (usually one founder), begin with the assumption that host-country cultures are different and that foreigners are difficult to understand," signifies a stage of growing awareness. The executives can draw on their extensive experience abroad that establishes the knowledge that "local people know best what is best for them" (Perlmutter, 1969: 12).

Two strikingly different interpretations are possible here: (1) whether "local management actually knows what is best for them" or (2) whether local people, embedded in a local institutional environment, know what is best for the MNE as a whole, not just for the local site. This is because they are deeply rooted in an intangible institutional context for outsiders. The first perspective implies that local management can deal with the existing headquarters standards much better than expatriates socialized there. The second interpretation favors the insight that local managers understand a complex institutional environment much better, which enables the subsidiary to be more adaptive to the existing local standards. In that context, we need to understand what Perlmutter probably meant by "polycentric." He claims that "a polycentric firm, literally, is a loosely connected group with quasi-independent subsidiaries as centers–more akin to a confederation" and he argued that "European multinational firms are more inclined to develop into that pattern" (Perlmutter, 1969: 12f). In cultural studies, these behavioral patterns are often trivialized as "let the Romans do it their way." What seems evident within the polycentric mindset is that an understanding of just how much the local situational context matters prevails. This remains a hotly debated issue, but the struggle to find out to what degree it matters is the motivating force to reverse identified stereotypes and organizational habits. New communication practices are thus endorsed to question the existing belief systems (Rattan & Georgeac, 2017).

The geocentric or "world-oriented" approach, whose design emanated from multinational firms' need to rely more on the existing and emerging repository of capabilities of foreign locations is supplemented by the implicit agreement between top executives that it is tedious to implement one's *standards* everywhere. Moreover, the geocentric orientation overcomes a costly misconception, namely the enforcement of a rigid and uniform solution developed by the headquarters, while the real problem is causally rooted in a constantly changing, heterogeneous environment (Perlmutter, 1969: 13). The term *geocentric* indicates that some if not all geographical regions matter more for the multinational as a whole.

However, we still need to establish why and how they matter. Nevertheless, the increasing status of subsidiaries in foreign countries is due not only because they act as "hosts" there but also because subsidiaries are the key to generating a better and deeper understanding of local markets. The identity of these subsidiaries is changing from a unit receiving orders, advice, and information from the presumably omniscient headquarters to an entity providing "skills" and more and more "advanced technical knowledge." Perlmutter concurred with the chairman of Unilever, who claimed in the late 1960s, "We want to Unileverize our Indians and Indianize our Unileverans" (quoted in Perlmutter, 1969: 13).

Reading this quote today, we feel it is inappropriate to speak of "our Indians" but the progressivity hidden in the claim, "we want to Indianize our Unileverans," signifying an attitude of preparedness to learn from the other, is also a totally reversed understanding of the upcoming role of managing the differences in the multiple subsidiaries of a multinational firm.

The above quote expresses the intention of Unilever to implement not only their extant mindset in India, and thus figuratively socialize the local hosts with the existing home-grown rules based on their standards, but also to open up the mentality of Unilever to Indian ways and values. This is remarkable because, in 1970, two-thirds of Unilever's profits, sales, and capital were generated in Europe, about 15% in North and South America, 14% in Africa, and only about 7% in the rest of the world (Unilever, 1970: 8).

However, the mere use of "ours" and "us" to signify the importance of affiliates does not imply a confederation, which is a union of sovereign units or affiliates that establish common governance between increasingly independent units.

Perlmutter's notion of the multinational firm as a confederation is probably based on perceiving it as ideal cooperation between headquarters and subsidiaries and predates or is similar to the concept of heterarchy developed by Gunnar Hedlund (Finkelstein, 2018; Hedlund, 1986). In a truly confederated system, all members remain sovereign and reserve the right to withhold consent, which is often akin to blocking joint measures. Subsidiaries, conversely, are neither sovereign nor do they have a factual right to withhold such consent. However, between subsidiaries and headquarters, and even without a common formal approach, implicit and informal dependence is a common denominator.

Relations within the multinational firm remain hierarchical but adopting a more moderate and inclusive management approach may allow headquarters to explore and exploit subsidiary knowledge developed in multiple other regions. It thus remains an elusive question over whether governance systems can ever be non-hierarchical or a heterarchy (Hedlund, 1986).

Perlmutter's perception of the mental mindset ("Geisteshaltung") of top executives assumes that managers endorse stereotypical patterns in dealing with foreign affiliates that are often caricatured in the media and television. It would be too much of a digression here to delve into the origins of the conception of how exactly the individual might have produced stereotyped images about foreignness. Nevertheless, stereotyping cultural traits into two opposing poles generates discrimination, thereby further separating management from its foreign subsidiaries.

Zygmunt Bauman asserted that the ambivalent alteration of identity established by the home-grown, local, "us" delineates one group's identity from the "other" (i.e., foreigners). He argued that any attempt at coordination to achieve symmetry is an illusion, as it merely reproduces subalternation (Bauman, 1990). Although subalternity is a term usually employed in ethnography and sociological studies, it perfectly fits the tensions arising in modern multinational firms attempting to control, integrate, and coordinate different products and activities in scattered nations. The expressive denomination of ethnocentrism in Perlmutter's metaphorical account in the 1970s captured multinational corporations prevailing system of thoughts that characterize the existing attributes of modern management approaches that try to instill allegiance and loyalty within and beyond a network of business activities performed by dependent but essentially disconnected agents. Nonetheless, Perlmutter recognized the fragility of each mechanism. Indeed, multinational firms are more dependent on a narrow hierarchical order established across affiliates' systems and do not function like a confederation of subsidiaries. The ethnocentric management mentality was, in certain ways, the unquestioned approach for running a multinational firm in its heyday when multinationals were rapidly expanding into unknown territories.

These early approaches to the management of international business firms can be categorized by how they deal with the problem of their home-grown capacity to effectively manage multiple foreign locations and how the perception of foreignness affects management embedded in somewhat path-dependent mental frames such as ethnocentric, polycentric, and geocentric mind maps. The solution was sought in management skills that enable the firm to deal more effectively with the difficulties arising from heterogeneous political, economic, and cultural environments.

A somewhat simplified answer may be that all these approaches were confined to the task of overcoming the problems of transferring established business practices at home to multiple foreign locations. An extension of that perspective led to management approaches that focused once more on the question of how structure befits an international firm's strategies. Thus, the failure and success of multinational firms were explained not by a lack of strategy or indeed a wrong strategy but by a fundamental misfit between strategy and structure (Qiu & Donaldson, 2012).

The classical account of the intricate relationship between strategy and structure in multinational firms was elaborated by Stopford and Wells in 1972, which is discussed in the following section.

7.5 The Stopford/Wells Model

The multinational firms' need to respond to multiplied complexity and deal with increasing uncertainty in diversified and unfamiliar markets was widely acknowledged in the 1960s and early 1970s. However, the real challenge was in changing the organizational structure of the multinational firm, which was rapidly growing and expanding faster into multiple foreign markets with ever more products. This challenge was the result of increasing difficulties in managing multiple international markets. Management needed information and a new totalizing concept by which to organize the tensions between numerous independent and highly diversified products and markets.

In their classic study "Managing the Multinational Enterprise," Stopford and Wells (1972) explored how rapidly expanding multinational enterprises were pressured to find an organizational structure that would fit the heterogeneous needs of steadily growing international markets. The problem that Stopford and Wells observed was twofold. On the one hand, there were firms expanding into multiple markets with the same or similar products. The question was then how these firms could effectively manage this challenge. On the other hand, such firms needed to organize the multiplicity of products they had to offer. In other words, the underlying cause of the problem was not the number of different markets but rather the number of products, each of which required idiosyncratic treatment. However, the information flow within the organizational structure at the time did not fully support these two evolving growth trajectories.

Stopford and Wells conducted their study as a part of the larger "Harvard Multinational Enterprise Project" that began in 1965 under the auspices of Raymond Vernon. What the authors had initially recognized was that all multinational firms in their sample "varied widely [in their] response to the complex nature" caused by the challenging pattern of internationalization (Stopford & Wells, 1972). The authors further observed that, during such international expansion, these firms adapted their formerly domestic organizational structures in several stages (Stopford & Wells, 1972: 41).

Stopford and Wells were probably the first to recognize the tension between firms' headquarters and subsidiaries and the challenge resulting from the need to coordinate and control the diverging relations between them in multiple countries under a "common strategy" (Stopford & Wells, 1972: 5).

A major assertion in their study was that "multinational firms differ dramatically in their ability to move products, money, technologies, and managers around the world" and the authors started to explain these differences by focusing on how firms "have altered their structures" (Stopford & Wells, 1972: 5). To address these intriguing questions, they examined how the top management tried to maintain control with more sophisticated strategies in an increasingly complex business environment (Stopford & Wells, 1972: 5). However, upon looking at the prevalent strategies, it became clear that keeping or regaining control required substantial changes in how multinational firms were organized.

In their empirical study, the authors showed that many firms expanded internationally simply by increasing the volume of sales, thereby expanding with a single product group across multiple markets (i.e., John Deere). Firms first internationalized with a product line in which "they had the greatest experience and expertise," as such, exploiting home-grown firm-specific advantages. Firms with a diversified product portfolio that sold successfully in their home markets, however, started to expand into a few foreign markets with many products. Such firms were forced into a different trajectory (Stopford & Wells, 1972: 9). Some of them (e.g., General Motors) assigned the responsibility for all those international markets to one senior executive. Still, others tried to share the responsibility among a small group of executives (Chandler, 1962, 1977).

The general evolution was described as a change from an organizational structure built around specialized functions (U-Form) to a more elaborated multidivisional form, also referred to as the M-form. Stopford and Wells empirically examined these changes in multinational firms by separating them into three stages.

In the first stage, the business firm is managed by a single entrepreneur, the owner and founder of the establishment. In this stage, almost no delegation of administrative tasks takes place and the owner-entrepreneur depends on his personal strengths and weaknesses to manage the firm's affairs. As long as the firm remains small, this does not pose a significant problem.

However, firms growing in size and increasing diversity may come to expect too much from such owner-entrepreneurs who do not have the time and capability to take care of everything. The standard solution is to organize similar activities operating in the so-called functional department, called the second stage by Stopford and Wells. The pooling of functions increases the specialization. However, ever-increasing specialization requires more coordination. Managers responsible for a single functional department need to have the right to make decisions in their area of responsibility, and this right must be delegated to them (Kieser & Kubicek, 1992: 73–75). In every organizational structure, decisions depend on information that is either available, intentionally provided, or is lacking. How organizations cope with information and process critical data is no trivial matter (Perrow, 1999). Increasing size and diversity requires more information to flow smoothly to and from the responsible manager.

Stopford and Wells outlined this transformation from the second to the third stage, which is necessary for firms to be "capable [. . .] of accommodating considerable growth" (Stopford & Wells, 1972: 11). Each of these product divisions (see Fig. 7.1 on the lower left side) was administered by an appointed manager responsible for reporting to the president and managing the functions in his/her department. However, as these firms at stage three started expanding into foreign markets, the inherent diseconomies accelerated. Sooner or later, growing firms still dependent on a traditional functional structure recognized that the current organizational form had become ineffective.

One key observation of Stopford and Wells was that "enlarging the existing structure" did not help but only added complexity (Stopford & Wells, 1972: 15).

Their sample of firms identified a sequence of changes, which they described as changes that occurred at three junctures. Firms with autonomous subsidiaries (from a total of 88 firms in their sample) switched from Stage 2 to Stage 3. Stage 2 (describing the functional structure) was transformed by adding general product managers for each product and additional organizational level. As Fig. 7.1 illustrates, the adaptation of Stage 2 to Stage 3 did not solve the problem but rather added more complexity.

Stopford and Wells delineated the issue by stating, "In large systems the organizational 'distance' between subunits can be so great that a message in any form passed from one to the other becomes lost in the 'noise' introduced by the successive actions to the coordinators" (Stopford & Wells, 1972: 13).

What this early study on organizational change identified was that "the costs of delays and distortion in communication" were huge. Large organizations and their many managerial hierarchies have a limited ability to assimilate and process the information they ultimately receive, which is heavily filtered and distorted. Stopford and Wells demonstrated that the firms in their study could not adequately transform their organizational structure to a more global orientation. This meant that Stage 3 tried to enact a decentralized structure, wherein the multinational firms expanded into multiple markets with more and highly diversified products, which proved to be a better solution than the functional organizational structure. However, the Stage 3 structure was still a suboptimal solution because it evolved within a largely domestic environment.

Nonetheless, these gradual adaptations seemed a pragmatic approach to reacting to the growing challenge in these early days. Stopford and Wells recognized in their study that only 14 firms in their sample of 170 firms had switched from Stage 2 to Stage 3 directly,

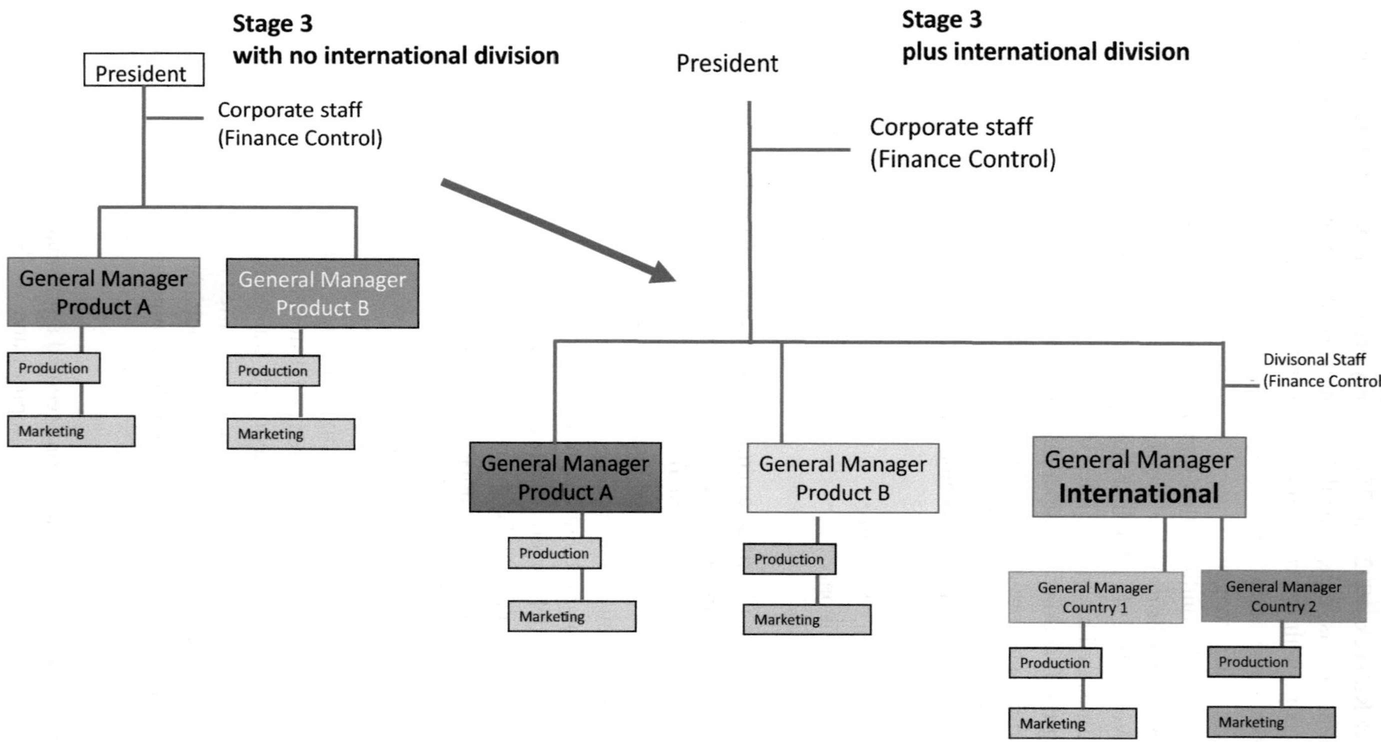

Fig. 7.1 Simplified visualization of changing from stage 2 to stage 3 (Stopford & Wells, 1972: 16)

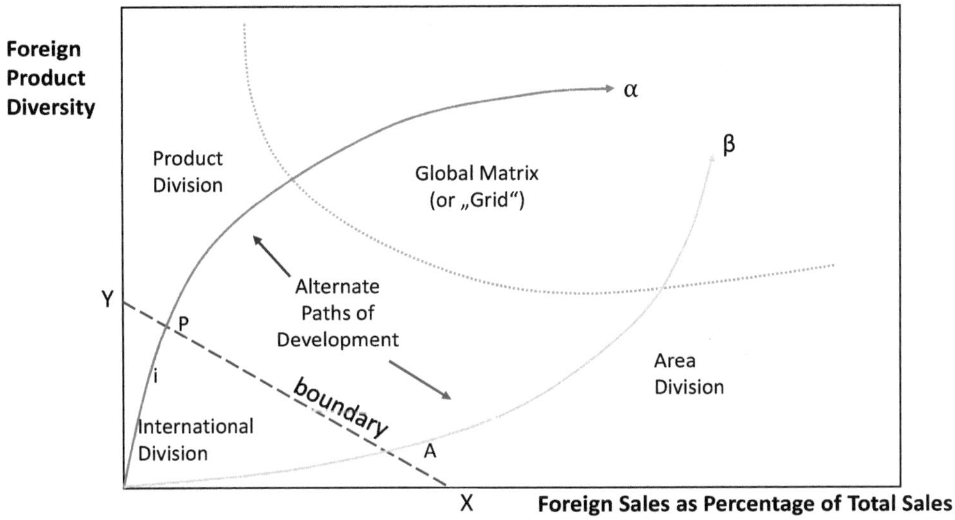

Fig. 7.2 Strategic choices in a multinational firm (source: Stopford & Wells, 1972: 65)

thereby adding to their existing structure an international division (see Fig. 7.1 on the right side).

Change is never simple, however, as it inevitably encounters resistance and all the potential benefits of introducing an international division were offset. Repeating an existing organizational design in a different setting with new personnel does not guarantee that well-established procedures and practices will be replicated elsewhere with the same efficacy. Against that background, incremental and gradual change makes more sense than radical change. However, expansion abroad increasingly demands more feasible autonomy in existing subsidiaries, something which could not be provided by the new international division.

In Fig. 7.2, the vector from Y to X marks the limits of the international division in which it is still possible to operate effectively according to the needs of a firm's product and markets simultaneously. Starting from this hypothetical boundary, Stopford and Wells delineated how to build a global structure beyond that boundary. The boundary is an approximate estimate, and Y indicates the point corresponding to the case wherein one product accounts for the majority of sales, while X indicates the area where the volume of foreign sales corresponds to the sales of the largest domestic product division. The lines denoted as "Alpha" and "Beta" illustrate two typified growth trajectories representing two possible strategic choices. The course of the Alpha curve marks the obvious (possible) strategic options over an unspecified period of time, whereby A indicates the beginning of a more rapid expansion of foreign sales. An international division, responsible for all foreign business, is established in the period denoted by i, and is replaced by a worldwide product-oriented division denoted by *P*. The second firm started internationalizing in a similar fashion but followed a trajectory exemplified along the Beta line. This firm established an area division at point A. Each of the trajectories in Fig. 7.2 is an idealized development path, and Stopford and Wells remind us that much of the needed change in an organization occurs with a severe time lag (Stopford & Wells, 1972: 66).

Example
Firms like Philips, Shell, and Nestlé that established area divisions early on could exercise more power and autonomy in host country markets but experienced greater difficulties in coordinating the development of products and maintaining scale economies in the manufacturing process. Firms that established global product divisions were significantly more sensitive to the local needs of host countries but were less effective in integrating activities across countries to exploit synergies (Birkinshaw & Terjesen, 2003).

Stopford and Wells proposed a structural innovation that would enable multinational firms to effectively manage these two conflicting demands. In Fig. 7.2, parallel trajectories are shown for two hypothetical firms, indicating that a solution may be to establish an international area division and/or an international product division. However, both structural solutions will become increasingly entangled in conflicts that will take up more and more of their precious time (Birkinshaw & Terjesen, 2003: 116). The final solution to the increasing complexity of international growth became known as the grid structure or matrix organization. A simplified version of the grid structure is illustrated in Fig. 7.3.

The critical switching part of the grid structure is where the general manager of product A in country Aaa reports to two superior management levels. One is the general manager leading the international division (1) and the other is the general manager (2) heading the regional (area Aa) department.

The grid structure not only integrated different communication flows between separated divisions but also soon became the source of conflicts. In cases where the matrix structure did work, it was less the result of the structural design than the strong personality of the leading manager (Stopford & Wells, 1972: 89). Consequently, after a few years, many multinational firms returned to either an area division or a product division.

After the hype of the 1980s, most firms "retreated from the pure form" (Birkinshaw & Terjesen, 2003: 117). Further, the research on the strategies and structures of multinational firms was largely marginalized in the early 1990s by other emerging topics focusing on the role of subsidiaries and the challenge of organizing knowledge flows.

The matrix organization was intended to curb the tendency of the diverging product and country-oriented divisions to become more and more independent, as its aim was to ensure the integration of different departments without losing customer and market proximity. The main advantage of the matrix organization was the broadening of perspectives (cf. Schreyögg, 1999: 184) that was intended to unite two different orientations in the company without losing too much from its functional specialization. However, this form of

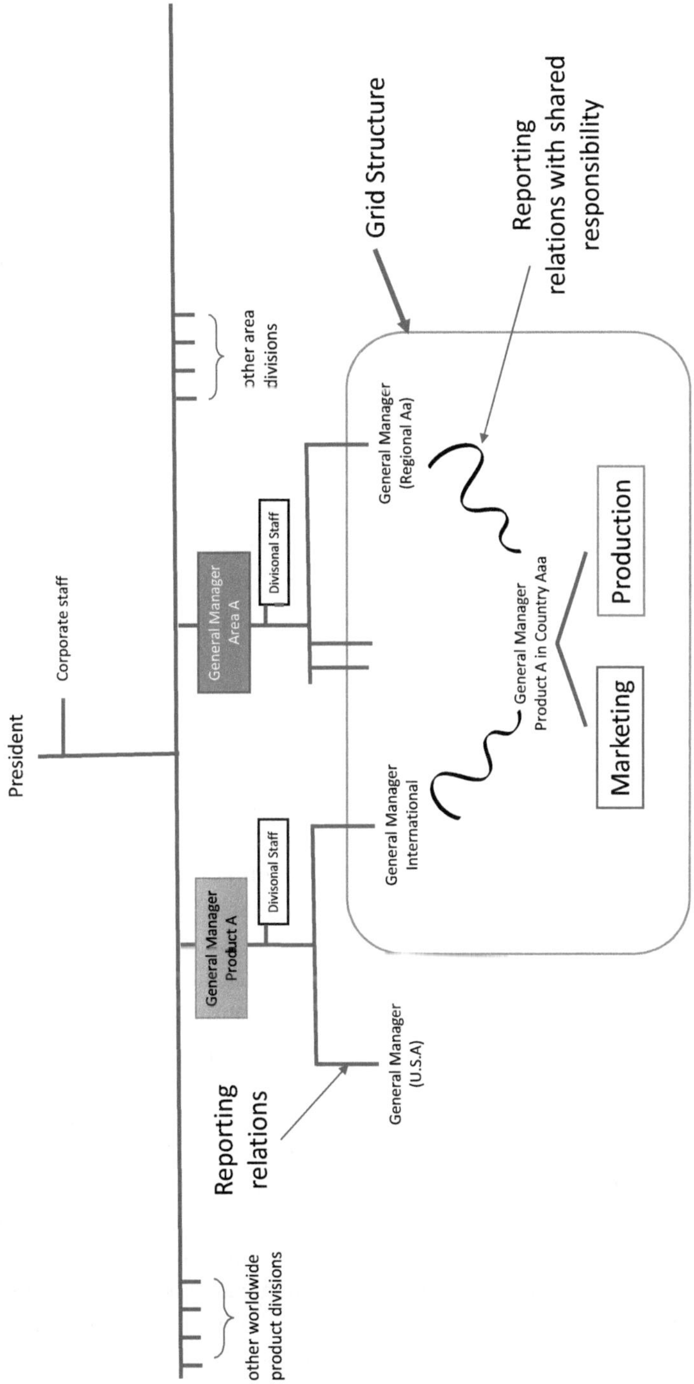

Fig. 7.3 A grid structure (source: Stopford & Wells, 1972: 88)

organization required complex and sometimes conflicting voting procedures. The primary objective was to facilitate the central coordination of decentralized units without losing their flexibility and strength (Egelhoff & Wolf, 2017; Wolf & Egelhoff, 2002, 2013).

Dow Chemical was one of the first companies to introduce the global matrix structure designed by Stopford and Wells; after years of bad experiences, however, it returned to its traditional method of responsible area directors. It turned out that the proposed organizational matrix was in practice too slow, conflictual, inflexible, and associated with high information costs caused by extensive travel and many meetings. Even today, Dow is still advocating for the permanent integration of the multiple perspectives of all its employees and departments.

Example

"Every day, Dow's 43,000 employees in 40 countries—our human element—combine their different perspectives to constantly improve our organization and the products and services we deliver. Because we know that the diversity of our employees gives us a distinct competitive advantage, our vision is to build a workforce that reflects the populations we recruit from in the places we do business today and tomorrow. We make an effort to ensure that our beliefs about the importance of diversity and inclusion enhance our employees' experience at Dow" (www.dow.com/diversity).

However, by and large, the matrix organization could not solve the upcoming problems of highly diversified international firms expanding to multiple markets. However, several authors continue to argue that "the matrix structure is a familiar but poorly understood" structural design (Egelhoff & Wolf, 2017: V; Wolf & Egelhoff, 2013). The key argument for the matrix organization is that this "most complex form of organization" is still capable of addressing the critical challenges of organizing and managing a large multinational firm (Egelhoff & Wolf, 2017: 1).

Although we lack space here to elaborate on this insightful critique of the apparent misunderstanding of the matrix structure, the key point that Egelhoff and Wolf made above seems to be that the matrix design still offers superior capacity for more effective and efficient information processing (2017: 37).

Organizational designs provide the underlying formal and informal framework for how information is produced, collected, and delivered, and each design also determines how all this information is interpreted. In this context, interpretation is broadly defined as how information X from person A is understood by person B, embedded in the same or different subunit. Egelhoff and Wolf emphasize that we need to understand the existing "information-processing framework" and highlight that communication is determined by the "organizational distance" (closeness) maintained by a "formal organizational structure" (Egelhoff & Wolf, 2017). They further clarify that the macrostructure (an accepted and agreed measure) determines the type of information used in a company and that the "processing" of information is affected by its intentional "purpose and perspective" of communication (Egelhoff & Wolf, 2017: 49).

A highly informative literature review provided by Egelhoff and Wolf focusing on prevailing conflicts in existing firms reveals that the significant frictions in a matrix structure are caused by tensions arising from power struggles among key managers (e.g., Philips) while a strong common culture may moderate conflicts (e.g., ABB). Conflicts may escalate when regional managers directly address top management while bypassing others (e.g., Bosch). Moreover, disputes often arise due to tensions between functional departments and business units (e.g., Serono), while in strong multi-product competitive markets (e.g., Procter & Gamble), a source of conflict may be tensions between regional and product managers (Egelhoff & Wolf, 2017: 111).

Nevertheless, the core objective of any matrix structure was to allow the exploitation of scale economies and to increase synergies between seemingly autonomous divisions, formally designated as area or product-oriented (Kieser & Kubicek, 1992: 270). The issues surrounding the exploitation of potential benefits arising from economies of scale and synergies resulting from economies of scope were later discussed under the heading of 'ambidexterity' (Birkinshaw et al., 2016; Christofi et al., 2021; Raisch & Birkinshaw, 2008; Scuotto et al., 2020).

7.6 The Heterarchical Multinational Firm

Gunnar Hedlund's approach to analyzing the structural problems of multinational corporations is based on his contention that the existing modern theories of the multinational firm can provide only a narrow answer to the most intriguing questions the subject raises (Hedlund, 1984, 1986, 1993, 1994). Traditional theories of the MNC are focused on the question of hierarchy. Managing the impediments in large organizations beyond those caused by the benefits derived from hierarchical relations has always remained a question of how structure affects the performance of an organization. While structure is always part of the solution, Hedlund addressed the question of organizational patterns from a new angle. Using "hypermodern" as a prefix to the multinational firm, he claimed that the traditional descriptions of the modern multinational firm do not adequately portray the most critical developments because they neglect the tension that is infinitely evolving in a constantly changing environment.

What hierarchy means is lost in the everyday use of this term, so Hedlund regretted that "[w]e have [become] so accustomed to the concept of hierarchy that we forget exactly what it is that we want to conceive with it" (Hedlund, 1986: 10). Hedlund thus favored the term "heterarchy"; he conceded, however, that it was no less problematic but was nevertheless superior to "hierarchy," a term which should not be conflated with the meaning of hierarchy in transaction cost economics.

As companies grow and expand abroad, coordination problems are intensified by more complex and uncertain environments. As the number of positions and organizational layers in the firm multiplies, it becomes increasingly challenging to coordinate the activities of the several jobs distributed throughout a heterogeneous organizational entity, such as headquarter functions, affiliates, business units, etc., to accomplish a common corporate goal. Coordination between similar and diverse activities turns out to be more arduous because of the lack of communication.

Hierarchy is constituted by a strict ranking of authority enacted by a chain of orders in the way that superior organizational ranks (i.e., managerial positions) exert command over lower ranks. We understand hierarchy as a mechanism that establishes order in a world facing potential chaos.

This old prejudice has remained in focus since Thomas Hobbes's opus magnum *The Leviathan* in 1651 (Martinich, 2021; Orbell & Rutherford, 1973). The creation of order—in the conventional and more commonly accepted conception—is associated with dominance. However, Max Weber's conception of *Herrschaft* (referring to rule, domination) has not been easy to attain. Weber knew that the concept of domination is not unambiguous. Weber confessed the shoemaker rules over him, but in a certain sense, he rules over the shoemaker.

A version of *Herrschaft* is understood as being capable of commanding and forcing a free person to carry out particular actions or omissions (Weber, 2015, 21/4: 5). Weber defined *Herrschaft* as follows: "Herrschaft in its most general concept, not related to any concrete content, is one of the most important elements of collective action. It is true that not all common action shows a dominant structure" (Weber, 2015, 21/4: 5). The important point to note here is that the ability to rule is needed for organizing collective action. It is perceived as one of the most important elements of collective action although not all common actions are based on following a prescribed rule (i.e., *Herrschaft*). Weber thus also added, "Without exception, all areas of collective action show the deepest influence of a dominant design (*Herrschaftgebilde*)" and pointed at the *common goal* to which each form of rulership (*Herrschaft*) pertains some form of rationality (Weber, 2015, 21/4: 5). Returning to the problems of structure in multinational firms, Hedlund's conception of heterarchy alludes to the instability of common goals that he diagnosed as the major problem.

Diagnosing the problem that way seeks a feasible solution to the dilemma of finding a common goal and a shared corporate culture. Hedlund argued that hierarchies create relations of domination that are supposed to guarantee the integration of different objects and actions. However, large multinational firms do not necessarily have a single common goal but rather strive toward many (often contradicting) objectives and perform several highly diversified activities within and between firm boundaries. The solution is then not solely about maintaining the effective integration of different and scattered actions but rather lies in an inherent dilemma in large organizations. The common resolution aims to address differences and how they can be avoided or assimilated. The panacea is seen in an all-encompassing and unifying common cultural identity. Therefore, building common ground becomes the primary responsibility of management.

Any traditional approach sees hierarchy as an intentional measure to fulfill different tasks by ensuring effective coordination. Coordination is necessary to accomplish order and hierarchy (originally meaning 'holy order') is needed for maintaining and implementing order among different activities (and different people) distributed among different organizational layers, locations, and persons. Small collectives can, however, also share a common 'holy order' that is much more accessible, no matter how metaphorical or mythical it is. Their reciprocal and close relationships and the close ties that exist among individuals sharing the same characteristics make it easier to construct a shared belief system. However, when people, who may never meet and who do not know much about each other, are asked to adopt a common belief system, they need to construct an abstract or artificial commonality. Bridging multiple organizational layers, locations, and people thus relies on a solid form of hierarchy to enable effective coordination in large complex organizations (Kieser & Kubicek, 1992: 82). The evident and traditional answer to this problem seems to be a proper hierarchy. It is a hierarchy that first needs to be established. Hierarchical relationships work only if the universal legitimacy that enacts them is accepted. With growing differentiation and more significant heterogeneity, the once established and sound mechanisms of hierarchical control may get into difficulties because the objects and actions no longer share a common ground or identity, causing the hierarchy to lose its legitimacy, which was gradually developed much earlier in different environments in much smaller and more cohesive groups, and cannot be re-enacted (Bauman, 1990).

Hierarchy is based on a conflicting model for managers; subordinates expect respect, tolerance, forbearance, and participation from those in superior positions who in turn expect the efficient execution of assigned tasks (Neuberger, 1995: 88). According to Weber (2015, Vol 21/4: 6), employees are dependent on employers, but employers are also reliant on employees. Nevertheless, enacting hierarchy in large organizations marginalizes the aspect of the inherently important reciprocity in such relationships.

Staehle et al. denote that the vertical formation of jobs in a hierarchical design is defined as "a hierarchical structure of positions [that] is the result of asymmetrical distributions of power. Positions are placed in a system of superordinate, inferior, and subordinate ranks. The ranking of a job in the pyramid is primarily determined by the task, whereby those with predominantly decision-making tasks are given the right to issue instructions (line approach) and are given a position in the upper and middle sections of the hierarchical pyramid and those with predominantly operating tasks (operating functions) are placed at the base" (Staehle et al., 1999: 701).

Given that a system of relationship structures alone cannot fix problems arising from such asymmetrical relations, communicative effectiveness does not necessarily depend on a firm's information-processing capacity.

However, a hierarchical system is more effective in accomplishing this purpose under certain conditions, such as when the framework of what is done (the task itself) and the environment (in which this task is carried out) significantly changes or not. In presumably stable environments, hierarchy is considered more efficient because many decisions in routine situations do not need to be repeated. Heterarchy stems from the Greek terms *heteros* and *hetero* meaning "the other" and, according to Hedlund, can be interpreted as the "other" source of hierarchy, based not necessarily on the strict hierarchical ranking of authority and its rigid system of lines of order. Heterarchy in Hedlund's approach is searching for a different, less hierarchical source to govern "hypermodern" multinational firms.

The question, then, is *where* this source comes from and *how* it is defined. The heterarchical multinational in Hedlund's conception is "different on both in structure and strategy" (Hedlund, 1986: 20). The dominant strategy exploits the advantages grown and nurtured in several subsidiaries. The strategy of Hedlund's heterarchical firm rests not on the capability to identify those factors in an industry environment that defines the competitive forces but in the capacity to "define [multinational firm's] structural properties and then look for strategic options" that emerge from their structural capabilities (Hedlund, 1986: 20). In Hedlund's heterarchical concept, structure defines the strategic opportunities that management develops in order to stay competitive.

Hedlund's heterarchical conception focuses on the potential strengths of motivating the "multiplicity of contributors or centers" in a multinational firm, thereby signifying multiplicity as the critical source of a firm's competitive advantages. Hedlund's three types of multinational firms—illustrated in Table 7.3—show how through different orientations these firms cope with the emerging problem of increasing complexity in foreign markets. The table introduces the differences in approaches between the ethnocentric, the polycentric, and geocentric organizational forms across markets. Each firm variant exploits the multiplicity of firm-specific advantages at different locations (Hedlund, 1986: 21). Consequently, management in a multinational subsidiary is conceived as a responsibility "not only for [the subsidiary itself] but for the [multinational] as a whole" (Hedlund, 1986: 22). While in the traditional version of strategy in the multinational firm, a "top-down" (see the ethnocentric version in Table 7.3) approach was dominant, "hypermodern multinationals" are governed by a non-hierarchical model, fueled by the vision of an almost symmetrical network of not only interrelated subsidiaries (again, see the types of interdependence in Table 7.3) but of interactions within the organizational structure that are not one-sided but are, to a large extent, equal. Not surprisingly, such a major shift diminishes and substantially shifts the role of headquarters (or core centers) as it implies a shift between home and host country relations wherein all *hetero*geneous locations contribute to "a corporate level strategy [. . .] in a geographically scattered network" (Hedlund, 1986: 22).

7.7 Diverging Worlds in Global Strategies

The antithesis to this debate on organizational efficiency was popularized by an influential and successful book authored by George Yip, who programmatically titled his answer to the question of how much local responsiveness is needed in multinational firms as the Yip (1995). Success was linked to the implementation of a global approach to managing

Table 7.3 The heterarchical structure of the MNC

	Ethnocentrism	Polycentrism	Geocentrism
Importance of Foreign Business	Marginal	Substantial/dominant	Dominant
Basis for International Strategy	Exploit firm specific advantages	Market size, scale and scope economies, finance	Competition, multinationality as such
Expansion mode	Gradual, concentric, green-field	Market driven, acquisitions, cash-constrained	Quick, direct, competition driven
Organization structure	Mother/daughter international division	Mother/daughter, international division, holding company	Global Division, or matrix organization
Type of interdependence	Sequential center-subsidiary	Pooled center-subsidiary	System of sequential and reciprocal
Governance mode	Hierarchy	Market	Normative, coercive
Specialization value added chain	Specialization up-downstream, HQ subsidiaries	Duplication	Specialization up-downstream between subsidiaries
Control style	HQ-derived, coercive, normative	Calculative	Normative, coercive
MNC Internationalization environment	Placid-random type I	Placid-Clustered Type II	Disturbed-reactive, turbulent, Type III => IV
Subsidiary Environment	Type I, II	Type I, II, III	Type III => IV
Autonomy of Subsidiaries	Low medium	High	Low-Medium
Strategic Role of Subsidiary	Implement local strategy	Formulate + implement local strategy	Implement + adapt to global strategy
Recruitment and Rotation	Home-country managers, much rotation	Local managers, little rotation	Mixed, TCNs, much rotations

Source: Hedlund (1986: 17)

the multinational firm. Even though the term "global" became more and more controversial in later years, it still dominated and continues to dominate the debate on how to manage a multinational firm (Rugman & Verbeke, 2004). However, another landmark study shifted the narrative on managing standardized global corporate policies to how a firm can be more responsive to an increasingly divergent foreign environment. This approach was popularized by Sumantra Ghoshal and Christopher Bartlett in their bestselling study titled *The Transnational Corporation* (1989). It was enacted years later by Yves Doz and his coauthors in a book called *From Global to Metanational: How Companies Win in the Knowledge Economy* (Doz et al., 2001). The authors addressed the notion of radical change that looked at building efficient and integrated clusters of production, sales, and services performed in many globally dispersed subsidiary locations to respond to the new challenge of sourcing the knowledge and opportunities needed to develop technologies and markets. The mission statement was thus updated from "penetrating markets around the world" to "learning from the world" (Doz et al., 2001). The notion of metanationality points to the merit that a multinational firm generated if it succeeded in overcoming national barriers. The core idea behind this premise is that a firm benefits from leaving national concerns behind, thereby breaking free from the burden of different geographies. The benefits come from the newly generated capability to learn from worldwide, divergent, and ever-present locations translated into steadily emerging innovations.

Pertinent examples of this new version of the multinational firm include Airbus, IBM, and Hewlett-Packard. It is argued that these companies successfully managed to access, mobilize, and leverage globally dispersed knowledge from their subsidiaries around the world as well as their key suppliers and customers (Doz et al., 2001: 3). The key to such success, according to the authors, lies in exploiting the knowledge that exists outside their subsidiaries as it is embedded in the globally existing network of operations (Doz et al., 2001: 3). This approach argues that the management of such multinationals need to build a skill set that would allow them to identify any potentially valuable technology. Next, management must focus on mobilizing these technologies by converting them into new products which need to be developed to capture their full profit potential (Doz et al., 2001: 8–9). One key message proffered by the authors is that these potentials cannot be exploited and leveraged in purely national markets or with a few lead domestic customers; indeed they can only be harnessed by becoming *metanational.*

Behind all these allusions and book titles, we can identify an ongoing tension between the need to coordinate and configure conflicting goals and activities across a scattered network of firm affiliates and markets. Most approaches can be understood as an attempt to overcome the old highly ethnocentric and logocentric approach to managing the multinational firm. Most of these approaches argue that a successful firm needs to adopt a mentality or mode of organization that fits the complex diversity in international companies and markets. Therefore, whether the individual—often cross-departmental—value-added activities within the multinational firms are described as global, international, multinational, or transnational is very often related to the fact that most of these studies addressed the need of top executives to grasp the challenges of a dynamically changing and complex world. Rugman (2005), a committed campaigner against the unreflective use of the usually vaguely defined label "global," demonstrated in a study that few multinational firms deserve the "global" epithet. Some multinational firms can be classified as "multinational" or as "global" and still others as "metanational" or "transnational" but the types of organizational definitions adopted in the literature are always to be understood only as ideal concepts that rarely fit the day-to-day reality.

Behind all these attempts to find a uniform definition of an internationally active company remains the ever-present challenge of designing the right strategy and the appropriate structure to match the goals and objectives of the internationalizing firm. This is not only a question of finding a suitable administrative design to carry out different activities within a scattered firm network but also how to establish normative values and develop an organizational mentality or culture that would fit different modes of coordination and configuration of core value-adding activities in different foreign environments.

7.8 The Transnational Approach and the Needs of the Multinational Firm

The search for an appropriate organizational structure for the diversified multinational firm has remained an important question in international business management. Christopher Bartlett and Sumantra Ghoshal claimed in a popular study (Birkinshaw & Terjesen, 2003: 117) that deficiencies in structure are responsible for the inefficiencies of many multinational firms. These authors claimed that "the disappointments and failures [that] some companies have encountered in their international operations were not due primarily to inappropriate strategic analysis, but to organizational deficiencies" (Bartlett & Ghoshal, 1989: 4).

One of the insights yielded by their clinical studies of nine multinational firms (General Electric, Philips, Matsuhisa, Procter & Gamble, Unilever, Kao, ITT, Ericsson, and NEC) was that they were curious about how sensible and knowledgeable managers had been to recognize the sources of the global competitiveness in their firms.

Therefore, the authors declared that the problem seemed not so much knowing what to do but how to implement what these firms already knew. Still, the answer presented was far from simple, as the proposed structure that allows a better fit in multiple (i.e., not one) dynamically changing environments was needed. The apparent answer revolved around how the multinational firm seems to be better prepared to generate the knowledge, know-how, and organizational capabilities to attain a more sustainable or proper fit (Bartlett & Ghoshal, 1989). However, the real challenge lies in developing those capabilities within a dynamic firm network of plural relationships that enable the firm to implement what is necessary (Table 7.4).

A central question in managing a multinational firm has always been how to align diverse needs within and across different countries. As mentioned, international business is focused on the study of the international activities of the firm.

As discussed in Chap. 4, it was primarily discussed as the problem of finding a suitable entry mode that would fit an unfamiliar environment.

The dynamic structure of the global economy, numerous disruptive technologies, and volatile markets pushed multinational firms to rethink traditional concepts such as location,

Table 7.4 Structure and Strategy and the MNC

Features	MNU	Global	International	Transnational
Configuration of skills and assets	Decentralized and autonomous at national level	Centralized and focused on global fixed cost degression advantages	Sources of centralized capabilities are centralized, others decentralized	Distributed, interdependent and specialized
Role of subsidiaries	Identify and implement localization requirements	Implementation of the guidelines of the parent company	Application and implementation of the competences of the parent company	Differentiated contributions of the national subsidiaries in an integrated network
Development and diffusion of knowledge	Knowledge is developed in the subsidiaries and remains there	Knowledge is developed in the parent company and transferred to the subsidiaries	Knowledge is developed at the center and transferred to subsidiaries	Knowledge is jointly developed and shared worldwide.

Source: Bartlett and Ghoshal, Managing Across Borders, 1989

competition, firm-specific resources, firm boundaries, knowledge, and learning. Choosing the most suitable entry mode is then transformed into the problem of how to operate and control a set of multiple entry modes while adapting each to dynamically changing environments.

Managing the multinational firm is, therefore, often thought of as coordinating different business groups or integrating fragmented value-adding activities carried out by subsidiaries, different divisions and departments, and often a long list of suppliers. Therefore, management needed to coordinate their actions not only to compete but increasingly to also cooperate with rival firms. Managing a multinational firm for that reason required strategies to coordinate and organize people—despite significant variations in their national origins and culture—within and across the boundaries of the so-called single multinational firm (Buckley & Casson, 2019; Foss, 2002; Jones, 2002; Kale & Singh, 2007; Teece et al., 1997).

7.8.1 Managing Conflicting Demands Within the Multinational Firm

Depending on their size, most firms organize operations by finding a structure that will fit their strategy.

The most common firm structure was based on the need to lead divergent business divisions that were profiled historically, following the requirements of mainly nationally operating companies. In most cases, the ethnocentric national firm was not well prepared for the challenges posed by international business activities (Perlmutter, 1954, 1969; Perlmutter & Shapiro, 1957). Others, for example Bartlett and Ghoshal do not entirely depart from this view but shift their focus to establishing how to manage a multinational firm. Based on their study, they start with the assumption that three major tasks need to be organized within an existing multinational network of relations. First, management needs to focus on maintaining operational efficiency throughout the firm. Second, firms cannot ignore the pressure from local markets for responsiveness. Third, success depends on the capability to enact worldwide learning within a network of relations operating within the multinational firm (Bartlett & Ghoshal, 1989: 10–13). None of the three capabilities—focusing on enhancing efficiency, elaborating responsiveness, and firm-wide learning, respectively—are in any way new. Nevertheless, the argument that multinational firms that are focused on one capability can shift their strategy and structure to symmetrically and equally strongly exploit all three capabilities throughout the firm network was an entirely novel conception.

7.8.2 The International Management Mentality

The *international management mentality* is characterized by highly formalized, unidirectional, and asymmetrical relations between headquarters and subsidiaries. As summarized in Fig. 7.4, the knowledge flows from headquarters to the subsidiary with no substantial communication the other way round. The role of a subsidiary is thus to follow headquarters instructions and implement its technologies. Subsidiaries are thus merely replicating the knowledge and competencies delivered from a highly centralized headquarters. The supposed network pattern, if there is one, is hierarchical and one-sided, thereby limiting the autonomy of the subsidiary and sacrificing any potential opportunity for exploring alternatives more appropriate for the local environment. The subsidiary's role is narrowed down to exploiting the headquarters' knowledge and capabilities, doing no more than implementing what it receives.

The headquarters is conceived of as the main and exclusive source of business policy. Product and pricing policies in the subsidiary markets are thus designed by the head office. The advantage of this structural mentality is no more than increasing possible scale economies. Products developed by the parent company are sold in foreign markets and raw materials and other resources are supplied back to the parent company. Figure 7.4 schematically outlines the unidirectional and one-sided relationships between headquarters and subsidiaries.

The prevailing mentality of management reflects the superior position of the domestic market of the international firm. With an international mentality, products are primarily produced for the domestic market and technology and know-how are transferred from the

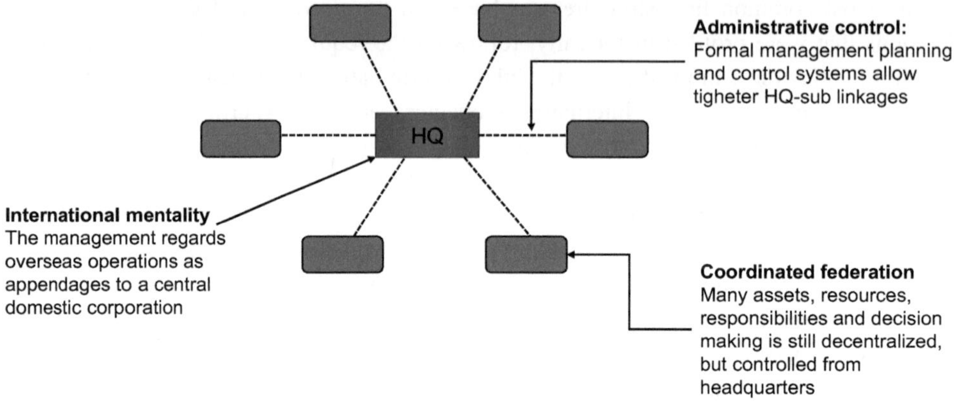

Fig. 7.4 The international management mentality from Bartlett and Ghoshal (1989: 35), reprinted with permission from Harvard Business Press. Copyright 1989 (C) Bartlett & Ghoshal

headquarters, but strict guidelines and tasks are assigned to the subsidiaries. The technology and knowledge of the parent company are used but not further developed by the subsidiaries.

Companies with an international strategy benefit from the diffusion of the parent company's core competencies. Such competencies are developed exclusively at a firm's headquarters. When foreign markets differ from one location to another, this form of organization develops a product-oriented organizational pattern, with a tendency to increase autonomy from the parent company. Headquarters nonetheless keep strict control over the subsidiaries. Stand-alone strategies are associated with this type of structurc wherein operational decisions are decentralized and all strategic decisions of the company are centrally aligned. Low interdependence in operational areas corresponds to the low utilization of potential benefits and in functional areas (e.g., purchasing, production, and sales), no cost advantages are realized through integration.

7.8.3 Global Management Mentality

Bartlett and Ghoshal's second type of management mentality is referred to as a "global mentality." The authors argue that this organizational type was developed and modified by early industrial pioneers such as Henry Ford and John D. Rockefeller, who established global manufacturing capacities to sell standardized products shipped to many foreign markets "under a tightly controlled central strategy" (Bartlett & Ghoshal, 1989: 58). Global managers stayed focused on global markets and tried to manage key capabilities by centralizing their assets and resources. The role of foreign subsidiaries was to assemble and sell products locally and enact strategic plans and policies designed in the headquarters. The headquarters in such an organizational design thus becomes a "centralized hub" that

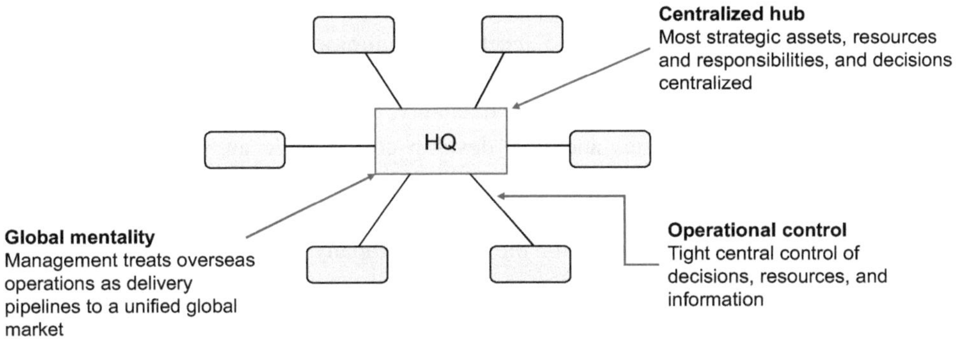

Fig. 7.5 Global management mentality from Bartlett and Ghoshal (1989: 58), reprinted with permission from Harvard Business Press. Copyright 1989 (C) Bartlett & Ghoshal

perceives local subsidiaries as "pipelines to a unified global market" (Bartlett & Ghoshal, 1989: 60). This global management mentality seems a replica of the concept that was enthusiastically sold by Levitt packaged in the message, the "future belongs to those companies that sell the same product, with the same characteristics, all over the world" (Levitt, 1983: 92). The strong competition among subsidiaries blocks any diffusion of assets and knowledge between them. However, direct exchange between subsidiaries is not yet practicable because the head office wants to secure its role as the chief decision-maker in asset allocation. The global orientation of business activities requires the company to have implemented tight central coordination and configuration. The success of the global management mentality is largely determined by the actual globalization of products and successful centralizing coordination and configuration are the key concepts in the global enterprise. The management in global firms are focused on global products, developed in the headquarters (see Fig. 7.5). Contrary to other mentalities, management have a stronger focus on world markets and so subsidiaries receive little or no independence. The world market is designed as a single market. Compared to the other mentalities, the global orientation allows almost no autonomy go exist in subsidiaries and headquarter managers are somewhat obsessed with keeping control on "flows of goods, knowledge, and support" (Bartlett & Ghoshal, 1989: 59).

7.8.4 Multinational Management Mentality

The multinational management mentality was the most widely adopted "classic organizational pattern" (Bartlett & Ghoshal, 1989: 55). The sales and a large share of the profits were generated by the subsidiaries in foreign markets. The distribution of firm resources and responsibilities is thus defined as a decentralized federation wherein a firm's headquarters makes only minor use of the strategic opportunities offered by its subsidiaries in foreign markets. In such a setup, managerial control is based on strong personal relationships and informal, normative processes. Nonetheless, subsidiaries are capable of modifying products and strategies to meet the requirements of their local customers; further, management strategies can be modified to fit the needs of important national markets. In the multinational management mentality, the subsidiaries follow and generate independent business strategies and thus develop considerable autonomy in important markets.

The multinational mentality focuses on exploiting the advantages that the localization of assets and responsibilities generate for the whole company but it has limited success in transferring these assets across subsidiaries. Managerial control is exercised through strong and selected personal relationships supplemented by "simple financial control systems" (Bartlett & Ghoshal, 1989: 56). The multinational firm perceives its core tasks in a loose coordination of relatively independent decentralized federation of subsidiaries, exemplified in Fig. 7.6. However, there is no or only limited intra-subsidiary exchange of innovation. Subsidiaries serve their own markets and do not intentionally share their knowledge and assets with other subsidiaries. Subsidiaries with high sales will attain a high degree of autonomy.

Strong subsidiaries develop strategic assets that will serve their strong alignment with the local needs of their national market. However, relatively high autonomy does not necessarily allow for an optimal multinational-wide integration of subsidiaries. One of the reasons for this neglect is that the headquarters do not rely on a tight system of financial control, while each subsidiary remains organized as an independent unit (Bartlett & Ghoshal, 1989: 56).

7.8.5 A Transnational Solution?

Each of these three management types has a specific strength generated within their organizational pattern that has emerged from their specific environmental-strategic-

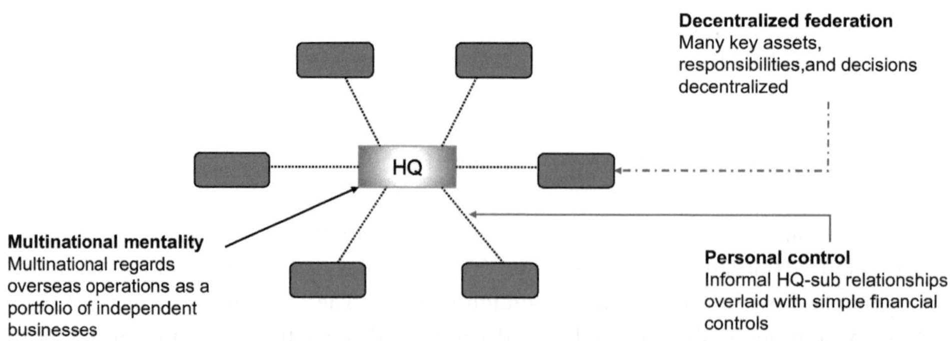

Fig. 7.6 The multinational management mentality from Bartlett and Ghoshal (1989: 57), reprinted with permission from Harvard Business Press. Copyright 1989 (C) Bartlett & Ghoshal

structural context (Bartlett & Ghoshal, 1989: 60). The solution capable of integrating firm-specific assets, which Bartlett and Ghoshal term "transnational," combines the following three competencies: global integration, national responsiveness, and worldwide learning. The solution is provided through the design of an integrated network in which all the previous contradicting forces are equally enacted and maintained within the so-called transnational firm intended to transcend the negative effects of the headquarters' and subsidiaries' national identities. However, the problem of balancing these different centripetal forces remains. The concept initiated an attempt to define and strengthen the roles of subsidiaries (Ambos et al., 2006; Barnard, 2011; Birkinshaw et al., 1998; Gaur et al., 2019; Schmid & Maurer, 2011). The integrated network is further confronted with the need to strike a balance between these three strategic options. Each option (see Fig. 7.7) can be organized across the entire firm or at the level of product division.

Global integration primarily means the consolidation of functional and cross-divisional activities at centralized locational hubs (Ghoshal & Bartlett, 1990; Mees-Buss et al., 2019). For example, establishing the central management of a firm's purchasing activities will result in substantial cost-saving potential. Firm-wide coordination depends on uniform accounting practices. The global integration of geographically dispersed yet jointly coordinated activities promises considerable synergies across specialized activities.

Globally, strategic coordination is fundamentally the coordination of functional activities across divisional boundaries with the aim of exploiting complementary synergy effects. Coordination supplements any managerial decisions on the cross-divisional

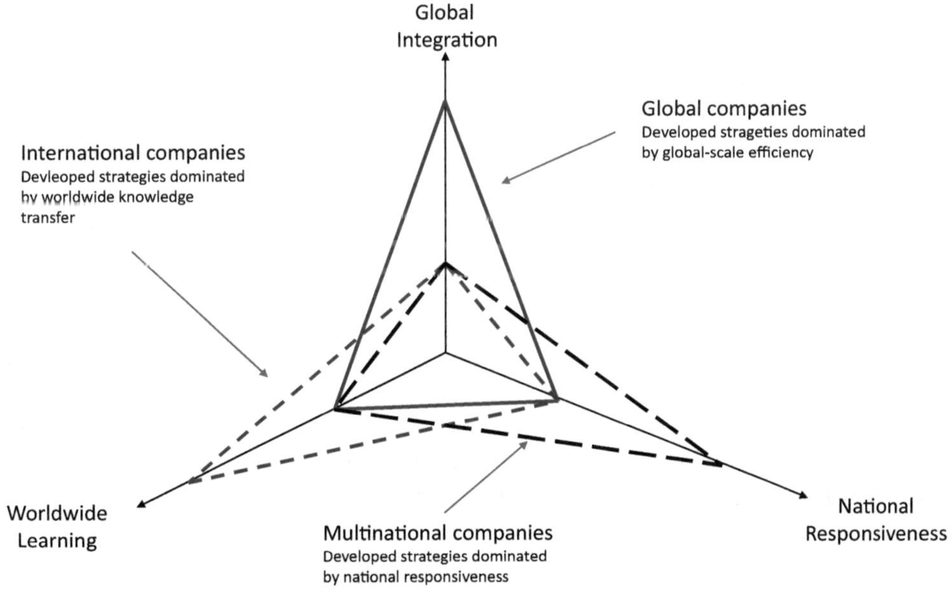

Fig. 7.7 Strategic imperatives from Bartlett and Ghoshal (1989: 66), reprinted with permission from Harvard Business Press. Copyright 1989 (C) Bartlett & Ghoshal

allocation of resources. However, any management decision on the degree of global integration relies on several tacit or implicit activities that need to be coordinated which elude any formal instructions from the center.

7.9 Global Integration or Local Responsiveness

What Bartlett and Ghoshal diagnosed as the key challenge for the transnational firm was a prevalent issue in organizing the diversified multinational firm, especially in the 1980s and 1990s. The underlying rationale for this approach was in finding the right fit between the structure of a multinational firm and its strategy (Donaldson, 2001; Hoskisson et al., 1999; Zott & Amit, 2008). The multinational firm, characterized as an ideal diversified (multibusiness) multinational corporation (DMNC), became increasingly confronted with the multiplicity of demands to coordinate and configure their multiple and diversified business units in a much more competitive environment (Comment & Jarrell, 1995; Prahalad & Doz, 1987). At the same time, a greater interest in multinational firms emerged amid the supposed theoretical advances made in multinational strategy theory and how it could be translated into a more feasible set of policies applicable to managerial behavior (Inkpen, 2004).

As a result, it has become more attractive to take a more integrative approach; in particular, C.K. Prahalad and Yves L. Doz presented an approach closer to the actual "business situation [that] managers in multinational firms [faced]" (Prahalad & Doz, 1987: vii). Strategy for the diversified, multiunit multinational business enterprise became a salient feature and a core subject matter in international business.

However, such a renaissance in strategic approaches has also been criticized for being less grounded in any robust and sound theory (Elango, 2004; Tallman, 2004; Westney, 1993). Nevertheless, the response to these studies was significant. The integration–responsiveness framework, or I/R grid, was not only well-received but was the empirical result of the close observation of firm strategies used by large multinationals to successfully exploit international markets. This new approach defined a novel strategy that was widely applied by practitioners and subsequently entered the strategy books (Doz, 2016; Tallman, 2004).

The successful multinational firm did not only grow considerably but also diversified in multiple markets operating in multiple businesses. The rising competition in multiple markets put more pressure on top management and identifying an ideal fit between structure and strategy in such multi-market competitive environments became more complex (Mees-Buss et al., 2019; Westney, 1993, 2006).

Corning Glass

Corning Glass Works, which was renamed in 1989 to Corning International, was founded in 1851 by Amory Houghton in Somerville, MA, where he opened a small shop specializing in glass manufacturing. In 1877, with the advent of industrialization and the impact of the railway industry, Houghton designed signal lanterns and used his expertise to enable the mass production of Edison's lightbulbs (Bartlett & Yoshino, 1998; Corning, 2022). In 1915, Corning developed Pyrex®, a form of cookware that sold very successfully, first in the US market and later internationally. In 1939, the company diversified into the production of TV cathode tubes, making the technology available to millions of people across the globe. In the 1950s, the company expanded into specialized products for the aerospace industry and in 2007, it invented the Gorilla® Glass used in billions of mobile devices around the world (Corning, 2022).

However, the company struggled to manage its six highly diversified business units, producing nearly 60,000 products for its home and international markets in the early 1970s. Rivalry among subsidiaries abroad, coupled with an absent or weak controlling and auditing system, and decreasing profits, forced the management to change its strategy and structure (Bartlett & Yoshino, 1998).

Corning Glass Works was plagued with the archetypical problems of a fast-growing and highly diversified international firm, and its management was forced to act on the huge losses sustained on the stock market. The company needed to know how to redesign its business strategy as a "large, diversified (multibusiness) multinational" (Prahalad & Doz, 1987: 1). The firm was compelled to act and initiated a profound transformation of its business strategy, starting with a restructuring process that stretched over more than a decade and suffered many setbacks.

In their bestselling *The Multinational Mission: Balancing Local Demands and Global Vision*, Prahalad and Doz proffered that the top management of large DMNCs need to "understand [. . .] the often conflicting forces that affect" their businesses (Prahalad & Doz, 1987: 4). The source of conflict arises from the different forces that either demand more integration or more local responsiveness, both of which cannot be fully harmonized against each other.

Prahalad and Doz identified three major layers that generated the framework for the top management of DMNCs. In each *industry* segment, economic forces exist that affect scale and scope economies; in each market, different *political environments* trigger often uncommon needs for adaptation; in each strategic business unit, several *organizational imperatives* dominate how firm resources can be exploited and mobilized.

Corning Glass Works may have lost its strategic foresight over its six major business units in the 1960s and 1970s (see Fig. 7.8 for an overview) as all were governed by

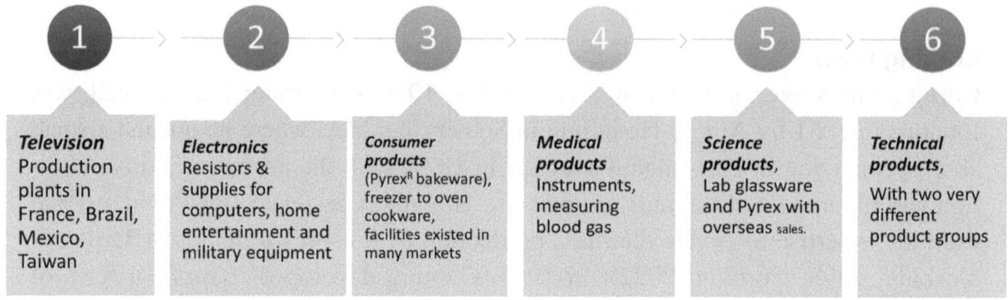

Fig. 7.8 Diversified business units from Bartlett and Yoshino (1998), reprinted with permission from Harvard Business Press

different centripetal forces emanating from heterogeneous organizational demands, economic rationales, and varying political environments.

Each of the six Corning Glass Works business units had been developed amid different environmental landscapes, moving into path-dependent trajectories that provided distinctive challenges and opportunities. However, none of these business units could work internationally on the same unifying business strategy.

While the TV unit had strong country subsidiaries that could exploit scale economies and local markets by supplying key Original Equipment Manufacturers (OEMs), the electronics divisions were kept dependent on a few specialized customers. Nevertheless, mass production was not a key problem, as those few key customers defined how to deliver products and did not require much product differentiation. The bakeware business unit, which manufactured and sold the Pyrex® cookware, was strongly oriented toward the needs of local markets and depended on the strength of its idiosyncratic but very country-specific sales forces. Nevertheless, single-country managers did export to rival markets served by other Corning subsidiaries. The science unit was driven by its strong R&D mentality and was configured along with the needs of three large country markets responsible for almost two-thirds of the total output of the business group. The technical products divisions were highly diversified in products and markets, and only a few manufacturing locations became responsible for exporting to selected overseas markets, although their exports remained marginal compared to the domestic sales of each unit.

The most challenging question for the top management in a DMNC like Corning Glass Works was how to reconcile all the conflicting demands, and how to explore and exploit the firm's extensive resources and capabilities within and across such heterogeneous business units. These business units operated in many different locations (running production facilities in 90 plants, several laboratories, and numerous sales offices) in more than 20 countries managed by more than 300 managers, staffed by almost 46,000 employees (Bartlett & Yoshino, 1998).

7.9.1 Staying Global or Becoming Multi-Domestic

To solve the issue of vastly diverging needs for defining a feasible strategy for the global and multi-domestic multinational firm required determining what is meant by being "global" or "multi-domestic."

> Prahalad and Doz define "global" as any activity that potentially gains by integrating it across country borders and describe "multi-domestic" as a local business carried out across multiple locations (Prahalad & Doz, 1987: 18).

The mere fact that each business is affected by different pressures triggered by (1) the industry environment, (2) competitive markets, and (3) idiosyncratic technological properties result in a bundle of both supporting and contradicting forces that push or pull the business unit (within the multinational firm network) to become either more global (integrative), or stay locally responsive, and/or try to balance both global integration and local responsiveness. All these efforts aim at gaining an adequate (or practicable) fit between structure and strategy in an evolving environment in which the respective business operates.

To make a feasible judgment, Prahalad and Doz (1987: 18–22) identified a total of seven dimensions as the source of generating the pressure needed for a more rigorous *global strategic coordination* and five dimensions affecting the need for local responsiveness.

7.9.2 Forces that Legitimize a More Rigorous Global Strategic Integration

How important is the customer across multiple nations? Each business unit is dependent on the specific needs of its customers. In the case of Corning Glass Works, the TV tube business unit sold a significant volume of its overall production to a few large OEMs (at that time, for example, to Philips and Sylvania). These large OEMs enforced competitive prices on their suppliers and required great effort to support and service the supplied products. Although production may be located in many countries, sales contracts are often negotiated at the headquarters with OEMs pushing for global coordination.

In the case of Corning Works, local responsiveness can be stronger in heterogeneous markets in which customers are less clearly defined and greater in homogenous markets, where customer segmentation is determined by a well-defined value perception of key products.

The number and presence of rival MNCs. A DMNC in markets with a number of rival firms competing for customers must respond to the actions of competing firms. However, each action can be driven by local responsiveness or global integration, depending on the characteristics a business unit has generated in each market over time. The answer will never be simply more global integration and less local responsiveness, or vice versa. The tension that exists between these two "general approaches" can be high or fairly low. Depending on the industry type, a DMNC can exploit its advantages in a limited set of market scale economies; in other markets, however, it needs to explore more locally responsive adaptations. Prahalad and Doz argue that it is essential to know the strategic intent of rivals and to understand the dynamic development. In order to respond to potential threats from competitors, it is necessary to globally pool the sources of firms' capabilities across countries and industry units. Heterogeneous markets, defined by many different but important customer segments, and local cultural traits that affect the marketing and sale of products, may require a large degree of effort to be locally responsive, but these responses need to be balanced against potential losses/gains exchanged for the potentially lower exploitation of advantages from global integration.

Capital-intensive manufacturing processes and expensive R&D industry environments. High costs in building up manufacturing facilities and multiple plants in different regions push the management of DMNCs to leverage synergies through various options for global integration. Uncertainty and costs related to R&D can be shared throughout multiple affiliates, but common efforts and costly resources need to be pooled for common exploration and exploitation within the industry units.

The high-tech industry in a DMNC needs to share its existing repositories of intellectual property throughout multiple locations. Prahalad and Doz (1987: 19) argue that a limited number of production facilities makes it easier to control the quality, cost, and product development process (Bao et al., 2006; Chaudhry & Zimmerman, 2012).

Forcing the industry toward cost reduction. Global sourcing within the multinational network of plants, R&D locations, and sales offices allows firms to pool supplies and input from low-cost locations. Affiliates can profit from exploited scale and scope economies within the network of locations in the DMNC. The DMNC can optimize its supplier relationships by using endogenous information asymmetry in its relations with competing, often smaller, and dependent firms (Li, 2020).

The universal character of global products. Some products remain independent from final use and are highly universal and will thus only be slightly adapted in multiple country markets, which allows firms to integrate common value-added activities. Some electronic products supplied for large OEMs in the automobile, computer, and mobile phone industry "[do] not vary by country" (Prahalad & Doz, 1987: 20). Corning's bakeware Pyrex®, although based on the same technology, is manufactured in both France and the UK with almost the same processing technologies. However, the country differences between the UK, the US, and various European markets in the use of these products in the kitchen when cooking with very distinct ovens, cookers, refrigerators, and dietary habits trigger a very strong differentiation. Such country market differences imply that R&D activities may have great potential for integration, but the optimal design, distribution, and marketing of the product is based on local responsiveness in multiple and different country markets.

Managing the *access to raw materials and energy*. High energy-consuming manufacturing processes and the dependence on key inputs can trigger the preference for specific locations that offer either cheap energy or allow processes to be simplified or streamlined, thereby reducing their cost. For example, combining two independent production steps creates considerable cost advantages (Kaufer, 1980). Access to capital in a large multinational firm due to the ability to issue bonds to raise capital can likewise provide significant cost advantages in financing. Thus, it may be appropriate to explore many different opportunities to integrate value-adding activities within the network of DMNCs to capitalize on apparent cost reductions. However, all efforts to integrate must be balanced against the tension that arises from losing advantages stemming from local adaptations.

7.9.3 Forces that Push the Business Units Toward More Local Responsiveness

Prahalad and Doz claim that a DMNC "does not operate in any one type of business—either global or multi-domestic. Each of its businesses is subject to a different combination of pressures toward global coordination and integration and toward local responsiveness—pressure that elude a simple 'either-or' classification" (1987: 22).

Five categorizations that allow firms to push the value-adding activities for a closer focus on the potential gains derived from adapting to local market factors are identified by Prahalad and Doz as follows:

Differences in customer needs. A business product or service that does not meet a clear and strong customer preference will constantly struggle with many often-secondary problems without sustainable success. An accurate and clear understanding of customer needs is essential, but gaining it is not a trivial matter. However, in large DMNCs, products and services are often created for large regions or very large customer groups, as any specific differentiation is considered too costly. There are a number of companies that still seem to believe that product customization is a necessary evil in selling a product or service. Subsidiaries in large DMNCs with considerable sales markets in their locations tend to adapt and generate products for their country-specific customer base. Much of the effort to develop a good product for the local market, which may enable the subsidiary to remain a strong competitor in that single market, is inaccessible for other subsidiaries. Components in product development that contain universal properties that may fit easily into other country market products remain unused within the DMNC network. The strength of being responsive to the needs of particular country markets can thus be regarded as a weakness simply because the product improvements and insights gained in the local market are not passed on to others.

Differences in distribution channels. Many country markets are still characterized by huge differences in the way goods and services are distributed. How a firm may promote, price, position, or advertise its products and services differs from country to country. Even digital products such as movies are priced differently and distributed in different cycles. Large multinationals put great effort into establishing efficient distribution channels for their products in national markets. Although it seems that large multinationals such as Samsung, LG, Apple, or Microsoft sell the same product across different nations, while adapting to the language used in each country, their pricing policies and promotions differ considerably from country to country.

Heineken and Kärcher

Heineken, one of the largest beverage multinationals, promotes beer in Europe and Africa with entirely different concepts: "The Dutch beer giant controls two-thirds of the Nigerian beer market. In good times the gross margins are above 50%, making Nigeria the second most profitable market for Heineken, after Mexico. In fact, for Heineken selling beer in Nigeria is more lucrative than selling their products in the UK, even though consumption in the latter is 2.5 times higher, according to Heineken in Africa (Dünnbier, 2019). The multinational has managed to become part of Nigerian society through strategic promotion and sale of 'local' brands (International Movendi, 2022).

Kaercher, a world-leading manufacturer of cleaning equipment, is a family-owned company based in Baden-Württemberg, Germany, that had at some point tried to establish nationwide distribution in India with a local joint venture partner. After a short period of time, the joint venture was terminated and Kaercher set up its own sales department, which was organized in accordance with its corporate values. Due to the need to adapt to the conditions of the Indian market requiring a great deal of training and a high level of personnel input, their efforts did finally result in the successful adaptation of the company's sales model to the Indian environment (Kaercher India, n.d.).

The number of potential substitutes for products designed for a particular national market requires a continuous and sensible push for local responsiveness. Sales and distribution thus need to differentiate against existing substitutes in a local market. For example, Corning's Pyrex® cooking ware was an elaborate and technologically advanced product, but in country markets like Italy, Corning had great difficulty in convincing existing customers of its superior product quality and convenient handling and storing features. Making the decision to leave the market or adapt is never an easy choice but the size of the market will ultimately affect the decision.

Market structure. Market structure is a classical concept that has been used in industrial economics since the 1950s and 1960s to analyze the impact of structure on firm performance (Scherer et al., 1975). Market structure conceives the important impact of "local competitors compared to multinational ones" and considers industry concentration as the key determinant in competitive forces that shape the behavior of the firms. In general, barriers to market entry increase—or correlate strongly—with the concentration rate in the industry (Affeldt et al., 2021). Conversely, a highly fragmented market structure (i.e., many small market participants) can indicate that there are few or hardly any barriers to market entry (Prahalad & Doz, 1987: 21). However, market concentration in attractive industries tends to be very high.

Market Concentration
In Germany, the market concentration in food retailing is around 76% (reported for 2019) with the companies Edeka, Rewe, the Schwarz Group with Lidl and Kaufland, Aldi, and Metro accounting for just over three-quarters of total sales in food retailing (Wirtschaftsforschung, n.d.). Austria has a concentration level of 84% among the three largest market participants in food retailing, Rewe, Spar, and Hofer (regiodata.eu). In the pet food industry, the five biggest multinational firms include Mars Inc., Nestle, J. M. Smucker, Hill's Pet Nutrition, and General Mills, whereby the two leading firms—Mars and Nestlé— account for more than 50% of total sales worldwide in this business segment (Petfood Magazine, June 2021). The market structure does not only affect the gains from deep knowledge about the new market segments emerging in key markets, but different product segments profit from joined R&D efforts in product development. Economies of scale and scope in these highly concentrated industries are the key determinant of market success (Makino et al., 2004; Meyer et al., 2011; Scherer et al., 1975; Uli, 2018).

Host governments (i.e., demands from foreign institutional contexts). Especially in the 1970s and 1980s, a number of host governments tried to increase local content rules for foreign manufacturers to increase the value-added activities generated in the host economy (Hassler, 2012). However, worldwide, it seems that protectionism is again widely used to deliver buoyancy aid for threatened companies (Feenstra, 1992; Long et al., 2013; Shen & Shang, 2019). Host governments maintain relationships with multinational corporations in order to attract foreign direct investment (FDI) but are also striving not to foil local value creation and the sustainable development of their own country.

Prahalad and Doz (1987: 7) elaborate their key approach on several levels that affect potential strategies that, in turn, have certain managerial implications for DMNCs. The first level focuses on determining how a business unit fits into an existing worldwide business strategy. At this stage, the management (relying on information from its business units) prepares an overall assessment of push and pull factors that influence the degree of integration and local responsiveness at the business level. In the next step, which relies on the outcome of the first, the business unit managers are required to think about the strategic intent of the business division.

The main focus in that stage is on identifying the common value-adding activities that can either be pooled in more for better integration or assessing the needs that legitimize greater local responsiveness.

The integration-responsiveness approach suggests that managers need a clear vision of how to develop their different business groups. To find out what to do is described as the "work of top management in DMNCs" (Prahalad & Doz, 1987: 7). The outcome should be a feasible strategy for how the diversified multinational can exploit the synergies of integration and of local responsiveness. The approach allow to identify a group of multifocal businesses that exert some integration potential and others that need more local responsiveness. Essentially, the problem is how to find a balance between these two forces. Push and pull factors operating in a particular industry are decisive. By "push factors," the approach define industry-specific factors that affect integration, such as economies of scale that force manufacturers to coordinate production capacities across multiple plants. By "pull factors," the approach describes country-specific market factors that affect require a greater local responsiveness.

Some business units may show a high rate of change, while others may exert a low need for change or reveal an unclear pattern. However, in each case potential drivers may require either moving toward more integration or becoming more responsive locally.

Study Questions

1. Describe and define the essence of Henri Fayol's conception of managerial tasks. Think about the means to carry out these tasks effectively within a large organizational structure.
2. Discuss with your colleagues the limits of the functional organization structure. What forced Du Pont and General Motors to implement such a change?
3. Describe the major characteristics of the multidivisional organizational structure. What was the inherent rationale for implementing that new corporate form?
4. Discuss the types of managerial mentalities analyzed by Howard Perlmutter. Why did he title his essay "The Tortuous Evolution of the Multinational Corporation"?
5. How did Stopford and Wells argue that the matrix organization (grid structure) can solve the problems of the diversified multinational firm?
6. Compare the meaning of hierarchy with that of heterarchy. What is the assumed merit of introducing a heterarchical organizational structure?
7. Discuss with your colleagues the different management mentalities elaborated by Bartlett and Ghoshal. Compare the strengths and weaknesses of each management mentality in leading the multinational firm effectively.
8. Try to characterize the need for local responsiveness and the pressures for global integration by using the case of Corning International. Define your conception of how to evaluate local responsiveness as well as how to measure the need for global integration.

References

Affeldt, P., Duso, T., Gugler, K., & Peichucka, J. (2021). Marktkonzentrationstrend steigt in Dienstleistungsmärkten deutlich. *DIW Wochenbericht, 20*, 340–247.

Ambos, T. C., Ambos, B., & Schlegelmilch, B. B. (2006). Learning from foreign subsidiaries: An empirical investigation of headquarters' benefits from reverse knowledge transfers. *International Business Review, 15*(3), 294–312.

Bao, H., Xu, M., & Gu, S. (2006). 'Patent pool' initiatives in manufacturing clusters in Zhejiang. *Innovation: Management, Policy & Practice, 8*(1–2), 153–159.

Barnard, H. (2011). Emerging multinationals benefiting from subsidiaries located in more developed countries: Drivers for the sharing of capabilities. *Innovation and Development, 1*(2), 187–203.

Bartlett, C., & Ghoshal, S. (1989). *Managing across borders: The transnational solution*. Harvard Business School Press.

Bartlett, C., & Yoshino, M. (1998). *Corning glass works international (A); Harvard Business School Case 381-160*. Harvard University Press.

Bauman, Z. (1990). Modernity and ambivalence. *Theory, Culture & Society, 7*(2–3), 143–169.

Birkinshaw, J., & Terjesen, S. (2003). The customer-focused multinational: Revisiting the Stopford and Wells Model in an era of global customers. In J. Birkinshaw, S. Ghoshal, C. Markides, J. Stopford, & G. Yip (Eds.), *The future of the multinational company* (pp. 115–127). Wiley.

Birkinshaw, J., Hood, N., & Jonsson, S. (1998). Building firm-specific advantages in multinational corporations: The role of subsidiary initiative. *Strategic Management Journal, 19*(3), 221–242.

Birkinshaw, J., Zimmermann, A., & Raisch, S. (2016). How do firms adapt to discontinuous change? Bridging the dynamic capabilities and ambidexterity perspectives. *California Management Review, 58*(4), 36–58.

Buckley, P., & Casson, M. (2019). Decision-making in international business. *Journal of International Business Studies, 50*(8), 1424–1439.

Chandler, A. E. (1962). *Strategy and structure: Chapters in the history of the industrial enterprise*. MIT Press.

Chandler, A. (1977). *The visible hand. The managerial revolution in American business*. The Belknap Press of Harvard U Press.

Chaudhry, P., & Zimmerman, A. (2012). *Protecting your intellectual property rights, understanding the role of management, governments, consumers and pirates* (pp. 125–140). Springer.

Chia, R. C. H., & Holt, R. (2009). *Strategy without design*. Cambridge University Press. https://doi.org/10.1017/cbo9780511642234.001

Christofi, M., Vrontis, D., & Cadogan, J. W. (2021). Micro-foundational ambidexterity and multinational enterprises: A systematic review and a conceptual framework. *International Business Review, 30*(1), 101625.

Comment, R., & Jarrell, G. A. (1995). Corporate focus and stock returns. *Journal of Financial Economics, 37*(1), 67–87.

Corning. (2022). Corning glass history. Company information. *Life in the Glass Age*. Retrieved from https://www.corning.com/life-in-the-glass-age/en/history.html

Donaldson, L. (2001). *The contingency theory of organizations*. Sage.

Doz, Y. (2016). Strategy and structure of the multinational enterprise (MNE). In M. Augier & D. Teece (Eds.), *The palgrave encyclopedia of strategic management*. Palgrave Macmillan. https://doi.org/10.1057/978-1-349-94848-2_447-1

Doz, Y., Santos, J., & Williamson, P. (2001). *From global to metanational. How companies win in the knowledge economy*. Harvard Business School Press.

Dünnbier, M. (2019, February 14). *Heineken in Africa*. Retrieved from https://movendi.ngo/media-release/not-a-love-story-heineken-in-africa/

Dweck, C. S., & Leggett, E. L. (1988). A social–cognitive approach to motivation and personality. *Psychological Review, 95*(2), 256–273.
Egelhoff, W. G., & Wolf, J. (2017). *Understanding matrix structures and their alternatives, the key to designing and managing large, complex organizations* (pp. 43–74). Springer.
Elango, B. (2004). Geographic scope of operations by multinational companies: An exploratory study of regional and global strategies. *European Management Journal, 22*(4), 431–441.
Feenstra, R. C. (1992). How costly is protectionism? *Journal of Economic Perspectives, 6*(3), 159–178.
Finkelstein, S. (2018). *The Palgrave encyclopedia of strategic management* (pp. 655–656). Palgrave.
Foss, N. J. (2002). "Coase vs Hayek": Economic organization and the knowledge economy. *International Journal of the Economics of Business, 9*(1), 9–35.
Frese, E. (1998). *Grundlagen der Organisation. Organisationsstruktur der Unternehmung*. Gabler Betriebswirtschaftlicher Verlag.
Gaur, A. S., Pattnaik, C., Singh, D., & Lee, J. Y. (2019). Internalization advantage and subsidiary performance: The role of business group affiliation and host country characteristics. *Journal of International Business Studies, 50*(8), 1253–1282.
Ghoshal, S., & Bartlett, C. A. (1990). The multinational corporation as an interorganizational network. *Academy of Management Review, 15*(4), 603–626.
Hassler, M. (2012). Macroregional economic integration in Southeast Asia: AFTA and the automobile industry from a Thai perspective. *Singapore Journal of Tropical Geography, 33*(1), 124–136.
Hedlund, G. (1984). Organization in-between: The evolution of the mother-daughter structure of managing foreign subsidiaries in Swedish MNCS. *Journal of International Business Studies, 15*(2), 109–123.
Hedlund, G. (1986). The hypermodern MNC—A heterarchy? *Human Resource Management, 25*(1), 9–35.
Hedlund, G. (1993). *Organization theory and the multinational corporation* (pp. 211–236). Springer.
Hedlund, G. (1994). A model of knowledge management and the N-form corporation. *Strategic Management Journal, 15*(S2), 73–90.
Heider, F. (1958). *The psychology of interpersonal relations*. Wiley.
Hoskisson, R. E., Hitt, M. A., Wan, W. P., & Yiu, D. (1999). Theory and research in strategic management: Swings of a pendulum. *Journal of Management, 25*(3), 417–456.
Inkpen, A. C. (2004). Theories of the multinational enterprise: Diversity, complexity and relevance. *Advances in International Management, 2004*, 43–52.
International Movendi. (2022, September 11). Nigeria. *Heineken pushes further for beer market domination*. Retrieved from https://movendi.ngo/news/2020/09/11/nigeria-heineken-pushes-further-for-beer-market-domination/
Jones, G. (2002). Business enterprises and global worlds. *Enterprise and Society, 3*(4), 581–605.
Kale, P., & Singh, H. (2007). Building firm capabilities through learning: The role of the alliance learning process in alliance capability and firm-level alliance success. *Strategic Management Journal, 28*(10), 981–1000.
Kano, L., & Verbeke, A. (2019). Theories of the multinational firm: A microfoundational perspective. *Global Strategy Journal, 9*(1), 117–147.
Kärcher. (n.d.). *Kärcher in India*. Retrieved June 15, 2022, from https://www.kaercher.com/in/
Kaufer, E. (1980). *Industrieökonomik* (Industrial economics). Vahlen Verlag.
Kelly, G. A. (1955). *The psychology of personal constructs*. Norton.
Kieser, A., & Kubicek, H. (1992). *Organisation* (3rd ed.). de Gruyter.
Levinson, H. (2013). *The exceptional executive: A psychological conception*. Harvard University Press. https://doi.org/10.4159/harvard.9780674424715
Levitt, T. (1983, May–June). *The globalization of markets* (pp. 92–102). Harvard Business Review.

Li, C. (2020). Supplier competition and cost reduction with endogenous information asymmetry. *Manufacturing & Service Operations Management, 22*(5), 996–1010.

Long, A. G., Kastner, J. J., & Kassatly, R. (2013). Is food security a new tariff? Explaining changes in sanitary and phytosanitary regulations by World Trade Organization members. *Global Economy Journal, 13*(1), 25–46.

Makino, S., Isobe, T., & Chan, C. M. (2004). Does country matter? *Strategic Management Journal, 25*(10), 1027–1043.

Martinich, A. P. (2021). *Hobbes's political philosophy* (pp. 1–14). Cambridge University Press.

Mees-Buss, J., Welch, C., & Westney, D. E. (2019). What happened to the transnational? The emergence of the neo-global corporation. *Journal of International Business Studies, 50*(9), 1513–1543.

Meyer, K. E., Mudambi, R., & Narula, R. (2011). Multinational enterprises and local contexts: The opportunities and challenges of multiple embeddedness. *Journal of Management Studies, 48*(2), 235–252.

Mintzberg, H. (1994). *The rise and fall of strategic planning*. New York.

Morgan, G. (1986). *Images of organizations*. Sage.

Neuberger, O. (1995). *Führen und Geführt werden* (5th ed.). Enke Verlag.

Novicevic, M. M., Buckley, M. R., Clayton, R. W., Moeller, M., & Williams, W. A. (2009). Commemorating Chandler through the lens of his revisionists. *Journal of Management History, 15*(3), 313–322.

Orbell, J. M., & Rutherford, B. M. (1973). Can leviathan make the life of man less solitary, poor, nasty, brutish and short? *British Journal of Political Science, 3*(4), 383–407.

Parker, L. D., & Ritson, P. (2005). Fads, stereotypes and management gurus: Fayol and Follett today. *Management Decision, 43*(10), 1335–1357.

Peaucelle, J. L. (2016). Henri Fayol face aux grèves. *Entreprises et Histoire, 83*(2), 36.

Peaucelle, J. L., & Guthrie, C. (2015). *Henri Fayol, the Manager* (pp. 171–182). Routledge.

Penrose, E. T. (1959). *The theory of the growth of the firm*. Blackwell.

Perlmutter, H. V. (1954). Relations between the self-image, the image of the foreigner, and the desire to live abroad. *The Journal of Psychology, 38*(1), 131–137.

Perlmutter, H. V. (1969). The tortuous evolution of the multinational corporation. *Columbia Journal of Word Business, 1969*(1), 9–18.

Perlmutter, H. V., & Shapiro, D. (1957). Stereotypes about Americans and Eurpeans who make specific statements. *Psychological Reports, 3*, 131–137.

Perrow, C. (1999). *Normal accidents. Living with high-risk technologies*. Princeton University Press.

Petfood Magazine. (2021, June). https://www.petfoodindustry-digital.com/petfoodindustry/library/document/june_2021/

Piaget, J., Garcia, R., Davidson, P., & Easley, J. (1983). *Toward a logic of meanings*. Erlbaum.

Prahalad, C. K., & Doz, Y. (1987). *The multinational Mission*. The Free Press, MacMillan.

Qiu, J. X., & Donaldson, L. (2012). Stopford and Wells were right! MNC matrix structures do fit a "high-high" strategy. *Management International Review, 52*(5), 671–689.

Raisch, S., & Birkinshaw, J. (2008). Organizational ambidexterity: Antecedents, outcomes, and moderators. *Journal of Management, 34*(3), 375–409.

Rattan, A., & Georgeac, O. A. M. (2017). Understanding intergroup relations through the lens of implicit theories (mindsets) of malleability. *Social and Personality Psychology Compass, 11*(4), e12305.

Rugman, A. M. (2005). *The regional multinationals. MNEs and global strategic management*. Cambridge University Press.

Rugman, A. M., & Verbeke, A. (2004). A perspective on regional and global strategies of multinational enterprises. *Journal of International Business Studies, 35*(1), 3–18.

Scherer, F. M., Beckenstein, A., & Kaufer, A. (1975). *The economics of multiplant operations*. Harvard University Press.

Schmid, S., & Maurer, J. (2011). *Internationale Unternehmungen und das Management ausländischer Tochtergesellschaften* (pp. 53–83). Springer.

Schreyögg, G. (1999). *Grundlagen der Organisation* (The foundations of organizations). Springer Gabler Verlag.

Scuotto, V., Garcia-Perez, A., Nespoli, C., & Petruzzelli, A. M. (2020). A repositioning organizational knowledge dynamics by functional upgrading and downgrading strategy in global value chain. *Journal of International Management, 26*(4), 100795.

Shen, W., & Shang, S. (2019). Tackling local protectionism in enforcing Foreign Arbitral Awards in China: An empirical study of the supreme people's court's review decisions, 1995–2015. *The China Quarterly, 241*, 144–168.

Staehle, W. H., Conrad, P., & Sydow, J. (1999). *Management: Eine verhaltenswissenschaftliche Perspektive*. Vahlen Verlag.

Stopford, J. M., & Wells, L. T. (1972). *Managing the multinational enterprise: Organization of the firm and ownership of the subsidiaries*. Longman, Basic Books.

Tallman, S. (2004). Strategic management and the role of the MNC in a post-industrial world market. In M. A. Hitt & J. L. C. Cheng (Eds.), *Theories of the multinational enterprise: Diversity, complexity and relevance* (Advances in international management) (Vol. 16, pp. 53–64). Emerald Group Publishing Limited. https://doi.org/10.1016/S0747-7929(04)16004-6

Teece, D. J., Pisano, G., & Shuen, A. (1997). Dynamic capabilities and strategic management. *Strategic Management Journal, 18*(7), 509–533.

Uli, V. (2018). A co-evolutionary perspective on business processes. *Business Process Management Journal, 24*(3), 00–00.

Unilever. (1970). *Annual report 1970*. Retrieved September 5, 2022, from https://assets.unilever.com/files/92ui5egz/production/bf7c5396028e0f83ed552a210b1929129ce8df38.pdf

Weber, M. (2015). *Max Weber-Gesamtausgabe*, Band 1/25, Wirtschaft und Gesellschaft (Eds. Hanke E. & Morlok Ch.) (1. Aufl.). Mohr Siebeck. Retrieved from https://doi.org/9783161581441

Westney, D. E. (1993). *Organization theory and the multinational corporation* (pp. 53–76). Springer.

Westney, D. E. (2006). The regional multinationals: MNEs and 'global' strategic management. *Journal of International Business Studies, 37*(3), 445–449.

Whittington, R. (2008). Alfred Chandler, founder of strategy: Lost tradition and renewed inspiration. *Business History Review, 82*(2), 267–277.

Wilson, J. F., & Thomson, A. (2006). *The making of modern management. British management in historical perspective*. Oxford University Press.

Wind, Y., Douglas, S. P., & Perlmutter, H. V. (1973). Guidelines for developing international marketing strategies. *Journal of Marketing, 37*(2), 14–23.

Wirtschaftsforschung, D. I.. (n.d.). *Marktkonzentration*. 2021. Accessed June 15, 2022, from https://www.diw.de/de/diw_01.c.413344.de/%20

Wolf, J., & Egelhoff, W. G. (2002). A reexamination and extension of international strategy–structure theory. *Strategic Management Journal, 23*(2), 181–189.

Wolf, J., & Egelhoff, W. G. (2013). An empirical evaluation of conflict in MNC matrix structure firms. *International Business Review, 22*(3), 591–601.

Yip, G. S. (1995). *Total global strategy: Managing for worldwide competitive advantage*. Prentice Hall.

Zott, C., & Amit, R. (2008). The fit between product market strategy and business model: Implications for firm performance. *Strategic Management Journal, 29*(1), 1–26.

Correction to: Theories of Internationalization

Correction to:
Chapter 3 in: Fuchs, *International Management*, https://doi.org/10.1007/978-3-662-65870-3_3

The original version of this chapter was incorrectly having in Chapter 3, Figure 3.1, p84, source information for the figure was omitted by mistake.

The correct figure caption should read as:

Fig. 3.1 International trade and technology gaps (reprinted with permission from Oldenbourg Verlag. Copyrights by Kutschker & Schmid, 2012:397)

The updated original version for this chapter can be found at https://doi.org/10.1007/978-3-662-65870-3_3

M. Fuchs, *International Management*,
https://doi.org/10.1007/978-3-662-65870-3_8

MIX
Papier aus verantwortungsvollen Quellen
Paper from responsible sources
FSC® C105338

If you have any concerns about our products,
you can contact us on
ProductSafety@springernature.com

In case Publisher is established outside the EU,
the EU authorized representative is:
Springer Nature Customer Service Center GmbH
Europaplatz 3, 69115 Heidelberg, Germany

Printed by Libri Plureos GmbH
in Hamburg, Germany